Standing Fast

Standing Fast

THE AUTOBIOGRAPHY OF ROY WILKINS

by Roy Wilkins

with Tom Mathews

THE VIKING PRESS   NEW YORK

First published in 1982 by The Viking Press
625 Madison Avenue, New York, N.Y. 10022
Published simultaneously in Canada by
Penguin Books Canada Limited

LIBRARY OF CONGRESS CATALOGING IN PUBLICATION DATA
Wilkins, Roy, 1901–1981
    Standing fast.
    Includes index.
    1. Wilkins, Roy, 1901–1981. 2. Afro-
Americans—Civil rights.   3. United States—
Race relations.   4. Afro-Americans—Biography.
I. Mathews, Tom.   II. Title.
E185.97.W69A37   323.4′092′4   [B]   81-70185
ISBN 0-670-14229-8   AACR2

Grateful acknowledgment is made to the following for
permission to reprint copyrighted material:

Viking Penguin Inc.: Four lines from "Lift Every Voice and
Sing," from *Saint Peter Relates an Incident: Selected Poems* by
James Weldon Johnson. Copyright 1935 by James Weldon
Johnson. Copyright © renewed 1963 by Grace Nail Johnson.

Walter White's letters to Roy Wilkins are reproduced by permission of his daughter, Jane White Viazzi.

The letter from Percy Sutton to Roy Wilkins is reproduced by
permission of Percy E. Sutton.

All photographs not credited are courtesy of the
Estate of Roy Wilkins.

Printed in the United States of America
Set in CRT Primer

OCT   '82

FOR MINNIE

CONTENTS

Standing Fast

1   DIDN'T MY LORD DELIVER DANIEL?

I was not born in Mississippi, but my story begins there all the same, deep in the rolling hill country of northern Mississippi. If you travel far enough into the heart of those hills, not far south of Holly Springs you will come upon an old dirt road wandering off the black-top highway that races on to Senatobia. The dusty road goes down a dip, winds around a slight curve, then comes to a stop right at the front door of a little country church called Beverly Chapel, a spare wooden building painted white and filled with pine pews. There is no stained glass in the windows, no steeple atop the roof; only a gnarled bell tower of cypress poles weathered hard by the sun and rain stands out front. On Sundays an old iron bell used to clang from the bell tower's rickety crossbeam, calling black people from the farms and countryside to worship. The bell is gone now. Most days the only sounds that break the peaceful quiet of the place are the soft drone of honeybees, the lilting call of bobwhites, and the chirp of small blackbirds nesting in a hole above the weather-beaten church door. A footpath bordered with wild daisies and tangled weeds threads its way to the Negro cemetery out back, where my grandfather and grandmother, Asberry and Emma Wilkins, lie buried. A tall stand of cypresses overlooks their graves. They have no other markers: no headstones, no dates or epitaphs carved for the ages, nothing. My grandparents were slaves—and the soil of Mississippi has swallowed them as indifferently as it produced them in the 1850s, ten years before Abraham Lincoln set them free.

Lost among the untended graves, my mother is also buried out behind Beverly Chapel. Except for good fortune I, too, might have disappeared into the earth there. This particular burying ground holds the first truth about my family: go back two generations and our freedom vanishes; go back any farther and the family itself disappears. We have been Americans for well over two hundred years, but for much of that time we were a family without a name and for most practical purposes without a country. Up to the time of the Civil War the branches of our family tree rustled with bills of sale, not birth certificates. We were sold by sex, age, and weight, not by name, and as a consequence of this loathsome traffic in human flesh, my ancestors from the third generation back are now as lost as any missing tribe of Israel.

The few fragments of our early history that survive were handed down by Grandfather Wilkins, a tall man with skin as black and lustrous as polished ebony. He had deep brown eyes that burned with intelligence and a steady warmth, and his sinewy arms could keep a span of mules plowing a straight furrow all day or tuck a protesting grandchild gently into bed at sundown. He had received his education at the end of a hoe and an eleven-foot cotton sack.

During the winter of 1914, when I was thirteen years old, I spent Christmas on his little farm outside Holly Springs. Looking back, I can see only a few shiny fragments of that holiday so long ago. It was very warm for December, and the townspeople of Holly Springs shot off fireworks in honor of Christ's birth, almost as if they were celebrating the Fourth of July. Grandfather Wilkins lived just across the road and down a small hill from Beverly Chapel, a rural outpost of the colored Methodist Episcopal Church. He was a tenant farmer, hardworking, sober, thrifty, up first from slavery, then from the misery of sharecropping. His own people called him a good Christian man. The white folks of Holly Springs called him a "good nigger": that is to say, a black man who did nothing to expose the gap between the pretensions of the white South to Christian virtue and the unholy way most white Southerners treated their black brothers and sisters all year round.

Grandfather Wilkins was born in 1851, six years by the calendar of race before the United States Supreme Court told Dred Scott the Negro had no rights a white was bound to respect and forty-five years before it told Homer Plessy that separate-but-equal citizenship was good enough for descendants of slaves. If the Civil War had liberated Grandfather Wilkins, the Supreme Court had circumscribed his possibilities. Like millions of other Negroes, he responded by becoming a stoic; he endured. I inherited his staying power, but not his patience. Chattel slavery and the damnable nineteenth-century race rulings of the Court divided my people—Grandfather Wilkins along with them—into two camps: victims of bondage and segregation who abided their sufferings passively hoping for a better day and rebels who heaped coals of fire on everything that smacked of inequality.

I have spent my life stoking the fire and shoveling on the coal. My grandfather had to keep his head down—or get his neck stretched.

Grandfather Wilkins owned a mule named Kel, a few clothes, his tools, and his Bible. The relics of his past were equally meager. The name of his father, which has survived only as an illegible scrawl on a death certificate buried in the archives of Mississippi, appears to have been Mound Jeffries. There is no mystery to this discrepancy in surnames between my grandfather and my great-grandfather: before 1863 slave fathers and their children were so abjectly powerless that they might not even share the same name. White masters commonly named their slaves after themselves; in all probability, a white Jeffries who owned my great-grandfather sold the son of Mound Jeffries to a white Wilkins, and this Wilkins in turn bestowed upon Grandfather Asberry the last name that has come down to the rest of us.

There is no record of when Great-grandfather Jeffries was born. In that respect he was no different from most slaves. Frederick Douglass once observed that he had never known a slave who could fix his birthday more precisely than planting time, harvest time, cherry time, or fall, and my great-grandfather wasn't even able to pass down that information. My guess is that he was born in the late 1820s. Land records and slave lists for the area around Holly Springs suggest that he belonged to a white planter named William Jeffries, who moved from the upland of the Carolinas to Mississippi during the great cotton boom of the 1840s. These Jeffries connections stretch back through the eighteenth century to St. Michael's and St. Phillip's parishes near Charleston, South Carolina, a city that first came to prominence as a slave port, and there my family's chains touch the Atlantic.

It is beyond my power to leap the last thousands of miles across the Atlantic to Africa. All I can do is wonder about this terminal gulf in my past. South Carolina started importing African slaves in the last part of the seventeenth century; so far as I know, none of my relatives can lay claim to arriving on the first slaver that reached the coast of the Carolinas. It is far more likely that sometime during the eighteenth century my more distant ancestors were kidnapped and sold into slavery in West Africa, packed like black spoons in the silver chest of a slaver plying the Middle Passage, and sold on the block in the Charleston slave market. One way or another, the line leading to Mound Jeffries wound up in Mississippi. From the beginning we were shanghaied Americans, possessing only our minds, souls, and muscles—and a set of hand-me-down names.

By ship, wagon, and footpath, my ancestors were removed from Africa to South Carolina, then on to Mississippi, where Grandfather Wilkins became the first of us to outlast slavery. Our new home soil, hill country along the border between Mississippi and Tennessee, was a land of forests, hills, and fertile bottoms watered by the Tippah and Tallahatchie rivers and the Pigeon Roost, Chuffawah, and Coldwater creeks. Local histories record that when white settlers like Jeffries arrived with my great-grandfather in tow, they found the virgin forests of oak and beech, hickory and maple, walnut and cypress alive with bear and deer, possum, squirrels and rabbits. Doves, quail, passenger pigeons, and wild turkeys flew among the trees, and plums, blackberries, and wild grapes grew everywhere. In the very heart of this fine territory there was a spring ten feet deep and thirty feet across. Its banks were shaded by holly trees with green leaves and bright red berries. The Chickasaw Indians to whom the land belonged unchallenged until the white men came said the berries commemorated the blood of an Indian warrior and maiden who died in a lovers' quarrel at the spot; so first in myth, later in reality, passion and violence watered my root soil.

After wresting the Treaty of Pontotoc from the Indians in 1832, Mississippi carved twelve full counties out of the Chickasaw cession. Marshall County, named after the Chief Justice of the United States Supreme Court, was the largest. Near the old holly spring, white planters like Jeffries—slaveholding Methodists, Baptists, Presbyterians, and Episcopalians from Virginia and the Carolinas, Alabama, Georgia, and Tennessee—built a town and made it the county seat. They called the place Clarendon, then Paris, before settling on the less affected name of Holly Springs. The slaves of Great-grandfather Jeffries's generation slashed down forests, built imposing plantation houses with towering Corinthian columns and cool verandahs, and planted cotton. By 1850, the census takers found that the local population stood at 29,419—14,271 whites, 15,147 slaves—and one free Negro.

Whoever that solitary black man was, he wasn't any relative of mine. Great-grandfather Jeffries, a field hand, had jumped the broomstick, marrying my great-grandmother, whose name is now lost. Their boy child was strong and very black, two credentials that fitted him perfectly for the place the white folks of Marshall County had reserved for him: down at the bottom.

For a very long time, it looked as if the bottom was where Grandfather Wilkins would stay. The year he was born there was a drought in Marshall County. The cotton and corn crops withered; planters were reduced to cutting barren cornstalks early and to laying in turnips for winter fodder; the fighting in Washington over the Compromise of 1850 fired Mississippi with threats of secession. A small child could not have started out in life with much more against him. The United States Constitution itself considered him only three-fifths of a human being, the fractional representation in the human race that was granted to determine the number of white Mississippians who would fight year after year in the Congress of the United States to keep him a slave. It was a hard time. But at night the North Star twinkled brightly in the sky, showing him the way to New England and Canada, where blacks could be free. And in the slave quarters after dark, his mother would lie by his side telling him stories about an all-powerful, loving God.

"He is the father of everyone and he lives in the sky," she told him one night. "He will come through the clouds one day and deliver his black children into freedom."

Grandfather Wilkins became the family's first recorded doubter. He told me that even as a child he found it hard to accept his mother's simple faith and vision. I must have picked up some of his skepticism; I have never been able to bring myself to believe that Christian forbearance alone is powerful enough to remove the obstacles that whites have thrown in the way of equality for Negroes.

Grandfather Wilkins was tormented by a child's relentless literalism, by questions that would not leave him alone: Was God white or black? Was one side of God white and the other side black? How could God say He loved black people when He allowed them to be slaves?

In the darkness of the cabin one night he slipped up to his mother and asked her to answer his questions. She looked at him, then told him gently, "Hush, child. You must wait." How many millions of black mothers have been forced to tell their children the same thing? Waiting is a sentence not a solution, but back then, there wasn't much else Grandfather Wilkins could do but wait.

As a child, he lived on two large slave plantations outside Holly Springs. When he was nine years old, his first master sold him to another white planter, who took him from his mother, gave him a new name, moved him to another farm, handed him a hoe, and put him to work in the cotton fields. There he was left to make his way in the world.

Records in the courthouse at Holly Springs show that half a dozen white Wilkins families owned slaves and land near the town in 1860, the year I believe my grandfather became the first official Wilkins in our family. Only four of the white Wilkins families on the courthouse lists owned land enough to fit my grandfather's memory of a childhood spent on large plantations. The slave census for 1860, the last before the Civil War, shows only two Wilkinses owning a nine-year-old slave boy the age of Asberry Wilkins: William Wilkins, a white merchant planter from South Carolina, and William's brother Moses. Between them, the Wilkins brothers had nearly a thousand acres of land on a mountain south of Holly Springs, a high, cool corner of Marshall County that lies within easy walking distance of Beverly Chapel, the center of Grandfather Wilkins's universe, and his last resting place.

I can't be certain whether William or Moses owned Grandfather Wilkins. The slave census lists 17,000 chattels not by name but by age, sex, and color alone—as if they were the livestock of their owners. The names of William and Moses Wilkins appear in the fine flowing hand of nineteenth-century clerks at the head of their lists of anonymous slaves, each with an entry for a nine-year-old boy who might be Asberry Wilkins. Which is it to be? The circumstantial evidence points just one way. The white census records show that William Wilkins named two of his sons William and John; many freed Negroes also named children after those of their master; and as it turns out, my grandfather also named two of his own sons—my uncles—William and John. William DeWitte Wilkins, born in 1878, two years after the collapse of Reconstruction, was my father. The details prove nothing, but as I read them, I can only conclude that one white William Wilkins who moved from Union County, South Carolina, to Marshall County, Mississippi, in the late 1840s was my father's namesake—and my grandfather's old master. And for those particular honors, I assume *he* will have to do some very fancy accounting come Judgment Day.

As a field hand Grandfather Wilkins worked each day from "c'ain to c'aint." "C'ain" came each morning when it got light enough for him to see a hoe hit the ground before it hit his foot; "c'aint" arrived in the evening when it got too dark to hoe the weeds without cutting up the cotton. In the summer he wore homespun shirts and trousers and went barefoot; in the winter he wore heavy brogans with brass toes. At night he plodded home to a log cabin made of hewed logs chinked with mud: the floor was dirt, the shutters and door were made of rough wooden planks, and the wind whistled through them.

The possibility of escape seemed as remote as his mother's vision of the Second Coming. The slave cabins were grouped in rows within sight of the master's house, and the whites could watch every move he made coming and going from the fields. At night, white patrollers with guns, whips, and dogs circled the plantation on foot and on horses, ready to grab and return any slave bold enough, reckless enough, or desperate enough to make a break for freedom.

Up to the time of the Civil War, there were at least as many slaves as white people in Marshall County. I'm sure the arithmetic gave the planters many troubled nights. Settlers from South Carolina still had fresh memories of Denmark Vesey's uprising in 1822; those transplanted from Virginia could not have forgotten Nat Turner's rebellion in 1831 or its body count of seventy whites. The planters crushed even the slightest hint of self-assertion among their chattel. The aim was to suppress slave revolts, but in practice the impulse led to gratuitous acts of sadism. My grandmother Emma Wilkins, a midwife who delivered half the babies in the hills and bottoms around Beverly Chapel, was the victim of one of those mindless acts. On her arm she had an ugly triangular scar. She had once worked as a house slave for a white woman in Holly Springs. One morning while ironing she scorched her mistress's best dress. The mistress came home and found her in tears. Eyes afire, that gentle white lady seized the hot iron and clapped it, sizzling, on the arm of her young slave. Grandmother Wilkins carried the brand for the rest of her life.

The memories of the Reverend John Aughey, a Presbyterian abolitionist who passed through Holly Springs in the 1850s while Grandfather Wilkins was a small child, show that the slaves of Marshall County could do little but suffer those cruelties, praying for better white folks or the Lord to deliver them. A white lady named Mrs. Dunlop told Dr. Aughey that one evening she had noticed a group of slaves assembling in a cabin near her home. Curious, she tiptoed up to a back window and peeped in. She saw a "well-dressed, burly African talking earnestly to the slaves." In crabbed dialect, Aughey transcribed his message.

"I tells you, ladies and gentlemen . . . we is all gwine to be free befo' long. We won't be slaves no longer and be whipt and cufd by de white folks."

"How duz you know all dat?" said Whit Jim, an octoroon.

"Why didn't I heah Massa Jeff Davis say so? I done drove him out in de carriage to dat stan' where he 'dressed de people today, en I have to wait to bring 'im back. From whut he sed, de people of de Norf is comin' down to set us free and dey'll jes mow dez Southern people down like dey mows de grass. An he sed de Northern people believed in negro 'quality, dat de white folks up dar wuz willin' to marry our daughters, and let us marry theirn. . . . Jes be ready, as de hym ses: 'Your redemption draweth nigh.' "

A glorious vision, but it was another nine years before redemption came. For most of Grandfather Wilkins's childhood, the North and Northerners seemed as remote as Heaven and the Heavenly Host itself. Not until 1862 did Ulysses Grant and the Grand Army of the Republic march on Mississippi. According to local chronicles, the first Yankees fell upon Holly Springs in early 1862. A party of raiders approaching the town from the south happened upon an elderly Negro.

"Who is the richest man in town?" asked one of the raiders.

"Mr. William Mason," replied the old man.

Spurring hard for town, the raiders seized the Mason house, jabbed bayonets through the eyes of the family portraits hanging on the walls, and gutted the keyboard on the piano. Then they put the china outside on the sidewalk and shot it to smithereens.

When Grandfather Wilkins was about twelve, Holly Springs became a supply depot for the Union assault on Vicksburg. Holly Springs annalists note that Mrs. Grant arrived with a Negro maid named Julia who had been "given" to her by her father; thus, a touch of Northern racial hypocrisy came to town right alongside the commander.

In December 1862, with the Union troops moving out toward Vicksburg, a swashbuckling Confederate cavalry officer named Van Dorn swept into town at the head of his own party of raiders. He attacked Grant's rearguard, capturing a train loaded with food and clothing bound for the Vicksburg front and putting to the torch hundreds of bales of cotton piled high in the courthouse square. By four in the afternoon, Holly Springs looked like the set for *Gone With the Wind:* Confederate raiders were shouting, shooting, and rattling their sabers; Yankees were scrambling for cover; abolitionists were pleading for their lives; and as a black cloud of smoke rose above the town, the white ladies of Holly Springs, their hair afrazzle, their dresses billowing in the wind, stood on doorsteps cheering the raiders.

In the countryside where Grandfather Wilkins watched the carnage of the war, crops were burned, fences ripped down, and livestock driven off, but neither the North nor the South managed to gain the upper hand. Late in the summer of 1863, after Vicksburg fell, Grant confidently ordered the planters of Holly Springs and the rest of Mississippi to comply with the Emancipation Proclamation. The planters just as confidently ignored him. But they couldn't hold out forever. On April 9, 1865, down at the railroad depot in Holly Springs, the telegraph wires hummed with the terse message that finished the Confederacy: "Hell's to pay. Lee's surrendered."

The Union victory didn't liberate the slaves of Marshall County overnight. A troop of Union soldiers was stationed in Holly Springs. What happened next—embellished over the years—became Grandfather Wilkins's favorite story. One day in the summer of 1865, the overseers herded Grandfather Wilkins and the other slaves on his plantation into a large group at the edge of one of the cotton fields. Just at noon, the master came out of his house and walked slowly down to the fields. When he reached the waiting slaves, he studied his boots for a few minutes. Finally, he looked up and spoke to them.

"The Yankee soldiers say y'all free. I don't hafta feed you or take such good care of you anymore—unless you want to stay on the plantation and keep working for me."

For a moment there was silence. Then, softly, one of the older slaves began to sing. The words of one of the old Sorrow Songs suddenly full of joy rose and rolled across the plantation:

> Didn't my Lord deliver Daniel,
> Deliver Daniel, deliver Daniel?
> Didn't my Lord deliver Daniel?
> An' why not every man?

One by one the other slaves began to sing, and when they finished they fell to their knees out in that cotton field and gave thanks to God—my great-grandmother's God of deliverance. Grandfather Wilkins had doubted. But on that day of jubilation, it looked as if his mother had been right all along.

2   AN ESCAPE FROM JUDGE LYNCH

When Grandfather Wilkins got up off his knees on Emancipation Day, his old master and the overseers were still standing there looking at him, and he obviously had a problem. He had been a slave one minute, a freedman the next; but he was still black all day long, and not a white planter in Holly Springs was eager to help him. To say that the vanquished whites of Marshall County merely opposed his liberation would be to do them an injustice; they considered it a war crime against them—and they did everything they could to undo it. He owned no house or land, no mule, no seed, no tools, no food, not even the clothes on his back. By force of brutal necessity, his first free choice was a hard one: to stay on the plantation.

It didn't take long for the white planters and politicians of Mississippi to get together in Jackson to patch up their losses in the Civil War. "Ours is and ever shall be government for white men," Governor Benjamin Humphreys promised the state in his 1865 inaugural address, and the legislature lost no time in translating the rhetoric into action: it passed the notorious and ferocious Black Code, which all but reestablished slavery in Mississippi.

Given the provisions of this code, Grandfather Wilkins's decision to stay put was probably the better part of valor. He had just turned fourteen. One of the new statutes bound all Negro orphans under eighteen—and all Negroes under eighteen who had no job—as "apprentices" to masters who could work them, beat them, and run them to the ground if they ran away. Another "antivagrancy" statute stipulated that by the second Monday in January 1866, all freedmen, free Negroes, and mulattoes in Mississippi had to produce written evidence proving that they had a job and a place to live. Local mayors, aldermen, and justices of the peace were given the power to arrest anyone charged with violating the law and to conduct trials without juries for the hapless suspects. Those convicted could be fined $50 and clapped in jail for ten days. To pay the fines, local sheriffs had the power to hire out penniless violators to their old masters.

The penalty for speaking up against the Black Code or insulting a white man or preaching without a license was a fine of up to $100 and thirty days in jail. As things stood, Grandfather Wilkins could be arrested almost as quickly for kicking a mule as for mixing with white folks. He could not carry a knife or gun, and the penalty for intermarriage, an idea I'm sure never occurred to him, was life in prison. The code was so transparently evil that radical reconstructionists in the U.S. Congress seized upon it to justify imposing martial law upon Mississippi and granting suffrage to the freedmen, the two devices of Reconstruction that the white folks of Holly Springs hated above all others.

It never fails to astonish me when members of white ethnic groups ask in indignation why Negroes should represent a special historical case, why they haven't made the same progress as the Irish or the Italians, the East European or Jewish immigrants. The question bespeaks a hostile indifference to the great gap between the starting points of black Americans and other ethnics. In the beginning Grandfather Wilkins had only two assets to count: the patrollers no longer dogged his every step, and he didn't have to sneak off into the woods simply to worship as a Christian. To keep black people out of the white pews in Holly Springs, planters encouraged the freedmen to build their own churches. Before long, chapels were sprouting on hilltop and bottom all over the county. Freed slaves from the Wilkins plantations built a church at the foot of a high hill near the farm of Moses Wilkins, politely calling it Wilkins Chapel. On Sundays the little church resounded with hymns, prayers, and sermons. Grandfather Wilkins and the others gathered there to talk out their troubles and to plan for the future, violating three or four Mississippi race laws every time they said amen.

The little country chapels were the only organizations Grandfather Wilkins and the other blacks of Marshall County could call their own. Bishop Elias Cottrell, who learned preaching by studying the sermons of a white minister over a pine-knot fire at night, rode circuit among them and later rose to great prominence in the colored Methodist Episcopal Church (now the Christian Methodist Episcopal Church). Hiram Revels, who represented Mississippi in the U.S. Senate during Reconstruction, was also a Baptist preacher in Holly Springs for a time. His flock called him "Parson Revels." He got on so well with the white folks that he was buried under an imposing monument in the main cemetery in Holly Springs, a long way from the weedy patch of ground where Grandfather Wilkins now lies.

My grandfather was a Methodist until the day he died. I believe his first name represents a corruption of Asbury, taken after Bishop Francis Asbury, an early saddle-back revivalist of the Methodist Episcopal Church who imported a rugged article of Methodist faith from England: "Slavery is contrary to the laws of God and man and hurtful to society." That tenet gave the Methodists an early and strong call on the loyalties of black Christians like Grandfather Wilkins. John Wesley himself laid claim to converting the first black believer to the faith that has sometimes sustained and sometimes subdued Negroes for more than two hundred years. In his diary for November 29, 1758, Wesley recorded that he had ridden

> . . . to Wandsworth and baptized two Negroes belonging to Mr. Gilbert, a gentleman lately from Antigua. One of these is deeply convinced of sin; the other is rejoicing in God her saviour, and is the first African Christian I have ever known. But shall not God, in his own time, have these heathen as his inheritance?

I find it harder to say who will be redeemed and who will be had when Judgment Day arrives. But no matter how it comes out, the Methodist Church supplied Grandfather Wilkins with a faith that served him well all his life.

At a prayer meeting one night he met my grandmother, a thin young girl named Emma. She had a quick smile, bright eyes, and the neck of a swan. Her skin was very black; she had small delicate hands—and that scar. Grandfather Wilkins was twenty-two years old, and she swept him away. Late in December 1873, he enlisted his brother Nelson to go with him to the courthouse in Holly Springs to take out a marriage license. The two brothers walked five miles over hill and ridge to reach the courthouse, a brick building two stories high, topped by a cupola and the town clock. They made their way through the town square, past mules and horses, goats and squawking chickens. Penetrating the high cool corridors of the courthouse, the two young men found the Marshall County clerk's office, a bailiwick run by a one-armed Confederate war hero named George B. Myers. Myers listened while they swore to a bond of $200 guaranteeing that Grandfather Wilkins's marriage plans were proper and in good order. In a bold hand, Myers signed the license for them, and they scratched their X's, the signatures of men forcibly deprived of education as slaves, where Myers told them to. Those timid little crosses comprise the earliest literary relics of my family.

Two days before Christmas, the Reverend B. H. Ford married my grandparents. The neighbors came from farms all around for the wedding. In later years Grandfather Wilkins would smile to himself when he thought back on that day. The celebration was just like when white folks got married, he would say, " 'cept the bride didn't have no white dress and there wasn't no fancy cookin' for a weddin' supper."

At the peak of Reconstruction, Grandfather Wilkins was a married man and a sharecropper. His old master staked him to a mule, seed, manure, food, clothes, and a cabin, in return for his labor and a 50–50 split of his cotton crop at harvest time, an arrangement that left him half slave and half free. The white planters kept the power to sell the cotton crop in Holly Springs, setting prices, collecting what they could, and returning what they chose to their croppers, a system built for boodling. Year after year, Grandfather Wilkins finished the harvest feeling that he had been outwitted or just plain cheated. But he was able to put aside a little bit of cash. Finally, he managed to rent a small farm several miles up the road from the Wilkins plantation, within shouting distance of Beverly Chapel, where he had become an elder. That move upward from cropper to tenant farmer imparted its kinetic energy to the Wilkins family, and we have been driven onward ever since.

Reconstruction opened the ballot to black people around Holly Springs, and Grandfather Wilkins became as fervent a Republican as he was a Methodist. In Marshall County, the G.O.P. was made up of Negroes, a few highly principled old-line Whigs who hated Democrats more than they hated black people, some Southern scalawags snuffling after postwar spoils, and a few carpetbaggers from up North. All through Reconstruction, the Republicans spent most of their energy figuring out how to outfox or outhate the Democrats.

The leading carpetbagger in Holly Springs was a tall, thin, ugly fellow named Nelson Gill. Gill organized the freedmen into political clubs called Loyal Leagues. The leagues encouraged the blacks of Holly Springs to vote a solid Republican line, partly for their own benefit, even more for the greater glory of Gill himself, who held more offices than any other man around: postmaster, head of the Freedmen's Bureau, president of the Board of Supervisors, and sergeant-at-arms in the state legislature. In Jackson he outraged Southern Bourbons by replacing white page boys with black children.

Gill was a greater talker and organizer, and the Loyal League gave my grandfather and the other freedmen their first instruction in the political harangue. The annals of Holly Springs record that there were great parades, processions a mile long of freedmen dressed in flaming-red sashes and great badges of red and blue marching through the streets. At night blazing torches lit the way, and in the day a horn and drum beat out a cadence for the marchers. During one particularly hot campaign, there was a float carrying a tree with branches full of possums, next to which stood a giant black man sharpening a knife. As the float passed through the streets he shouted, "Carve that possum, nigger, carve him to the heart." Then he yelled at the shuddering whites, "Carve that white man, nigger, carve *him* to the heart."

On Election Day the black voters of Marshall County rode to the polls four abreast on horses and mules. Gill met them at the courthouse gate, handing out great wads of Republican ballots, from a carpetbag at his feet. The performance outraged white Democrats, who quickly took to stuffing ballot boxes and stealing elections themselves. They got so good at it that in the election of 1875 they wangled back all the power Reconstruction had cost them.

Politics thereafter became a dangerous game for Grandfather Wilkins. Henry C. Myers, the brother of the county clerk who signed my grandfather's wedding license, was elected sheriff in 1875. According to local historians, Sheriff Myers also happened to be Cyclops in the Ku Klux Klan, which had about fifteen dens in Marshall County. The Klansmen of Marshall County wore red and black regalia and practiced a catechism so simple that the dimmest cracker could master it. ("Question: What are the objectives of the Ku Klux Klan? Answer: To suppress the Negro and keep him in the position where he belongs and to see that the Democratic Party controls this country.") After Reconstruction, torchlight parades and black political power flickered out, not to reappear for nearly one hundred years.

As Reconstruction waned, our family began to grow. Grandfather Wilkins's first son, Robert, was born in May 1876; my father two years later; a daughter and two more sons—Eula, John, and Oran—followed in the 1880s. By the time the census takers came around in 1900, there were three sons, a daughter, a grandson named Sam, and a granddaughter named Beatrice living with Grandfather Wilkins, and his little farmhouse could barely hold all the clan.

My father hated farming. He was a stocky man with brown skin and a chronic scowl. Around Holly Springs everyone called him Willie. He went to a one-room school for black children near Beverly Chapel, spending all the time he could steal from the chores with his nose buried in Grandfather Wilkins's Bible. Grandfather Wilkins strapped him for lazing, but encouraged him to get an education.

Eventually he managed to talk his way into Rust College in Holly Springs, which was run by the African Methodist Episcopal Church. Back then Rust was more like a high school than a modern college, but it was an improvement over the unpainted, one-room shacks that Mississippi considered good enough schools for its black children.

At Rust, my father began to court my mother, a willowy young country schoolmarm named Mayfield Edmundson, who taught in a little school near Beverly Chapel. She was very pretty and rather frail. She wore dresses that buttoned up to her chin and down to her wrists, and she had a look of perpetually surprised innocence. Her friends called her Sweetie Mayfield.

My mother had a café-au-lait complexion. Her sister Elizabeth was fairer. Their father was Peyton Edmundson, one of the first black Baptist preachers in Marshall County. The Edmundsons provide the second of the two anomalies in my family tree: a paternal grandfather named Jeffries and, on my mother's side of the family, a great-grandfather who was probably white. The fair skin of the Edmundson sisters had to come from somewhere. There is no way to know for sure, but I suspect that Parson Edmundson or his wife—perhaps both of them—were light-skinned children from one of those unions white masters so commonly forced on black women in the slave quarters or the woods after dark.

In early June 1900, my father proposed to Sweetie Mayfield and made the same trip to the Marshall County courthouse that Grandfather Wilkins had made before him. There was, however, an improvement in the marriage license Willie Wilkins obtained: he signed the document himself in a clear, confident hand. No more X's—we were making progress.

William Wilkins and Mayfield Edmundson were married on June 7, 1900. For a while my father worked as a porter, the best job he could get after graduating from Rust College. The work was bone-wearying and poorly paid. He had to call the son of his boss "sir," even though the white boy was younger than he was. He had to step out of the way every time a white man approached him on the street. In return, the white folks of Holly Springs saluted him as "boy"—or "nigger."

My father had enough education to realize that the equality of all men as set forth in the Declaration of Independence wasn't exactly common policy around Marshall County; he became the family's first hell-raiser. Since he talked back to white people whenever he felt like it, people around Holly Springs began to worry about him. They said he was on his way to becoming a troublemaker, bum, and all-round bad nigger. I have the same traits buried somewhere in my chromosomes. I don't like to be mistreated. I don't like to see other people mistreated. I believe in fighting back.

The rebelliousness of my father finally broke into open insurrection in midsummer 1900. One day not long after his marriage, he was walking down a dirt road near Grandfather Wilkins's farm. It was a hot day, and dust kicked up in red whirls as he scuffed along, deep in thought. Suddenly he heard a voice bellow behind him: "Nigger, get out of my way."

For a second he stood there transfixed. When he turned around, he saw a white farmer sitting on a wagon in the middle of the road. The farmer was leering at him, waiting confidently for him to jump out of the way. A lifetime of insult finally boiled up and over within my father. He took a quick step forward, swung up onto the wagon, and smashed the smirk off his tormentor's face. Then he kept right on swinging until the white man lay in the wagon bed, bloody and groaning. Finally, trembling with rage, he stepped back down into the road and walked home to the farm.

In those days, by the book of Judge Lynch, for a Negro to hit a white man meant death in the Deep South. Word of what had happened quickly raced through the county. Late that afternoon, a worried white friend for whom Grandfather Wilkins did chores came calling at the farm.

"Uncle Asberry," he said, "you better get that boy Willie out of town. He's making trouble for both of us. There's nothing I can do for him. He's heading for a lynching sure."

The same night, in the darkness, Grandfather Wilkins anxiously bundled Willie and Sweetie Mayfield into a wagon and drove them to a railroad station up the line from Holly Springs. Early the next morning, they caught the first train north. Willie Wilkins had lifted us from mute suffering to open war against the injustices of race. The Lord may have delivered Daniel from the lion's den and Grandfather Wilkins from slavery, but it was the Illinois Central that delivered my father from Mississippi—one step ahead of a lynch rope.

A Jim Crow railroad car carried my parents to safety in the North. Passing through Memphis, they rode the Illinois Central straight to St. Louis. The train rattled along, clicking up the tracks, coughing great billows of white steam and black smoke, grinding up the grades, whistling at the crossings, leaving the Deep South farther behind at every milepost. My father's explosion had propelled him from boy to man almost as fast as Grandfather Wilkins had made the passage from slave to freedman. The transformation must have been exhilarating, but the road ahead looked a little grim: he had a new wife, no home, no job, and only a pitiful lump of savings in his pocket. Still, he no longer had to bow, scrape, and say, "How high?" to every cracker who ordered him to jump. He had broken the double code of white supremacy and black passivity that had kept him a prisoner of race, and he was headed to the North, where things had to be better—just as fast as that shabby Jim Crow car could take him.

The train deposited my parents at Union Station in St. Louis, a tower of stone built to imitate a French château. Between the hissing train and the main depot stood a long line of high iron gates topped by imposing clocks. Hoisting their bag, the two refugees made their way through the gate and into a new world. The first thing they did was set off to find the colored washroom. Much to their surprise, they couldn't locate it. Puzzled, they then began looking for the colored waiting room. It was missing, too. Jim Crow had reached the schools, hotels, restaurants, and theaters of St. Louis, but hadn't bothered with the railroad depot. The white people of the city still found it possible to share the soap, basins, and toilets at the train station with black folks. The change was small enough, but my father used to say that to him it looked like a miracle.

On a scrap of paper in his pocket, my father had the address of a friend who had moved North earlier at a much less desperate pace.

The friend lived in a house on Papin Street, but neither of my parents had the slightest idea where Papin Street was. For a few moments they stood in the depot feeling very lost. Finally, they saw a black janitor sweeping up outside one of the train gates. When they walked up and eagerly showed him their scrap of paper, he said, "Ain't never heard of it." With a shrug that made Papin Street seem as remote as the moon, he went right on sweeping.

Their hearts sank. Then, to their surprise, an elderly white man walked up and asked politely if he might help them. They showed him the little slip of paper; he gave them directions. They seemed bewildered by all the twists and turns, so he invited them to follow him. Leading them out of the depot, he boarded a waiting trolley. "Give these people two transfers," he told the white conductor. "Let them off at Jefferson Avenue and point them on to Papin Street." After that he tipped his hat to them and went on his way.

They climbed aboard the trolley and moved toward the rear, only to discover that the car was full of black people sitting wherever they pleased. A few white people were sitting in the back seat. The strange sight made them laugh out loud. Mississippi was obviously a long way behind them. Things were definitely beginning to look up.

When they finally found the little house on Papin Street, the owner took them in like long-lost relatives and fed them a bountiful welcome-North supper. Three adults and four children were already jammed into the house, but they immediately moved over to make room for the newcomers. Such generosity was common at the time. The great migration of Southern Negroes was still over the horizon, but by 1900, the vanguard was already settling in up North. Many Negroes fled the South as my parents had done. The luckier ones found the help, shelter, and welcome that the people on Papin Street offered the Wilkins family.

The following morning my father set off to find work, and found out soon enough that St. Louis did indeed have a color line. It began at the payroll office, and its warning was all too clear: "If you're black, step back." For two weeks, in increasing anxiety, he left the house each day only to return downcast and empty-handed in the evening. Finally, he found a job in a brick kiln in East St. Louis, across the Mississippi River. The job paid poorly, but it enabled him to move my mother out of Papin Street to the first-floor flat of a two-family house at 2818 Laclede Avenue in a black neighborhood. A year later I was born in that flat. Dr. Ottoway Fields, a Negro physician, delivered me. I have a mortifying baby picture that captured me as a chubby infant in a long, white dress, smiling in hopeless innocence, as if all the world had been created for my larger benefit. My mother and father named me Roy Ottoway Wilkins, slipping the doctor's fancy name into my own, which was two-bits plain in all other features. As a little boy I disliked that middle name and dropped it as soon as I learned how to write.

My earliest memory has nothing to do with blackness or whiteness. The first thing I can remember is wandering the aisles in Mr. Nevins's grocery store. At the turn of the century Mr. Nevins was the only Negro grocer in St. Louis. I can still see him, a tall, friendly man in a white apron. His store was a cool, mysterious place that smelled of sawdust, flour, and fresh-ground coffee. Up by the front counter, he kept a great barrel of dark sorghum molasses. On shopping days he would smile at my mother as he dipped sweet streams of molasses into a jar for her. I can smell that molasses to this day. If I could wangle my way back into childhood, I would be there in Mr. Nevins's grocery right now, craning out from behind my mother's skirts, studying that magic barrel, dreaming of biscuits and molasses come suppertime.

We lived in a clean little flat in a row house. I dimly remember a long hall with four rooms opening off to the sides. We didn't own anything much to brighten them up. From time to time, my father brought home bricks from the kiln. My mother covered some with scraps of carpet and painted designs on others. That was all the interior decorating we could afford. On hot summer evenings I used to sit out on the steps in front of the building and watch the horses and buggies passing by in the street. There was a red brick police station a few doors down from us, and burly policemen in blue uniforms walked by all the time. They always stopped to smile and say hello. Squeezing my shoulder or patting me on the head, they would walk off on their rounds. I liked them and trusted them. Years later when I saw a less worthy generation of police officers wading into peaceful demonstrators with clubs, dogs, and cattle prods, I found it hard to believe what I was seeing.

I don't remember many children on Laclede Avenue: most of the time I played by myself. Even then I was a loner, and I have stayed a loner all my life. I'm not particularly proud of this trait—it can make a man seem a little distant or even aloof—but it has helped pull me through some tight spots and hard times.

I went to kindergarten at the Banneker School, a segregated grammar school. At the time, it didn't strike me as unusual that all the children in the class and out on the playground were black. The truth is that at first color doesn't mean very much to little children, black or white. Only as they grow older and absorb poisons from adults does color begin to blind them; blacks and whites alike are susceptible to this sad change.

There were integrated neighborhoods not far from Laclede Avenue, and although the usual white bigots were skulking around them, I don't remember many. Missouri was a border state, less virulent in its racism than Mississippi, and thus I was able to start life a long leg up on my father and grandfather. St. Louis had an aristocracy of Negroes—all white or nearly white in appearance—whose ancestors had owned property in the city before the Civil War. Black newcomers from the South were as foreign to them as any Japanese might have been. To these aristocrats, I imagine, my family must have looked like a raggedy crew of outsiders.

The crew gradually grew bigger and bigger. In 1903 my sister, Armeda, was born, and my brother, Earl, arrived two years later. Earl was a plump little baby with the widest, most trusting eyes I have ever seen. Standing over his crib, peering in, admiring him, I saw him as a mysterious present. To me, he was the most important person in the whole house. When he grew up he became a trusted confidant. Armeda was a quiet little girl with mischief in her eyes. I used to tickle her under the chin until her giggles brought our mother running. Then all three of us would tumble down on the floor, rolling over one another, laughing until the tears came.

As the years passed in St. Louis, such happy moments in my early childhood became increasingly rare. Work in the brick kiln soured my father's spirits, and he became sterner and more remote. He had the inner resources to make the passage to St. Louis, but the spiritual and physical effort of the change seemed to exhaust him. Each morning he picked up his lunch pail and headed to work, and at nightfall he returned with brick dust on his boots and a scowl on his face. Eventually he and my mother joined the African Methodist Episcopal Church in St. Louis. After that he turned to religion for answers to all his quandaries and comfort in his woe.

I have never had much natural talent as a Christian. This weakness goes back to the first time my parents took me to church. I sat there in my best clothes, my hair all brushed down and parted neatly, my eyes blinking at what I saw. Up front on a stage a tall man in flowing black robes stood there yelling at us. The grownups sitting around me started yelling right back. Amens broke out on all sides. Finally, there was a lot of singing. My ears rang. All I wanted to do was get up and go home.

At dinnertime my father always read endless passages from the

Bible, delaying the real business of getting down to the biscuits and gravy. I didn't pay much attention to what he was reading. All I could see was that the food was getting cold as he droned on. But I didn't dare touch a thing until he finished the verse, closed the Bible, and picked up his own fork.

Several years after my mother moved to St. Louis she developed a frightening cough. During some of her bad spells she had to stay in bed for a week at a stretch. Whenever she was sick, kind ladies from the A.M.E. Church would come in and help with the cooking and cleaning.

About the time I was five years old, the bad spells began to come more frequently, and the doctor told her what she had long since guessed: she had consumption. The disease did not break her spirit, but she became weaker and weaker, and when her strength had ebbed dangerously low, she wrote a letter to her sister Elizabeth, who had married and was living in Minnesota. I found the letter years later; it read:

> Dear Sister,
> My cough is getting worse. I am afraid I cannot last much longer. Please promise me you will raise the children. Willie cannot handle three babies himself. I am afraid he will send them to his mother, and I do not want my children raised in Mississippi.

The appeal changed my life. One afternoon I came home from school to find the flat bustling with church ladies. My father and Dr. Fields were in the bedroom with my mother, who was lying very quietly in bed, paler than I had ever seen her before. Suddenly Earl started to cry, and when one of the church ladies picked him up, a rage came over me.

I shouted, "Let my brother go."

The startled woman called my father, who took me off to a neighbor's house. I stayed until bedtime. That same night my mother died.

Two days later, a tall, plump, fair-skinned woman arrived from St. Paul. Sweeping Earl, Armeda, and me up in her arms, she hugged us and told us we were to call her Aunt Elizabeth. We were all frightened by my mother's death, but Aunt Elizabeth swooped into the vacuum, filling it before we had a chance to feel very sorry for ourselves. She was a wonderful, buxom woman, high-spirited, cheerful, resistant to the worst adversity. This warm angel of mercy quickly took charge of the household. My father couldn't raise enough money to pay for my mother's funeral, so Aunt Elizabeth arranged with an undertaker back in Holly Springs for a burial on the installment plan.

She sent $10 down on the $70 bill. It took her several years to pay off the balance, but her sister received a proper funeral.

So my mother didn't quite escape from Mississippi, after all. Her body was shipped back to Holly Springs, and she, too, was buried in the graveyard behind Beverly Chapel. Her grave, like those of Grandfather Wilkins, who died of a stroke in 1917, and Grandmother Wilkins, who was burned to death in a brushfire in 1928, has disappeared in the weedy ground.

I nearly wound up back in Mississippi myself.

One morning Aunt Elizabeth put on her coat, picked up her purse, left the flat, and went off to the telegraph office. Armeda and I were sturdy little kids, and she planned to send us back South to Grandfather and Grandmother Wilkins. But Earl was still a baby, so she sent a telegram to her husband asking his permission to bring Earl home with her.

The following day she received a short return telegram from St. Paul:

I WON'T BREAK UP A FAMILY. BRING ALL THREE. SAM.

When Aunt Elizabeth received the telegram, she had a long talk with my father. She persuaded him that with Sweetie Mayfield gone, his only course was to let her take care of us. Although Aunt Elizabeth had been married for twelve years, she had no children. Since the Wilkinses had become a family looking for a mother, and since our father couldn't pick up the pieces left by Mother's death, she would do the job.

Several days later she packed our clothes in small suitcases, dressed us in our Sunday best, and prepared a hamper full of food. We took the trolley to the railroad depot, where my father and mother had made their first, hopeful entry to the North five years earlier. Both my parents had become wayside casualties of the black exodus from the South. We said goodbye to my father, boarded a train, and headed for St. Paul, Minnesota.

That journey northward was my first train ride. I sat glued to the window as the countryside of Missouri rolled by, giving way to the dark soil and rich fields of Iowa. Even when Aunt Elizabeth opened her hamper of cold fried chicken I could barely tear myself from the window. The trip transformed my prospects. A violent protest drove my father to Missouri, halfway North; the death of my mother drove Earl, Armeda, and me all the way North, so far beyond the reach of the South that for years I made the mistake of thinking it could never catch up with me.

The train finally rattled into Union Station in St. Paul, a great, homely barn of a station without any of the French pretense of the depot in St. Louis. Aunt Elizabeth gathered us up like a mother hen with a new brood of chicks. Clinging close to her, we got off the train. For a second or two she looked up and down the platform. Then she beamed. Coming toward us was a tall man in a dark suit. There were knife-edge creases in his trousers, and he wore a somber businessman's hat. At first glance he looked a little forbidding. While Aunt Elizabeth was as fair as any St. Louis black aristocrat, the face of this stranger was sculpted like a rugged ebony mask. He had high cheekbones and a straight powerful jaw. His full lips were pursed with concentration as he approached; but when he reached us, he broke into the friendliest smile I had ever seen and kissed Aunt Elizabeth. Peering down at Earl, who stared right back from his perch in Aunt Elizabeth's arms, he laughed and chucked my wide-eyed baby brother under the chin. He studied Armeda and me for a few seconds. "My, what two fine young people we have here," he said. Then he hugged Armeda and soberly shook my hand.

That was my introduction to Uncle Sam Williams, my stand-in father. He was the warmest, kindest man I have ever met. Over the years he taught me that the world was not the universally hostile place my own father had taken it to be; that a man could get along if he had faith in the goodness of other people, kept his eye peeled for their weaknesses—and believed in himself. Everything I am or hope to be I owe to him.

Uncle Sam bundled his new family aboard a trolley outside the depot and took us home. After bouncing and jostling its way out of downtown St. Paul, the trolley hummed westward up a gentle slope. The day before, I had been living among brick flats and noisy city streets; now there were sun-dappled sidewalks lined with trees, and houses with neatly trimmed lawns.

We eventually reached 906 Galtier Street, a small clapboard cottage painted white and fitted out with a little porch trimmed with Victorian posts and railings. Uncle Sam owned the cottage. He was proud to be an owner, not a renter, an important distinction in St. Paul. He was a railroad man, the chief steward on the private rail car of Howard Elliott, president of the Great Northern Pacific Railroad. As far as I know, he never earned more than $85 a month, but he bought that cottage, saw three children through college, and left Earl and me the deed, mortgage paid in full, when he died.

The day we arrived on Galtier Street, the little cottage had only four rooms. Within a few days Uncle Sam had the carpenters in, hammering, sawing, and working up great clouds of dust. In short order there was a new upstairs with three rooms and a bath; bright rooms where yellow beams of sunlight streamed in, giving the far-thest corners a warmth and security I have never quite felt since I left them.

Aunt Elizabeth enrolled me at the Whittier Grammar School on Marion and Wayzata streets, about four blocks from our house. The evening before I set off for my first day at the new school, Uncle Sam sat me down and gave me some advice. He told me I had to keep my fingernails clipped and clean, something I had never tried. Then he said, "Education may be the most important thing in life. You should go to school and be the best. If you find that you can't be the best, then *do* your best—that's almost as good." No one, he went on, can steal an education from a man. Whenever I tell children the same thing today, I can see Uncle Sam Williams sitting there at my side, earnest, intent, offering the best advice I have received in my life.

The next morning Aunt Elizabeth marched me off to school. She had a natural talent for disciplining kids, and as we walked along she gave me a running lecture. I was to say, "Yes, ma'am," whenever a teacher talked to me, and I was to pay close attention to everything that was said in class. "Nothing is more important than a good edu-cation," she said, echoing the counsel Uncle Sam had drilled into me the night before. I was just starting on the road to wisdom, she said, warning me with a look that I had better start off right.

When we arrived at Whittier, a red brick school with a playground and a flagpole outside, Aunt Elizabeth ushered me into the principal's office and enrolled me in the first grade. Then she left me. Before sweeping out the principal's door, she left one last order: "Come straight home as soon as school is out."

The principal was a nice enough old man. He took me by the hand, walked me down a hall, opened a door, and nudged me into the first-grade class. I looked around at my new classmates with the timidity any new child feels in a new school. I got a quick shock. All the chil-dren were white.

In St. Louis, the children at Banneker School had all been black. I was six years old, and this was the first time I registered the differ-ence between black skin and white. I sat in the classroom until 10:30 that morning, totally absorbed by this strange new development. When the bell rang for recess, I ran all the way back to Galtier Street. Aunt Elizabeth greeted me with surprise.

"What are you doing, child?" she asked.

"You told me to come straight home when the bell rang," I sput-tered.

She looked at me severely . . . then laughed and sent me gently back to school. For some time I remained suspicious of the place, but after several weeks and the usual new-boy hazing, my classmates accepted me. I settled in and buckled down to work.

It was winter when we moved from St. Louis to St. Paul. When we left Missouri it had still been warm; now each morning the skies sparkled blue and I could see my breath in frosty white puffs as I set out for school. After school, neighborhood children in bright red, yellow, and green mittens, mufflers and snowsuits, skated on the silver ice at nearby Lake Como. Snow came sifting through the air in the evenings, and women bundled in heavy winter coats rushed off to do their Christmas shopping.

As Christmas approached, Aunt Elizabeth and Uncle Sam said the time had come to write Santa Claus; Armeda sent off her letter, but I ignored them. I had too many things to do outside in the snow. I couldn't make up my mind what I wanted, anyway.

Two days before Christmas I fell into bed and had a wonderful dream: I heard bells tinkling and I was sliding faster and faster down a long hillside covered with snow. I glided to a stop, and when I woke up, my list for Santa was complete: what I wanted was a red sled with silver bells. The next morning, with a child's innocence of price tags and shopping-days-left-to-Christmas, I announced brashly that if there really was a Santa Claus, he would bring me that sled. Uncle Sam and Aunt Elizabeth said nothing.

On Christmas morning Armeda and I woke early and tiptoed downstairs. In the living room was the largest Christmas tree I had ever seen—a towering green fir with boughs bending under glittering ornaments and ropes of cranberries. There were pairs of snowshoes, ice skates, and roller skates. A baseball and bat, a doll and a doll carriage were lying among mountains of fruits and candies. And in the center of all these riches, at the foot of the tree, there was a red sled with silver bells.

4 SOME LESSONS IN RACE

O f the two Edmundson girls, Aunt Elizabeth had obviously married the better provider. Wafting along with the tantalizing smells out of Aunt Elizabeth's kitchen, that first Christmas in St. Paul returns to me now in memory as a nostalgic vision of the secure world into which Earl, Armeda, and I had so suddenly fallen. Aunt Elizabeth set the table with fine linen and silver. She brought out oysters. At the time I didn't even know the Lord had created shellfish. Then she disappeared into the kitchen and came back with a great, steaming platter. On it was the largest "chicken" I had ever seen, cooked a golden brown. My eyes widened. "You mean you've never seen a turkey, child?" Aunt Elizabeth asked. "No, ma'am," I said, with embarrassment. "Well, *that's* a turkey," she said, pointing to the platter in front of Uncle Sam. "And from now on you'll see one every Christmas."

In time, life in the warm little house on Galtier Street undid the damage that a forbidding home and a dour father had worked on me in St. Louis. My father had made the journey halfway up the Mississippi before his spirit failed him; I had come nearly as far up the Mississippi as I could travel. The river still connected me symbolically with Holly Springs, but throughout my childhood, the South and its way with race were safely behind me. St. Paul was a sturdy melting pot full of Swedes and Germans, French, Irish, and Jews. James J. Hill and the Northern Pacific had made it a great railhead. The city had drawn Uncle Sam up from Mississippi, and unlike my mother and father, he and Aunt Elizabeth had put down strong roots and prospered.

I have never met a more trustworthy individual than Uncle Sam. When my mother's death threw my father into spiritual and financial default, it was left to Uncle Sam to teach me how to become my own man. He accepted the responsibility without protest. He was not a hard man, nor was he soft. He ran the household on a few simple rules: he believed that children should behave, and he wouldn't tolerate lying; he taught us the value of hard work, but he also saw to it that we had fun.

Uncle Sam had followed the railroads north from Holly Springs to Minnesota, picking up whatever work he could find along the way—porter, waiter, toter of bags—the main jobs open to Negroes in the days of Hill and the robber barons of the railroad era. When he reached St. Paul, he caught the eye of Howard Elliott, president of the Northern Pacific Railroad. Elliott hired him to run his private railroad car. The car was furnished like an elaborate hotel full of plush chairs. At one end were the state rooms, at the other a formal dining table. An observation platform was at the rear. With the help of one waiter, Uncle Sam presided over this empire, doing everything including the cooking. I have an old photograph that shows him aboard the car somewhere out on the Northern Pacific line. The picture captures a strong, compact man in a straw hat and boiled white shirt, sitting in a wicker chair under a wall of gleaming mahogany, smiling, master of all he surveys.

That white shirt betrayed Uncle Sam's vulnerability. How different it looks from the conservative business suits he wore when he was away from the railroad. The uniform of service and the coat, vest, and trousers of the middle-class man did not really contradict one another. Around the turn of the century and for many years afterward, most Negro communities of any size had a few doctors, lawyers, and professional men; but railroad porters—men hired for their impressive physical stature and trustworthiness—were also an important component of the black middle class. On the road Uncle Sam may have been little more than the butler of a rich white man, but at home he was a pillar of the community. This was the price respectability exacted of him. The country yielded it to Negroes only with great reluctance, and it yielded it only to brave souls who refused to be broken by the crushing, slow pace of progress.

Uncle Sam's boss was a tall, thin man with a neat little mustache and a pugnacious jaw. He had come to the Northern Pacific by way of the Burlington, which he ran until Hill lured him away. He was a Harvard man and an engineer; he claimed a bloodline running back to John Elliott, an Englishman who arrived in Boston in 1631. During the ten years he presided over the Northern Pacific, he built 377 miles of new road in the Far West, 230 miles of it along the winding Columbia River, over which he built what was then one of the country's most imposing railroad bridges. He added sidetracks and double-tracks to the Northern Pacific's main line, gentling curves, improving grades; he bought locomotives like toys and built round-houses like other men build toolsheds. His engineering works and his public-relations fights with the trustbusters of the U.S. Justice Department kept him out on the road in the private car for weeks at a time. And when he went, Uncle Sam went with him.

Sometimes Uncle Sam was gone a week, sometimes a month; we never knew when to expect him home. His absences were one of the few hardships that befell us. Aunt Elizabeth was not a moping woman, and she bore up well under the strain, bustling about the house, cleaning, cooking, sewing. But she missed him. A palpable melancholy would fall on 906 Galtier Street until the day we finally heard the familiar brisk footfall coming up the walk and the quick steps across the wooden boards of the front porch that announced Uncle Sam's return.

Between road trips, Uncle Sam worked as Elliott's general factotum. Each morning he got up before dawn, dressed, and made the trip across St. Paul to the Elliott house, where he served breakfast to the entire Elliott family. Then he spent the rest of the day at the Northern Pacific offices working as Elliott's messenger. In the late afternoon he returned to the Elliott house and served dinner. It was usually after dark when he came home to 906 Galtier Street for his own supper. He worked at least twelve hours a day. For this Elliott paid him a pittance.

Aunt Elizabeth was the disciplinarian around 906 Galtier Street. Uncle Sam did the spoiling; he left enforcement duties to his wife. Whenever he came back from his road trips, he would lavish presents on us. Whenever we earned a spanking, Aunt Elizabeth did the paddling.

One of Aunt Elizabeth's first tasks was to break me to the traces of religion. My father's Bible thumping and subsequent collapse the first time a true spiritual crisis presented itself had left me with no kind feelings toward the church. She and Uncle Sam were members of the flock at St. James's African Methodist Episcopal Church on Jay and Fuller streets. The minister there was the Reverend Henry P. Jones, a stomping preacher. He used to get so carried away with his own hellfire sermons that he'd talk right through the time set aside for Sunday school. The first time we went to church together, I made faces, laughed, and imitated the forensic gestures of Reverend Jones, much to the amusement of Armeda. Aunt Elizabeth was shocked. Afterward she enrolled me in the children's choir. Scrubbed to a high polish, we sat up front in full view of the congregation. From then on, I had no choice but to mind my manners.

St. James's was an old-fashioned frame church that could hold about 250 worshippers. On nice days the sun flooded through its stained-glass windows, bathing the pews in warm yellows, reds, and blues. Gradually I softened in this pleasant atmosphere and became a less rebellious Christian. I worked for a while as the janitor; my job was to prepare the church for prayer meetings on Wednesday nights and to sweep up Saturdays before the long run of Sunday services. I didn't do this purely as a matter of Christian charity; Reverend Jones paid me two dollars a week for the job. When I got older, I also became superintendent of the Sunday school. We had eight teachers, and I watched over all of them. There were separate Sunday-school classes for boys and girls. I taught a class for little girls. They were polite and they loved Bible stories. I don't think I've ever had a nicer job.

St. James's and the Pilgrim Baptist Church—a more imposing structure with a tall steeple—were the two social centers of black St. Paul. Their congregations probably accounted for half the Negro families in the city. Sundays were the days I saw friends like Walter Miner and Henry Johnson, who lived on the other side of town. All the good-looking girls went to Pilgrim Baptist. Walter, Henry, and I used to wander over together just to stare at them.

Strictly speaking, St. Paul did not have a black ghetto, though a great many Negroes lived around Rondo Street and St. Anthony Avenue. In my neighborhood, there were only three other Negro families. Richard Anderson, a headwaiter in a private club, owned a house nearby. He was prosperous by local standards. I remember that he used to put in his coal in April; no one else, not even the white people, could afford it. Phil Anderson, a lieutenant in Engine Company 22, the all-Negro fire brigade just around the corner, also lived near us. His house was the best kept in the neighborhood. The Davises lived not far off. They had several children who appeared to be poorer than the rest of us: their clothes were more frayed and they had fewer toys.

I suppose the faith I have in integration comes from the days I spent in a schoolboy's cap and knickers chasing around the quiet tree-shaded lanes that stretched off and away from our little cottage. The men who owned the tidy frame houses in my neighborhood were white: Swedes and Norwegians, Poles, Germans, and Irish—first- and second-generation immigrants. They worked as carpenters, patching up boxcars in the nearby yards of the Northern Pacific, or as laborers and janitors, watchmen, policemen, and firemen. I don't remember any rich people living in our part of town.

Most of these hardworking white people were still struggling to learn English. In that regard, Aunt Elizabeth and Uncle Sam had an advantage over them. Aunt Elizabeth used to read letters for the neighbor ladies. The Irish, who had no language problem and were the dominant political force in the neighborhood, were the least friendly; many of the other European newcomers looked up to Aunt Elizabeth and Uncle Sam as steady people, friendly and willing to help them through the difficulties of starting over in a new country and with a foreign language. Everyone around us, white and Negro alike, was struggling to support a middle-class outlook on a poor man's income. Hard work, thrift, education for the children, a sense of pride in home and country, faith in the future—those were the ruling values up and down Galtier Street.

A Swedish family named Hendrickson lived next door to us. Mr. Hendrickson worked as a janitor in an office building downtown. He was a sober man, wiry and blond. He worked long hours, returning home late at night, and his children rarely saw him during the week. On Sundays he would put on his best clothes and gather his family. As we set off for St. James's, we would usually see the Hendricksons heading for the Lutheran church.

Mrs. Hendrickson was a plump woman; she always wore an apron tied around her ample waist. She spoke Swedish at home, and her cares and energies centered entirely around her children. Leonard Hendrickson was about my age. After high school I went to college, and he became a clerk for the Great Northern Pacific Railway. Melvin Hendrickson, a little older than I, joined the police force, working his way up to lieutenant. Mrs. Hendrickson treated me as one of her own sons. There were times when she smiled and hugged me, but whenever I got out of line, she aimed a torrent of Swedish at my ears and a hard swat at my backside. A few years ago, during a trip back to St. Paul, I stopped by the nursing home where she was living to see her. She was sitting in a wheelchair, but when she saw me come in, she rose to her feet and cried, "My boy, my boy." We both cried a little after that.

Perhaps I'm a sentimentalist, but no one can tell me that it is impossible for white people and black people to live next door to one another, to get along—even to love one another. For me integration is not an abstraction constructed on dusty eighteenth-century notions of democracy. I believe in it not only because it is right but because I have lived it all my life. Where there are decent, loving people like the Hendricksons, integration works. Where decent white people are missing—that's where the trouble begins.

My best friend in those days was a shy blond boy named Herman Anderson, who lived about six blocks away on the east side of Rice

Street. Rice was the main business street in the North End, a bound-
ary line between my quiet neighborhood and the turf belonging to the
Rice Street Gang, the toughest kids in the city. The word "nigger"
was part of their equipment, along with other brickbats. I was a tall,
lean kid; I towered over most of them, so for the most part they left me
alone. Herman resisted them, too.

Herman and I never talked about black and white. People no longer
believe me when I tell them that there was a time when it was possible to pass over such things. It wasn't until Herman was seventy-six
that he finally told me how he regarded the race question. He said, "I
was taught by my mother that skin didn't make any difference and
that color didn't make any difference: the thing that mattered was the
kind of person you were." These days everyone seems to be so sensitive about their racial and ethnic roots that such old-fashioned goodness has withered away. If only we could find it within ourselves to
bring it back to life.

I had met Herman at Whittier Grammar School, to which we
trudged slowly each morning, toting our books in a strap. The lower
grades were on the ground floor; the upper grades on the second
story. In the basement there was a little wood shop where we made
boxes and plant stands. Herman was a very quiet boy; his motto was
"Still water runs deep." The two of us had charge of the school's
Edison disc phonograph. I can remember hauling the polished box
with the great horn around to the rooms of the lower grades for concerts. At the noon recess and at the end of the day, Herman and I
would carry it out into the hallway, crank it up, and play marches.
The strains of the "Washington Post March" and "Under the Double
Eagle" blared from the horn as the pupils filed out two by two. On
Lincoln's Birthday the teachers always called on me to read the Gettysburg Address. I see now that they picked me because I was a
Negro; at the time I thought rather vainly that it was because I was
the best reader in the class, a standing that was very important to me.

When I reached the seventh grade, Miss Lulu Converse, a stout
woman who wore long, black dresses and button shoes, took me
under her wing. Miss Converse was strict but very fair, a fine, no-
nonsense sort of teacher who wore her hair parted down the middle,
pulled back at the sides, and tucked into an austere bun. We sat at
wooden desks arranged in orderly rows before Miss Converse's great
oak desk, a bastion of authority looming up at the front of the room.
Behind her was the blackboard. It looked like the wall of a firing
squad to some of the slower pupils in the class. Standing before that
board, Miss Converse would consult her bottomless store of simple,

compound, and complex sentences. After writing out a snaking tangle of words on the board, she would turn, fix us with a dark eye, and call for volunteers to identify all nouns, adjectives, adverbs, verbs, and participles. "What's this word, and *this* and *this?*" she would bark, pointing to the words chalked on the blackboard. Heaven help the poor student who couldn't fire the right answers back. We learned spelling by rote, surviving bees and spelldowns once a week. We studied the Palmer method of writing, a style of penmanship requiring great, looping rotations of the arm and wrist. It produced elegant handwriting for the more artistic students. In me it produced a chronic writer's cramp.

Away from the blackboard, Miss Converse was one of the most popular teachers in the school. One day Miss Shaw, a martinet who served as St. Paul's music supervisor, came to Whittier on an inspection tour. "Miss Shaw is coming and she is going to test you on singing," Miss Converse warned us. "If you get a compliment from *her,* I'll buy you a box of chocolates." We thought Miss Converse was just fooling, but when our reedy voices drew praise from Miss Shaw, Miss Converse rushed right off to the sweet shop and returned with a big box of chocolates. I will always be grateful to her for attending to another vital part of my education—she taught me to dance: white schoolmarm and gawky black scholar gingerly waltzing to the thumping chords of the piano—the Ku Klux Klan would have been beside itself.

Out in the schoolyard we played football until the knees of our knickers wore out, and marbles until our knuckles ached. The boys carried cloth bags of the common clay marbles we called "commies," more expensive "red eyes"—glass marbles containing a glowing cat's eye—and the steel ball bearings we used for shooters. We shagged after one another in breathless rounds of "Run, Sheep, Run," and a game like baseball, except that the fielders threw the ball at the runner to put him out. I can feel the sting of the rubber ball to this day. In winter we tramped out round diagrams in the snow and played pie tag, and when spring came we had a baseball team after school. Barney Simpson, Russ Nelson, and Bobby Schmidt, all big kids, were our stars. I was the manager. We played at a ball field at Rich and Lawson streets. I stood behind first, coaching and keeping score. In the last inning of a game against our old enemy, the Hancock School, I ordered a double steal and we won 2–1. It was one of life's sweet days. Herman still talks about it.

This idyll lasted until I was about nine years old. Then a shadow fell: after several years of aimless work in Missouri, my father turned up in St. Paul. Following my mother's death he had wandered off; he hadn't even sent Earl, Armeda, and me birthday or Christmas cards. We had practically forgotten him, but suddenly there he was, husky and dour as ever, a new burden on the doorstep of 906 Galtier Street.

Uncle Sam got him a job as a fireman at Engine Company No. 22, which was just up the hill and around the corner from our house. The firemen were heroes in blue uniforms with soft caps and gleaming brass buttons. Since they were black and the neighborhood was mostly white, the fires were all integrated: white victims, with black men riding to their rescue. The fire barn, a two-story brick building on Matilda and Front streets, had a hayloft where Mike and Tommy Gibbons, two white boxers, trained Tommy successfully enough to get a crack at Dempsey in 1924. Between alarms the firemen played handball against the brick walls of the barn. They slept up in the loft. When the alarm bell went off, they came hurtling down a slick brass pole to the stable, where matched teams of three white horses stood waiting, their heavy harnesses dangling from a contraption on the ceiling. At a signal, the harnesses dropped down, the firemen buckled the horses up and threw open the doors of the fire barn, and the horses, three abreast, charged into the street. One team pulled a hose cart loaded with ladders. Another hauled "The Puffer," a shiny, coal-burning water pump that thundered along, belching clouds of black smoke from its fat, round chimney. As a Mississippi farmboy, my father had had plenty of experience with horses; he became the Puffer's substitute driver.

Footloose, my father very soon got restless. One day he told Aunt Elizabeth that he was ready to reclaim his children. When she asked him just how he planned to take care of us, he told her vaguely that he would probably send us back down to his parents in Mississippi. My mother's last letter had not faded from Aunt Elizabeth's memory. She decided to put a stop to such talk once and for all. Stalling for time, she took Uncle Sam aside; then the two of them went out and found a lawyer.

Although this emergency took place less than seventy years ago, finding a black attorney in St. Paul wasn't all that easy. Most blacks in the city worked at unskilled or service jobs, and the Negro middle class was composed mostly of St. Paul's waiters, barbers, and Pullman porters, with an occasional postal worker, fireman, or policeman thrown in. There were two black doctors, a dentist, one pharmacist who owned his own drugstore, and one newspaper publisher, but there were no black teachers, no hospital workers, few clerks, and no real politicians. Minnesota's total black population at the time was about 7,000, not enough to produce a Negro vote of much consequence. But fortunately for Earl, Armeda, and me, St. Paul did have several black lawyers.

The man my aunt and uncle settled on was W. T. Francis, an elegant young lawyer with fair skin and features. He parted his hair in the middle, wore high white wing collars, soft silk ties, and a red rose in his lapel. He came from Indiana, and he had learned his law clerking in the legal department of the Northern Pacific, where Uncle Sam had met him. He had just opened his own office in the N.P.'s building in downtown St. Paul. Later he would become the Republican Party's black whip in the upper Midwest and Herbert Hoover's minister to Liberia. Earl, Armeda, and I were one of his first cases.

Aunt Elizabeth and Uncle Sam had a simple plan for defeating my father: Aunt Elizabeth would become our legal guardian. Francis took on their suit and won. On February 25, 1911, he sent Uncle Sam a short, formal letter with the good news. "In the matter of the appointment of Mrs. Williams as Guardian of Roy, Armeda and Earl Wilkins," it read, "I am pleased to inform you that the appointment has been made, all papers filed and the matter is now closed, the bond having been accepted and approved by the court." Since our father hadn't even been able to cope with our mother's funeral expenses, how he could have taken care of the three of us I will never know. The judge apparently felt the same way. W. T. Francis submitted a bill for $25 to Aunt Elizabeth, who quietly paid it, and from that moment forth, in the eyes of the law and in our own, she and Uncle Sam were our mother and father.

There was another lawyer in town to whom Aunt Elizabeth and Uncle Sam might have turned. His name was Frederick L. McGhee, a lean man with silvering hair and fiery black eyes, the son of slaves from Aberdeen, Mississippi, and the first Negro admitted to the bar in Minnesota. He was in poor health in 1911, which may explain why Aunt Elizabeth and Uncle Sam didn't hire him to handle the custody case, but he was an important figure to St. Paul and to us all the same. It was McGhee who served as the link between St. Paul and the militant civil rights movement of the day. He was a friend of W. E. B. Du Bois and with Du Bois one of the founding fathers of the Niagara Movement. In 1906, he had gone from St. Paul to the first gathering Du Bois called on the Canadian side of Niagara Falls (the hotels on the American side wouldn't rent rooms to Negroes). A year later he had gone down to Harpers Ferry to sign the Niagara Movement's manifesto denouncing the spread of Jim Crow in the United States.

That particular document argued: "Stripped of verbose subterfuge and in its naked nastiness, the new American creed says: fear to let black men ever try to rise, lest they become equals of the white. And this in the land that professes to follow Jesus Christ. The blasphemy of such a course is only matched by its cowardice." At a time when Booker T. Washington's racial temporizing and fraternizing with rich white millionaires, philanthropists, and the Republican Party were the rule of the day, these were radical views. McGhee was a man who practiced what he preached. A white lawyer once made the mistake of telling him that he wouldn't stand in court with a "damned nigger." McGhee spat in his eye.

We knew McGhee, and it was through him that the National Association for the Advancement of Colored People reached St. Paul and 906 Galtier Street. In the summer of 1908, when I was not quite seven years old, there was a bloody race riot in Springfield, Illinois. On the first night a mob lynched a black barber; the following night it lynched an eighty-four-year-old black man who had committed the unthinkable crime of being married to a white woman for over thirty years. It took 4,200 state militia to restore order, and before the mayhem ended, 2,000 Negroes had to flee for their lives.

A young Southern journalist named William English Walling happened to cover the Springfield riots for a muckraking magazine called *The Independent.* He wrote that if the spirit of the abolitionists, of Lovejoy and Lincoln, was not rekindled, the race wars of the South were sure to spread to the North. His article caught the eye of Mary White Ovington, a wealthy white social worker and philanthropist who lived in New York City. She got in touch with him, and with the help of Dr. Henry Moscowitz, another social worker, they drafted a call for racial justice. In 1909, on Lincoln's Birthday, the call was printed in the New York *Evening Post* by publisher Oswald Garrison Villard, the grandson of the abolitionist William Lloyd Garrison. The document came at the nadir of race relations in the United States. In later years it always surprised me to hear Southern racists talk about the sanctity of Jim Crow, as if he had been around forever. Actually, he didn't gain full strength until the years after *Plessy vs. Ferguson.* The call pointed out that Georgia had just completed a second confederacy by joining all the other states of the old South in disenfranchising the Negro; that the Supreme Court had made it a crime for white and black people to shop in the same marketplace at the same time; that state after state was denying black children equal education; and that lynching and other brutalities against black men, women, and children were afflicting the North as well as the South. "Silence under these conditions means tacit approval," the call argued. "This government cannot exist half slave and half free any better today than it could in 1861." Dozens of prominent white liberals—from Jane Addams to Rabbi Stephen Wise—signed the call. They later met in Cooper Union in New York City and laid plans to turn the manifesto into a permanent organization. In 1910 these plans led to the birth of the N.A.A.C.P.

Those founding white liberals had the best of hearts—and one rather embarrassing problem: while the new N.A.A.C.P. was long on conscience, it was very short on contacts with Negroes. The problem was solved when enough money was raised to hire Dr. Du Bois as director of publicity and research. He had been having troubles keeping the Niagara Movement in funds, and when he joined the N.A.A.C.P. he brought his friends and followers with him. Very quickly it became the most important civil rights organization in the country.

With Du Bois came his old friend McGhee, with McGhee came St. Paul, and with St. Paul came our house. In 1912, shortly before he died, McGhee began to recruit members for what he called the Twin Cities Protective League, a civil rights group that he hoped to affiliate with the N.A.A.C.P. The league died with him. A year later, in the summer of 1913, Du Bois took soundings around St. Paul to find out what had happened to McGhee's plans. In response, a new flurry of organizing led to the founding of an official N.A.A.C.P. branch that fall. The local folks sent $27 to cover the annual fifty-cent dues for fifty-four members. On receiving the dues and the membership list, the national office in New York sent out a charter. Not long ago I found a wrinkled copy of that list of charter members in the Library of Congress. Member number 42 was Uncle Sam Williams; so as things turned out, my family and the N.A.A.C.P. were entwined practically from its creation.

We started to receive *The Crisis*, the magazine Du Bois edited with such skill, peppering Woodrow Wilson for extending segregation in Washington, excoriating the lynch spirit in the South, printing prose and verse by black writers who went begging at the slick white monthlies, urging the talented tenth—his own black aristocracy—to pull the race up by the bootstraps. The St. Paul branch responded to his prodding. Dr. Valdo Turner, our family physician, was head of the local branch. When the Minnesota legislature took up a bill banning intermarriage, Dr. Turner led a delegation to protest. Reverend Jones went with him. With a little logic and a whiff of hellfire they succeeded in getting the politicians to drop the idea.

Most of the branch's other activities were a good deal more tame. St. Paul had no segregation in its schools or on public transportation, and virtually none in housing. The main sore spots were job discrimination and a mean color line at the hotels and restaurants. The branch once caught Kresge's five-and-dime using separate glasses for black and white customers at its lunch counter and raised an effective uproar. But to most Negroes in St. Paul, the great issues of color seemed to be confined to the South. Some even seemed to feel just a touch superior, thinking mistakenly that they were immune to the afflictions down the Mississippi.

In 1913, the fiftieth anniversary of the Emancipation Proclamation, Uncle Sam undertook his own campaign of personal emancipation. That summer, the New York, New Haven, and Hartford Railroad hired Elliott as president—for $100,000 a year. This was a lot of money—one hundred thirty times or so what Elliott paid Uncle Sam—and Elliott's new job was to clean up the legal mess the New York, New Haven, and Hartford had made in trying to monopolize rail traffic in the Northeast. One day Elliott confidently took Uncle Sam aside and said he expected Uncle Sam to go with him back East. We debated the offer over the dinner table for several days. But in the end, Uncle Sam decided that he had let Elliott drag him around long enough, and he turned down the offer.

The decision represented an important psychological step forward for our family. Grandfather Wilkins had been held a slave, then freed by forces beyond his control. My father had had a brief fling with independence, only to retreat into religion. Uncle Sam's path couldn't have been more different. He studied matters carefully, made up his own mind, and took action, doing what he thought was right. No one had any strings on him. I never forgot the example he set that summer.

Uncle Sam knew a vice president of the Northern Pacific named Woodward, who also had a private railroad car. He signed on with Woodward, and life became almost normal: we didn't uproot, there ware fewer inspection tours and long absences, and Uncla Sam got home for dinner every night. The new boss was a relaxed, kindly man, and one summer, when he took his own family off in the private car for a vacation in Canada, he let Uncle Sam take me along. We rattled thpough Quebec and into the Maritkie Provinces, where I got my first glimpse of the Atlantic Ocean. After we parked the railroad car on a siding, I ran down to the beach, dove headlong into the rolling waves, and got a shock that shivered me to my toenails. "Lord deliver me from this cold water," I spluttered as I came up through the frigid surf. To this day I am leery of strange waters, and I distrust plunging and plungers in any form.

On June 13, 1915, the year Booker T. Washington died, I graduated from the eighth grade at Whittier Grammar School. The graduating class sang "The Mill in the Forest," a ballad about a sturdy blacksmith pounding his anvil deep in a lonely wood—the only words I can remember are "Clang, clang, clang." That fall I went on to the George Weitbreit Mechanical Arts High School, the best high school in the city, where I registered for a pre-engineering course: four years of math—including trigonometry and college algebra—chemistry and physics, mechanical drawing and machine shop, along with English and history. I was brash and confident in those days. I remember saying to myself, "You might as well take the toughest course and see how you do."

I don't know why I settled on engineering. Perhaps I wanted to outdo Elliott at his own game. Whatever the case, it turned out that I hadn't been born to become an engineer. The teacher who influenced me most was Miss Mary E. Copley, a tall, plump woman who wore long dresses that nearly touched the floor. She taught English. The day I turned in my first composition she asked me to stay after class. When I arrived at her desk she had my paper lying in front of her. I wondered what disaster I had committed. For a few agonizing seconds Miss Copley studied me, then she said briskly, "You have ability, Roy. You must develop your writing skills."

With that my plans to become an engineer melted in a new lust for books and writing. Whitman once said that he was simmering, simmering, simmering until Emerson brought him to the boil, and that is precisely what Miss Copley did for me. The high school had an excellent library, and I read everything I could lay my hands on: Chaucer, Homer, Shakespeare, Longfellow, Robert Burns, Gerard Manley Hopkins, and Tennyson. The melodious syllables of "Invictus" had me in a lather ("Out of the night that covers me, / Black as the Pit from pole to pole, / I thank whatever gods may be / For my unconquerable soul"). I also read *Souls of Black Folk*. I knew by heart the basic axiom of Du Bois—"The problem of the twentieth century is the problem of the color line"—and his presentation of the psychological dilemma of Negroes: "One ever feels his twoness an American, a Negro; two souls, two thoughts, two unreconciled stirrings; two warring ideals in one dark body, which dogged strength alone keeps it from being torn asunder." At thesame time I was young, Jim Crow had left me mostly alone, and while I loved the beauty of Du Bois's writing, his arguments were still a little abstract to me. I was too young to go to the N.A.A.C.P. meetings that Uncle Sam attended twice a month. There was no color line at the lake house where Herman and I went boating; there were no colored seats on the trolley which we rode all over town, no colored toilet at the Ice Palace, the great, glistening castle of ice that went up each year at Winter Carnival. I was sheltered, and I went my way not knowing that Du Bois was exactly right, that a tremendous shock was waiting for me.

After that first meeting with Miss Copley, I put myself under her guidance. She believed in originality in composition and encouraged me to develop my own style. In my junior year I became editor of *The Cogwheel*, the school's literary magazine. The English Department awarded the job on the basis of compositions submitted during the first three years of high school. I can remember the teachers crowding around me, wringing my hand, and congratulating me. It was a wonderful day, and with it came a great surprise. When *The Crisis* reached our house that month, I found a one-paragraph news item tucked inside: "Roy Wilkins has been elected president of the Mechanical Arts High School Literary Society of St. Paul, Minnesota, over two white candidates." It would be years before I met W. E. B. Du Bois in person, but my scrivening had somehow attracted his attention. After that paragraph it no longer occurred to me to be an engineer.

As president of the Literary Society, I also became editor of the yearbook during my last year in high school. I still have a tattered copy, bound in paper with a large block letter *M* printed in blue on the cover. The date is summer 1919, and in opening it, I can almost feel those innocent days pouring forth in a rush. There is the extravagant ad calling all athletes to buy Vanderbee's Ice Cream ("It sticks to your backbone") and the more homely pitch of the Consumer's Milk Company ("Just try it. That's all"). The waist-seam suits we wore in those days sold down at McCluskey's Department Store for $20.

I loved the job of running the Literary Society and editing the yearbook. As I recall, the great influenza epidemic of 1918 struck down my staff in the fall, but in the spring we made a strong comeback. On St. Patrick's Day we put on Lady Gregory's play *Spreading the News*, and in May I organized a reading of Paul Laurence Dunbar's poems. I see in turning the pages that I suffered from the usual editorial arrogance. I filled nooks and crannies of white space between short stories and essays with howlers taken from student test papers, probably leaked to me by Miss Copley, though I have forgotten the source. There I am, exposing one ten o'clock scholar for writing "Gaius Gracchus passed the Corn Cob Laws" and sneering at the literary moralist (probably a Methodist) who wrote, "Poe drank heavily—and gamboled."

I was the salutatorian at our graduation in June 1919. President Burton of the University of Minnesota was the commencement speaker, and I went on to the universitu myself that fall. Minnesotans were fiercely proud of the university, and I didn't think of going anywhere else. Tuition, a healt charge, and other fees came to about $115 a year; books, meals, and carfare were extra. Since I didn't have to live in a dormitory, I could save on expenses. Each morning our household began to stir about six o'clock, with breakfast at seven. Afterward I caught the Rice Street trolley near our home, transferring to the Como-Harriet Line for the run to campus. The trolleys were painted yellow and were round in the front and rear. As you got on at the rear, a conductor collected the fare—a nickel through St. Paul and another nickel on into Minneapolis. I could get to school for twenty cents a day and a little lunch money or dinner money whenever I stayed late.

Uncle Sam offered to help all he could with the school bills, but he didn't have enough money to pay them all. I made ends meet with a series of summer jobs that gradually put an end to the innocence that had blessed most of my childhood. For a time I was the only Negro caddy at the St. Paul Town and Country Club. The golfers were mostly Main Street businessmen, bankers and the like, all tight as ticks. I never saw a tip bigger than a nickel or a dime. After that I worked for a while as a redcap at Union Station in downtown St. Paul. The station was a huge, echoing cavern with tile floors. Those of us on the late shift spent two hours each night swabbing them with mops. I watched the trains steam out of the station and dreamed of following them one day.

One summer I worked at the Minneapolis Steel and Machinery Company, making artillery shells for the U.S. Expeditionary Force in Europe. We worked eight hours a day with ten minutes for lunch. Another summer I worked as a clean-up man in the beef and pork kills at the Swift and Company slaughterhouses. I wore rubber boots. At times I was up to my ankles in blood. My station in the pork kill was twenty minutes from the live hog; the job was to split the back bones, separate the pork chops, and clean up the floors and the trays on which the dismembered hogs came shuttling to us. After the first day I thought I would never eat again in my life. Back home the only thing I could get down was a piece of Aunt Elizabeth's cake. By the end of that summer, however, I had a cast-iron stomach. I used to toss raw pork loin in a bucket which I hung from a pipe by the steam escape. The hot steam cooked me a free lunch every day.

Finally, Uncle Sam got me a job as a waiter in the dining car of the Northern Pacific's North Coast Limited, a crack train that pulled out of Union Station in St. Paul at eleven o'clock in the morning and highballed west across the Dakotas, Montana, Idaho, and Washington, reaching Seattle forty-two hours later. Those trips come back now as a pleasant blur of rattling Pullmans rocketing along behind a great locomotive that filled the days with clouds of black smoke and the nights with the eerie wail of its whistle. During the run we worked like house slaves on roller skates, serving breakfast, lunch, and dinner, cleaning up, then starting all over again, seven meals in all. At night we slept on the cleared tables. We ate whatever the cook had left over. He served pie to the white folks only the first day out, keeping the moist desserts for the last part of the run; so only the white folks ate watermelon on our train.

I was the youngest waiter; the cook and the other waiters were hearty, friendly men. Some were old enough to be my father, and they broke me in as gently as they could. All the way out to the coast they talked about going to the "Chinaman's." When I asked them to explain themselves, they only winked. It turned out that the Chinaman's was a little hole in the wall in Seattle run by an enterprising man of color (yellow in his case) who owned and operated a one-man lottery. Hitting a number at the Chinaman's could win a man more than a month's pay, and they used to make his place our first stop. I put up in a rooming house that catered to dining-car waiters and Pullman porters. The next day I killed time sightseeing around Seattle. Then I hopped a return run to St. Paul.

It was grueling work, but it offered me my first sense of the sweep and expanse of the country. For the first time I began to look beyond the comfort and safety of St. Paul to the larger, harder world beyond. The waiters used to call passengers who left small tips "snakes," and I will never forget one of those particular reptiles, an unpleasant woman with two unruly children. I served the three of them all their meals from St. Paul to Seattle. After breakfast on the last day, just as we were approaching Seattle, this lady reached into her purse, rummaged around, looked up, and handed me a nickel. I looked hard at the coin she had pressed into my palm. Then, to her astonishment, I threw it out the window next to her. It was my first real act of rebellion, and I've never felt better.

I was not a street kid of the ghettos or a child of the South: I did not suffer as they do, nor did I become hard as quickly as they do. But a few weeks after the University of Minnesota let out for the summer of 1920, I lost my innocence on race once and for all.

I still feel a shock every time I think back on what happened that summer when the John Robinson Show hit Duluth. The John Robinson Show was a traveling circus. In mid-June, it came lumbering into Duluth with a manifest of elephants and tigers, lion tamers, trapeze artists, strong men, clowns, and about two dozen black roustabouts, whose job was to feed the animals, carry water, clean the grounds, and pitch the big top. About 10 P.M. on the night of the last show, as the roustabouts were hauling down the canvas and loading the circus train for the overnight run up to Virginia, Minnesota, James Sullivan, a white boy from west Duluth, and his girlfriend, who was not quite eighteen, stood watching. Sullivan later told the newspapers that a group of six Negroes suddenly stepped from the darkness behind him, pinned his arms behind his back, put a gun to his head, and told him, "Keep still or we'll blow your brains out." He also told the police that the attackers had carried his girl off into a ravine and assaulted her.

At 3 A.M. that night, just as the circus train was getting up steam, John Murphy, Duluth's police chief, and a flying squad of cops descended on the circus grounds. Stopping the train, Chief Murphy dragged every Negro in the John Robinson Show into a predawn lineup. Sullivan and the girl managed to implicate twelve black men, something of a feat, since it doubled the number of attackers who had supposedly taken part in the rape. The police sweated their suspects, obtained three "confessions," hauled six of the luckless roustabouts down to police headquarters, and let the circus train go on its way. Within a few hours, however, the terrified suspects had produced such a welter of confessions and conflicting testimony that Chief Murphy and his chief of detectives, Frank Schulter, set off for Virginia and arrested ten more John Robinson Show roustabouts, making sixteen arrests in all. The thought that at least ten innocent men were caught in the dragnet didn't seem to cross Chief Murphy's mind. It's a wonder he didn't arrest every black man in Minnesota.

The next morning wild rumors and false reports about the attack began to swirl through Duluth, and at about 2:30 in the afternoon, an informer called police headquarters with a disquieting report that hotheads in a poolroom in west Duluth were talking up a lynching. The police ignored the call and the pool hall boiled over. Around 7 P.M. a group of young white men found a rope, rounded up a truck, and set off for police headquarters, a three-story building on Superior Street, where the suspects were under lock and key. For a while these thugs stood on the back of the truck whirling their lynch rope around in the air, shouting, "Come on, join the necktie party. Help get the niggers." Then they tossed the noose into the street and dragged it behind them. From the curbs and sidewalks dozens of white men and boys stepped forward, grabbing the snaking rope. Before long a mob of 5,000 white citizens converged on the jail.

Up in the boys' jail, one of the roustabouts named Isaac McGhee cowered in his cell. Finding him, the mob produced a set of steel saws and went to work on the bars. For over an hour the saws rasped. Then, losing patience, the crowd improvised a battering ram from some heavy timbers and smashed a hole two feet wide and three feet high through the sixteen-inch masonry wall on one side of McGhee's cell. A few men scrambled through the hole, seized McGhee, dragged him out, pushed him down the stairs, rushed him out the front door, and hustled him up Second Avenue to First Street, where an electric-light pole stood on the corner facing the Shriners' Auditorium. It was a tall pole with an arabesque arm curving out above the light. A small boy shinnied to the top, and the mob tossed him a rope, cheering as he fed it through the iron curlicue and dropped it to outstretched hands below. Father W. J. Power, a Catholic priest from Duluth's Sacred Heart Cathedral, managed to climb up a telegraph pole overlooking the executioners. The priest cried out, "Men, you do not know that these Negroes are the guilty ones. . . . In the name of God . . . I ask you to stop."

Jeers drowned out the priest's voice.

"To hell with the law."

"Remember the girl."

"Lynch the dirty black snakes."

The mob returned to its work. McGhee shouted that he was innocent; he begged for mercy. But a noose was placed around his neck.

White hands yanked the rope.

The black boy swung aloft—and the rope broke.

As McGhee fell to the street, the crowd pressed forward. Men jumped on his chest, kicking his head. The rope was mended, and on the second pull it held. McGhee gasped and kicked. Then he twisted quietly in the soft glow of the streetlamp.

Back at the police station a second crew of wreckers was busy with the locks in the main jail, where the other suspects waited in terror. One by one the locks on the cells were broken. The mob set up a kangaroo court that summarily judged Elmer Jackson, twenty, and Elias Clayton, eighteen, guilty of rape. The two were marched out of the police station and dragged to the lamppost.

As the noose tightened on Jackson's neck, he reached into his pocket and took out a pair of dice. "I won't be needing these," he said, tossing them to the mob. The executioners pulled at the rope. Jackson jerked up into the air. His body twisted violently. Then it was still. The mob lowered it to within a few feet of the ground, stripped it naked, and left it dangling.

Elias Clayton was forced to watch Jackson's execution. He wept and begged the mob to spare him. His arms were still raised in a last prayer for pity when the hangmen pulled their rope for the third time.

By 11:30 P.M., McGhee, Jackson, and Clayton were dead. Just then the phone jangled down at Fort Snelling in St. Paul, where the Sixth Minnesota Infantry was stationed: the Duluth authorities had finally decided to call for help. The troopers arrived at 8 A.M. the next morning, just in time to turn around and go back home. By 1 A.M., the mob had dispersed. The police went to the lamppost, cut down the bodies of Jackson, Clayton, and McGhee, and carried the three corpses off to Grady and O'Horgan's Funeral Parlor.

The next day the triple lynching made headlines all around the country. The better white people of Duluth were as horrified as everyone else by what had happened. That, of course, was no comfort to the three dead men, or to the other thirteen left in jail after the lynching. The Duluth, St. Paul, and Minneapolis branches of the N.A.A.C.P. raised $1,200 to defend the Duluth 13. The national office stepped in from New York with more money and advice. There was no real evidence linking any of the roustabouts to the rape. A jury acquitted one of the thirteen suspects, and the court dismissed five other cases for lack of evidence. The cases of six other suspects were dismissed at the request of the Minnesota state prosecutor. Max Mason, the thirteenth man, was found guilty of rape and sentenced to thirty years in prison. No one around the N.A.A.C.P. believed he was guilty, but it took several years of legal work to free him.

I was just short of nineteen the night that the bodies of McGhee, Jackson, and Clayton swung from a light pole in Duluth. I read the stories in the newspapers and put them down feeling sick, scared, and angry all at the same time. This was Minnesota, not Mississippi, but every Negro in the John Robinson Show had been suspect in the eyes of the police and guilty in the eyes of the mob. What bothered me most was the way those 5,000 white Northerners had gotten together on the lynching. The mob was in touch with something—an awful hatred I had never seen or felt before. For the first time in my life I understood what Du Bois had been writing about. I found myself thinking of black people as a very vulnerable *us*—and white people as an unpredictable, violent *them*.

5   A FRONT-PAGE APPRENTICE

fter my summers in the slaughterhouse and on the North Coast Limited, I could tell that I was not cut out to butcher hogs or wait on tables—or sleep on them. I buckled down at the University of Minnesota. I suppose I'm a Middle Western leveler—I don't believe bright young people have to go to an Ivy League school to get along in this world. Good minds and fine teachers are where one finds them, and there were plenty around the University of Minnesota. In the English Department, Professor E. F. Stoll taught Shakespeare; R. Richard Burton was the expert on George Bernard Shaw, and Joseph Warren Beach was a master on the craft of Henry James. Beach used to tell his students that Theodore Dreiser couldn't write well enough to pass English at the University of Minnesota: his pronouns and antecedents didn't match regularly enough. The Sociology Department was also a lively place. At the time, the evolutionists from the Natural Science Department and the fundamentalists from the Religion Department were going at one another tooth and nail, and the bloodshed spilled over into our sociology classes. During one battle, the school *Literary Digest* published a symposium on the incendiary question "Shall Moses or Darwin rule Minnesota schools?", a topic that brought Rev. H. J. Habel of Minneapolis brachiating right out of his pulpit. He made a ferocious attack on the school's young instructors for trying to "impress [on] the class that every intelligent person now accepts the theory of evolution," and sneered at such teachers as men of no convictions, intellectual flappers following the crowd. His attack drew a calm response from Rev. Frank J. Bruno, the university's rector, who also appeared in sociology classes from time to time. Rev. Bruno's reply was that, if pursued long enough and honestly enough, all the uproar over evolution could only end in better religion and better science. Such moderation dominated the University of Minnesota in my student days. I absorbed it, and it has sustained me many times over the years.

Professor Rarig, the public-speaking instructor, gave me lessons in how to keep a banquet audience awake while the rubber chicken is going down. In the spring of 1922 I gathered my thoughts on the Duluth lynchings and entered the annual Pillsbury Oratorical Contest. I made it to the finals with a speech titled "Democracy or Demonocracy?" The six finalists were judged on platform presence, subject matter, and rhetorical finesse. Sidney Benson won first prize with a stem-winder on Soviet Russia. I thought I had a sure winner, and I was disappointed when I won third prize. But the $25 in prize money came to a quarter of one tuition bill. I put it to good use, and I have been in the speaking business one way or another ever since.

I was not a big man on campus, for in the twenties black students were banned from fraternity row at the University of Minnesota. A few of us got together and formed a chapter of Omega Psi Phi, a national black fraternity founded at Howard University. The other charter brothers were George King, F. D. Inge, Hutchin Inge, Theodore Inge, Robert Harris, Albert Butler, B. W. Harris, and Earle Kyle. We invited Duke Slater, Iowa's famous black tackle, to a smoker after the Iowa-Minnesota football game, and when Charles Gilpin played the Emperor Jones in Minneapolis, we threw a party for Brother Shields, a member of the cast who had been an Omega Psi Phi man at Michigan. In 1922 the *Minnesota Gopher* published a picture of us standing starchily on the steps of a classroom building on campus. We looked more like a crew of hopeful bankers than hell-raisers, but it was the first time in the history of the university that a black organization had appeared in the yearbook.

During my sophomore year, I tried out for the staff of the *Minnesota Daily*. R. R. Barlow, a newsman from Iowa, had taken over the school's Department of Journalism. Barlow was a fine man and a great doer, a member of Sigma Delta Chi, the national newspaper fraternity, and a proud professional. He talked the university into letting the *Daily* set up offices in an old music hall on campus, and that bailiwick became a home away from 906 Galtier Street. On one occasion, J. M. Thomas, a pugnacious teacher in the Rhetoric Department, baited us by assigning his pupils to write themes attacking yellow journalism. I believe the topic he set was "If the spirit of the modern newspaper were incarnated in a human being, we should set the dog on him wherever he appeared on the doorstep." Professor Thomas told the *Daily* that his bile had been stirred by a run of "battles, murders, and sudden death . . . on every page of the newspapers." Barlow crushed him. "There are plenty of clean newspapers for all of us to read—if we want them," he told Thomas. "Most newsfolk are as respectable and as generous in their service to society as anyone else, and I am sure you wouldn't kick them off your doorstep if they called on you." These were sound views. I listened to Barlow and began to consider becoming a newsman myself.

The *Daily* drew me like a bee to clover, and if I'm not mistaken, I became the *Daily*'s first black reporter. My exhilaration at the breakthrough was deflated somewhat when I picked up the paper and saw that the editors had listed me on the masthead as Ray Wilkins, and it took nearly a month for the paper to get my name right. I started out as a lowly cub, chasing after two- and three-paragraph items on the lowliest doings around campus. We ran plenty of stories along the lines of "How Y'Gonna Grow Your Fall Mustache—They're in Vogue." After a time I became editor of the *Daily*'s *Official Student Bulletin*. My first big job was to print a notice from Bill Freng, the Varsity Rooter King, announcing that he did not plan to run for reelection as yell leader—and inviting all comers to try out for his job at a pep fest on Friday night. During my last year in college I became a night editor. In the afternoons, at about four o'clock, after classes were over, I hoofed over to the *Daily* office, where I read and edited stories brought in by reporters who had picked up their assignments earlier from the day editor. The managing editor and I then decided the news play for the next day's edition. I laid out the front page, wrote six- and seven-column banner and streamer heads for the big news, smaller heads for double column boxes, and captions. I also corrected galley proofs, approved the final page proofs, and put the paper to bed at a print shop in Minneapolis. It was often after midnight when I finished. The next morning the managing editor or his assistant blue-penciled errors and posted a copy of the *Daily* on the bulletin board for the mortification of any sloppy night editor. Most of the time I escaped their mangling. I edited the paper once or twice a week, earning three dollars for each stretch at the print shop. Those were probably the happiest nights I spent at college.

The *Daily* was supposed to earn enough money to pay its own way, but we were usually hard put for cash and subscriptions, and in the fall of 1922, we organized a monumental subscription drive. John K. Mortland and John M. Bridge, two *Daily* livewires, hired a steam calliope, mounted it on a truck, and went out on a Monday morning cruising the campus. Their tootling drew the eyes of teachers, students, and helpless civilians to a sign plastered on the side of the truck HAVE MUSIC IN YOUR HOUSE AND THE MINNESOTA DAILY IN YOUR POST OFFICE BOX. Unfortunately, the noise also offended the bluejackets down at the East Side police station. The law tracked down

Mortland and Bridge, took them into custody, and hustled them off in a Black Maria. Luckily the desk sergeant was a tolerant man; he released them—but only after they had promised to stopper their calliope.

In mid-January 1923, our circulation fell to a perilous 1,100, and we were reduced to putting out the *Daily* in the form of a little three-column pamphlet. I have a copy of the January 16, 1923, issue, which marked our humiliation. In the lead story George Dworshak, the managing editor, said testily, "This is not a souvenir or pocket edition of the *Minnesota Daily*. It represents the type of issue which we will continue to publish until we have the support of at least 3,000 more students." We did find space in the middle of our stubby little edition for one very serious story. A peculiar wooden fortress had turned up on the Knoll, a hill and campus landmark. Above the odd structure flew a sinister black flag, and the campus was soon full of rumors that the Ku Klux Klan had used the place for an initiation ceremony. The St. Paul and Minneapolis newspapers quickly got on to the story, and after the Minnesota legislature began to talk about an investigation, Dean E. E. Nicholson promised that the university would see if the Ku Kluxers were at work. But Dean Nicholson also said, "We would naturally make inquiry so as to be able to classify them with the rest of the student organizations." Everyone except me got a good laugh out of that.

Journalism was the one profession that offered me a way out of the dead-end jobs that St. Paul had to offer. In the spring of 1922, a friend of mine named Walter Chestnutt founded a little weekly called the *Northwestern Bulletin*. Chestnutt was not quite twenty years old at the time. He had been two years behind me at Mechanical Arts High School and hadn't been able to go on to college, but somehow he managed to raise several hundred dollars to get the *Bulletin* going. He was the businessman of the operation, and for a while I edited the paper. To my delight, Melvin J. Chisum, who was field secretary of the National Negro Press Association, called the *Bulletin* "the best appearing of all the fifty-odd exchanges" he was getting, "with the bare exception of the *Chicago Defender*."

I became more set than ever on getting ahead in the news business. In the fall of 1922, John Quincy Adams, editor of the *St. Paul Appeal*, was hit by a car and killed. Adams's son, John Quincy, Jr., was a tolerable enough printer, but he knew nothing about editing and putting out a newspaper; so in desperation, Mrs. Adams, who was a member of the congregation at St. James's A.M.E. Church, turned to me for help. She had followed my work in high school, on the

Daily, and with the *Bulletin*. She asked if I would be interested in becoming the new editor of the *Appeal*. I quickly accepted. The University of Minnesota was chuckling at the Klan; the *Daily* was little more than a handbill; the *Appeal* offered me a paper all my own.

But the *Appeal*, once a fine newspaper, had fallen on bad days. Adams was a stout man who looked like a Caucasian. He had organized the first Afro-American Press Association in the country and served as its president for two years. He loved to argue, but his manners were always flawless, and his main theme appealed greatly to me. "Remove all barriers on account of race and color," he would say, "and like water, we will find our level." Over the years Booker T. Washington, William Monroe Trotter, the hot-tempered editor of the *Guardian* in Boston, and Dr. Du Bois had all stayed at his home, a jumble of Victorian spindles, turrets, and stained glass on St. Anthony Avenue.

By the time I stepped in as editor, the *Appeal* had lost its voice as a crusading weekly. It was little more than an advertising throwaway, and on Valentine's Day and Easter ads from local businesses filled the entire front page. Other days, it was larded with odd feature stories. My favorite was a story on maple sugaring season in New England. With fine disregard for nature or husbandry, the *Appeal* ran the same story spring, summer, and winter alike, whenever there was nothing else to fill the yawning front page.

In December 1922, prepared for revolution, I became editor. I did not, however, succeed in transforming the paper overnight. I had just turned twenty-one, and my news experience was limited to reporting, copy reading, and editing a high school yearbook, a college daily, and the *Bulletin*. The *Appeal* wasn't the New York *World*, but it did have an image to maintain, along with four pages of news, church happenings, and social gossip that made it the voice of St. Paul's black community.

I started as diplomatically as I could to change the paper. In January I published a New Year's editorial hinting to our readers that more news, local and foreign, and fresher news than the *Appeal* had been serving up for some time, was on the way. My plan was to buy what I could get cheaply and to crib major stories by rewriting the metropolitan papers around the country. I managed to talk the Adams family out of selling the whole front page for ads, and I announced my new era with a second editorial later that month in which I promised not to play up crime or sensation. I now see in looking at that editorial how young and earnest I was. I said, "The editor will strive to make the paper a medium of information on questions of the day, as they affect the race, and a stimulus to thought. As in the days of its founder and veteran editor, the *Appeal* still will cry out for justice and fair play for the colored Americans." Then I waited to see what would happen.

St. Paul seemed largely indifferent to the editorial. I found myself in an awkward position—having to make good on my own rather inflated promises. By February, I was still running stories about the French birth rate, an ax murder, and the saga of a Poland China hog that had crawled under a haystack in Madison, Nebraska, living forty-seven days without food and water. I was a great admirer of H. L. Mencken in those days, and so I also printed a story about the misanthropic whim of Mrs. Sidmon McHie of New York, who had ordered a mason to carve an unusual epitaph on her tombstone: "The more I saw of people, the more I thought of dogs."

The more I saw of the *Appeal*, the more I was disgusted with myself. In the next issue, however, I finally managed to turn the paper around. I kept the familiar makeup—a grim row of tombstoned headlines—but I brightened the content of the stories, shifting toward more substantial Negro news. I began by dusting off a report that a number of important race leaders were urging Warren Harding's Attorney General to prosecute the epaulettes right off the burly shoulders of Marcus Garvey. I ran the story along with a piece on the migration of unskilled Negro workers from South to North and a report that suggested optimistically that lynching seemed to be on the wane. Instead of Mrs. McHie and the Poland China hog, I had a brief item on a group of black ministers from Knoxville, Tennessee, who had denounced Billy Sunday as a Ku Kluxer after the evangelist made the mistake of inviting them to a Jim Crow prayer meeting.

Winter edged into spring, and the *Appeal* began to turn into a decent little newspaper. As managing editor, I had a front-row seat whenever anyone of news significance to Negroes stopped in St. Paul. But the best part of the job was the early vantage it gave me on the tougher issues of leading the race. In late April of that year, Oswald Garrison Villard, vice president of the board of the N.A.A.C.P., arrived from New York on an organizing and fund-raising trip. Villard was white, a latter-day abolitionist, the first I had seen up close. He was a little overeager to dispense solutions for all Negro problems, a failing common to many good-hearted white liberals, but he was sincere, and he knew how to stoke up a crowd, and he filled St. Peter's Church. "Among colored people," he said, "there are the great church and fraternal organizations, but on the question of common welfare there is no solidarity. . . . A vigilant organization such as the National Association should be supported so that it can ever be on the watch."

I had joined the St. Paul branch of the N.A.A.C.P. in 1922, and at the time of Villard's visit I was serving as its secretary. The branch was no hotbed of revolution, but it stood far in advance of the local churches and lodges. As a result, we had terrible problems raising money. Villard's visit had an ironic side effect: three weeks after he left, a large group of St. Paul citizens got together and raised $575— to found a branch of the Urban League.

A month later, Representative Leonides C. Dyer came to St. Paul to speak at the Pilgrim Baptist Church. Dyer was then a prime mover in Congress for a federal antilynching law. His bill would have given Congress power to carry out the equal-protection clause of the Fourteenth Amendment, a step that was needed because the South chose to prosecute every crime except lynching. Dyer had succeeded in getting his bill through the House, but it always died in the Senate. "When you send these cowardly mobbists to the penitentiary, they'll stop this damnable crime," Dyer said that day. But he left the burden of achieving that goal to Negroes. "Colored people as a people are all right. But instead of standing together upon issues in one compact organization, they fight among themselves about who shall 'lead' or 'hold office.' " Of course, he didn't say why black people should be any better than anyone else at standing together; perhaps he thought that blackness can work like glue, a very white notion. The argument that blacks should entrust all their interests to a single organization has always been wrong; black interests are too broad and varied to be contained in such tight compass. But there has also been a tendency among us to carve one another up over questions of leadership, when discrimination and inequality have provided more than enough targets to shoot at, more than enough work to go around.

The greatest leadership dispute that summer concerned Marcus Garvey. The battle was exhilarating. Garvey stirred feelings like a black Moses and raised money like a black Croesus. His problem was that he made enemies like a black Kaiser. In those days I agreed with A. Philip Randolph, who gave credit to Garvey as a tremendous organizer, while attacking his autocratic ways and his talk of empire at a time when most Negroes were still struggling manfully to make democracy work. "Garvey must go" was a slogan that turned up regularly in the pages of *The Messenger,* the magazine that Randolph edited with Chandler Owen. At one point, there were rumors that Garvey had been dickering with the Ku Klux Klan. Randolph jumped all over him and the United Negro Improvement Association. Before long, Randolph got a package in the mail containing a severed human hand and a note from the Kluxers in New Orleans. The note said, in effect, if you are not in favor with your race movement, you can't be with ours, and gave Randolph about a week to put his "name in your nigger improvement association as a member, paid up too . . . or we may have to send *your* hand to someone else."

In *The Crisis*, I watched W. E. B. Du Bois try to come to terms with Garvey. The first articles were temperate, then Garvey denounced Du Bois as "purely and simply a white man's nigger." I suppose Garvey made the charge because he suspected that Du Bois was trying to sabotage the U.N.I.A. to protect his own Pan-African Congress movement. In 1920 Du Bois was calling Garvey an "honest and sincere man with a tremendous vision, great dynamic force, stubborn determination, and unselfish desire to serve." In a few years he was calling him "the most dangerous enemy of the Negro race in America."

From my restricted vantage in St. Paul, I sided with Randolph and Du Bois. As Garvey's fraud trial proceeded, I splashed the stories across the front page of the *Appeal*. Looking back at the editorial page, I see that we hit below the belt every now and then. One of the editorials that spring reads, "Imagine if you can the kind of impression created by a pudgy black man striding back and forth across the courtroom pulling his moustache majestically, twirling a gold monocle, dramatically bellowing out ridiculous questions with every move and syllable showing more plainly his inordinate vanity. . . . The best that could be said for him is that he stole in millions, not in dimes; and dreamed in empires, not city lots."

When the jury rendered its verdict of guilty, we broke out the big type at the *Appeal:* GARVEY GETS FIVE YEARS IN PEN. But even if Garvey was guilty, the verdict didn't quite account for the hostility he managed to arouse. His success alarmed black leaders as well as white prosecutors. Even then, I thought his back-to-Africa ideas marched in the wrong direction, but he commanded an awesome power to raise broken spirits and to reach that nine-tenths of the black population that the Talented Tenth of Du Bois left out. When Garvey called out, "Up, you mighty race—" the people moved. I underestimated that power back in the twenties.

In opposing Garvey, I was not just put off by the style of the man; I did not like his ideas of separatism. There was nothing personal in this. When I detected the same ideas in Du Bois, I boiled him in oil, too. I see that I ran one editorial called "Du Bois' African Jack-O-Lantern" that put the case this way: "In 1921, W. E. B. Du Bois was gallivanting over the country from the Atlantic to the Pacific talking Pan-Africanism when he should have been using his talents to aid degraded America. Du Bois acknowledges that 'Pan-Africa' is a dream. And so it is. But lynching, disenfranchisement, segregation, and a thousand and one evils are not dreams. They are terrible realities. Du Bois should cut out his wild dreams and use his time and talents in fighting the awful things that be."

I quote these yellowed documents to show that I have believed all my life that the fight of Negroes lies in America and that one's duty is to wage it, not take flight. Still, my attacks were callow, as only youth can be. Du Bois was fifty-five at the time; I was twenty-three. Years later, Stokely Carmichael, H. Rap Brown, and company would cut me much as I had cut Du Bois. Times change; the souls of young men and old men don't seem to.

Part of my animus came *ex officio*. I was for a time secretary of the Urban League as well as a member of the St. Paul N.A.A.C.P. There was plenty for both organizations to do that summer of 1923. In August, the Ku Klux Klan held a rally at Little Bass Lake, seven miles north of St. Paul. More than a hundred Klansmen donned their bedsheets and burned a cross twenty feet high in a hollow near the lake, and nearly four hundred citizens turned out for the festivities. Cars with headlights and spotlights trained on the access roads prevented outsiders from breaking up the rally, which lasted from nine o'clock in the evening to about 11 P.M. The enemy was striking very close to home. How to fight back?—that was the question.

I found an answer a few weeks later when I went to Kansas City for the N.A.A.C.P.'s 1923 Midwestern Race Relations Conference, which ran from August 29 to September 5. I took the train from St. Paul in great spirits. There was to be a silent march against Jim Crow, disenfranchisement, and injustice, a week of gatherings on race topics, and a mass meeting in Kansas City's new convention center. George Washington Carver of Tuskegee was to receive the N.A.A.C.P.'s Spingarn Medal for his scientific advances with peanuts, pecans, and sweet potatoes. And it was my first chance to see the leaders of the N.A.A.C.P.—James Weldon Johnson, the poet, playwright, diplomat, and gentleman; Walter White, a light-skinned Negro who had investigated some of the most revolting lynchings in the South; Du Bois; and William Pickens, the droll field organizer who had once said, "Why, I never kick when a man gives me the right change. It is only when he short-changes me that I protest."

Perhaps 500 delegates from twenty-eight states were there for the conference, and 10,000 black people from Kansas City and nearby towns crowded into Convention Hall for the great mass meeting on Sunday. I had never seen anything like it. A haunting chorus of 200 Negroes in white robes sang Dett's "Listen to the Lambs." On the platform, the old accommodationist ways of Booker T. Washington were swept aside by the fighting doctrine of Du Bois.

A white emissary named Mr. Brown, sent by Governor Arthur M. Hyde of Missouri, stood to address the crowd.

Before he had been on his feet for a minute, he dropped the word "darky." There was a mighty roar of outrage in the hall. For six minutes, feet stamped and hands clapped, drowning out Brown when he attempted to resume his speech. Finally Arthur Spingarn, a white lawyer and prominent member of the board of directors of the N.A.A.C.P., persuaded the audience to quiet down. Mr. Brown then read a letter from Governor Hyde that urged the delegates to pursue "devotion to fundamental institutions . . . industry, thrift, individual achievement, rather than the pursual of so-called equality."

There was an ominous silence as he sat down. Soft yellow light came pouring through the high windows of Convention Hall as James Weldon Johnson rose to reply.

"His Excellency advised patience, industry, thrift, and intelligence," Johnson said softly. Then his voice rose. "Patience? We know that patience is a foundation upon which we have built. Who has been more patient than we? Who has endured more hardships, suffered more insults, bent to more humiliation than we? Thrift and industry?" he said, looking at Brown. "Look around you, sir, at these thousands who by thrift and industry, by study and by devotion to church, have made themselves worthy to enjoy the rights of American citizens. But, sir, do they enjoy them?"

There was a tremendous roar of applause. Johnson turned. Facing the governor's man squarely, he pounded his hand down upon the table before him and said, "We are here to serve notice that we are in a fight to the death for the rights guaranteed us as American citizens by the Constitution."

Ten thousand black people rose to their feet. They cheered and clapped until their voices were hoarse and their hands stinging with pain. As they cheered, the soft sunlight streamed down around James Weldon Johnson, and I knew I had seen a great leader—and found my own cause.

6 JIM CROW AND THE HARD HEART OF AMERICA

When I went to Kansas City that summer, I was very green, a new graduate with college behind me and no job in sight. St. Paul had little to offer beyond redcapping or following Uncle Sam out on the railroad, and I didn't earn enough editing the *Appeal* to keep body and soul, or a family, together. I was at a loss over where to try my hand next. At just that moment, my father reappeared, this time with some real help to offer.

After Aunt Elizabeth and Uncle Sam had taken legal custody of Earl, Armeda, and me, our father had gone back to Missouri, where he remarried and began to study for the ministry in a little seminary run by the African Methodist Episcopal Church. The affairs of this world may have defeated him, but he did quite well in the other-worldly business. He left the seminary a preacher, a very good one. Starting with small country parishes in central Missouri, he gradually rose to a larger church in Kansas City. By chance, he had his Sunday programs printed on the Missouri side of Kansas City at a job-lot print shop owned by Chester Arthur Franklin, a successful black businessman who also published the *Kansas City Call*. The *Call* was a small, thriving weekly, much stronger than the *Appeal*, but it had developed a few growing pains. One day, when my father strolled into the print shop to pick up his Sunday programs, Franklin mentioned casually that he was in the market for a trained news editor. To the preacher, the passing remark looked like the Lord's hand at work. "My son is studying journalism in Minnesota," he told Franklin quickly, adding that I might be the man he was looking for.

Franklin wrote me shortly before the N.A.A.C.P. convention that summer, asking me to come down to Kansas City to talk things over. After getting off the train, I hopped a streetcar and set out to find him. The office of the *Call* was near the corner of Eighteenth Street and Vine, at the hub of Kansas City's black business district. A little trolley that looked like a piano box on wheels let me off just up the street in a noisy, colorful world that made St. Paul look very small and far away. Up and down Vine, shiny Packards, Marmons, and Hupmobiles purred alongside honking Fords and Chevies. On laundry lines stretched across front porches, flannel and linen flapped in the breeze, and the ladies of the neighborhood raucously called out "How y'all?" to friends passing by.

I made my way through the hubbub to the *Call*'s office, where I found Franklin working calmly at his desk. He was an intense man in his early forties. His silvering hair had retreated from his forehead, leaving him a high, deeply crinkled brow, on which sat his ferociously bushy eyebrows, and he had a square, solid jaw. He wore a dark, three-piece suit with a silk tie, knotted neatly and tucked within his vest. He was all business.

"I need a news editor," he said abruptly.

"I'm your man," I replied.

I tried manfully to sound more confident than I felt. Franklin studied me. I couldn't have made much of an impression. I was a tall, gangly kid with big hands that shot from the sleeves of my suit, and I looked more like the Boy Scout master and Sunday-school superintendent I was than the hard-bitten newsman I hoped to become.

Whatever Franklin thought he kept mercifully to himself. He considered things for a few moments; then he told me he was willing to see what I could do and assigned me to cover the N.A.A.C.P. convention. I spent the next week reporting harder than I had ever done in my life. When I handed in my story of James Weldon Johnson's speech in Convention Hall, Franklin took it and flipped through the pages. Then he looked up briskly.

"You'll do," he said.

He put my by-line on top of the copy and handed it to one of his assistants, who carried it off. He turned to me and offered me $100 a month to work for him.

I went back to St. Paul feeling like a million dollars. I had to do some persuading when I got home. Aunt Elizabeth didn't much care for the idea of sending me off to a sinful place like Kansas City, and the Adams family was not happy about losing an editor for the *Appeal*, but after a few days, everyone agreed that Franklin's offer was too good to pass up. I packed my bags, kissed Armeda and Aunt Elizabeth goodbye, shook hands with Earl and Uncle Sam, and took the train back to Kansas City. On October 1, 1923, I went on the payroll of the *Call*. For the next eight years, through the wildest days of the Roaring Twenties, I had an orchestra ticket to a wonderful theater of experience—the Black Front Page.

When I first moved to Kansas City I had no place to stay, so I put up at the Paseo Y.M.C.A., a segregated facility. I had a monastic little cell with a bed, chair, desk, and bureau. The window looked out on nowhere, but the rent was only four dollars a week, and there was a decent cafeteria downstairs where neighborhood businessmen gathered for lunch. One of my fellow boarders was Joe LaCour, Franklin's business manager, a tall, thin young man who wore suits with wide chalk pinstripes and pointed lapels. Joe had come to Kansas City from Omaha. He had a warm smile and a hot salesman's patter, and he was bringing in more advertising than Franklin had ever imagined. "What we need is circulation. Then we can really make this damn rag hum," he told me the first time I met him. My job was to build that circulation.

I liked Joe immediately. He was a fiercely independent man and a great scoffer. He loved pretty women and potable whiskey, and he hated the affectations of Kansas City's black middle class. His best friends were Homer Roberts, a hearty fellow who owned a Hupmobile dealership, and Wilbur Woods, a skinny druggist.

The job at the *Call* didn't leave me much time for pleasure. When I started, the paper was still printed by the Western Newspaper Union, a white outfit that printed many other black weeklies throughout the Middle West. The paper came out on Fridays, and during the early part of the week I reported, wrote and edited stories, and kept the office running. On Thursday night, Joe, Franklin, and I put the *Call* to bed. As the evening wore on, the three of us made up the paper page by page, then sent the final locked-up and proofread forms over to W.N.U. Early Friday morning the finished copies came back. We stuffed some of them in envelopes, made bundles of the others, and toted the edition off to the post office and distributors in Franklin's car, then adjourned to the publisher's house. Franklin lived with his mother, and she always had a big breakfast waiting. Stuffed with eggs, bacon, and biscuits, Joe and I would drag ourselves back to the Y.M.C.A. and collapse for a few hours' sleep before starting all over again. The work went on that way for several years.

Franklin was a good man and a good boss. His main articles of faith were "Nothing is too good for the customer," "A Negro can deliver the goods," and "I'm optimistic about the future." He had been around newspapers from the time he was eleven years old. His father had been a barber in Omaha, and when Franklin refused to follow him into the business, the barber used his savings to open a small newspaper. Franklin's mother, Clara, hand-set the sticks of type for that first small weekly. When the paper failed, the Franklin family wandered off to Denver, then to Kansas City, scratching out a living as itinerant printers. His father died, but in 1919 Franklin managed to scrape together enough money to found the *Call*. At first he had farmed out his typesetting and presswork to a white print shop, but after a few years he was able to buy his own Linotype machine. The machine sat in the shop for eight months before Franklin got the hang of how it worked, because the white printers' union in Kansas City refused to let any of its men teach him how to use the thing.

Franklin was fond of saying, "People work with me, not for me." He was willing to accept suggestions, even from a greenhorn, on how to improve the paper, but there was no question about who was the boss—Franklin ran the show. He was a dyed-in-the-wool Republican, but he was also a fierce moralist, and he detected few grays between black and white. During one tight election I saw him turn down a $1,500 check from a Republican leader who made the mistake of trying to buy the *Call*. "Anyone who can pay can buy space in the *Call*," Franklin roared at the retreating fixer, and he cheerfully printed ads from Democrats and from Republicans right up to Election Day.

Franklin was a notorious penny pincher who thought nothing of leaving the office on errands with 15 cents in his pocket. It was always dangerous to accept a dinner invitation from him as he seldom carried enough money to pick up a check, and he had no compunction about sticking a cub with the bill.

At the time I joined the *Call*, Franklin was living in a trim little two-story brick house with his mother, but soon thereafter he went to Atlanta on a business trip and returned with a bride. Her name was Ada Crogman, a handsome woman from one of Atlanta's most distinguished families, and she made a new man out of the editor of the *Call*. I have never seen a fonder husband. Franklin became cheerful and generous and, to everyone's surprise, suddenly began prying time away from the sixteen-hour days he put in at the newspaper to be with his new wife.

Franklin was a practical newspaperman. "Nothing too good for the customer" often translated into no murder too bloody for the front page of the *Call*. During the first few months I worked on the paper, our headlines ran like this:

WIFE MURDERED IN COLD BLOOD
HUSBAND SAYS HE COULDN'T
STAND HER "ARGUMENTS"

GIRL'S THROAT CUT IN FIGHT OVER MEN
COULDN'T CHOOSE WHICH

MANIAC RUNS AMOK
BAREFOOT MADMAN
SHOT ON 12TH ST.

As gently as I could, I urged Franklin to dilute some of the blood and gore with more serious news. By December he agreed to give banner headlines to stories about the Republican Party and the Negro vote, but as a hedge against this sudden infusion of civics, he printed the political stories right next to another bloodcurdler more up our line:

SKULL CRUSHED
WHILE HE
SLUMBERS

I don't want to leave the wrong impression—those headlines do not give the full picture of Kansas City. In the glow of sunshine, Eighteenth Street was something to marvel at, to drink in, to feel glad about. On Sunday mornings in early April, the neighborhod around the *Call* would bloom under the soft touch of spring. Faithful Christians and their hangers-on—the Sunday Morning Strutters—would look out at the golden sunlight, test a stray sweet breeze, and head for the churches, where there were sermons, announcements, hymn after hymn, a dozen collections—frenzy. The crowds were patient through the service, quietly anticipating the delicious afternoon and evening ahead. After dinner the streets filled with the rich and poor, the low-down and dignified, crooks and choir singers, riders, strollers, and "just standing." Men in snap-brim hats and gray suits with knife-edge creases in the trousers walked along with topcoats hung carelessly over capable arms. You might see a black man in a pearl-gray hat and a spotless gray suit, somber as any undertaker, except for one touch—a vivid, pink and blue moiré scarf; or four men in dark suits and gray spats, Niles and Mosers cigarettes dangling from their lips. You saw slick hair, flashing teeth, ladies' legs clad in silk—some good, some maybe not so good.

Then there were the cars: a cream-colored Chrysler, a blue Chevy with the top down, soft cow horns, gleaming nickel trimmings; a doctor crawling by in his Buick, another in a gleaming Cadillac; dozens of new Fords and scores of old ones. Positively beautiful black women, but then I was no fair judge because black women have always been beautiful to me. Eighteenth Street could laugh at the sheer joy of being alive in the sunshine of spring. From corner to corner, from window to window, it waved, sang, and yelled out greetings. The next winter might be worse than the last, but no one cared. The neighborhood came out of its cocoon, tested its new wings, preened its feathers, strutted its glory to the world.

White Kansas City was an entirely different place, a Jim Crow town that nearly ate my heart out as the years went by. It wasn't long before I was introduced to its ways. I still remember the sunny afternoon I told everyone at the *Call* that I was going to take half a day off to go down to Muehlbach Field to watch the Kansas City Blues play a visiting baseball team from St. Paul. People looked at me strangely, and when I reached the ball park I found out why. It turned out that Negroes could sit only in the last section of the bleachers, a few yards farther from home plate than the right fielder. I skipped the Blues from then on. Not long afterward I went to Muehlbach Field to watch the Kansas City Monarchs of the Negro National League play ball. It was the first N.N.L. game I had seen, and when I arrived I discovered that the stands were full of white people scattered among the Negro fans, the same white people who could not bear to sit beside Negroes when a white team was on the field.

After that came my full initiation into the city's racial code. One evening on the way home from the *Call,* I jumped up to offer my seat in a streetcar to an elderly white lady. She eyed me frostily, turned her back on the seat, and snapped to a white man standing next to her, "I'm not old enough yet to accept a seat from a nigger." A few days later I was standing in line in front of a theater ticket window. A white woman immediately in front of me suddenly whirled around.

"I wish you wouldn't stand so close to me," she said.

"But, madam," I answered, "I am not close to you."

"Yes, you are," she hissed. "Entirely too close. I don't want you to touch me."

Hate in her eyes, she looked down to where the hem of my topcoat was grazing her coat. Then she flounced out of the line, going all the way to the rear to avoid me.

I was stunned. Back in those days, even good manners could be a crime for a black man in Kansas City, and if the light touch of a topcoat's hem could bring down such wrath, God only knew what anything more substantial might bring.

Kansas City called itself "the Heart of America." The claim was partly geographical, partly psychological, a concoction of boosterism and Babbitry that glossed over the fundamental fact that the place was a Jim Crow town right down to its bootstraps. Except for the

streetcars, which had somehow escaped the color line, neighborhoods, schools, churches, hospitals, theaters, and just about everything else were as thoroughly segregated as anything in Memphis. In
its feelings about race, Kansas City might as well have been Gulfport,
Mississippi.

In this respect, the town only practiced what much of the rest of
America also believed. The main themes of antiblack propaganda at
that time were the same that had been used against Negroes from the
day they first hobbled ashore in Jamestown in 1619.

Negroes are good manual workers, but they are not good thinkers.

Negroes can't absorb abstract learning.

Negroes imitate, but can't originate.

Negroes have no geniuses.

Negroes are born rapists and thieves.

Negroes owe their progress to white blood in their veins.

How Negroes could owe anything to folks who swallowed such
wretched lies escapes me, but the unhappy fact was that in Kansas
City and elsewhere, millions of whites swallowed dozens of other
misconceptions as smoothly as mashed potatoes. Back then I was a
fervent reader of *The American Mercury*. One day I picked up a copy
and found that H. L. Mencken had printed an essay by James Weldon
Johnson, who had observed that whites tended to view the Negro as
"a simple, indolent, docile, improvident peasant; a singing, dancing,
laughing, weeping child; picturesque beside his log cabin and in his
snowy fields of cotton; naïvely charming with his banjo and his songs
in the moonlight and along the lazy Southern rivers; a faithful, ever
smiling and genuflecting old servitor of the white folks of quality; a
pathetic and pitiable figure. In a darker light . . . an impulsive, irrational passionate savage, reluctantly wearing a thin coat of culture, sul-
lenly hating the white man, but holding an innate and inescapable
belief in the white man's superiority; an everlastingly alien and irre-
deemable element in the nation; a menace to Southern civilization; a
threat to Nordic race purity; a figure casting a sinister shadow across
the future of the country." I reprinted the piece on the editorial page
of the *Call*. Its cornucopia of racist stereotypes spilled forth all that
Negroes in Kansas City and the rest of the United States were up
against: a deep, unreasoning, savagely cruel refusal by too many
white people to accept a simple, inescapable truth—the only master
race is the human race, and we are all, by the grace of God, members
of it.

The casual, almost offhand way that race prejudice intruded into
the lives of Negroes in Kansas City was part of what made it so infuriating. Down at Wolfe's Department Store, clerks refused to let

black women try on clothes or hats; black customers had to take such goods home on approval to see if they would fit. At the railroad depot, the Santa Fe wouldn't sell a black traveler a Pullman berth to Chicago without a knockdown fight. I remember standing in a market one day behind a black woman who had just ordered a pack of Beech-Nut gum. The clerk tossed a package of some other brand on the counter. When she protested, he shrugged and said, "How would you know the difference, anyway?" I could have killed him.

At Christmas, when the civic organizations of Kansas City held a great fund-raising drive for charity, dividing the city into sections, there was a charity "ladder" on a billboard downtown to show the progress of each division toward its contribution goal. The Negro division always had a separate ladder. Since most Negroes contributed to the drive where they worked, not in the ghetto where they lived, the Negro division always stood at the ladder's bottom rung. This humiliation was unfair, but it took a long time for the white folks to find enough charity in themselves to correct it. Some of the other nastiness was not so subtle. One year the white women's clubs of Kansas City got the idea that interracial marriages were on the rise (I believe they had heard that twelve such marriages had taken place in Chicago). Consternation set in. The Kansas City Council of Clubs, an umbrella group for these ladies, passed a resolution that said, "There is no condition extant in the country that is more demoralizing to the people of America than the practice of miscegenation, particularly with reference to the white and African races." The white ladies then set out to enact a law banning intermarriage. They ignored the fact that in the South, where such laws had been in force the longest, hundreds upon hundreds of thousands of children of mixed blood had been born. The vicious antimiscegenation laws of the sort they were proposing stripped every vestige of protection from Negro women, leaving them mercilessly exposed to the lust of white men. In reality, what the ostensibly enlightened ladies of Kansas City were fighting for was legalized rape and bastardy, though that truth never dawned on them. Another year, the Council of Clubs sponsored a performance of the Freiburg Passion Play, which was a dramatization of the ministry, suffering, and death of Christ enacted by a cast from Europe. As the day for the performance drew near, the Jenkins Music Company in Kansas City announced that seats for colored people would be available "in a very nice section on the east side in the upper balcony." In other words, Negroes were being told that they could come and take a peek at the white folk's Christ—but only from a Jim Crow balcony. The legitimate and vaudeville theaters in town were also segregated. Several times a year I held my temper and made my way to the Orpheum Theater's Jim Crow alley entrance. From there I climbed the set of stairs leading to the skylights and the last row of seats in the highest gallery, which was way up and right under the roof. From that roost I could watch Miss Ethel Barrymore and other stars of her magnitude. Every time I climbed those Jim Crow stairs I was climbing Jacob's ladder backwards; every step higher brought me one step farther down. Later, I organized a boycott of the theaters. We didn't crack the race line, but it wasn't fashionable to go to a Jim Crow theater after that. The roost went empty.

Kansas City had a large black ghetto. Most Negroes in town were jammed into the central east side, which was almost entirely zoned for business and light manufacturing. There were other pockets of blacks in part of the North Side, where Italians and Negroes lived easily side by side, and down in the Bottoms, the fragrant part of town near the stockyards. But the residential neighborhoods, the nicer sections of Kansas City, were all white. There were ads in the Kansas City *Star* that talked of $5,000–$7,000 houses that could be bought for $750 down—if you were white. A Negro had to cough up at least $1,000 to buy a smaller house, then run the risk of being "persuaded" out because he dared to wander away from the railroad tracks and the factory sites. Baffled, bewildered, and poor, the lone Negro had nowhere to turn. Negroes who took a stand against this system had to make their bed among bombs.

There didn't seem to be any limit to what the white people would do to keep blacks from moving up. One group of Kansas City whites formed an organization called the Linwood Improvement Association. Their plan was to keep black people penned north of Twenty-seventh Street. At one point, the Linwooders even went to the Kansas City park board to demand that it condemn sixty-three Negro homes to make a park along this border. They argued that the park would serve as a "dead line" separating the races. The park board refused to go along with the scheme, but anyone who could feel comfortable in his home or optimistic about the future when those Linwood snakes were at work was a bigger fool than I was prepared to be.

I did what I could to fight them in the *Call*. On one occasion, a Linwooder raised a fuss about twenty Negroes who had tried to buy homes in white neighborhoods when, she charged, there were 251 vacant apartments in the Negro district good enough for colored. We took a look at her list. Most of the buildings were ramshackle dwellings that hadn't been painted or repaired for years, places that had siding patched with tin, sagging porches, and even a few outside toilets. It also turned out that some of these shanties belonged to slumlords who were members of the Linwood Improvement Association. The woman also claimed that she knew of at least 40,000 square feet suitable for building new homes in the black part of town. What she didn't say was that with the district zoned for light manufacturing, a hardworking black man might plunk all his savings into a new house only to find a barbecue stand, foundry, machine shop, garage, gambling den, cabaret, or whorehouse going up next door. When Franklin finally began paying me enough to move out of the Y.M.C.A., I rented a room in a new house that had a boilermaker's shop as a neighbor. A friend of mine lived across the street from a combination barbecue stand, dance hall, and taxicab stop, where a grinding phonograph, laughter, and the roar of gasoline motors kept him company day and night.

About the time the Linwooders were in full howl, the Ossian Sweet riot erupted in Detroit. Ossian Sweet was a rugged black doctor who had dared to buy a house in one of Detroit's white neighborhoods. On the night of September 9, 1925, a white mob surrounded his house; there were shots, and a white mob member fell dead. It was not clear who had fired the fatal shot, but it was clear that Dr. Sweet had simply stood his ground on the "man's home is his castle" principle hallowed in English common law. Even so, he, his wife, two brothers, and seven friends who were in the besieged house the night the mob arrived were all clapped in jail and charged with first-degree murder. The N.A.A.C.P. recruited Clarence Darrow to handle the defense. Darrow was an agnostic who didn't acknowledge the divinity of Christ but who honored the Golden Rule far better that most white Christians, and he won the case. One night, while the jury was still out, I went down to the Kansas City *Star* to see if any of the wire services had word of a verdict. It was the most important housing case of the twenties, but when I asked a white news editor about the story, he looked up at me blankly and mumbled, "The Sweet Case? Never heard of it."

The *Star* had a similar blind spot for most black news in those days. It fulminated over bombings among racketeers in Chicago, and it ran a tough editorial when a bomb was thrown into a cathedral in Sofia, Bulgaria, but when bombs exploded at black homes on Montgall Avenue and Park Avenue in Kansas City, the *Star* was silent. For years it refused to print even a photograph of a Negro. The first black to break this tradition was Tom Lee, a boatman from Memphis who rescued a group of white engineers from a sinking riverboat. To show the survivors, the *Star* had to show Lee, too: he was right there in the middle, and there was no way to get him out.

The police in Kansas City were not like those I had known and liked in St. Louis and St. Paul. In those days the Kansas City Police Department was heavily politicized and often corrupt. Some of the stories that made their way off the police blotter were hard to believe. One night a bluecoat picked up a Negro drifter named James Price, offering to slip some quick money Price's way if he would undertake a little job. The drifter took the offer, and the two men drove to a filling station. It was closed, but there was a stack of oil barrels out back, and the cop told his hired hand to roll them out front while he got a truck to pick them up. The drifter started to work. When he appeared with the first barrel, the cop shot him nine times. The next day the cop claimed a $25 reward offered by a local oil company for stopping petty thefts. Unfortunately for the entrepreneur, the drifter was a tough bird; he lived long enough to identify the man who had gunned him down. When we ran the story in the *Call*, the cop received so many death threats that he had to get out of town.

One day I was sitting at my desk when the phone rang; the caller was a relative of the departed cop.

"Let my brother come home," he begged me.

I told him that the *Call* had nothing to do with his brother's problems, but he obviously believed that the newspaper's stories had inspired the death threats. Maybe they did, I really don't know, but I do know they couldn't have happened to a nicer fellow.

Getting Kansas City's police to enforce the law in black neighborhoods was almost impossible. For a time we ran a "Murder-a-Week" campaign in the *Call* to draw attention to the bloodshed that took place at approximately that rate all through the twenties. The official attitude seemed to be, "Well, there's one more Negro killed—the more of 'em dead, the less to bother us. Don't spend too much money running down the killer—he may kill another."

With this policy in effect, all a murderer had to do to escape punishment was walk around the corner, step across the hall to another flat, or take the trolley to Independence. Nothing was ever done; within a week or ten days the culprit could return home scot-free. I remember standing alongside a detective in the balcony of a popular dance hall one night watching couples swinging by while a band filled the night with Kansas City jazz.

"Yes, it's a pretty party all right," the detective said as he watched the dancers. "They look nice, don't they? But already since

I've been here I've seen four men who have killed someone—either a man or a woman."

To the white policeman of Kansas City, the greatest crime imaginable was for a black man to be seen in public with a white woman. I remember a bright, sunny afternoon when Muriel Stewart, a Negro high school girl who looked white, went riding with her boyfriend, a black kid who had borrowed his father's car. A patrol car stopped the two young people. They were arrested and hauled off to the police station, where their captors threatened to book them on a morals charge. Muriel cried hysterically for her mother, and the police relented long enough to call Mrs. Stewart. She, too, was very light-skinned and normally as proper as any lady from Boston, but she stormed into that station house shouting all the cusswords she had ever heard. She gave those police officers a quick lecture on the reason some Negroes look white, and abashed, they let Muriel and her boyfriend go.

Joe LaCour ran into a similar problem. One day he was out driving with a light-skinned young woman named Edith Evans. A cop caught sight of them and flagged them down.

"That a white woman you're driving with?" the cop asked grimly.

"Yep, but she's not Caucasian," Joe replied, setting the cop back with the six-bit word. "You *do* know what Caucasian means?" said Joe, pressing his advantage.

"Well, no," the cop admitted.

"Have you ever heard of Mendel's Law?"

"No," said the cop in increasing alarm.

"Well, you better go back to the station and look it up," Joe said sharply.

That poor cop couldn't tell a gene pool from a car pool. He probably thought Joe was going to run *him* in for breaking Mendel's Law. He just shook his head and drove away.

The stupidity of the police was legendary. People used to laugh over the story of a bluecoat who came across a dead horse in the middle of Highland Avenue. The discovery required a written report, but the cop didn't know how to spell Highland. Scratching his head, he stood over the corpse for a moment. Then, brightening, he dragged the horse around the corner to Vine Street, where his spelling was up to his paperwork.

The joke offered poor comfort against the daily harassment by the police and the courts. In North Side court, Judge Carlin P. Smith used to ladle out $500 fines against any black man seen with a white woman, but he would wink and give $10 fines to white men caught with black women. Judge Smith kept a picture of Stonewall Jackson

when we arrived at the Atheneum, a young white woman acting as usher met us at the door. She forced a stiff smile. "We have a lovely little balcony for you," she said.

So it was to be up in the roost for the black folks while Horner gathered at the altar of art. As we sat down in that lovely little Jim Crow balcony, Dawson came in. "This is Missouri," he said with a grimace.

It turned out that the officers of Horner had told him—as nicely as they could—that he wouldn't be allowed to graduate with the white students. He was not to worry, they said, since they would give him his degree the next day.

We all considered walking out right then, but stayed only because we wanted to hear Dawson's composition, a piece for violin, cello, and piano titled "Romance." A violinist and a cellist from the Kansas City Symphony Orchestra and a pianist from Horner came onstage, sat down, and began to play. As the melody bewitched the audience, Dawson sat in the balcony watching, his face drawn, following the music from measure to measure and instrument to instrument.

When the musicians finished, the audience broke into applause that swelled, diminished, and rose all over again. The program identified the composer, and the ovation clearly called for a bow, but Dawson had to sit silently in that balcony looking down at the rest of his class—a great sea of white faces. He said nothing.

Then Senator Henry J. Allen of Kansas rose to give the commencement address. In stentorian tones, Senator Allen said that character determined culture, and he congratulated Horner on the way it was building character into American manhood and womanhood. He said nothing, of course, about the way Horner had exiled one of its most promising students to a perch among the pigeons simply because he was black. I shifted angrily in my chair as the mockery went on. Then came the final slap.

Charles F. Horner, president of the institute, rose to hand out the diplomas. He passed them one by one to two little white girls, who carried them off to the beaming new graduates. Looking down at his list, Horner suddenly called out loudly, "Bachelor of Music—William L. Dawson."

He handed a roll tied with a white ribbon to one of the little girls. Somehow the folks at Horner had forgotten that Dawson was a Negro, that he was to get his degree out by the back door the next day. The little girl looked around, then stood still for a moment, wondering where to find Mr. Dawson. There were some hurried whispers.

Hands reached out, the little girl was tugged back, and the diploma with the white ribbon was laid to one side.

After that, the audience rose to sing "America." As I looked down, I saw a young Filipino student—darker than any of the six of us in the balcony—sitting between two white students, and I understood something that had eluded me before. The color line wasn't really based on color at all: it was simply meant to keep down Americans who were Negroes. The singing of the people around me turned to a terrible jumble, and the words of "America" died on my lips.

7 THE RESTLESS TWENTIES

I

f white Kansas City was mean-spirited and low, black Kansas City also had its faults. Allen Hoskins, the little boy who played Farina in the movies, paid a visit, gave Kansas City a quick going-over, and announced that the place was "kind of a dead ole town." I had to agree with him. To liven things up, I joined a small group that organized a black concert company. The first performer we pursued was Paul Robeson, who was quite famous in the East by then, but still had no professional manager. In those days, he city-hopped with his wife, singing for $1,000 a concert. He agreed to stop in Kansas City for $750 because we were amateurs with little working capital.

We made arrangements to hold the concert in the Grand Avenue Temple, a spacious white church in downtown Kansas City. The *Star* carried advance notices but refused to print Robeson's picture in its news columns or in our advertisements. Our seating plans shocked white Kansas City. Since we were selling pews, not numbered seats, and since we were not in the Jim Crow business, we simply set up rows at $3 and $2—75 cents in the balcony—and threw them open on a first-come, first-served basis. It wasn't long before we started getting anxious calls asking if we were going to reserve a section for white people. Our answer was a very firm no, and advance ticket sales went poorly. On the night of the concert the box-office take threatened to fall short of Robeson's guarantee, and there was a real question about whether he would go onstage. I was nervously raking through the cash box when Robeson stepped forward and smiled at me.

"Don't worry, Mr. Wilkins," he said in that fine, deep bass. "I will sing for my people."

I can still feel the warmth of his promise. Those were less complicated days, before Robeson took to giving lectures between acts. The concert was a success. White folks decided they couldn't stay away, and we got an integrated house, one of the largest Kansas City had ever had. In the end we were able to pay Robeson's fee and clear about $300.

Such memories still brighten the twenties, now sixty years gone, for me. Those were restless but valuable years. As they passed, I changed from a soft-shell boy to a well-armored Kansas City slicker.

Some of my friends today are surprised by how hot my blood ran back then. After one brutal lynching not far from Kansas City, I decided to organize a band of young Negroes to raid towns where such murders had taken place. Retaliation was my goal; what I had in mind was a black Robin Hood band that would pounce and punish with no warning. It didn't take me long to realize how ridiculous the idea was. We could not have made the fantasy work; we would have invited our own deaths instead. In this country, black people are a permanent minority and we will never have the numbers or the guns to stage a successful armed revolution. This is a hard reality, and it makes revolutionary cults little better than suicide cults.

When I cooled down, I joined a study group made up of teachers, doctors, lawyers, preachers, and other young professional men that met once a month. Our philosophy was to outthink and outfox the white man; we believed that if we thought deeply enough and talked long enough about the hostile white world around us, we would find a way to overcome it. In the end, however, most of our discussions were reduced to the question: What do we want for our children? The motivation for change *now* was very slight. I was disappointed, but not really surprised. These were elite, middle-class people, most of whom were content to live with what they already had.

I was not; I burned for change. If I could not accomplish it overnight, I promised myself, I could at least speak out against a status quo that left only society's dregs to Negroes. The main difficulty was how to make my case effectively. At just this time, Franklin offered me a signed column on the editorial page of the *Call*. I labeled it "Talking It Over," and from its inky battlements I was able to shoot at Kansas City's fattest targets: white bigots, the Linwood Improvement Association, the police and the courts, the school and park boards, Jim Crow stores, restaurants, and theaters—everything loathsome about the town.

To a neophyte columnist in his twenties, H. L. Mencken offered a model of style, and the white folks of Kansas City supplied endless material. I remember how gleeful I felt when the local police arrested a carful of white bandits caught red-handed with a load of chickens. What a blow to tradition! The old slur had always been that only Negroes stole chickens, carrying them off in gunnysacks, but here were two white men and a white woman going South with a whole Ford-load of poultry. I went to my typewriter and fired up the keys. Another day I stumbled upon a cafeteria that had posted ads all over town for watermelon at 15 cents a slice. This cafeteria refused to serve black people, so it was white folks that were being lured to the table. Ne-groes were supposed to be the only Americans crazy about water-melon, but those cafeteria signs conjured up a whole new set of images: of the little, blue-eyed, straw-haired, barefoot Nordic, his face buried up to the ears in a dripping slice of red melon; of the fat, natty, businessman licking his chops as the waiter at his club plunked down a huge wedge of watermelon before him; of paleface ladies in backless gowns and men in dinner jackets chatting about golf scores, market quotations, foreign trade, and the Riviera season—while mountains of chicken and watermelon sat on a groaning table waiting for them to smack their thin lips and begin gobbling.

Other racial turnabouts came every day. In Chicago, the police ar-rested a twenty-year-old white girl and called her the world's best crapshooter, a designation that had hitherto been reserved for black experts at "African golf." The Windy City cops also nabbed a Gold Coast matron who waited in the dark for her husband's mistress one night and slashed her with a razor. At about this time, the Great Sun-tan Craze of the late twenties became so frenzied that hotels in Wash-ington, D.C., that very Southern town, had to hire colored spotters to maintain the color line without insulting browned-up white folks at the door. Who could tell what the changeable whites would do next. First they stole the blues, jazz, crapshooting, corn bread and greens, tap dancing, the Charleston, watermelon, fried chicken, spirituals, and voodoo; then they turned to razors and knives. Now they seemed to be out to steal our brown skins. Jacob taking Esau's birthright was nothing by comparison.

It would be comforting if I could fix blame for the poisonous racial atmosphere of Kansas City entirely upon the whites, but the reality was much more complicated. A lot of the things we suffered came as wrapped, perfumed presents from ourselves.

I was something of a prig back in those days, but I couldn't help wince when I saw my own side play into the hands of its worst ene-mies. In the seventh decade after Emancipation, Negro illiteracy had fallen below 20 percent, the death rates were dropping, the net worth of Negroes had risen from zero to more than $2 billion, the era of one-room shacks for schools was giving way to universities and long lines of honors graduates. Even so, there was still a witch woman in

Kansas City who sold sawdust for one dollar a box as "bring back" powder and gave advice for five dollars a session on numbers that couldn't miss, unless something went wrong (it always did). Her business was so good that when the police finally arrested her, she paid her bail in cash and drove away from the courthouse in a Pierce-Arrow.

When I went to see John Barrymore swashbuckle his way through *General Crack,* the seats were full of black women giggling louder than Clara Bow and Louise Fazenda put together, and the dialogue was drowned out by two old servitors loudly comparing notes on what time their white folks were up for breakfast and what "Miss Anne" wore to the country club. One dismal night at Central High on the Kansas side, I watched two innocent black kids turn up onstage as Petie and Jakie—"Two Little Coons"—in a fairy operetta called *The Pixies.* The program announced that little white fairies would sing "Hail to the Morning Sun" and other cunning numbers, while Petie and Jakie were to sing "Mammy's Black Lambs" and "Jolly Picka-ninny." The lines of the latter song went something like this: "We are little sons of Ham, all we want is someone to grease our lips with jam." Here were black children, reduced—with the compliance of their parents—to pickaninnies and stuck with jam instead of the bread, meat, salad, and dessert of life. "Tell them about Frederick Douglass, Booker T. Washington, W. E. B. Du Bois, and hundreds of others," I groaned to myself. "Spare them this cooning and these coon songs."

I was also badly goaded by the timid souls who always seemed to say "Go soft" or "Go slow" to anyone who sought to accelerate the progress of the race. One morning I opened a copy of the Moberly, Missouri, *Monitor-Index* and discovered that a Mr. N. C. Bruce, state superintendent for Negro schools—and a black man—had told the local school board that Negroes should be taught scrubbing, cooking, laundry work, and nail driving instead of "high book learning." Mr. Bruce told the board, "Negroes make the best servants and the best house workers of any race when they are taught pride in their work." His philosophy might as well have come from white race baiters like Cole Blease or Pitchfork Ben Tillman. From a black man it was in-credible; yet it represented an attitude that still existed in the twen-ties. I did all I could in the *Call* to root this self-image out, and as a result, plenty of soft-shoe, half-a-loaf Negroes called me half baked, a sorehead, a radical, and just about everything but a black mili-tant—that term hadn't been coined yet.

As I warmed to the fight in Kansas City, I got a terrible series of shocks from St. Paul. When I had left, Earl was a freshman at the

University of Minnesota and Armeda was about to begin her second year at Hamline College. Earl was a bright kid with a smile that could have thawed Nome in January. He made friends easily, one of whom was Harold Stassen, who later became the wunderkind governor of Minnesota. Uncle Sam and Aunt Elizabeth loved to talk about the way Earl had looked in a tuxedo at his first college prom. Armeda was a quiet, introspective young woman who hoped to pursue a career in teaching. Uncle Sam and Aunt Elizabeth had great expectations for both.

At the end of her sophomore year at Hamline Armeda developed a frightening cough and dropped out of school. At first we all believed that the illness would soon clear up, but instead, she grew more and more frail. She was hospitalized for a while; then, when she seemed to grow stronger, she spent some time in a sanitarium. Her recovery was very slow, and, discouraged, she began to study Christian Science. Finally, she embraced that faith completely, renouncing all medical care. We could do nothing to sway her, and tuberculosis carried her mercilessly away. She died in November 1927.

Her death touched off a chain reaction at 906 Galtier Street. A terrible sadness fell over the house. Two months later, in January 1928, I received an urgent telegram from Earl telling me that Aunt Elizabeth was critically ill. I caught the first train out of Kansas City, and on arriving in St. Paul, I rushed to the hospital and discovered that Aunt Elizabeth had suffered a massive heart attack. Earl had also sent a wire to Uncle Sam, who was traveling on the railroad when Aunt Elizabeth fell ill. He immediately set off for home. On the way he suffered a massive stroke and died forty hours after he was brought to St. Paul. Aunt Elizabeth picked out the suit for his burial; then all the fight and life seemed to go out of her. Two days later she died. Earl and I arranged a double funeral for them. In little more than the blink of an eye, Armeda and the two loving people who had saved us from Mississippi were gone forever.

The deaths of Armeda, Aunt Elizabeth, and Uncle Sam snuffed out the home we had in St. Paul. Among Sam's few papers, Earl and I discovered an insurance policy that covered the expense of the funeral and all of Uncle Sam's unpaid debts, a paid-up mortgage, and a will leaving the house to the two of us. It was one last gift from the good man who had raised us, a final testament to his belief in self-help and breaking ground for the generation that follows. My uncle marked a clear path; I have tried to walk it ever since that last sad trip home to St. Paul.

Earl had graduated from the University of Minnesota a few months before that bleak winter, and he had planned to work for a year and then enter law school. The deaths in the family shattered his cheerful optimism. He told me he felt he could settle Uncle Sam's small estate, but he had always looked up to me, and I could see that he needed some help himself. As I rode the train back to Kansas City, I turned this problem over in my mind, and when I returned to the *Call,* I made a few inquiries and discovered that Joe LaCour was looking for an assistant. I also stumbled into a teacher from Lincoln High School who was taking a year's sabbatical and who needed to sublet his apartment. I did some quick selling to Joe, snapped up the apartment, and wrote Earl to pack his bags.

In February 1928, he sold the house and came to Kansas City. Earl was a very quick study. He had had no experience selling newspaper advertisements, but Joe adopted him and he made rapid progress. Before long he was courting old advertisers so smoothly and bringing in new ones so fast that Joe had to step lively to keep ahead of him. Chester Franklin was delighted.

As bachelors and newspapermen, Earl and I eventually got around to most corners of black Kansas City, some nice, some not so nice. Deep divisions separated the town's social classes. At the bottom was a floating world of hustlers, torpedoes, fly-by-night artists, and easy women. The center was held by solid workingmen, railroad porters, hod carriers, and truck drivers, a labor force that was far larger than anything I had seen in St. Paul. At the top was a prosperous upper middle class of doctors, lawyers, dentists, pharmacists, teachers, school principals, and a scattering of businessmen. It was this top-drawer crowd that Joe loved to sneer at, and he didn't spare Earl or me when we mixed with it.

Kansas City's black society was a tight little circle, dominated by the Ivanhoe Club for men. Almost all entertaining was done in the home, because the Jim Crow laws barred black people from most public watering holes, theaters, and the like. Each year at Christmas, the Ivanhoe Club, whose president was a school principal named Joe Herriford, gave a great ball at the Paseo Hall. Since invitations to the Christmas Ball were highly prized, Herriford was a very powerful social arbiter around Kansas City. The dance was a white-tie affair; anyone reckless enough to show up in a tuxedo was turned away at the door. This meticulous attention to outward style was heroic and sad at the same time. It was meant to prove that black people were the equal of whites in social graces, but unhappily, it also showed that they could be every bit as affected as the worst white snob from the country club district.

Society Row was up on the Paseo, a hill overlooking the great boulevard that ran the length of Kansas City. Joe Herriford had built a house there, as had many other prosperous black residents. The members of that little enclave of black people were well educated, intelligent, hardworking, successful people whose standard of living matched anything in the surrounding white community—and whose ethics were higher than those of the local white community. Yet they were penned in those fine homes, barred from everything beyond them simply because their skins were not white. There was Dr. A. Porter Davis, for example. Dr. Davis bought an American Eagle biplane that carried three passengers, had a top speed of 103 miles per hour, and could climb to 17,000 feet. He painted the fuselage black and the wings orange, bought himself goggles, leather boots, and a flying cap, and took six hours of flying lessons, advancing far enough to feel comfortable soaring at 3,000 feet. At that point the white folks at the local airfield told him he would have to take his plane somewhere else: he was drawing too many black people to their field. Dr. Davis and the residents of the Paseo—like black people from one end of the country to the other—were victims of a ruthless system of apartheid that made a mockery out of the Republic's promise of equality.

Organizations like the Ivanhoe Club were not going to topple this system, but such groups did take some of the pain out of everyday life. Kansas City also had dozens of clubs for black women—the Merry-We Social, the Matinee Matrons, the Forget-Me-Not Girls, the Radiant Home Art Club, the Mysterious Few Whist Club—brave little outposts of middle-class normalcy in a hostile white world. Corinne Wilson, the *Call*'s society editor, presided over this gay, chatty empire, and out of her constant activities came the luckiest day of my life.

On Thursday evening, March 1, 1928, at the Community Center on Lydia Avenue, Corinne held a meeting to organize the eleventh annual fashion show for Wheatley Provident Hospital, the only private hospital for black people in Kansas City. The public hospital for Negroes was called City Hospital Number 2. Any Negro run down on the very steps of City Hospital Number 1, the white hospital, would be carried, bleeding, perhaps dying, across town to Number 2 before receiving treatment.

The Wheatley Provident fashion show was a benefit, the centerpiece of the spring social season, and its guiding spirit was Mrs. Minnie Crosswaithe, a matron in her late sixties. Under her watchful eye, Corinne had been preparing the show for months, and had spent several days in Chicago studying the latest fashion pageants at Marshall Field and Co. That night at the Community Center she announced plans for what she called an "Artists and Models Revue Glorifying the Kansas City Girl."

We reported this exciting news the next morning—along with the fact that Corinne was looking for "a young man above average in height and medium weight for a very important and pleasant role." She picked me. My solo role was that of a painter with a weakness for revelry and an insatiable demand for models, an easy enough assignment for a twenty-six-year-old bachelor. Corinne dug out a blue beret and a smock from somewhere, and I was in business.

The benefit took place in Convention Hall, and more than 6,000 black people filled the arena that day. As I recall, the show opened with Mrs. Roy Barker and her police dog, Pal, circling the ring in a shiny La Salle sports Phaeton, followed by Mrs. Alberta Gilmore in one of Homer Roberts's flashing Hupmobiles. The young ladies of Lincoln High School staged a "Bathing Beauty Revue," and then came my turn. I stood in the center of the arena, my beret cocked rakishly, a brush clutched in my hand, and a palette crooked over my arm. One by one I had "dreams" of Youth, Modesty, Innocence, Beauty, Charm, Passion, Vanity, a Blonde, a Brunette, an Opera Singer, and Pep, each played by a beautiful young woman. The applause was overwhelming. So were the models. At the party afterward, the Cotton Club orchestra of Harlem played, and Ethel Waters, then a slender young torch singer, fired up everyone. Just as I was settling comfortably into the lascivious swing of things, I heard someone call my name. When I turned around I saw Mrs. Corinne Eagleson, a chatty woman whose husband, Albert, was a well-known dentist in town. Standing next to her was a thin girl with a wonderfully smooth olive skin and the largest, darkest, most hypnotizing eyes I had ever seen.

"I'd like you to meet Miss Badeau from St. Louis," Mrs. Eagleson said. I fell in love faster than a French Impressionist.

After talking with this lovely girl for a few moments, the Blonde, the Brunette, and even the Opera Singer slipped out of my mind. "Why have I never seen her before?" I asked myself. It turned out that Miss Badeau had arrived only that day on the midnight train from St. Louis. She had come to take a job with the Kansas City Urban League, and planned to live with the Eaglesons in their home on the Paseo.

"May I call on you?" I asked, doing all I could to conceal the tumult I felt.

"Please do," she replied.

The next morning I telephoned the Eaglesons and asked Miss Badeau when we might meet again. She agreed to go with me to the movies the following Saturday night. Saturday came and I discovered quickly that she was extremely intelligent and well informed. She had a quick, wicked wit and a wonderful sense of the ridiculous; she was frank, broad-minded, quick to laugh at herself. And her eyes mesmerized me. At the end of the evening I blurted, "It's so nice to talk to a girl who reads books." She told me to call her Minnie, as her friends did—and thus started a love affair that has lasted more than fifty years.

I knew from the beginning that I would have to move fast to keep Minnie to myself. Kansas City was full of rakehell bachelors, all of whom I had to outcourt. I owned a dented old secondhand Dodge coupe, and I drove it to the Urban League not long afterward to offer Minnie a ride home through a spring downpour. When I opened the door for her, she looked at me a bit dubiously. I eased back behind the wheel and saw why: rain was pelting in through a large hole in the roof. I looked sheepish. She laughed, and our romance survived. Somehow I managed to make up through persistence what I lacked in transport. Mrs. Eagleson kindly did what she could to advance the match. One day I arrived just before a rich old rake in a slick Packard stopped by the Eaglesons' home, hoping to take Minnie out for a drive. The older man began to drop unkind words about my coupe— until Mrs. Eagleson cut him off. "Now, what would a beautiful young girl want with an ugly old man like you," she said, and I drove Minnie away in triumph. All young lovers should be blessed by such a fairy godmother.

Minnie was an innocent—or so I thought. Kansas City moved at a faster, rougher tempo than St. Louis, and I determined to become her protector. One day she told me that one of the city's black professional men had asked her to a party at his office. Groaning to myself, I quickly offered to go as her escort. When we arrived, the old lecher was sitting by himself, waiting. There was no one else in the office. He was flabbergasted when he saw me.

I said, "Minnie told me you were throwing a party tonight—so we came right over."

He looked up and blurted, "I had a gift for you."

I knew he hadn't bought anything for me, and Minnie got the drift, too.

"Well, I hope you give it to your wife," she said, looking him right in the eye. Obviously she could take care of herself far better than I had thought.

My courting days were the happiest of my life. Minnie and I took long, wandering drives through Swope Park, and on Sundays we went to the Eblon Theatre, a movie palace owned by an irrepressible man named "Jap" Eblon. Jap had hired a talented young musician named Bill Basie to accompany the silent movies on the organ, but on Sundays he gave performances without the distraction of the movies. Later he became known as Count Basie, and played his way from the darkened Eblon to Carnegie Hall.

Joe LaCour and I spent many long hours trying to shake Minnie's faith in the Republican Party, but we didn't succeed until the G.O.P. gave us some unexpected help. In 1928 the Republicans held their national convention in Kansas City. To improve its prospects in the South, the G.O.P. had been angling for some time to make itself lily-white, and it made no effort to crack Kansas City's Jim Crow line on behalf of its own black delegates. I remember one black banker named Hawkins who arrived from Washington with his chauffeur and limousine. He was a delegate and he obviously wasn't poor, but he had to stay in a private home because none of the hotels would take him in. Minnie saw what was going on and for the first time began to listen to Joe and me a bit more closely.

Minnie had been born and reared in south St. Louis in a house built by her grandfather in the center of a German neighborhood. Her childhood playmates had all been white, and she didn't really encounter the problems of race until the time came for her to enter grammar school and her best friend enrolled in the Monroe School a few blocks from the Badeau house. Minnie's mother told her that she had to go to the Delaney School, where her Aunt Virginia was a teacher. Since the schools in St. Louis were segregated, Minnie's mother hoped the excuse about her aunt would spare the little girl some pain, but Minnie saw what the score was. In the interest of upholding a vicious race law, a little white girl and a little black girl who had been inseparable all their lives were torn apart. Segregation scarred two more victims. How many millions of times must this have happened over the years, each time making a deeper cut in our country's honor and soul.

Minnie was from an old family in St. Louis and met many of the individuals who were to become famous in black history. One of her favorite memories was the meeting she had had as a child with Booker T. Washington, who had come North from Tuskegee on one of his periodic fund-raising expeditions. "He gave me a nickel for candy," Minnie told me.

Minnie was a dedicated social worker. The Urban League had hired her to organize a neighborhood program, and she had many adventures along the way. One of the handsomest men in Kansas City back then ran a big policy wheel, Kansas City's version of the numbers. Someone jokingly told Minnie that this sharpie had more money than anyone else in town, so when the time came to collect for the Community Chest, she went over to the headquarters of the policy boys and marched right in. The sight of a proper young lady in a cloche and a plain cloth coat dumbfounded all those in shirtsleeves and suspenders. There was a long silence. Minnie said a few words to the policy king, who listened and roared with laughter.

"This lady is collecting for charity," he told his men. "I want every one of you to give her ten dollars." And they did.

I did what I could to steer Minnie through the tougher parts of town. She was shocked by the misery of the poor. Her theories for rooting out poverty made her sound like a regular Bolshevik, though I am sure that to this day she has never opened a volume of Karl Marx.

One day Franklin called me in and said he wanted me to go to St. Louis on some business for the *Call*. When I told Minnie, she suggested that I telephone her mother to ask if I might stop by and meet her during the trip. I made the phone call. Mrs. Badeau did not seem overjoyed at the notion of sitting down with me. She was polite—but icily distant. Undaunted, I took the train to St. Louis. After completing Franklin's assignment, I set off for the Badeau home. It was an old-fashioned house with a front and back parlor and an air of shabby gentility. Mrs. Badeau received me graciously, but with no more warmth than she had registered over the phone. She looked Caucasian: she had freckles, a slightly pug nose, and a thin-lipped smile, and her reddish hair was sprinkled with gray. While it is unchivalrous of me to say it, she looked old enough to be Minnie's grandmother.

As things turned out, Mrs. Badeau was not terribly impressed with me, either. After I left she lost no time in writing Minnie that I did not meet her qualifications for a suitable husband. First, she had never heard of my family, a serious blot. Second, she was shocked that Minnie would show interest in a black newspaperman, a notoriously poor breed of fellow. Finally, I was a Protestant, and the Badeaus were Catholics.

Most of Mrs. Badeau's reservations were unfair, but so far as the financial ones were concerned, I had to agree with her. Fortunately, the *Call* continued to prosper throughout the late twenties. In March 1928, Franklin bought a 32-page Goss Straight Line printing press, a wonder of steel and ink drums 19 feet long, 5 feet 6 inches wide, and 13 feet high that could print and fold 24,000 papers an hour. When we installed it just after the *Call*'s tenth birthday, it gave us the second-best printing plant for Negro newspapers in the country—right behind the *Chicago Defender*. With the *Call*'s circulation increasing, my own fortunes improved, and I was able to think about marriage.

The longer I lived in Kansas City, the more the racial atmosphere and smug provincialism of the place ground on me. The same restlessness unsettled many of my friends, some of whom successfully escaped.

Homer Roberts and his business partner Kenneth Campbell moved their auto dealership to Chicago. Even though they relocated during the coldest February Chicago had shivered through in many years, their first month in business they amassed $38,000 in sales. Homer was still a Negro, but he could fly higher and in wider circles than I could in Kansas City. When he was doing business near the Loop, at lunch or dinnertime, he didn't have to race back to the "black district" to buy a sandwich. If he wanted to go to New York, Cleveland, Buffalo, Pittsburgh, or Philadelphia, he could buy a good berth on the Twentieth Century Limited or the Broadway Limited—the world's finest, fastest trains—without going through a battle at the ticket window. He could sit in the orchestra, first, second, or third balcony of any theater he chose. And if he wanted to play golf, he didn't have to go to court to prove he was a citizen and entitled to play on municipal links maintained with the taxes of black people. In Kansas City, Negroes were not permitted to use the four municipal courses because, the head of the park board announced, "Negroes don't like to play golf"—and that was that. A black millionaire farmer known as the "Potato King of the Kaw" contributed a few acres for a Negro golf course where Earl and I went to do our hacking and slicing.

I knew many others who put Kansas City behind them. David Crosswaithe, a son of the dowager who ran the Wheatley Provident fashion show, was a bright young graduate of the city's ward and high schools. He wanted to become an engineer at a time when that idea was considered crazy for Negroes. He graduated from Purdue University, got a job with a heating and ventilating company in Iowa, took out patents, wrote articles for technical magazines, and wound up designing the ducting system for the giant Stuyvesant Town housing project in Manhattan.

William Dawson left for Chicago not long after graduating from Horner Institute. For a time he read and arranged music for a large publishing house there, and the year I met Minnie, Roland Hayes, the famous singer, was using one of Dawson's arrangements of spirituals in his concerts. Later he composed the Negro Symphony, which

Leopold Stokowski and the Philadelphia Orchestra debuted. Dawson, too, was on the rise.

Aaron Douglas, a painter who taught art at Lincoln High School, also broke out of Kansas City. During the state convention of art teachers, the works of Aaron's students were hung separately from those of the white children, and his own paintings were treated no better in a town that prided itself as a cultural center. He moved to New York City and became part of the Harlem Renaissance. He and his wife, Alta, had a cozy studio apartment on Edgecombe Avenue. There, high atop Sugar Hill, they mixed freely with poets from England, magazine publishers, and Park Row newspapermen. Eugene O'Neill used to turn up at the little apartment for parties. It was a far cry from the Paseo in Kansas City.

My own itching grew worse in the spring of 1929, after I made my first visit to New York City. I saw Broadway all awash in white light, the towering hotels and apartment buildings of Fifth Avenue, Central Park, Grand Central Terminal, the subways and elevateds, Chinatown—and, at last, Harlem: Seventh Avenue, 125th Street, 135th Street, all purring with commerce; Lenox Avenue, Striver's Row, 409 Edgecombe Avenue, and the other luxurious apartments on top of Sugar Hill.

One evening I went over to Broadway to buy tickets for *Blackbirds,* the year's best black revue. At the box office window, all the clerk said to me was, "How many and what price, please?" At the Shubert box office in Kansas City, the ticket vendor debated only whether to let black people sit in the last row of the topmost balcony, or maybe—on very special nights—in the next to last row. I sat in that Broadway house enthralled. Behind me, in front of me, and to the right of me sat white women, while on my left sat three black women, one of whom was snuggled into a squirrel coat that would have cost me most of a year's pay. On the stage, brown women sang "I Can't Give You Anything But Love, Baby" and "I Must Have That Man." Then Adelaide Hall stepped out wearing little more than a shoulder strap and beads to sing her "Diga Diga Doo" song. Under the spotlight, her velvety brown skin glowed, and I heard a young white thing behind me gasp to a friend, "Girl, hasn't she got a beau-*u*-tiful color?" At the Ziegfeld Theatre I saw *Show Boat*—not from a Jim Crow roost, but from right up front. During the first act, Jules Bledsoe, a Negro baritone from Waco, Texas, sang "Ol' Man River" and had to come out for five curtain calls before the audience would turn him loose.

But it was Harlem, petted, pampered, and lied about, mighty Harlem, that I had really come to see. Harlem was then a city of 200,000

Negroes. Whatever lower Manhattan had, Harlem had as well. There were apartments, hotels with canopies from curb to doorstep, marble lobbies, uniformed attendants, telephone operators, and swift, silent elevators. Businesses, theaters, nightclubs of every description were all around me. Black people were everywhere, some hardworking, others free and easy; loafers and home lovers, steady folks, and gadabouts. The place didn't have the boastful, hard-boiled, go-getting quality of Chicago's South Side.

And the races mixed—like nowhere else in America. I went to a breakfast dance at one of Harlem's large casinos, where I saw perhaps 300 whites in a crowd of 2,000 black people. At the dance I was introduced to a publisher of books and magazines, a white man. As we looked out over the floor swirling with dancers—white and white, white and black, black and black—I said to him, "Well, one thing is certain: this could not happen in Kansas City, because any policeman in town knows that stopping race mixing is a more sacred duty than stopping any bank robbery."

"But, my dear young man," said the publisher, "can *anything* happen in a place like Kansas City? You see," he went on, "the significant thing about this interracial association in New York is that it is not wholly a black-and-tan sporting proposition such as you have in Chicago. I would ask you to dinner not because I want the 'thrill' of having a colored man at my table, but because I want *you*."

8   A TIME OF TESTING

The spring and summer of 1929, those last giddy days before the Great Crash, were a fine time for courting. I was twenty-seven years old, as devious as a young man in love can be. In those days it was possible to obtain a marriage license in Kansas City without informing the prospective bride. The marriage bureau downtown at City Hall would grant a license to anyone of age who could produce a character witness willing to swear to the honor of his intentions. I enlisted Earl, went to the marriage bureau, and took out a license on Minnie, almost as if I were going hunting. I told Minnie nothing about my preparations, but from then on, whenever I called for her, I had the license tucked away in my pocket just in case. I carried it around for quite a while before I found the courage to propose. On September 15, 1929, Minnie agreed to marry me, but when I reached into my breast pocket for the marriage license, all I pulled out was a handful of air: on the one day I needed the thing, I had left it home. I thumped my pockets and began muttering to myself. Minnie looked at me quizzically. When I owned up to my little game, she just laughed. We drove to my apartment, found the missing license, and set off to find a justice of the peace. It was a Sunday, and the search took some doing, but we finally found a kindly old J.P. who married us and sent us on our way. Two weeks later we were wed in accordance with the rules of the Roman Catholic Church sanctioning the marriage of Catholics to Protestants. Only then did we work up enough nerve to inform Minnie's mother that she had a new son-in-law.

Mrs. Badeau made peace with this unwelcome surprise, and Minnie and I began a new life. We settled into two rooms and a dinette in the Dade Apartments, a new, eight-family building not far from the *Call.* The owner of the building was a man named Luther Dade, a frugal black entrepreneur with a sharp eye for the main chance. He had served in a Jim Crow army unit during World War I, and saved his pay to make loans at hefty rates of interest to his comrades, rustling up customers at crap games around the barracks. After the war he invested his earnings in a limousine, which he hired out for weddings and funerals, making enough money to build the Dade Apartments. The building was as immaculately kept as his car. At first he kept one of the eight apartments for himself; then, rejecting this show of luxury, he rented half his own quarters to a roomer. Other landlords in Kansas City flaunted their wealth; Mr. Dade modestly hid his. He wasn't too proud to pull on overalls; he worked as his own janitor.

After Minnie and I were married, Earl was left on his own. He was a handsome bachelor, much more of a catch to the young ladies of Kansas City than he realized, but he had no interest in using his advantage. He was deeply in love with a young woman back in Minneapolis named Helen Jackson, who had been his college sweetheart. When Helen was elected to Phi Beta Kappa, Earl was as proud of her as her own parents had been, but Mrs. Jackson took as dim a view of Earl's qualifications as a husband as Mrs. Badeau had taken of mine, so the courtship went on at a distance and with many separations before Earl and Helen were married in 1930.

In the meantime, Earl spent much of his time with Minnie and me. On evenings when I could get away from news work at the *Call*, the three of us would go out to Paseo Hall and other night spots, where we heard Bennie Moten, Cab Calloway, George Lee, and their bands rattling the roofs with numbers like "The Elephant's Wobble" and "The Evil Man Blues." In those dance halls, you had to keep your hand on your wallet. The men used to jam their fedoras on the backs of their heads and dance in their overcoats.

During Prohibition, bootleg whiskey, easy women, and everything else that went with them weren't hard to come by in Kansas City. Garden-variety sinning didn't bother me much, but there was one small vice—the policy game—that I didn't like. Over on the Kansas side of town there were two big policy wheels: the Black and White, and the Black Gold. The numbers writers for these wheels offered odds of about 5,000–1 to their gullible takers, siphoning off quarters and dollars from thousands of black folks who could least afford to be suckered. In the fall of 1929, the Black and White suffered a number of big hits—and then took nearly a week to pay off on them.

I decided to expose the Black and White in the *Call*. The wheel's headquarters were in a little speakeasy called the Musicians Club on Twelfth Street, and although the police had raided the place nearly a hundred times, they never found any evidence worth prosecuting. After each raid, an Italian bail-bond company quickly got the policy boys back out on the streets. Everyone was satisfied with the arrangement until the cost of protection and staying out of jail began to affect the wheel's profit margin. The unexpected hits that fell also hurt the wheel's cash flow.

Not long before Christmas I got word that the policy boys were salting the black community with rumors of more big hits—$50, $500, even $1,200—as an enticement to play. The new hits, of course, had all been faked. I exposed this sorry scam on the front page of the *Call*, under a headline that no one could misunderstand: WINDY TALE OF WINNERS . . . IS JUST BAIT FOR SUCKERS. I told our readers straight that those $100 bills the Black and White was supposed to be spreading around town were scarcer than watermelons in Siberia.

The story drew plenty of blood. A few days later, a detective from the Kansas City Police Department called me up with a friendly warning: he said the policy boys had made me a marked man. There had been no by-line on the exposé, but the cop told me the boys had concluded that I was "the only nigger over there who could figure out what was going on." He offered only a warning, no protection.

There was no choice but to grab the threat by the horns. I wrote a column pointing out that a slugging or a shooting on a dark street after midnight was not the work of a mastermind but the act of a tinhorn sport, a man who could not take a beating with all the cards on the up-and-up. I don't think I shamed the policy boys into backing down—someone else may have saved me. When Minnie learned what was going on, she insisted on accompanying me wherever I went—even to the barbershop. I don't know whether her sociological training had taught her that the code of the hit man forbids shooting a victim in front of his wife, but whatever the case, the strongmen never materialized. Minnie was the most effective bodyguard I've ever had.

The strain of these adventures began to tell on me over time, and I developed some very raw nerves. One day Minnie and I walked down to the post office to mail a letter, and she stayed outside while I went in to buy stamps. When I came out, I saw a white man standing there talking to her. Fury welled up inside me. I rushed up, grabbed the stranger by the shoulder, and yelled, "What do you mean talking to my wife?" I had never done anything like that before in my life. The poor man looked scared to death. Minnie seemed surprised, too. She eyed me a minute, then said, "Why, Roy, this man is just asking the way to Vine Street. Aren't you ashamed of yourself?"

I felt sheepish, all right. Simply because the stranger was white I had concluded that he was out to insult Minnie and to injure me.

There were plenty of good reasons for making such a mistake, but lumping all white folks together was as wrongheaded as the behavior of Southerners who refused to have any contact at all with Negroes. My feelings shocked Minnie—and when I saw them, they shocked me.

A small change of venue seemed like a good idea. As Christmas drew near that year, Minnie and I decided to leave Kansas City for a brief vacation. She took me to St. Louis to visit her family, and for the first time I met Mr. Badeau, a short, thin, gentle man who looked almost white, and who obviously adored his daughter. I also met Minnie's older brother, Arthur, a handsome young man with a great sense of humor, whom Minnie accused of cornering all the good looks and brains in the Badeau family. Mrs. Badeau seemed to accept me. She gave a dinner party in our honor, inviting all Minnie's old friends and their beaux. That evening, as the guests began arriving, I was struck by the range the gathering of Negroes presented. I had never really thought about the variety of skin colors before. Most of the women were extremely fair—though their escorts ran from light brown to deep black. This parade of white Negroes fascinated me. When a blue-eyed blonde came in on the arm of a very black young man, I could restrain myself no longer. Making my way through the crowded living room, I found Minnie. Leaning over, I whispered in her ear, "When are the colored girls coming?"

Minnie shot me a dirty look, but she knew what I was talking about. In the late twenties and the thirties, the same scene could have been replayed in many big cities throughout the United States. Though it would be denied, fair skin was highly prized within middle-class Negro circles. The origins of this color consciousness were complex, although in a world where white made right, it wasn't hard to understand why a black person would covet a fair complexion. As far back as the years of bondage, house servants, particularly those sired by white masters, considered themselves a cut above the blacker slaves of the field. That pigmentation could produce such pathetic misconceptions has always saddened me. The black-is-beautiful concept of the sixties was only one more color-means-everything theory in reverse—though it did supply a welcome and much needed antidote to the poisonous doctrine of white-is-everything.

In the 1960s I became the first Negro on the board of trustees of St. Louis University. The job had a strong personal resonance for me. Minnie's father had told me during that trip years before, "There's a good Catholic University in St. Louis, but I had to send my son to the University of Chicago."

As discrimination grew worse in the 1890s and in the first decade of the twentieth century, many light-skinned Negroes in St. Louis and elsewhere simply resigned from the race and crossed over to the white world, never to be seen or heard from by their black friends. When I returned from Christmas in St. Louis, I gave a speech at the Sunday Forum of the Linwood Christian Church, whose pastor was a decent white fellow named Burris Jenkins. During the question period, a pretty young girl stood up and asked me with considerable agitation if it was true that many Negroes passed for white. I told her that it was, indeed, true. "Then that means a girl could marry a Negro and not know it, doesn't it?" she said. That possibility had just occurred to her, and in her view nothing in the world could have been more disastrous.

Those were memorable evenings at Reverend Jenkins's church, and I respected Reverend Jenkins, who courageously attacked Jim Crow from his pulpit. As I was riffling through some old copies of the *Call* not long ago, I stumbled across one of his sermons, and the man himself, warm, thoughtful, brave, suddenly came back to life. "The real problem," he said on that Sunday so long ago, "is that we have in America 11 millions of blacks set down to live side by side among 111 millions of whites, to serve the same nation, keep intact the same government, construct and hold together the same society. It is a problem. No use to not recognizing the fact. Do you hate Negroes? Do you even condescend to Negroes? Just in proportion to your hatred, dislike, condescension, you are a bad citizen of America. . . . 'God has made of one,' not one blood but one organism, a single entity, one being, one family, one body—all men. That's what Paul said. The same hopes and fears, loves, longings, struggles in all human breasts regardless of the pigmentation of the skin or the origin of the race. To treat all men alike, as human beings, children of a common Father. To do as we'd be done by—this is the gospel, and this is American citizenship." This was the message Reverend Jenkins delivered regularly, and if ever there was a town that needed it, it was Kansas City.

It was always surprising and encouraging to see how many white people were willing to listen to what Reverend Burris Jenkins had to say. On a Sunday evening not long before Christmas one year, more than a thousand of them turned out to hear Walter White, the field secretary of the N.A.A.C.P. and one of the most extraordinary men I have ever met. White was a Negro, the son of an Atlanta mail carrier, but he had blue eyes, blond hair, and skin as fair as his name. James Weldon Johnson had found him working for a Negro life-insurance company and had recruited him to work in the field for the

N.A.A.C.P. He made a specialty of passing for white—a ploy that enabled him to investigate lynchings incognito—and he risked the rope himself every time he went below the Mason-Dixon Line.

That fall White had investigated the Lowman "lynching" in Aiken, South Carolina, a particularly savage triple murder that he took as his subject at the Linwood Christian Church. The story he told was typical of the atrocities that happened virtually every other week somewhere in the South. Bertha, Clarence, and Damon Lowman had been convicted by a mob-dominated court of killing a local sheriff who had descended on them, guns drawn and without identifying himself, in search of moonshine whiskey. The Lowmans had clearly shot in self-defense, and higher courts in South Carolina had directed new trials for them. Before the injustice could be corrected, however, the mob carried the Lowmans off and shot them down in cold blood. White turned up a guilt-stricken former Kleagle of the Aiken Ku Klux Klan, who supplied the names of the ringleaders. One of the murderers told White, "We had to waste fifty bullets on the wench before one of them stopped her howling." White talked about his experiences that night. During the discussion period that followed, a young white man stood up and said in a thick Southern drawl that he loved Negroes so long as they "stayed in their places," but he wouldn't stand for any Negroes "stepping on his face and climbing any higher than he." White politely asked the young man how he had come to consider himself an arbiter of superior and inferior races. He added that his own experience had taught him to doubt the superiority of any man who found it necessary to trumpet his own.

White was one of the best talkers I have ever heard. When people asked him why he had chosen not to resign as a Negro, he told them a little story. It began with a race riot in Atlanta in 1906, when White was thirteen years old. Gun in hand, he and his father had stood guard by the windows of the front parlor one night as a mob from Peachtree Street marched on "darktown" to "clean out the niggers." The mob stopped just up the street. Walter and his father heard the voice of the son of a grocer with whom they did business call out, "That's where the nigger mail carrier lives. Let's burn it down. It's too nice for a nigger to live in." Walter's father turned to him and said, "Son, don't shoot until the first man puts his foot on the lawn and then—don't you miss." Someone up the street shot first, and the mob broke and ran. But Walter never forgot the lesson: though his skin was white, he was a Negro all the same, a target for the lowest of white trash.

I knew White by reputation, and I had seen him at a distance from time to time, but that night I saw for the first time how well he could operate at close quarters. I had become the secretary of the Kansas City branch of the N.A.A.C.P., and I made a point of getting to know White much better during his visit. A few days after he left I received a note from New York City. It said:

> Dear Roy,
>   I am sorry I did not have a chance to see more of you when I was in Kansas City. This is just a note to tell you how much I enjoyed that meeting. I hope some good comes of it.

This breezy greeting was the beginning of a friendship that was to last nearly thirty years. A few years up the road from that evening at the Linwood Christian Church, White re-entered and changed my life. In the spring of 1930 he was sitting in for James Weldon Johnson, who had taken a leave of absence as executive secretary of the N.A.A.C.P. to travel to Asia. At about this time, President Hoover nominated Judge John J. Parker, a circuit court justice from North Carolina, to fill a vacancy on the U.S. Supreme Court. White had looked into Parker's background and discovered that ten years earlier, in the heat of the campaign for governor of North Carolina, the *Greensboro Daily News* had quoted Parker as saying, "The participation of the Negro in politics is a source of evil and danger to both races and is not desired by the wise men in either race or in the Republican Party of North Carolina." No Justice with such views should be in the position to defend the Thirteenth, Fourteenth, and Fifteenth amendments, and White set out with his usual energy and boldness to torpedo the nomination.

At the *Call,* we received one of his first salvos: a telegram urging us to prod Negro organizations into pressuring their senators to demand that Hoover withdraw the nomination, and to vote against the nomination if Hoover refused to back down. The telegram also carried a tough warning. It said, "Negro voters will hold their senators accountable for their votes on the Parker confirmation."

The threat was big news. In our next edition we spread the story across the *Call*'s front page under a banner headline COUNTRYWIDE FIGHT ON PARKER—and published a photo of the judge, a quiet-looking man with mild eyes that peered through spectacles from under bushy eyebrows. Alongside that picture, we printed one of the more infamous quotes attributed to him: "If I should be elected Governor of North Carolina and find that my election was due to one Negro vote, I would immediately resign my office." This was obviously not an acceptable position for a Justice of the United States Supreme Court.

On the editorial page we said: ". . . for a man who would be judge, prejudice is the unpardonable sin. . . . It all comes back to the basic principle so often illustrated in American history—only those great enough to be just to the Negro, the humblest of Americans, are big enough to lead the nation to its highest destiny."

I sent one copy of the edition to President Hoover and mailed another to the city editor of the *Greensboro Daily News* to deflate that paper's claim that only "the colored highbrows of New York" were opposed to Parker. I then waited eagerly for the outcome of the N.A.A.C.P.'s campaign. In the Senate, the fight over the Parker nomination lasted for ten days as Southern politicians trotted out all their oldest tricks. First they refused to admit that the issue of race prejudice had anything to do with the uproar. Then they tried to bluff Northern senators, calling them timid, nervous, and afraid of the Negro vote. The Northern migration of Southern Negroes had created row on row of solidly black precincts. The Election Day tally sheets were something no Southern senator had to contend with; but few Northern senators could safely ignore them. The Southerners also bellowed that the N.A.A.C.P. was harming the cause of racial peace. The opposition to Parker made Hoover furious. Striking back, the G.O.P. held a soft-soap convocation of important Negro leaders in Washington. I worried for a while that black folks might get sentimental and forgiving and lose the fight. Many, many times before, Negroes had been on the verge of accomplishing something of great importance, only to get softhearted at the last minute and say, "Excuse me," to the white man—and quit. My fears were groundless. White kept up his drumfire and lobbying; telegrams poured in to the Senate. The American Federation of Labor—angered by a Parker ruling upholding yellow-dog contracts in a coal-mining dispute—also joined us, though the union's leader took care never to be seen in White's company. In the end, the Senate Judiciary Committee voted 10–6 against Parker, and the Senate rejected the nomination 41–39.

I was ecstatic. The victory made White a national figure, overshadowing Johnson himself, and the N.A.A.C.P. picked up hundreds of new members. Earlier, it had won a string of important legal victories outlawing grandfather clauses and other Jim Crow paraphernalia, and now it began to look quite adept at old-fashioned, brass-knuckle politics. Black voters meant to be counted. Still, Hoover seemed immune to learning anything from such affairs, and his thickheadedness cost him dearly two years later. The seismic shift of Negro voters away from the G.O.P. had been building for more than a decade, and the Parker fight helped push millions of wavering black voters away from the party of Lincoln and into the arms of Franklin D. Roosevelt. Not everyone made the leap, of course. Minnie's father remained a staunch Republican, and when he discovered that Minnie was thinking of voting Democratic, he wouldn't talk to her for weeks. "No daughter of mine would ever vote for the party of Blease and Vardaman," he said in disbelief. It was a long time before he finally forgave her.

The *Call* had given full play to the Parker case. To me the most intriguing aspect of the affair was the way the N.A.A.C.P. had taken to slugging under White's direction. Here at last was a fighting organization, not a tame band of status quo Negroes. One day, riffling through my mail at the *Call*, I discovered an impressive-looking letter from N.A.A.C.P. headquarters in New York, with the return address of W. E. B. Du Bois in the corner. I opened the letter and discovered that Dr. Du Bois was offering me a job. The Depression had played hell with the finances of *The Crisis*, and Dr. Du Bois wanted to hire me as the magazine's business manager, to turn things around. He suggested that I meet him in Chicago to talk the offer over. I was thrilled. I returned to the Dade Apartments that night waving the letter cheerfully in my hand. Dr. Du Bois was the most articulate spokesman of the race, and his invitation opened the way to joining the N.A.A.C.P. at a moment when it was poised for greatness.

Minnie was cool to the offer. She sat me down and reminded me of some things that I had forgotten. While Dr. Du Bois was the undisputed intellectual champion of the race, he was also a notoriously prickly fellow. During one of his many speaking tours, he had stopped in Kansas City. Because Negroes were barred from the town's best hotels, he stayed overnight in a private home, and his hostess had asked if she might give a reception for him. He had agreed to the polite offer, and she invited quite a few people in to meet him. Dr. Du Bois was upstairs when everyone arrived. He descended as far as the landing, then, like a sea captain scanning the horizon, he swept the room with an icy stare and told his hostess, "I don't care to meet them." With that, he turned on his heel and marched back upstairs.

Minnie also reminded me of a similar incident during one of Dr. Du Bois's trips to St. Louis, where he was to speak at one of the city's finest black men's clubs. On the evening of the speech, a contingent of clubmen in evening clothes stopped at his lodging to drive him to dinner. On the way, the car broke down. The clubmen got out and pushed the car as Dr. Du Bois stayed inside and was trundled forward like a potentate. He was a towering figure, and I revered him, but in his weaker moments he managed to give the impression that racial discrimination had been invented solely to make *his* life miserable. "Do you really think you would be able to get along with him?" Minnie asked.

I began to have a few doubts, and I decided to think the offer over more carefully. When I still couldn't make up my mind, I wrote a long letter to White asking for his advice. It reflected the way I was at the time: a young man with one foot in Kansas City and the other itching for bigger things, too restless to stay put, but still too cautious to break away.

> The Kansas City Call
> Kansas City, Missouri
> June 21, 1930

Mr. Walter White
409 Edgecombe Avenue
New York, N.Y.

Dear Walter:

I know you are busy getting ready for your annual conference, but I would be grateful if you could arrange to answer this, if only briefly, before you go up to Springfield. I would like a little information and confidential advice—given straight out. This is apt to be trifle long, but I ask your indulgence.

No doubt you are aware that I have been corresponding with Dr. Du Bois relative to accepting the business managership of *The Crisis.* . . . Dr. Du Bois in his last letter tells me he has conferred with his committee and passed around the correspondence and the members have also been favorably impressed.

Now all this puzzles me very much, for all the men in your office and in *The Crisis* office must know that I am not, and do not profess to be, a business manager. I have spent all my time on the news end of publications. What information I have of the business end has been picked up very casually. Yet these men appear to desire very much that I come as business manager. The offer has all the appearance of sincerity. Plans have been talked of which indicate that I am to consider it a permanent position.

What does it all mean?

The decision is rather important to me. I have reached the place on the *Call* where a change will be advantageous to me only if it means permanence, more money and opportunity to advance farther than I can here. It is not merely a question of changing jobs with me. I have too much at stake here to consider a mere change. At present I am getting a reasonably good salary—more than has been offered by *The Crisis*—and there is room for advancement beyond what I am getting. I have the best job I can get anywhere in the country on a Negro paper—as well paid and with more than the customary executive freedom. The job is what I make it and is mine as long as I care to have it and take care of it. My hours are my own, my weekends as well. No one to say nay. No committees or boards to please. A personal conference with the boss over troublesome questions of policy and on other matters at my own discretion.

The trouble with the job is that it offers no opportunity for growth in the work. It is to be a steady treadmill until the end. The greatest drawback is the place. There is no opportunity for cultural contacts, for the breathing of reasonably fresh air, for movement without the ever-present reminders of the slave system. For nearly seven years I have choked and squirmed and protested and the more I feel it, the sicker I get. Then, I am married, and wouldn't my children, if I am lucky enough to have any, have a hell of a time in a town like this?

I do want to come to New York and I'm not unduly conservative. I'll take as many chances as the next man, but I do not wish to leave a good position as positions go, for something which, after all, may be only an experiment with the people on the other end. I have heard, for instance, that Dr. Du Bois is very difficult to work with. He has assured me that I should have a free hand within the bounds of the magazine's policy. I prefer to believe him. Yet I cannot help asking myself if I can afford to give up a position of almost complete autonomy for one which may be terminated after a few months because of a marked difference of opinion.

If you can advance me any information or outline any conditions which will give me a clearer insight into the situation on your end, I will appreciate it a great deal.

Sincerely,

Roy Wilkins

I don't know what White thought when he received my cautious letter, but he wrote back promptly.

June 23, 1930

Dear Roy:

Your special delivery air mail letter came this morning just as I am getting ready to leave for Springfield.

I am glad to give you my best opinion on the matter of negotiations beween yourself and Dr. Du Bois.

I am a member of *The Crisis* Finance Committee and am one of those who felt and feel that you can do an excellent job as Business Manager of *The Crisis*. I can well understand your present mental situation for it is, in many respects, analogous to my own thirteen years ago when I was asked to consider the position of Assistant Secretary of the N.A.A.C.P. If anything, your problem is a little less perplexing in that the Association at that time had a membership of only around 10,000 and was not nearly so well established as it is today. At that time, I was Cashier of the Standard Life Insurance Company, which was then in its heyday. I have never for a moment regretted making the change though many of my friends in Atlanta told me at the time that I was very foolish to do so. It is true that I have not made nor will ever make, perhaps, the amount of money that might have come had I continued in business. On the other hand, work with the Association has given me contact with some of the best minds of both races in various parts of the world. There is compensation in doing work of this sort and in carving out a career for oneself.

Now, specifically as to *The Crisis:* it is by far the best known magazine of its kind, with a reputation so well established that it is a pity that reputation has not been better capitalized. Dr. Du Bois has worked very hard to make it what it is and I say this in no criticism of him, but what *The Crisis* needs most is expert business methods and, more than that, it needs energy, intelligence, youth and business foresight for its development.

I believe you can do a great job. I believe that Dr. Du Bois and you will get along without any difficulty and that he will not only be willing to accept but will welcome new ideas.

My measured advice is that you consider acceptance. I say this not only because of what I feel confident you can do here but also because of the Kansas City situation. I am sure I do not have to tell you that I personally will be delighted to do anything and everything I can to help you. It is a hard job, but knowing you as I do, I am sure that the very challenge therein implied will act as a spur and inspiration to you.

I am sorry I do not have time to go into this in greater detail, but I want to get this off to you before leaving for Springfield.

Ever sincerely,

Walter White
Acting Secretary

Despite these assurances, Minnie's reservations and my own second thoughts were stronger, and I wrote Dr. Du Bois a second letter telling him regretfully that I could not accept the job. In hindsight, I see that my letter was a bit impertinent, but at the time, it seemed to be the height of good sense.

Kansas City, Mo.
July 9, 1930

Dear Sir:

I am sorry it is not possible for me to accept definitely at this time your offer of the business managership of *The Crisis.* As I have stated in previous letters, your offer comes at a time when affairs on this publication are in a state of transition with more than an even chance that, as far as I am concerned, the new order will be much better than the old.

Added to this is the fact that the salary offer of *The Crisis,* as good as it is considering the magazine's finances and earning power, is somewhat less than I am drawing at the present on the *Call*. When the difference in living conditions and in expenses of moving be considered, it will be seen that a downward difference in salary is of some consequence.

Further than all this, I am here in my special field—news writing and editing. There is no strain here of having at once to learn a new angle to the business, of having to produce revenue or die, of having to adjust oneself to a new environment and new people. Do you see? Could I carry my little specialty under my arm I would ask nothing of any man or any city. Bereft of my tools in a strange city and with the business destiny of a publication on my hesitant shoulders, I would be something liké an expert launch engineer adrift in a sailboat.

But may I suggest, Dr. Du Bois, that whether the magazine secures a business manager at once or not, that especially during this business depression it make an effort only to hold its present circulation, to keep its accounts collected as near as possible to date, to scrutinize new business carefully and tighten up on the old accounts gradually, but effectively; in short, not to lose any money and if possible to accumulate a surplus so that a manager will have some money to begin the promotion program which will be necessary to the securing of more circulation and thereafter of more advertising.

The big advertising agencies will be absolutely deaf to proposals from a class magazine, and especially a Negro class magazine which cannot talk at least 100,000 audited and certified circulation. You can see that 50,000 would command no attention, for the average man knows that there are approximately that number of Negro families in the Greater New York area; therefore a magazine claiming a national, even international circulation and having only 50,000 would receive hardly an interview.

Getting circulation costs money and it would be better, in my judgment, for *The Crisis* to hire a man and call him "assistant business manager," that is, assistant to you in your capacity of business manager, pay him a moderate salary and lay aside the difference in his salary and that of a good business manager for use as a promotion fund when a good man becomes available. This may not be feasible but you can be the best judge of that.

I do not know that I shall stay in Kansas City forever; I hope not. But my wife and I will stick it out for another year, at least. We are both employed and we can save against the day when the right chance comes along. I am not unaware of the prestige of a connection with *The Crisis* and the N.A.A.C.P. and I am grateful to you for considering me as a member of the staff. Of course, I have no right to expect that this particular offer will be available then, but in another year, perhaps, I can see more clearly whether the rewards on this paper are going to compensate for the lack of freedom in this city.

Very sincerely yours,

Roy Wilkins

I was a newsman, not a businessman—that was the crux of the matter. The N.A.A.C.P. people in New York accepted my decision gracefully, and I kept in close touch with them. During the summer I wrote Walter another long letter alerting him that Senator Henry J. Allen, one of Hoover's field marshals during the Parker fight, was up for re-election in Kansas and vulnerable. "If Allen's head can be chopped off," I pointed out, "the unmistakable signal will have been given that Negroes resent his vote in the Parker fight." As most senators go, Allen had been relatively moderate on race, but the time was right for pressing home the momentum of the Parker fight. I was operating on a principle I had learned from Oscar DePriest, then the new black congressman from Chicago: DePriest's rule of thumb was, "If someone has something you want and he doesn't want you to have it, take it." Politics was a hard, ruthless, no-quarters game in the thirties. He who grabbed got.

I asked Walter to send Dean Pickens, the N.A.A.C.P.'s field secretary, out to Kansas. Pickens was as homely as a mud hen but beautiful to watch in action. He could be by turns witty, sarcastic, and moving. Pickens agreed to come, and Minnie and I drove him on a campaign circuit of Topeka, Coffeyville, Wichita, Parsons, Atchison, and Kansas City. He gave a tub-thumping speech in a church in Wichita, Allen's own back yard, telling a crowd of nearly 2,000 black and white voters that if the N.A.A.C.P. could remember Parker's racial slurs for ten years, the people of Kansas would certainly remember Senator Allen three months after the Parker fight. He also told those home folks, "A man who advertises himself as your enemy is not nearly so dangerous as the one who advertises himself as your friend in small things, then joins those who aim to destroy you when your most vital interests are at stake," and called Allen one hundred times more dangerous than Cole Blease. As we were walking out, I heard one impressed white woman whisper to a friend, "There must be some Irish in that man—he's so witty."

Despite Pickens's best efforts, Allen managed to win the primary, partly because he had three opponents who split the vote against him. But the total vote of the opposition (145,000) was far greater than Allen's own winning tally (118,500), and in Kansas City, where black precincts normally voted 75 percent Republican, Allen received only 27 percent of the vote. He lost in the general election that fall, so the outcome justified the effort we had put into it.

As I look back on 1930, I can see that it was a turning point for me: more and more I wanted to shift from passively recording Jim Crow's hard knocks to fighting them. One night that winter, Minnie and I set out from the apartment to go to Earl's place for his birthday. It was snowing that evening, and as we crossed the street we were caught for a moment in the lights of an approaching car. Neither of us paid any attention to the lights. Minnie walked on to the passenger side of our car, and I had just reached for the door on the driver's side when the approaching vehicle screeched to a halt and a policeman jumped out and started to frisk me.

Minnie looked over and saw that I hadn't slid behind the wheel. When she saw what was going on outside, she jumped out of the car and shouted to the policeman, "What are you doing to my husband?"

A second cop got out of the prowl car. "Get in your car and shut up," he told Minnie.

"I'll do no such thing," she shot right back. "What do you think you are doing to my husband?"

She had saved me again. Sensing the situation was getting out of hand, the police began to back off. They told us that they had been looking for a stolen car and left.

The next day I filed a complaint with the police commissioner. At a subsequent hearing the two officers said that in the glare of the head-lights Minnie had looked white and that they couldn't understand what she was doing with a black fellow like me. The commissioner knew the work I did for the *Call* and fined the two cops two days' pay.

There was not much comfort in such small victories. To push things further, I tried to educate the Negro community in Kansas City about its own economic power. One of the things I did was orga-nize a boycott of a local bakery that had heavy sales in the Negro com-munity but that refused to hire Negro drivers for its delivery trucks. The response was very satisfying. Negro housewives kept away from the company's bread and rolls, the bakery saw the light, and for the first time Negroes started driving its trucks.

But I longed to test myself at something more dangerous, and the opportunity finally came in early November 1930. As so often hap-pened, the adventure began with a ring of the phone on my desk at the *Call*. In those days we ran a string of small-town correspondents to keep us in touch with the news beyond the borders of Kansas City, and my caller was one of these stringers. He told me breathlessly that a lynch mob in Clinton, Missouri, had railroaded a jury into sentenc-ing two hapless black handymen to death for the murder of an elderly white recluse.

My curiosity overrode my better sense, and I decided to drive down to Clinton to investigate the case. First I telephoned Minnie. "There's a lynch mob at work in Clinton, and I'm going down there," I told her.

"If you're going, I'm going," she snapped, and nothing I could do would make her change her mind.

I picked her up and we set off for Clinton, a town sixty-five miles southeast of Kansas City. The drive took about two hours, and we were both nervous, but I didn't really feel afraid. I was naïve, intent on seeing the lynch spirit up close and on getting the story into print. After pulling into Clinton, we stopped at the office of the local newspaper to get our bearings. The editor was a courteous white fellow who made a point of calling me Mr. Wilkins, uncommon good manners in Southern border states. He told us that the murder had taken place in Windsor, Missouri, about twenty miles northeast of Clinton. The victim was an old lady named Elizabeth Neiman, who lived by herself on a lonely farm outside Windsor. She had dropped from sight for several days, and a relative calling at the farm had found her body. No one really knew when she had been killed.

The murder might have remained a mystery, but a freelance Burns detective in Kansas City had decided to make a case of it. He went up to Windsor and started poking around. After considerable scratching, he found a thirteen-year-old boy who told him he had seen Emmett Gallie, thirty, and Eual Richardson, twenty-two, leaving the Neiman farm about the supposed time of the murder. The two men had been driving a wagon owned by Gallie's father-in-law, Wesley Shockley, a one-armed black man. With nothing more than this slip of a story to go on, the Burns man arranged to have Richardson and Gallie arrested; they were taken to Kansas City, given the third degree, and beaten to a pulp. Richardson stood up under the beating, but Gallie, a frailer man who feared the cops might beat him to death, signed a "confession." The two suspects were then hauled back to Clinton and put on trial. Their lawyer was given less than forty-eight hours to prepare a defense, and when he requested a continuance of the case, the judge turned him down. Faster than you can say Jim Crow, an all-white jury convicted the two men of murder, and they were sentenced to death. At the verdict, a mob, which had jammed the courtroom and filled the entire courthouse during the trial, broke into cheers.

The irony was that only the death sentence had saved the two suspects from a lynching there and then. As he thought back on the mob scene, the editor of the *Clinton Democrat* told me, "There was rope in that crowd. The whole thing was the fault of our sheriff," he added. "I blame him. Ya know, Mr. Wilkins, our niggers down here vote Democratic."

His meaning was clear enough: you don't let lynch mobs form

when you depend upon Negroes to win elections. The issue was not that a lynching is a murder. What he was saying was, "Look out now, we are going to make these niggers vote Republican."

From Clinton, Minnie and I drove on to Windsor, which looked like a very peaceable little town. About twenty-five Negro families lived on the far side of the tracks in little white frame cottages with vegetable gardens out back. By the time we got there, dark had settled on the Negro section. An eerie atmosphere hovered over the neighborhood: the houses were dark, the streets were empty, everything was hushed.

We finally found the cottage belonging to the Shockleys. I got out of the car, walked up a small path to the front door, and knocked. I heard rustling inside, but no one answered. I knocked again. Again, no one came to the door. Looking at Minnie, I knocked for the third time and waited.

The door opened a small crack, and a terrified black woman peeped out. She pleaded with me to go away. It took all the balm I could find to persuade her to let Minnie and me through the door. Finally, the fact that I worked for the *Call*, a familiar name in the Missouri and Kansas countryside, got us through. Inside we found two women cowering in the dark. The lady who had answered the door was Mildred Shockley, the wife of the man whose wagon had allegedly been used in the murder. The other woman was Mrs. Gallie, the wife of one of the two accused men. They told me their husbands had been carried off so quickly that there had barely been time to hire a lawyer from Salina to defend them.

After hustling Richardson and Gallie to Kansas City, the police had ransacked the Shockley place in search of clues to the murder. One of the raiders triumphantly came up with a pair of blood-spattered boots, but the doctor in the party examined them and announced that the stains were only rabbit's blood. "You mean to say it's not human blood?" the disappointed cop had asked bitterly. The doctor turned his back and walked away, saying that the lawman could make of the find what he chose. The law chose to arrest Shockley on the spot. As they dragged him off, one of the raiders told his wife, "Never mind what we want your husband for. We are going to break his goddamn black neck."

Shockley had worked in Windsor for twenty-five years, and his wife worked for the town banker, but neither the banker nor anyone else in Windsor stood up to help them. Shockley was saved from a lynching at the Windsor jail only by an honest lawman who sneaked him out the back door as the lynch mob formed by the front.

If the white folks in Windsor had no doubt about who had killed

Mrs. Neiman, the black folks said there were plenty of things to wonder about. For one thing, Richardson and Gallie were accused of stealing a big sack of silver dollars from the dead white woman, yet none of the money had been found on them. For another, the small boy whose testimony had convicted them recited his story quickly and mechanically in court, as if he had been coached. Finally, although Mrs. Neiman, an eccentric old lady, had a running feud going with some of her relatives, no one suspected them—they were white.

As Mrs. Shockley and Mrs. Gallie told me these horror stories, I felt a terrible, helpless rage. The two black women were resigned to what was happening· their husbands were gone; they were mortally frightened themselves. Yet they accepted what had happened as something that could only be endured—believing that there was no hope of changing anything.

We were all talking to one another in whispers. Finally, Minnie asked if she might use the bathroom. The two women looked at one another and shook their heads: there was no indoor plumbing in the cottage. Very reluctantly the younger woman took Minnie by the hand and led her through the dark house to the garden and the outhouse. They then groped their way back. That was the way things were in Missouri in 1930. Mob "justice" was the rule, creating a terror so great that its victims did not dare to light a single candle against the night.

9 AN INVITATION FROM THE N.A.A.C.P.

What I had seen in Clinton shook me. For seven years I had been content with a newsman's guiding philosophy—seeing and reporting without bias—but the anger I felt as Minnie and I drove back to Kansas City demanded a different and larger satisfaction. I had seen enough to last a lifetime—*doing* something was the important thing. I could no longer hide behind my press card. Wherever I looked, I saw "me too, Boss" advocates arguing that the Negro should not make so much noise, not protest, not fight. These same people told Negroes to be meek, silent, forgiving, forbearing, patient, and long-suffering. But so far as I could see, meekness had never gotten the race anywhere. Militancy was the only approach that led to progress. Lynchings and burnings, job stealing, peonage, disfranchisement, inequality before the law, in schools, and in the ghettos—all the features of segregation—would yield to nothing less.

The 1930 elections were held a week after Minnie and I returned from Clinton. In New York, black voters elected a black state assemblyman and two municipal court judges; in Philadelphia, Cleveland, and Detroit, blacks won seats in the state legislature. In Illinois, a black congressman, a state senator, and five members of the state house of representatives were elected. In St. Louis they put a state legislator, one justice of the peace, and a constable into office. But in Kansas City, black voters, following Republican and Democratic machine bosses, elected whites even in the black precincts. I was furious. Only in Kansas City had we fallen on our knees and asked the white man, "Please, mister, how shall I vote?"

The problem of whether to hold my ground in Kansas City or fly the coop as so many of my friends had done pressed harder than ever. As I was wrestling with it, Paul Robeson came back through town on tour, and I went to his hotel and spent an hour talking with him. He leaned back in his chair with a smile that illuminated every corner of the suite and told me he planned to sail for England at the end of April 1931. He had a house in London at 19 Buckingham Street, the Strand. He wanted to stay in Europe studying German and Russian, perhaps doing *Othello* in Sweden or making a movie in Germany for a motion-picture company that also had Marlene Dietrich in its stable. He couldn't do a picture in the United States at that time as the major American studios wouldn't hire Negroes for serious roles because they feared the films would be banned in the South. I can hear Robeson rambling on about the world, not bragging, but talking matter-of-factly about Vienna, Berlin, Budapest, Paris, London, Stockholm, Moscow, and New York. New York City, he said, was all right so long as one had friends to act as "bumpers" against prejudice. I sat there, fascinated, yearning to make a break of my own.

About two weeks after Robeson left town, I was sitting at my desk at the *Call* going through my mail. Buried among the usual junk was a letter from Walter White in New York marked *Personal and Confidential*. My fingers trembled as I slit it open.

February 26, 1931

Dear Roy:

I am writing to you personally and confidentially to ask if you would be interested in an important executive position with the Association. As you of course know, Mr. Johnson has resigned as Secretary. We are faced, therefore, with the problem of getting the right man for the position of Assistant Secretary, which I formerly held.

Your name, among others, has been discussed at length for this position. I have been asked to find out from you if you would be interested. If you are, our Committee on Administration would like to present at the next meeting of the Board of Directors on March 9th, a proposal to invite you to come to New York for a conference, at our expense.

Please let me hear from you immediately. I am sure I do not need to tell you how pleased I would be, personally, to have you with us here. I am sure, also, I do not need to tell you that it offers an opportunity for a magnificent career.

Cordially,

Walter White
Acting Secretary

I read the letter several times, my heart thumping. This was no invitation to bury myself in the business department of *The Crisis* but an offer to work side by side with the most exciting civil rights leader of the day. I pulled out my typewriter and tapped out a two-paragraph reply. Anything overeager, I cautioned myself, might spoil my chances.

February 28, 1931

Dear Walter:

    I thank you very much for your letter of February 26. You may say to your committee on administration that I am interested and would be pleased to have it submit its proposal to the board of directors on March 9.

    I want to assure you that I consider it an honor to be approached with this offer. It seems wise to me to reserve any further discussion until a conference can be held.

Cordially,

Roy

    Ten days later White wrote to invite me to New York City for an interview. He suggested that I arrive by March 22, as the committee on administration wanted to look me over the next day. I was in the middle of pulling together a pre-Easter shopping edition for the *Call,* but I juggled my plans, booked a berth on the Pennsylvania Railroad, and wrote White that I would arrive in New York City on the twenty-second—two minutes before noon.

    I spent the next few days in eager planning and calculations. The N.A.A.C.P. was the most militant civil rights organization in the country. In the free air of New York City, they had pounded down the South's infamous grandfather clauses, exposed lynchings, and pushed for a federal antilynching law so long and loudly that the South was eventually humiliated into dropping the rope. The same Northern radicals had exposed the spread of peonage among black sharecroppers in the South, prodded the Supreme Court into throwing out verdicts reached by mob-dominated juries, and blotted out residential segregation by municipal ordinance. And in the fall of 1930 they had hired Nathan Margold, a young lawyer out of the Justice Department and Harvard Law School, to map out a nationwide fight against Jim Crow. These were people who were getting things done.

    The departure day finally came, and I settled into a seat on the Pennsy's Train Number 30, headed east. Just out of Indianapolis, a conductor came around, tapped me politely on the shoulder, and handed me a telegram: PLEASE TELEPHONE MY HOUSE FOUR HUNDRED NINE EDGECOMBE AVENUE ON ARRIVAL STOP. EXPECTING YOU TO DINE

WITH US. WALTER WHITE. 409 Edgecombe Avenue, the finest address in Harlem. As the train clattered and bounced along, I thought to myself, Kansas City won't hold you now.

At noon the next day I got off the train at Pennsylvania Station and took the subway uptown to Harlem. After finding a room at the Y.M.C.A. on 135th Street, I parked my bag and climbed up the gently sweeping curve of Edgecombe Avenue to the snappy canopy of the famous apartment building at its crest. A uniformed doorman ushered me in and pointed the way to the elevator. White greeted me at the door of his apartment, smiling as he grasped my hand and showed me in. His wife, Gladys, a wonderful cook, had fixed a splendid dinner. For several hours we sat at the table talking politics and turning over his plans for the N.A.A.C.P. At the end of the evening, I walked back down Sugar Hill and into Harlem, feeling happier than I could remember.

The following morning I took the bus downtown for the job interview. In those days the N.A.A.C.P. was in a loft building at 69 Fifth Avenue, just up from Fourteenth Street on the northern border of Greenwich Village. I took one final look up and down Fifth Avenue, gathered as much composure as I could, and went in. The full committee on administration was waiting for me. Dr. Du Bois was there, as were Arthur B. Spingarn and Joel E. Spingarn, two white liberals and brothers who did as much between them as any two white men to advance the cause of civil rights. Looking around the room, I could see White, Dean Pickens, and Robert Bagnall, the director of branches. Presiding over this assembly was Mary White Ovington, chairman of the board of directors, the N.A.A.C.P.'s wealthy maiden aunt. I presented my credentials as a black newsman. "And what *else* do you do, Mr. Wilkins?" she asked me pointedly. She could not believe that a Negro could make a living in the news business.

The interview went smoothly until we reached the N.A.A.C.P.'s most vulnerable spot—money. At that point, Dr. Du Bois and White adjourned with me to discuss my salary. I knew that the Depression had hurt the N.A.A.C.P., but I was not prepared to go broke working for it. At the time I was earning $2,600 a year at the *Call*, and I told Walter and Dr. Du Bois that I would have to have $3,600 a year to absorb the cost of moving and of maintaining Minnie and me in New York. As diplomatically as he could, White said that the board had been thinking about a salary along the lines of $3,000. I felt a stab of disappointment. I told him that the issue of money wasn't paramount, but that I would have to talk the matter over with my wife. We shook hands all round. It was clear that I had the job—if I could afford to take it.

I picked up a ticket at Pennsylvania Station, found my berth, dropped my bag, and ambled back to the club car as the train pulled out of New York City. The Hudson River was rolling by outside the window when I came into the bar. As I eased into a stiff Scotch, I looked out and smiled in anticipation of the overnight run to Chicago.

Absentmindedly I picked up a newspaper and unfolded it. There, below the fold, was a depressing story out of Scottsboro, Alabama. Nine black youngsters bumming on a Southern freight train had been arrested for the rape of two young white women. You didn't have to be a genius to figure out what kind of white women were hopping freight down South in 1931, and you didn't have to be a constitutional lawyer to guess what kind of justice the suspected rapists were going to get. The Scottsboro affair would soon balloon to an international scandal, and the Scottsboro Boys would soon have me running all the way from well-upholstered law offices in midtown Manhattan to seedy pawnshops in Harlem.

When I got home Minnie and I sat down to review the N.A.A.C.P.'s offer. We were both delighted at the thought of going to New York, but worried about the salary. Finally, I wrote Walter and told him that if the board could see its way to splitting the difference and paying me $3,300, with a raise up the road, I could sign on in New York by mid-August. The haggling succeeded. The board gave me what I was after, and as an afterthought it also approved a motion by Dr. Du Bois to pay an extra $10 for my ride aboard the Twentieth Century Limited.

My elation over the new job was tempered by the pain of breaking the news to Franklin. At last, we sat down and I told him what was going on. "I thought you wanted to be a newspaperman," he said. The rebuke gave me a real twinge. Then he told me a few other things. The *Call* was prospering mightily; by 1931 our circulation had risen from 4,000 to 20,000 copies a week. Since there were only about 14,000 black families in Kansas City, we calculated that we were reaching just about every black household and some of the whites as well. The figures were certified by the Audit Bureau of Circulation, a point of honor and great pride with Franklin. In those days, circulation figures were mostly guesses; publishers simply pegged their circulation and ad rates to what they thought the traffic would bear. The *Call* became the first Negro weekly in the country to secure official A.B.C. figures on its circulation. Franklin told me things were going so well that he planned to turn the *Call* into a $100,000 public corporation with his family and his employees as shareholders. Joe LaCour was to become a vice president, and there would be room for me to run the paper one day if I would give up wild notions like running off to New York.

The offer was tempting, but I told Franklin that the time had come for me to move on. "I won't stand in the way of any young man who wants to get ahead," he told me. Then he thumped me on the shoulder and said, "If ever those people in New York do not treat you right, come back. Not only will you be on the payroll from the moment you say you are coming, but a part of the company will be yours also."

The next few months sped by quickly. At the end of June I went to the N.A.A.C.P.'s twenty-second annual convention in Pittsburgh. At the opening session there was a polite burst of applause when I was introduced to the assembled delegates as the new assistant secretary. For the next forty-six years I would stand on that platform in different cities, watching the audience grow larger and larger as the N.A.A.C.P. grew older and stronger, but I knew from that first moment that I was standing exactly where I wanted to plant my feet.

Our headquarters for the convention was in the Pittsburgh Y.M.C.A., and one night the officers of the organization decided to go swimming. In those days it was the custom at the Y to swim in the nude. I can still see Dr. Du Bois, a man of enormous presence who carried a silver-headed cane to go with his three-piece suits, natty hats, and Vandyke beard, confronting this prospect. At the Y that night, the great man, naked as a jaybird, plunged ceremoniously into the pool. He emerged sputtering cheerfully, water dripping from the Vandyke, and I felt a fondness for him that lasted the rest of his long life. No man who made that plunge could have been so well starched as Dr. Du Bois affected to be when he was fully clothed.

At the closing meeting in Soldiers Memorial Hall, Joel Spingarn told the delegates that the N.A.A.C.P. was the only organization in the country that believed the United States Constitution meant just what it said. White then told them that the United States would have to give the Negro justice or see the race go over to Communism—a threat inspired by the early success of the Communists in exploiting the Scottsboro Case. There were 4,000 people in the hall that evening, and they all craned forward to see the major speaker, Clarence Darrow, the great agnostic, defender of Dr. Ossian Sweet. Darrow was a bear of a man, but he spoke slowly, taking his time, mixing wit with salty sarcasm. "This association really ought to be named the National Association for the Advancement of White People—they are the ones that need it," he said. After the laughter subsided, he continued: "If this had been any association other than the N.A.A.C.P. I would not be here to speak. I don't want to hand you any bunk. I hate bunk. But I do want to give you a little advice—and if you take it I will be more surprised than anyone else. Negroes are used to having white people speak to them who tell them about how they loved their old black mammies. Those whites did love their black folk—because blacks were their meal tickets. And the descendants of those white people love you today for the same reason—and that only."

Then he raised his right hand and shouted into the microphone of radio station KDKA, which broadcast the speech live that night: "The Negro from now on must save himself. The white people who will help him are growing fewer and fewer. He must fight his own battles." In a slow, deliberate voice, he added: "What weapon has the Negro with which to fight? Well, he better not depend on God, for if God intended to help him, he never would have cursed him first.

"The Negro does have the weapon which he can use if he will," Darrow said as he finished. "That is the vote. Disown the petty politicians of your own race who sell you out for money or for jobs. Get out from under the control of white or colored four-flushers. Vote strictly to advance the interests of your race. Thus you can ease your burden."

There was a burst of applause in the hall. It was impossible not to feel that the old ways were changing—and that the N.A.A.C.P. would be leading that change.

I returned to Kansas City and got ready to pack. At the end of July there was a going-away party for me at the Paseo Y.M.C.A. I didn't know I had so many friends. Looking out over the crowd of more than a hundred, I could see Earl and Helen, Joe LaCour, Bishop W. T. Vernon of the A.M.E. Church, the Franklins, dozens more. Franklin presented me with a calfskin toilet case and traveling bag from the employees of the *Call*, and Edward S. Lewis, executive secretary of the Kansas City Urban League, gave Minnie a dozen long-stemmed roses. I felt a lump in my throat as I rose to speak. "My office may be on Fifth Avenue, not Eighteenth Street, but I'll be fighting for you," I said—and sat down.

The next day, Minnie and I drove to St. Paul for a short holiday. There were five days of swimming and golf, and evenings of gaiety and good conversation with Dr. James Crump, St. Paul's only Negro physician, and other friends. The time in St. Paul passed quickly. As we drove back to Kansas City, the temperature reached 107 at Des Moines, and we decided to stay overnight and set out for Kansas City in the cool of the morning the next day. Only movie houses were air-conditioned in 1931, so we sought a movie where we could have a couple of hours of relief. As we entered the theater, an agitated usher rushed over to us and said, "Seats in the balcony, seats in the balcony." The main floor to which the white couple who were just ahead of us went was practically empty. I was getting out just in time.

Back in Kansas City, I threw my bags into the back of our car, and set off for New York with Minnie, who planned to ride with me as far as St. Louis. I hadn't gone far before I noticed in the rearview mirror that a car was trailing me. It was Earl, escorting me out of town. Finally, I pulled over to the side of the road and he drew up alongside. We shook hands; then my brother got into his car and headed back toward Kansas City. I watched his car disappear before slipping back into my own. My eyes had misted up. I blinked hard a few times, eased the car back onto the highway, pointed it east—and stepped on the gas.

10   UP IN HARLEM, DOWN IN THE DELTA

few hours later Minnie and I reached St. Louis. The plan was for me to go on to New York while she returned to Kansas City, after visiting with her parents, to finish packing and to wrap up her work with the Kansas City Urban League. On August 13, 1931, I kissed Minnie, boarded the Pennsylvania Railroad's Train Number 30, and set off for New York. My newspapering days were over; a new way of life lay just up the tracks.

I arrived in Pennsylvania Station the next day shortly after noon, and for the second time that year I picked up my bag, made my way out of that cave of hissing trains, harried passengers, and perspiring redcaps, and headed uptown to Harlem.

I had no place to stay. For a time I had toyed with the idea of putting up at the Y.M.C.A. until I could find better quarters, but the idea of starting out in New York the way I had started in Kansas City didn't appeal to me, and I came up with a better idea. In those days the Y.W.C.A. in Harlem operated a registry that inspected and approved rooms in private homes. I figured that any room clean enough and safe enough for the young ladies of the Y.W.C.A. had to be good enough for me. At the registry, a clerk gave me a slip listing a bedroom and bathroom with use of kitchen in the home of a Mrs. Millburn at 307 West 136th Street.

The Millburns' place was a well-kept brick town house on a quiet block off Seventh Avenue. Public School 136 was just across the street, and up on the hill at the end of the block, City College of New York overlooked Harlem. The house had a high stone stoop, narrow front doors, and a bay window on the parlor floor. When I knocked, Mrs. Millburn, a friendly woman, opened the door and showed me through the house. Even though it was August, the halls were cool and dark, and the rooms were comfortable, with large windows and plenty of sunlight. I rented a bedroom for five dollars a week, unpacked my bag, and hung up my clothes.

Walter had invited me to spend my first evening as a New Yorker dining at his apartment, so as dusk settled over Harlem, I left my room, hunted up a cab, and rode up Sugar Hill to 409 Edgecombe. Gladys White cooked another fine supper while Walter—a compulsive talker and a very good one—rattled on about the N.A.A.C.P., the Scottsboro Boys, and the Communists. He talked about books, about Gladys's skill as a cook, wife, and mother, about the year they had spent together in France on a Guggenheim Fellowship while he wrote *Rope and Faggot: A Biography of Judge Lynch*. The Whites' daughter, Jane, a pert little girl of kindergarten age, took an intense interest in everything that was said that evening. Their little boy, Walter Jr., whom they called "Pidge," played with a toy and ignored us completely. When the evening ended I left for my room feeling as close to Walter and Gladys as I had felt to old friends in Kansas City.

The next day I took the Sixth Avenue El downtown to my spartan working quarters at 69 Fifth Avenue. I discovered that I was to occupy a cramped little cubicle behind a glass partition that didn't reach the ceiling. Within this cell I found an ancient desk and chair. Must have come from some old abolitionist, I thought to myself.

It didn't take long to settle in. The staff's outstanding figure was Dr. Du Bois, the literary voice and intellectual dean of the N.A.A.C.P. Impeccably tailored, haughty, he patronized me as he did everyone else. He had a private office with an enormous double rolltop desk and a couch, a retreat where he could come and go without being seen or bothered by the rest of the staff. Then there was Dean Pickens, abrupt, informal, always on the move, a field secretary in a hurry who filed expense accounts right down to the half penny on his postage stamps. Robert Bagnall, a short, amiable man with an easy manner and a good sense of humor, was the director of branches; he had studied to become an Episcopalian minister, and he had a keen eye and a tolerance for human foibles. The office's chief bookkeeper was a quiet gentleman named Frank Turner; he kept to himself, avoiding the office politics and intrigues that drew everyone else like bees to clover.

Finally, there was Miss Richetta Randolph, the chief secretary and office manager. Miss Randolph wore black woolen dresses and a perpetual scowl. Her clothes looked as if they had come out of a trunk closed since the Civil War, and they smelled just as musty. Miss Randolph loved order and dreaded sin. She treated the secretaries under her command like girls in a boarding school. As they sat perched over their desks and chores, she would stride down the aisle looking for the slightest hint of an exposed knee. Such an infraction invariably brought a flood of scolding down upon any hapless secretary whose skirt didn't match Miss Randolph's standards of propriety.

I began my new job officially on August 15, 1931. The N.A.A.C.P.'s publicity department sent out a crisp little press release announcing that a new assistant secretary had arrived, "ready for work." And that was that. I had no way of knowing that I would spend the rest of my working life at the N.A.A.C.P.; if I had, I might have talked them into saying something more memorable.

My new duties involved a little bit of everything—writing, lecturing, organizing new branches, raising money for a treasury that was always Depression-dry, running the office while Walter was touring around the country. For a while I even reviewed legal cases. During those first few months I did everything from handle correspondence with the mothers of the Scottsboro Boys to organize the annual Christmas Seal drive. One of my first assignments was to protest the army air corps' policy of denying commissions to Negroes—I wrote General Douglas MacArthur at the War Department and got nowhere. I also handled the case of a Negro guard named Fred Harvey, who was convicted of first-degree murder when a white man fell under the wheels of the Hagenbeck-Wallace circus train. Harvey had the job of putting persons not connected with the circus off the train, and when a white man fell, Harvey found himself facing the death penalty.

The first few weeks passed rapidly. Claude Barnett, director of the Associated Negro Press, wrote me a letter asking me to write for them. From Kansas City, Chester Franklin lobbied to keep "Talking It Over" going at the *Call.* William C. Nunn, city editor of the *Pittsburgh Courier,* also wrote me a flattering letter: "I have noticed with great interest the way in which N.A.A.C.P. releases have been handled for the past two weeks and methinks that one can see the journalistic hand of Sir Roy in the background." Nunn said he would take up "Talking It Over" if Franklin dropped it. In the end I kept on writing for the *Call* with one hand, while doing everything else with the other. I was busier than I had been for years.

As those first weeks went by, I wrote Minnie every day and spent what spare time I could scrape together sightseeing. I wanted to be able to squire her comfortably into New York. Her trip turned out to be a little bumpier than I had anticipated. By early November she had finished her work in Kansas City and was ready to leave for the East. We owned a 1929 Ford coupe, and Minnie stowed the silver in the trunk, packed her clothes in the back, and drove to St. Louis, where she spent a few days with her parents, who tried to talk her out of driving East. Her mother's mid-Victorian ideas didn't include women driving by themselves for ten miles, let alone a thousand; she threatened to get on the running board and hold Minnie back if need be. No one, of course, got anywhere. Her brother finally drew up an itinerary for her, loaded her down with maps—and prayed.

Minnie has never bothered to read a map, but she took the stack her brother offered to make him feel better. She was to spend her first night on the road in Indianapolis, then make her way on at a gentle pace. To every stop along the way I sent telegrams saying BE CAREFUL. DO THIS. DO THAT. The first day she reached Indianapolis at noon. Seeing no point in spending a day and night there, she drove on to Columbus. That evening she telephoned me. She said that she was quite capable of driving the rest of the way alone, but I made arrangements to meet her in Buffalo in two days. She stopped in Cleveland for a visit with a childhood friend, but reached Buffalo well ahead of my train. I insisted on taking the wheel of the car myself.

"I don't mind driving," Minnie said mildly.

"Oh, you're tired," I said.

"You're a little out of practice, you know. You haven't driven for a couple of months."

"No, *I'll* drive," I insisted.

Two blocks from the station I collided with another car. The damage was slight but the embarrassment lasted for years. Two days later we arrived in New York City in good spirits—and with a large dent in the coupe.

Minnie had never seen New York City before. We drove into Manhattan feeling elated at breaking free from the provincial smugness and racial strain of Kansas City, but more than a little trepidation was also riding with us in the coupe. We were both Middle Westerners: we had spent our childhood there, we had been educated there, we had found our first jobs there, our relatives were still living there. For months we had heard about the frosty shoulder New York and New Yorkers turned on newcomers. We didn't say much to each other as we drove in, but both of us were wondering the same thing: would we take to this town—would it take to us?

I drove Minnie into Harlem and parked at the Millburns'. On the third floor of their town house they had a large bed-sitting-room with a kitchenette for rent at seven dollars a week. When I showed the little apartment to Minnie, she said it would suit her fine, so we moved out of my room downstairs the same day. Until the middle of the following summer that friendly little perch overlooking Harlem was our home.

New Yorkers weren't as unfriendly as we had been led to believe. After church on Sundays, the Millburns made a point of inviting us downstairs for brunch. Sally Alexander, an old friend from St. Paul, and her husband, Dr. Ernest Alexander, a prosperous dermatologist, gave a black-tie dinner for us in their home on West 139th Street, the block of Stanford White brownstones that had been flippantly tagged "Striver's Row" when Negroes began moving in. Sally Alexander was a formidable woman who had been the wife of Dr. Valdo Turner, our family physician in St. Paul. At forty she entered the University of Minnesota and earned her degree, graduating Phi Beta Kappa. Then she divorced Dr. Turner, moved East, married Dr. Alexander, and took a fierce interest in the activities of the N.A.A.C.P. She was a close friend and ally of Dr. Du Bois. At dinner that evening, the guests were all much older than Minnie and I. They talked knowingly about the strengths and shortcomings of Mayor Jimmy Walker and of the city's Negro politicians, and indignantly about the discrimination practiced by the British Cunard Line against black people crossing the Atlantic for grand tours of Europe. I nodded sagely at the cosmopolitan chatter—checking my tux for stray hayseeds when no one was looking.

After that welcome to Harlem, an avalanche of invitations descended on our little apartment on West 136th Street. Mr. and Mrs. Charles Toney adopted us like their own children. Charles Toney was a lawyer who later became one of the first Negroes elected to the Civil Court in New York; his wife was an old friend of Minnie's mother. Dean Pickens took us out to dinner with his wife, two daughters, a son and beautiful daughter-in-law. We ate at a downtown club; the membership was ultra-liberal, white, with a few blacks on the roll. The Bagnalls also had a dinner for us in their home. Mrs. Bagnall, a pretty, gray-haired woman who wore a long hostess gown that evening, liked a toddy and spoke her mind. She was particularly curdling about climbers who put on airs as the "cream" of Negro society. Walter and Gladys invited us to a large party at their apartment. Half the guests were white, a sight no one in Kansas City would have believed.

We also spent many evenings with Aaron Douglas and his wife, Alta, in their apartment at 409 Edgecombe Avenue. By then the Harlem Renaissance was fading, though painters like Aaron, singers like Paul Robeson, and writers like Jessie Fauset were still very much around. Chic white hostesses downtown seemed to feel that their parties were a flop without at least one or two Negro artists on hand. Taylor Gordon, the tall, rough-hewn butler who had written *Born to Be,* was still lionized by a few Park Avenue matrons. Aaron wasn't part of this fraudulent circuit. He was a free spirit and a generous one, and during the gloomy days of the Depression there was always a pot of soup simmering on Alta's stove for the painters, poets, and writers who flowed in and out of their apartment in an unending stream.

During those first weeks, Minnie and I ate dinner now and then at the Gold Leaf Tea Room on 137th Street. One evening a young man who was dining alone came over to our table. "You are Roy Wilkins, aren't you?" he said. "They say we look alike. I'm Hubert Delany." Hubert soon became the first black member of the Board of Tax Commissioners of the City of New York, one of Mayor Fiorello La Guardia's early appointments, and we saw a lot of him in the years that followed. William Andrews, who was a part-time counsel for the N.A.A.C.P., and his wife, Regina, a librarian, invited us to spend our first Christmas in New York with them. I also remember one decorous little tea party on the Upper East Side at the home of Joel Spingarn, the N.A.A.C.P.'s president. Spingarn's wife, Amy, had a strong social conscience. She was a fine, gritty woman with a good deal of money. The Spingarns lived in a small palace—that was the first time I saw an elevator in a private home.

I had a few rough edges back in those days. Not long after we had arrived in New York Walter invited Minnie and me to dinner and an opening night on Broadway. A bit apologetically he took me aside and said, "We dress for this occasion. You *do* have a tuxedo?" I didn't tell Walter that I had owned a tux for a long time; even in Kansas City we didn't go out in straw hats and coveralls.

Adjusting to the new climate around 69 Fifth Avenue took some time. The office was a world apart from the *Call*. It was friendly enough, but terribly formal. There was none of the camaraderie of a newspaper office, no joking, wisecracks, or kidding. The staff wrote volumes of memoranda "for the record" on the most trivial matters, affairs that could easily have been settled with a phone call or a face-to-face talk. And the pall of office politics and intrigue was thicker than smog in Los Angeles. I arrived the summer after James Weldon Johnson had stepped down as secretary of the N.A.A.C.P. Johnson's wife thought Walter had pushed her husband out, and Walter had yet to establish his own authority around the shop. Pickens, Bagnall, and Dr. Du Bois each believed he would have made a better secretary than Walter, and Dr. Du Bois was leading a campaign to topple him. I was somewhat naïve in those days, and it took me a while to get the drift of what was going on. Not long after Minnie arrived, we received an invitation from Dr. Du Bois to join him for brunch at his apartment. He was very cordial to us, but before long it became clear that there was an ulterior motive behind the ham and eggs. As it turned out, he was mustering support for his war against Walter. Walter had been a student of Dr. Du Bois's at Atlanta University, and I suspect that Dr. Du Bois found it hard to accept a former protégé as the N.A.A.C.P.'s chief executive officer. Walter's temperament was also far different from that of Dr. Du Bois: he was brash, outgoing, effusive, a great salesman, propagandist, and maker of friends. Perhaps Dr. Du Bois considered him a bit vulgar; perhaps he envied his popularity. Whatever the case, there was bad blood between them. As a plotter, however, Dr. Du Bois was hopelessly inept. During the brunch he received a telephone call, which he took just off the dining room. After a few words his voice suddenly dropped to a conspiratorial whisper and he began to speak in French. Minnie had studied French, and Dr. Du Bois's tactics made her furious.

Not long afterward, Dr. Du Bois circulated a memo that was extremely critical of administrative procedures around 69 Fifth Avenue. The memo made no mention of Walter by name, and I naïvely signed it, along with just about everyone else on the staff. When I got home, I showed the thing to Minnie, who pointed out that it was a transparent attack on Walter. The next day I removed my name from the offending memo. Later, at the prodding of the board of directors, the other staffers who had signed withdrew their names. But Dr. Du Bois, proud and inflexible, refused to back down an inch. As early as the fall of 1931 it was clear that he and Walter were heading for a terrible collision, though the smashup didn't take place for another three years.

In July 1932, Minnie and I moved out of the Millburns' house and rented our own small apartment at 409 Edgecombe, a thirteen-story building with 128 apartments that stood at the top of Sugar Hill overlooking the Polo Grounds. It had uniformed doormen and elevator operators for the two elevators, a switchboard in the lobby that announced all guests, large Oriental rugs over white tile floors. The vases on the sideboards near the elevators were always full of freshly cut flowers.

Our apartment was on the seventh floor, just down the hall from the Douglases'. It had three rooms, and the rent was $51 a month. As the Depression ground on, the landlord dropped the rent to $48; even so, for a time the Douglases and we were the only tenants on the seventh floor. Whenever we heard the elevator stop down the hall, we knew someone was going to see Aaron and Alta. After a time we traded up to a four-room apartment on the same floor. We lived there for twenty years, all through the worst blues of the Depression, the frenzy of World War II, and the tumult of the postwar years. The building was a way of life and a state of mind; after the stifling years we had spent in Kansas City, it liberated Minnie and me.

Downtown, my duties at the N.A.A.C.P. continued to expand. In 1932 I became a member of a "press conference" assigned to keep an eye on *The Crisis*, the magazine of the N.A.A.C.P., and the voice of Dr. Du Bois. *The Crisis* was Dr. Du Bois's personal bailiwick and creation. He had nurtured it lovingly for twenty years, turning it into the country's foremost journal on race, which at its peak in the twenties claimed a circulation of nearly 100,000. But by 1932 the figures had tumbled to little more than 12,000. Part of the problem was the Depression: black people needed every last dime for bread. Another aspect of the trouble, however, lay in the temperament of Dr. Du Bois, who was a superb literary man but no businessman. The chronic deficits of *The Crisis* put him at odds with the board of directors and with Walter. Because of my newspaper experience I was dragooned into helping *The Crisis* find its feet, even though Dr. Du Bois undoubtedly felt he could do quite well without my assistance.

I suggested that we move away from the magazine's lofty, ebony-tower approach and broaden its appeal, audience, and circulation. As a small contribution, I wrote an article on Negro athletes at the 1932 Olympic Games. While black athletes and athletics fill the sports page today, that wasn't true in the early thirties. This was four years before the feats of Jesse Owens at the 1936 Olympic Games in Berlin and a few years before the great fights of Joe Louis, the watershed for black athletics in the thirties. Still, the first ripples of a black athletic tide could already be seen. In 1932 Ralph Metcalfe, a 180-pound gazelle from Marquette, was approaching records or breaking them in the 100-yard dash, the 100-meter dash, and the 200-meter relay. Eddie Tolan, the "Spectacled Speedster" from Michigan, and Everette Beatty, a hurdler from Michigan State Normal, were also very promising young black runners. I wrote my article, and they suddenly found themselves in the pages of *The Crisis*, tucked among the most august literary and sociological thinkers of the race. I saw this as an improvement, and whatever Dr. Du Bois thought he kept to himself and graciously printed the story.

As diplomatically as I could, I also tried to supplement our coverage of politics beyond the loftier levels of constitutional and moral issues. Early in the summer of 1932 I took the train from New York to Washington and made my way from Union Station to Anacostia Flats, where the Bonus Marchers had set up a raggedy camp in the shadow of the Washington Monument. There I found black toes and white toes sticking out side by side from a ramshackle town of pup tents, packing crates, and tar-paper shacks. Black men and white men, veterans of the segregated army that had fought in World War I, lined up together for company messes, served together in camp councils, pulled K.P. duty and M.P. duty equally, perspired in sick bays side by side. For years the U.S. Army had argued that General Jim Crow was its proper commander, but the Bonus Marchers gave the lie to the notion that black and white soldiers—ex-soldiers in their case—couldn't live together. In the middle of the camp someone had put a piano up on a scarred wooden crate. A white kid and a black kid took turns playing it. As the black player tickled the keys, the "St. Louis Blues" trickled its way across the camp. Elder Micheaux's Gospel Choir was also there, belting out a morale-boosting hymn in stop time: "God's Tomorrow [will be brighter than today]." After a few days I went back to New York feeling a renewed sense of faith in the goodness of poor folks—and hoping the Elder and his choir knew what they were singing about.

That first year on the job I wanted desperately to prove myself as something more than a scribbler, and the chance to do so came when a team of investigators for the American Federation of Labor discovered that the U.S. Army Corps of Engineers was paying an average of 10 cents an hour to Negroes building flood-control dams and levees along the Mississippi delta. We received a number of reports confirming the A.F. of L. story. Helen Boardman, a brave woman and former Red Cross nurse who sometimes did undercover investigations for us, came back from a Southern tour with evidence that the army was paying Negroes a dime an hour for shifts as long as twelve hours a day. The Corps of Engineers angrily denied the whole story, but Senator Robert Wagner of New York got up an official investigation. When Wagner's probe bogged down in the Senate, we concluded that if we could produce eyewitnesses to actual conditions in the camps, we might be able to break the jam holding up Wagner's corrective legislation.

The trick was to find those witnesses. After thinking about the problem for several weeks, I finally took Walter aside and volunteered to go down to the delta myself. I suppose I was trying to match some of his own exploits when he had held my job, but he was very dubious about the proposal. He himself has always been able to work undercover by passing for white, but he told me that a black man who meddled around the river camps in 1932 might easily wind up dangling from a tree. His warnings were sound, but I was thirty-one years old, braver and more foolish than I am now, and eager to prove that I

could do more than give speeches out on the road or write stories for
The Crisis.

Because the mob was dangerous and because there was a lot of
ground to cover, I decided to recruit a second investigator to go along
with me. My man was George Schuyler, a mordant newspaperman
and freelance writer whose ambition was to become the black H. L.
Mencken. To a degree he succeeded; Mencken himself once referred
to him as "the uremic George Schuyler." George had just returned
from a trip to Liberia; he was knocking around Harlem at loose ends
and quickly agreed to join my expedition south.

Toward the middle of December 1932, the two of us sat down and
drew up careful plans for the trip. With the exception of my brief
Christmas visit in 1913, I had never spent any time in the Deep
South. George knew the territory better. He said—rather melodra-
matically, I thought—that we were risking our necks and that we
would have to protect ourselves from within and without. It was common in those days among some Southern Negroes to collaborate with
white sheriffs, informing on strangers, union organizers, radical Negroes, and the like. To protect ourselves against these quislings we
dropped a blackout on the trip. The plan was to run the mission under
deep cover until George and I were safely on the way home. The other
day I found a copy of the cloak-and-dagger memo I sent to the
N.A.A.C.P. staff before setting out:

> It is of the utmost importance that the absence of Mr. Wilkins from the
> office during the next two weeks shall be described merely as a busi-
> ness trip to the West, and that this description shall be given only when
> necessary. There is no need of explaining where Mr. Wilkins is unless
> direct and unavoidable inquiry is made, and in that case a western
> business trip will suffice for an excuse. The staff cannot be too careful
> in withholding even from their families and close friends the real na-
> ture of Mr. Wilkins's trip.

Having muzzled the staff, I went uptown and bought the nicest set
of lingerie I could find for Minnie. I had the present gift-wrapped, and
I arranged with a friend to deliver it to her on Christmas Eve. She had
better sense than I, and she was scared to death by the trip. I promised her that nothing would happen to me, but she wasn't very impressed. I hoped that the present would cheer her up while I was
gone.

With my alibi concocted and the lingerie stowed away, I set off with
George for the delta. We took the train from New York to Washington, where we had dinner with an old friend of the N.A.A.C.P. who

had connections with the House Committee on Labor. He was to supply us with a list of river camps and contractors, but as things turned out, he had nothing to offer. We would have to make our way without lists or maps.

The next day we boarded a Memphis-bound train and headed south. In Memphis we made contact with Robert Church, the black Republican boss of the city, who invited us to his home for dinner and some strategic planning. He offered to do what he could to help us if we ran into trouble, and for his own protection we arranged to send all communications to him through an intermediary, one of his local political operatives. I also asked Church if he could send Minnie a dozen roses from me on Christmas Day. Church was an old gentleman as well as one of the shrewdest black politicians in the South, and he agreed to carry out the small errand.

George and I left our luggage, our suits, white shirts, and city gear with Church, and the next morning went down to Beale Street to buy disguises for the trip. We found a dry-goods store and purchased corduroy trousers, work boots, overalls, and leather coats lined with sheepskin. We also bought two canvas bags, into which we jammed our new possessions. Settling on two threadbare aliases—George Smith and Roy Jones—we tucked $50 apiece in our socks, and the next morning hopped a Jim Crow coach on the Yazoo and Mississippi Valley Railroad and rattled on down from Memphis into the delta.

I planned to get off the train at Greenville while George continued on to Vicksburg. When the train pulled into the Greenville station, I clapped George on the shoulder, picked up my canvas bag, and stepped onto the platform. I was a spy deep within enemy lines, and I was on my own.

I spent the first night in a rooming house on the wrong side of the tracks in Greenville, a run-down place full of boarders from the levee work camps. In the front room was a potbelly stove that nearly burned through my disguise. It was chilly for December, and I put my hands out to the stove to warm them. The landlady, a wise, tough old bird, took a hard look at my palms.

"Mister," she said, "you don't look like no workingman. Your hands are too damn soft."

A few minutes earlier I had explained my accent by telling her I had come down from St. Louis. Now I had to do some faster talking. "I've been running an elevator in St. Louis," I said, palms sweating. "The Depression flattened me out. I lost my job, so I came down here."

The landlady eyed me suspiciously, but the story seemed to take.

She rented me a room for 50 cents a week. The roomers bought food from a pretty little girl who had built up a small business tending to local white businessmen at lunch. At noon she sold chicken and fish, which they ate at their desks. In the evening she sold us the leftovers, along with cold beaten biscuits, ham, and milk, the day's one big meal.

The next morning I got out of bed to find that the temperature had dropped below freezing; there was a light dusting of snow on the ground. Shivering, I called the landlady.

"How can a man get some heat around here?" I asked her.

"Fire?" she drawled, so it came out sounding more like "far." "You want far? Well, that's 25 cents a bucket for coal."

"Pretty steep, isn't it? Even in the morning?"

"Mister, morning, evening, it's the same. But the men around here don't need no far. In the morning they jes' jumps up, jumps in they pants, and goes to work. *They* don't need no far."

My greenness was showing through dangerously, and I warned myself to be more careful. When I went out on the street for the first time that morning, I couldn't escape the feeling of being on foreign soil. As I walked away from the boardinghouse, I overheard a woman behind me drawling loudly to a friend: "Ah don't know what ah'm gonna give her for Christmas. Ah reckon ah'm gonna give her a corset."

There was an explosion of bawdy laughter. I thought the women were Negroes and grumped to myself. But when I turned to look, I saw two plump white women. I was a long way from home.

I spent the next ten days trudging up and down the delta looking for work in the camps. It was icy cold that December and there was plenty of snow. When the snow finally abated and things warmed up, the frozen ground turned to an oozing sea of mud. The cold and the mud had closed most of the camps. Everywhere I went I was told, "No work here today. Machines froze up. Try down the road."

At the boardinghouses where I put up in the evenings, however, I found dozens of hard-luck cases who had been working in the camps. The men commonly started their shift at 6 A.M., staying out on the levees until 6 P.M., when a night shift took over. Some of these workers were farmers most of the year, poor blacks who exhausted their lives cropping shares for "Mistah Somebody." They got a bit of flour, pork, salt, and maybe a little chewing tobacco on credit in the country stores, along with a dab of cash come harvest time—nothing more. They had no choice but to try for jobs in the delta camps.

One day as I was walking down a country road, a nice young farm kid caught up with me. As we walked along we got to talking, and he invited me to spend the night at his place. He lived with his parents in an unpainted shack in the woods. The cracks in the floorboards were so wide I could see chickens scratching on the ground below. The boy's mother took me in, fed me biscuits and salt pork, and offered me all that she had. The next morning as I was leaving, I pressed three dollars on her. She stood there for a moment, numbly staring down at her hand.

"Mistuh," she said quietly, "that's the most cash money I've seen in a year."

Poverty kept these country black people in a state of abject peonage. The shortage of cash drove them to work on the levees in the off season between planting and harvest. At the time the federal government was spending over $300 million building and improving the levees, great, man-made ridges of dirt planted with grass designed to hold the Mississippi back at flood time, but those millions were dribbling out in nickels and dimes. Payday fell every two weeks when it came at all. Company commissaries plucked back most of what was paid out. I met one man who took home $12 for two months' work. Anyone who complained was fired; anyone who complained too loudly risked a beating or worse. All this was under the supervision of the U.S. Army Corps of Engineers, in mockery of the American flags that flew on staffs erected in the camps. It was a system of peonage organized by the federal government and paid for with American tax dollars. The more I saw, the angrier I grew.

Just after Christmas, I learned that George had run into some serious trouble down in Vicksburg while making the rounds of camps in Tallulah, Mounds, Delta Point, Natchez, Eyebrow, and Deer Park. One night he returned to a squalid room in a boardinghouse, bought a bucket of coal, built a fire, and got into bed. He was lying there reading a copy of *The American Mercury* when a brutal knock rattled the door. Two cops with drawn revolvers burst into the room, yelling, "Throw up your hands, nigger."

They hauled George to the local jail. It turned out that earlier the same day a pair of black bandits had held up a milk wagon in Vicksburg. The police had alerted their network of spies, and George's landlady had turned him in to the sheriff. This was exactly what George had said might happen when we were back in New York; he had been giving me the facts of life, not spinning out melodrama. Fortunately, his quick wits saved him. Taking a dollar from the treasury in his sock, he bribed a jail trustee to wire Walter in New York. Walter got in touch with Church, who got in touch with me. For a few hours we all prayed: Schuyler was married to a white woman from Texas, and he kept her picture in his wallet. God only knew what might happen to him if the picture fell into the wrong hands. Several hours passed, then a second telegram arrived saying that George had been released. The police ran him out of town, keeping $30 and his fountain pen.

We met in Memphis to review the situation. In New York, Walter had made our job harder by rushing out a press release on George's night in the Vicksburg jail; our cover was gone, but we were not satisfied with the investigation. We decided to go back south.

This time we stuck together. On a Tuesday morning early in January, we left for the delta between Lula and Tunica, Mississippi, hinterland country eight to ten miles from the nearest railroad. After some hard walking we reached the camp of the J. W. Noble Company, a mile or two outside Jeffries, Mississippi. The foreman told us he was "full up" and directed us to a second camp run by Mr. Noble a mile farther on across cotton fields and freshly turned levee dirt, now muddy from the rains. There, too, the camp was full, so we made our way on to the Brandenburg camp, then to two camps run by the Canal Construction Company.

At all the camps, the earth-moving machines were laid up waiting for the sun to dry out the mud. At noon we stopped under a big tree for a lunch of sardines packed in cottonseed oil, which we ate with our pocket knives. As the day wore on, we reached the camp of R. T. Clark, known to the local black folks as the terror of the river. But Clark's camp, like the others, was closed. As the light faded, we talked a black sharecropper into putting us up for the night.

The next day we tried our luck at Clark's again. The Negro straw boss at the camp was evasive when we asked for jobs. He told us that the men in the camp would go back to work the following day, but he said nothing when we offered to stay on. We hung around for a while, only to find that the night crew was short of men, which surprised us. A feeling of ugly hostility hung over the camp. That afternoon we decided it would be wiser to move on—fast.

We were already sore and weary, and we had a long tramp ahead of us. On the way back to Dundee, Mississippi, we found out what the stalling at Clark's had been about. As we were trudging down the road, a little sedan filled with white "crackers" drove up alongside us. The white boys motioned us to stop; then they pulled over to the side of the road, piled out, and headed our way. When they found out that we were not "boys" from the Norfleet Plantation, over which we happened to be traveling, and that we didn't have jobs at any of the levee camps, they looked at one another and fell silent. Finally, one of them stepped forward. Giving George and me a look that would have frosted hell, he said, "Y'all better be gittin' on up the road."

The men got back into their car, drove slowly ahead of us for a while, then disappeared. As night began to fall, George and I turned on the steam for Dundee. We passed a chain gang heading home from clearing out a drainage ditch. A gimlet-eyed guard rode herd on the gang with a shotgun, making us move all the faster.

We hove into Dundee at dusk, missed the last train to Memphis, and spent an anxious hour waiting for the last bus. At nine o'clock, with dark well advanced and lynching hours approaching, we finally made it out of town, and we reached Memphis shortly before midnight. It didn't take much talking from Church to convince us that we had finally pushed our luck far enough.

The next day Church bought drawing-room tickets for us so we could get out of Memphis by train without being observed. We made a stop in Chattanooga, hopped a second train, and headed back for New York. I arrived home on a Saturday evening with a three-day beard, a premature Afro, and a case of fever blisters that was so bad Minnie thought I had been beaten. An evening in a hot tub put me back together again.

On Sunday, George and I went up to the Abyssinian Baptist Church in Harlem, where Adam Clayton Powell, Sr., and Adam Jr. were preaching. They had made the church available to the N.A.A.C.P. for its annual January business meeting. Knowing that we were on the way, Walter had beaten the woods and drummed up a great crowd. The church was full to overflowing when we came in. We went over our findings, keeping the worst for the Senate; then sat down. From downtown, the Communists had sent a few provocateurs to disrupt the meeting. They stood upon the pews and shouted that George and I were fakes, that we had never gone to Mississippi, that we were out to fool the people with another N.A.A.C.P. trick.

I can still see those hecklers standing there yelling. I'd like to put a couple of those Reds in the middle of Coahoma County, Mississippi, I thought to myself that day. Let *them* find out how much of a trick it is to get out.

11   MY FIRST ARREST

Images of what I had seen in Mississippi—the grim little river towns, rain-soaked levees, suspicious white faces, poverty-beaten Negroes—stayed fresh in my mind for a long time. I returned from the delta determined to do something about them. The first problem, as it would be all through the Depression, was to broaden the range of the N.A.A.C.P., to get the association down to where the people were, where race cut the deepest, where the suffering was the worst.

It was the middle of the winter of 1933 when I got back home. In February the streets of Harlem were icy and the rooftops covered with snow. Down in Washington, Senator Robert F. Wagner of New York agreed to push for an investigation into the conditions George and I had seen in the delta. Southern senators immediately threatened to filibuster the planned investigation, but by fluke we managed to out-maneuver these gentlemen. Late in February, Senator Huey Long of Louisiana took the Senate floor and began a one-man filibuster against a bill that had nothing to do with our investigation. As Long settled down to droning, most senators fled the chamber, but Senator Wagner stayed to see what Long had to say. To Wagner's surprise, the Kingfish suddenly broke off the filibuster and walked out of the room. Scanning the Senate floor, Wagner discovered that all the opponents of the Mississippi investigation were out of the chamber. He jumped to his feet and put forth a motion for the investigation that passed just as the Southerners, who learned too late what was going on, arrived back in the Senate on the run. Hearings took place; there was a general public airing of conditions in the camps; the Corps of Engineers pulled in its horns, and wages went up.

We didn't turn Mississippi into Canaan, of course. I believe we only succeeded in pushing paychecks up by 10 cents or so an hour, but even that small amount doubled what some of the men had been receiving, and several million dollars made its way into the pockets of workers down on the levees. For me, the reward was even more substantial: we had proved that if you pushed the government long enough, hard enough, and in enough of the right places, change could be accomplished. I felt hope and renewed energy. If we could bring a few dimes to Mississippi, perhaps we could one day bring freedom.

That same spring, Franklin Delano Roosevelt swept into Washington. I eagerly read his inaugural address in the morning newspapers. It was easy enough for him to tell us all we had to fear was fear itself. I could think of a lot of things that still looked fearsome to me—lynching for one. But when F.D.R. said, "The nation asks for action, and action *now*," I was with him.

Not long after Roosevelt took office, there was a great Recovery Day parade in New York City. Minnie and I watched it from the office, and from the windows on the fourth floor of 69 Fifth Avenue, we looked out over rank on rank of marching men, men in work clothes and men in three-piece suits, citizens in heavy boots and citizens in wing-tipped shoes, all trudging earnestly and purposefully up the broad avenue, a new look of hope radiating from their faces. The parade lasted most of the day. That night we went back uptown to Harlem in high spirits. The gloom, the awful sense of foreboding that had settled on the country during the early years of the Depression, seemed, for that one afternoon at least, to be lifting.

The good feelings didn't last. I have always felt that F.D.R. was overrated as a champion of the Negro. He was a New York patrician, distant, aloof, with no natural feel for the sensibilities of black people, no compelling inner commitment to their cause. The New Deal, of course, was designed to help poor people, and some of the benefits were bound to spill over to blacks, the poorest of the poor. For that Negroes were grateful; but it wasn't as if F.D.R. and his brain trust had worked out a program for uplifting the country's Negroes from generations of neglect and centuries of servitude. In practice, the effect of F.D.R.'s alphabet agencies was often quite different. Checks from the Agricultural Adjustment Administration often wound up in the hands of white landholders, who withheld them from black tenant farmers and sharecroppers. The Public Works Administration set no minimum wage for Negroes and offered too few jobs. The National Recovery Administration countenanced differential wage scales, paying black steel workers in Birmingham far less than their white brothers in Pittsburgh. To get the Cotton Textile Code passed, F.D.R. threw Negroes to the wolves, exempting them from its provisions.

When Social Security was passed, it left out farmers, domestics, and casual labor—and millions of black people. For rallying the country during the Depression and for leading it through World War II, black Americans, like all other Americans, could be profoundly grateful to F.D.R., but as a patron saint for Negroes, he had plenty of red clay on his feet.

In Eleanor Roosevelt, however, the N.A.A.C.P. found a loyal and effective friend. I'm not sure when Mrs. Roosevelt first developed her interest in race and civil rights; even after she moved into the White House there was gossip that she referred to Negroes as "darkies." Her transformation was a tribute to her fundamental goodwill and decency, but it was also due to some deft lobbying by Walter White. After F.D.R. took office, it was Walter's idea to reach him through the First Lady. We courted her for several years. Not long ago I found a copy of the invitation I sent in an attempt to lure her to our silver jubilee convention in 1934.

Mrs. Franklin D. Roosevelt
White House
Washington, D.C.

My dear Mrs. Roosevelt:

We do not believe that anyone in America can doubt your deep interest in the welfare of all the people of the United States, and certainly this Association does not doubt it. For in addition to our general knowledge, we have the testimony of Mr. Walter White, our Secretary, who has had several personal conferences with you.

We know you are an extremely busy woman with engagements in all parts of the country, but we wish to invite you to do this Association and the colored citizens of America the great honor of speaking this year at the 25th Annual Conference of this Association in Oklahoma City, Oklahoma, Sunday afternoon, July 1, 1934.

This Association, which began in 1909 with a small committee of white and colored persons in New York City, has grown in twenty-five years to have 375 branches in forty states and the District of Columbia. It has both white and colored members, and the Board of Directors, as you can see from the letterhead, is composed of distinguished white and colored citizens. The Association is recognized as the foremost organization of and for colored people in the country.

We appreciate fully that your time is taken with many matters and that Oklahoma City is far in the Southwest. It is only because we are certain that the appearance of no other single person, excepting our distinguished President, could so hearten and inspire colored Americans in this period of rehabilitation than that of yourself, that we pre-

MY FIRST ARREST   129

sume to request this favor of you. We hope very much, and we know we are joined in our hopes by millions of fellow citizens, that you will find it possible to accept our invitation.

Very sincerely yours,

Roy Wilkins
Assistant Secretary

I had never used so much soft soap on anyone in my life, but in 1934 my presumption, apparently, was still too much. I received a polite note back from Mrs. Roosevelt's secretary saying that the First Lady was very sorry not to be able to accept the invitation but that she wished us success in every way.

The first rebuff did not daunt Walter. As he went about his lobbying for an antilynching law, he bombarded Mrs. Roosevelt with letters and telegrams and appeals for interviews. The lynching issue was powerful, and Walter was all but irresistible once he set his mind to something. In the end he prevailed, and he and Mrs. Roosevelt became friends. One unpleasant bit of gossip that made the rounds was that when F.D.R. heard that Walter used the First Lady's given name in talking about her, he vowed never to let Walter into the White House. The story must have been a fabrication, because as time went by, Walter found that he could get into the Oval Office in times of racial crisis. Still, F.D.R. wouldn't be budged much on the subject of lynching. He opposed it, of course, but that didn't mean he was willing to support legislation banning it. His argument was that to save the country he had to work with the tools at hand: the House of Representatives and the Senate. The seniority rule had put Southerners in charge of the most strategic committees in Congress, the bottlenecks through which the New Deal had to pass. Roosevelt's fear was that if he advocated an antilynching law openly, the South would punish him in Congress by striking down every bill he asked for. Whether this would actually have happened is a moot point, for F.D.R. chose not to test the South on the subject.

As the years went by, Walter kept after Mrs. Roosevelt, who needled her husband to be more forthright about lynching. He in turn evaded her. The little tug-of-war showed up in small ways. In the winter of 1935 there was a vivid, antilynching art exhibition in Manhattan to drum up support for the Wagner-Costigan antilynching bill, and Walter quickly invited Mrs. Roosevelt to attend. I have a copy of the note she wrote in reply. It shows the timidity that was such an obstacle to us back then.

The White House
Washington

My dear Mr. White,

The more I think about going to the exhibition, the more troubled I am, so this morning I went in to talk to my husband about it and asked him what they really planned to do about the bill because I was afraid that some bright newspaper reporter might write a story which would offend some of the southern members and thereby make it even more difficult to do anything about the bill.

My husband said that it was quite all right for me to go, but if some reporter took the occasion to describe some horrible picture, it would cause more southern opposition. They plan to bring the bill out quietly as soon as possible although two southern Senators have said they would filibuster for two weeks. He thinks, however, they can get it through.

I do not want to do anything which will harm the ultimate objective even though we might think for the moment that it was helpful and even though you may feel that it would make some of your race feel more kindly toward us. Therefore, I really think that it would be safer if I came without any publicity or did not come at all. Will you telephone me at my New York house at seven o'clock on Friday night? The number is Rhinelander 4-7428. You can then tell me how you feel.

Very sincerely yours,

Eleanor Roosevelt

Mrs. Roosevelt eventually agreed to attend the exhibition. She didn't care much for the art, and she later said she thought it could cause trouble if the exhibition went on tour around the country, but she had made a step into the public eye on our behalf.

Others soon followed. In the late thirties, after I had become editor of *The Crisis,* a group of women in Harlem joined together to help the magazine out of its chronic financial problems. The committee invited Mrs. Roosevelt to speak in Harlem, and to the surprise and immense delight of everyone, she accepted. It was the First Lady's first trip to the capital of black America since F.D.R. took office. I will never forget it. The meeting was at the Mother A.M.E. Zion Church on West 137th Street. The people of Harlem filled every pew and seat in the galleries, spilling over into the side streets stretching away from the church. Inside, people craned forward eagerly, leaning dangerously over the rails of the gallery; outside, they stood patiently, shifting from foot to foot, waiting to get just a glimpse of Mrs. Roosevelt.

Mayor Fiorello La Guardia also turned up that day, though he had made no arrangements to speak. His late appearance amused me. On matters of race, the Little Flower's heart was in the right place, but he was also a politician right down to his gaiters. Not long after his election, the N.A.A.C.P. invited him to attend a banquet, and he sent his regrets. On the evening of the banquet I noticed a tough-looking aide from City Hall sizing up the house and rushing for the telephone. The guests that evening included Governor Herbert Lehman and a number of other well-wired politicians and citizens. By the time the cigars were smoldering, La Guardia himself walked in, looking as if he had meant to be there all the time. From that evening he called me "Dr. Wilkins." Somehow it got into his mind that I was a physician or a Ph.D., and like Lyndon Johnson years later, once he had fixed something in his mind, for better or worse, he wouldn't drop it.

La Guardia wrung Mrs. Roosevelt's hand when she arrived. "It is encouraging to have on this platform the First Lady of the land," he said, beaming. "There are many publications that could not get Mrs. Roosevelt to the platform." I smiled in spite of myself.

Mrs. Roosevelt's own speech that day was titled "The Relationship of the Press to the Democratic Ideal." Standing at the rostrum, she looked out over hundreds of black faces. "In this country," she said, "we should all have equal rights, and minorities should certainly have them exactly as majorities do." There were cheers. She conceded that government programs "were only a drop in the bucket" of what needed to be done for Harlem. The crowd dared hope that the flow from Washington might one day increase and the bucket grow larger, if only F.D.R. would listen to his wife.

Roosevelt's refusal to support a federal antilynching law was extremely disappointing to me. All through the thirties, the N.A.A.C.P. pushed F.D.R. and the Congress to pass a federal law against this crime. We argued that since local sheriffs and state governors simply stood by while lynch murders took place, it was up to the federal government to step in and put a halt to them. In addition to Senator Wagner, our main allies at the time were Senator Edward P. Costigan and Congressman Joseph A. Gavagan, all of New York. Time after time one or the other of those brave politicians would succeed in breathing life into an antilynching law, only to see it throttled by the Southern bloc in the Senate. If Southern mobs used lynch ropes, guns, and knives to keep black people down, Southern senators used magnolia bluster and the filibuster to protect their state's right to string up any black man, innocent or not, who ran into trouble with the law, the ruling powers, and Roman holiday mobs down home.

The outrage I felt over F.D.R.'s expedient cowardice on the issue came to a head in the fall of 1934, when Attorney General Homer S. Cummings called a national crime conference to meet in Washington. It was a big affair: J. Edgar Hoover was to talk about the detection and apprehension of hard-case criminals, and the President himself was to address the opening session. The official program included everything from white-collar crime to old and new methods of dealing with vagrants, but when we got our copy, we discovered that not a single word was to be said about lynching.

I couldn't believe it: a national conference on crime, under the sponsorship of the United States Justice Department and the patronage of the President of the United States himself, that omitted from its agenda the most revolting crime of the day. We didn't intend to let Attorney General Cummings get away with it. On October 9, 1934, Walter wrote a letter to him. "My dear Mr. Attorney General," he said. "May we inquire if consideration of the subject of lynching is included in the program of the National Conference on Crime, which you have called to meet in Washington, December 10–13? And if it is not improper for us to offer such a suggestion, may we suggest that either Senator Robert F. Wagner or Senator Edward P. Costigan, joint authors of the bill introduced to the last session of Congress, which is to be re-introduced in the coming session, to make lynching a Federal offense, be invited to present to the Conference the subject of lynching?" A week later we received a brief reply from Joseph E. Keenan, an assistant to Attorney General Cummings. It said, "The program for the conference is not yet complete. Obviously it will be impossible to cover all phases of the crime problem in the short space of three days. No definite decision has been made with reference to the subject of lynching. I wish to thank you, however, for bringing this matter to our attention."

A respectful brush-off. The conference would take up such matters as "The Centralization of State Prosecuting Agencies" and "The Importance of Criminal Statistics." Time would be given to the windy Fulton Oursler, editor of *Liberty* magazine, and H. V. Kaltenborn, the radio commentator, to talk up the role of the press and radio in propaganda wars against crime. But the Justice Department would not look Judge Lynch in the eye.

At the time, lynchings were running at a rate of two to three a month, and before long the Justice Department's policy was splotched with blood. Toward the end of October that year, several thousand white citizens got together in Greenwood, Florida, to lynch Claude Neal, a young Negro who had been arrested on charges of killing a twenty-two-year-old white girl named Lola Cassidy. Neal had been arrested in Brewton, Alabama, a town across the state line from Greenwood. A mob of about a hundred white men formed, drove to Brewton, broke into the jail, seized their victim, and carried him back to Greenwood. Around noon, these murderous adventurers hid Neal in the woods near the Chipola River outside town; then they sent outriders to announce that there would be a public lynching that night between eight and nine o'clock. The plan was to take Neal to the Cassidy home and let the Cassidy family do whatever it wanted with him; then to hustle him on to the pigpen where Lola Cassidy's body had been found, for the formal lynching. After the festivities were over, the mob planned to haul Neal's body to the courthouse square in Marianna, nine miles away, and hang it up for a public viewing.

God only knows how many statutes, including the Lindbergh kidnapping law, this mob had violated. Although the leaders of the lynch party gave eight full hours' notice of their plans, neither the local sheriff nor the governor of Florida headed off the lynching.We sent a desperate telegram to state officials demanding that they take steps to rescue Neal—but we were too late. Somewhere deep in those Florida woods, Neal was stabbed, mutilated, and shot a dozen times. His body was tied to an automobile, dragged through the roads to Marianna, and strung up on a tree. The next day the Associated Press reported that Miss Cassidy's sixty-year-old father had complained that the mob had "done me wrong about the killing. They promised me they would bring him up to my house before they killed him and let me have the first shot. That's what I wanted."

I put down *The New York Times* that day feeling sick. If neither the Justice Department nor F.D.R. had the time or fortitude to talk about lynching during a national conference on crime, what kind of crime fighters were they? There was nothing I could do to bring Neal back to life; there seemed little I could do, period. But I did not intend to shut up or look the other way.

I suggested to Walter that the N.A.A.C.P. picket the crime conference. If nothing else, we could humiliate Cummings and the weak-kneed Justice Department. Walter took up my suggestion with several of his newspaper friends in Washington, who told him that there had been so many parades, pickets, and marches in Washington during the Depression that no one would notice ours. I didn't accept that. What I had in mind was not a stereotyped labor or protest parade. I was out to drive home the issue to General Cummings and J. Edgar Hoover in a way they would never forget.

Toward the end of November I went to Washington to talk things over with Virginia R. McGuire, president of the Washington branch of the N.A.A.C.P. She was a brave woman, and she responded enthusiastically to the idea of protesting the conference, but I could start no fires elsewhere in the branch. An atmosphere of excessive caution had all but paralyzed it. For many N.A.A.C.P. members back then, picketing was a radical act, and the thought of giving hell to the Justice Department and the President of the United States was more than enough to make them draw back. I returned to New York feeling discouraged but determined to push ahead. The first thing I did was to type out sixteen slogans for our pickets. As I rolled the foolscap out of my machine, I felt a little better. Some of my ideas were simple and factual ("5,068 Lynchings in U.S.A. in 52 Years"); some were a bit more rhetorical ("When Is Kidnapping Not Kidnapping? When Victim Is Black"); some were just plain angry ("Al Capone Got 11 Years. Lynchers Get Cheers").

Working quietly behind the scenes, Walter succeeded in talking Eleanor Roosevelt into persuading F.D.R. to mention lynching during his opening address to the conference. Then two days before the conference was to open, we tipped the black press to our demonstration. Whatever happened, we were sure to make ourselves heard.

I felt elated. Many members of the Washington branch remained cautious, but others, working with Mrs. McGuire, went to work painting our signs. George B. Murphy, Jr., head of the Washington bureau of the *Baltimore Afro-American,* Emmett Dorsey, a political science instructor at Howard, and Edward P. Lovett, an attorney who did legal work for the N.A.A.C.P., agreed to join me on the picket line. At the last minute, Charlie Houston, dean of the Howard Law School, drove in from the South and threw himself enthusiastically into the legal planning for the protest. The strategy of the Justice Department seemed to be to stall as long as possible and to hope we would back down. The conference was meeting in Constitution Hall. It was no more than 25 degrees at noon that day when George, Ed, Emmett, and I pulled on our overcoats, clapped on our hats, grabbed our picket signs, and drove to the hall. I had an improvised sandwich board that read AMERICA NEEDS FEDERAL ANTILYNCHING LAW. It wasn't very elegant, but I figured it would do. Less than ten minutes from the time we started marching, the law arrived. Captain Edward J. Kelly and Detective R. E. Talbot of the Metropolitan Police, backed by several other men in blue, walked up and stopped us. As politely as he could, Captain Kelly said that we would have to get permission from the superintendent of police to go on marching; without it, he said, we would be arrested.

Having delivered his warning, Captain Kelly looked at us impassively. We had applied for a parade permit: police headquarters had turned us down. We put our heads together for a few minutes and agreed to make a second trip to headquarters to try again. We were, of course, rejected once more. Our choice seemed to be to pack up or go to jail. We decided to go back and start the picketing in time to catch the delegates as they returned from lunch.

When we reached Constitution Hall, taxicabs were already pulling up and unloading delegates. Losing no time, we slipped into the sandwich boards and began to march. This time the law descended upon us even faster. "You've got one more chance," Captain Kelly warned us. If we tucked in our tails and ran, he wouldn't arrest us. There was only one answer to give him. We began to march. "Okay, that's it," he snapped, and arrested us on the spot. A Black Maria wheeled up; we were loaded aboard and hustled off to the city's Number Three Police Station, where we were charged with violating the municipal sign law, a law that had been designed to control outdoor advertising, not outdoor demonstrators.

Word of our arrest spread quickly through the N.A.A.C.P. Washington branch. The timidity that had dogged the demonstration vanished in a rush of indignation. Not only was the Justice Department going to wink at Judge Lynch, it seemed, it was also going to violate the spirit, if not the letter, of the First Amendment, arresting four men who had had the temerity to challenge its crime conference. In short order, the branch resolved to step up the protest. Charlie Houston sat down and got to work on ways of getting around the technicalities of the sign and parade laws. The branch recruited seventy pickets—lawyers, ministers, teachers, and students from Howard—to pick up where we had left off. About half the demonstrators were women, and there was one blind student. To beat the sign law, each picket was furnished with a placard less than one foot square. The pickets also were given nooses to drape around their necks, a fine symbol—and one that didn't fall under the sign law at all.

On Thursday morning, our people mustered at the Phyllis Wheatly Y.W.C.A. There a fleet of cabs waited to carry them to Constitution Hall, one by one and by separate routes, a device that foiled the parade law. The tactics took the police completely by surprise. They blustered and threatened to make arrests if the pickets didn't pack up and leave, but the demonstrators held their ground. Baffled, the police called in the federal park police, pointed out that the pickets were occupying park land across the street from the hall, and demanded that the park police make arrests. The park police refused. When an angry lawman from the Justice Department arrived and tried to prod the local police into breaking up the demonstration, our people warned the increasingly bewildered forces of the law that a barrage of false-arrest suits would greet any attempt to dislodge them. The police then made one last-ditch attempt to arrest the pickets when they left the hall. But once again the cabs arrived; once again the pickets were picked up one at a time; once again the parade law was circumvented. Our victorious troops returned safely to the Y.W.C.A. The police could do nothing but stand helplessly by.

The next morning the newspapers were full of pictures of the demonstrators: quiet, well-dressed, earnest people—with nooses around their necks. The conference was upstaged; Cummings was reduced to defensive sputtering. Walter sent telegrams congratulating all of us on our arrests. George Murphy quickly sent a cheerful return wire: "My going to jail for protesting against lynching in this country was a cost, though small, of which I shall always be proud." That said it for each of us.

12 A MONTH ON THE COLOR LINE

I have never kept a regular journal. I'm not entirely sure why, but perhaps it's because over the years events have tended to tumble one atop the other so quickly and in such confusion that capturing them in miniature entries at the end of each day seemed impossible. Or then, perhaps I'm just lazy. Whatever the case, the years have fled, unrecorded by me, and there seems no point in fussing over it now. In the winter of 1934, however, I did make a New Year's resolution to keep a journal during 1935. Like most such resolutions mine lasted barely until February; but for that brief span of time I was a diarist. I found my journal the other day. The red book I wrote in is now worn threadbare at the corners; the blue-lined pages are beginning to yellow with age. In rereading what I had jotted down so long ago, I was struck by the random way large issues of race and smaller day-to-day matters had run together in shaping my life. Over the years the specific issues and the daily humdrum have changed, but the fundamental rhythm has remained much the same.

January 1, 1935

We arose late today after New Year's Eve last night in Brooklyn. Judge and Mrs. Toney and Thelma and Elmer Carter made up our party. Breakfast about two, then to a movie and dinner out about 8. Home and to a badly needed bed so as to be ready for tomorrow at the office.

Minnie and I agreed we should be thankful that this new year of the Depression found us no worse off financially than the first of the slump. Nothing to brag about, but better than many who don't deserve their hard luck.

January 2

Back to the office bright and early because Walter is in Atlanta and there are odds and ends to be caught up with for the public mass meeting against lynching on Sunday. Read proof on the program first and rushed it back to the printer, only to have Miss Gardner of the Council of Churches telephone to say she had told Walter that the A.C.L.U. could not be listed as a sponsor with church organizations as they wouldn't stand for it. Walter evidently forgot, and would I straighten it out? Printing held up about an hour until I could talk to Roger Baldwin of the A.C.L.U. who was okay about it—no offense.

Miss Dixon, my secretary, is back today after three months' leave, and now perhaps I can get some work done. That substitute girl was a terror.

Charlie Houston wired from Washington that he had got a three-day stay of execution from the U.S. Supreme Court for Jess Hollins.

January 3

The morning's work was speeded by the Jess Hollins news, as we have been fighting for this Oklahoma man since August 15, 1932; he was sentenced to die January 4.

Tried to get some work done in *The Crisis* office, but it is practically impossible when Walter White is out of town. The separate telephones are a nuisance to us and our friends outside. Must see to putting all extensions through one switchboard.

Got all invitations to Sunday meeting in the mail and made final check on programs as well as got stories off to the dailies for Saturday or Sunday papers. Trying to arrange radio broadcast for Senator Costigan, but it looks like no go. Wire from Walter in D.C. saying he will be in office tomorrow. He is conferring with Costigan and Wagner on final revisions of antilynching bill.

January 4

Another unsuccessful attempt to do some *Crisis* work. Walter White telephoned that he had some important memos on Jess Hollins case suitable for a number-one news story and press release; but he did not get down until after 1 P.M. and delayed the release considerably. He looks very tired and is working much too hard. As usual, he had a lot of late ideas on this, that, and the other—and the Sunday meeting.

Had to pitch in and start dictating on odds and ends in the annual report for the N.A.A.C.P. as George S. Schuyler, being unfamiliar with many details in cases, has had to get it all out slowly.

New Masses, the Communist weekly magazine, appeared today giving N.A.A.C.P. hell.

January 5

Hectic Saturday morning—as usual. Walter was very grateful and much impressed when told Elmer Carter and *Opportunity* magazine had refused a $50 advertisement from *New Masses*.

Went about one o'clock with a subpoena server to the McCallister restaurant in Greenwich Village; serve papers on manager and hostess, who refused to serve Alice Mason, Isabel Tarkington, and me last August 31. The trial is to come up next Tuesday.

Notices off to the dailies about the N.A.A.C.P.'s annual business meeting next Monday. We get excellent stories in the morning papers on tomorrow's mass meeting, but strangely enough, nothing in the *Amsterdam News* in Harlem. That paper. I would hate to have the dailies beat me on a story in my own back yard, especially if I had it first as they did.

January 6

Up late and to the mass meeting at Broadway Tabernacle, Fifty-sixth and Broadway. Good crowd at 3 P.M., and more steadily coming in as it got underway about 3:15. All speakers were excellent, and by the time Senator Costigan spoke at 4:15 there were more than 1,000 present. *The New York Times* was there and *The Amsterdam News* and Baltimore *Afro-American*. Photographers got some shots of the senator. Looks like good meeting from publicity standpoint.

To dinner with Minnie and Alice Mason, here to live from Chicago. She went to the meeting with Minnie. Then Minnie and I went to the Carters' for a chat; but Elmer was away speaking on something to the white folks.

January 7

Practically whole day given over to annual business meeting. About eleven o'clock, for some reason, Walter had about fifteen Mt. Holyoke college girls in for conference. On this of all days.

We had heard a rumor that some of the "opposition"—meaning no particular people—were going to try and force through a resolution of censure for our conduct of the Crawford case. [N.A.A.C.P. lawyers had argued that George Crawford, a defendant in a North Carolina murder case, was out of state at the time of the murder for which he was charged; later, evidence showed that he *had* made a brief trip back South around the day of the murder, undermining his alibi.] Everything was sweet at the meeting—too sweet, almost. Smooth as clockwork. For the first time, nominations to the board from branches were on the ballot and voted upon; Louis Wright, a surgeon, was elected chairman of the board at a subsequent meeting. The board said it found it was "in error" when it thought it had adopted a budget for the *Crisis;* voted money for January and will ratify the budget at the February meeting.

Managed to get a little *Crisis* work done this morning.

January 8

Spent the entire day in municipal court, where our suit against the Alice McCallister restaurant finally came up. This restaurant refused to serve Miss Alice Mason, Mrs. Isabel Tarkington, and myself last August. After the waitresses (colored) and the hostess had ignored us for about fifteen minutes, the hostess said she could not serve us, etc., etc.—then she called a man she said was the manager and he said the same thing.

We placed the matter in the hands of Hubert T. Delany, who, being occupied with tax hearings in his capacity as tax commissioner, had one of his partners, Emil G. Kleid, handle it.

The restaurant's defense was that I "seemed to be under the influence of liquor" when I arrived, that I asked only for liquor, and that they refused liquor only and not a meal. The sole proof they offered of my intoxication was the testimony of the hostess that I had a "happy smile" on my face. The jury laughed and awarded us $200 damages each.

January 9

A long hard day at the office. Stayed downtown for dinner as I had to go out to Far Rockaway, L.I., for a branch meeting.

Raining; arrived 8:15 and wandered into the church only to find six people present at that hour. Program started about 9:10 and good crowd present when I started to speak at 9:40. Long, tiresome program. I finally had to leave them there so I could catch 11:11 train back to city.

To bed after midnight and no thanks for long day for "the race."

January 12

Just after breakfast at Thirty-third Street and Eighth Avenue, during which read of lynching in Franklinton, Louisiana. I decided to try to interview Senator Huey P. Long of Louisiana; he was in town today staying at the New Yorker Hotel, a block away.

Strange to say, no trouble getting to Long's suite. Kept waiting my turn for hour and quarter, but finally was ushered invg the presence of the man who calls himself the "Kingfish" and is known as the Dictator of Louisiana. He received me in maroon silk pajama pants only, barefooted and about to wash his teeth. He talked almost steadily for about thirty minutes. Said he was against a federal antilynching bill; couldn't help it because a Negro got lynched yesterday in Louisiana; was for education for them and public health care. Would not touch question of franchise for them. Meant that they should be included in his share-the-wealth program.

January 13

Up late and whipped Huey Long interview into shape for *Crisis,* sending it to Albany by mail. Also got off column to the *Call.* Dinner out— late—and back home to bed.

January 14

Nothing exciting today. Did manage to catch up a bit with *Crisis* correspondence, but made no progress on back N.A.A.C.P. letters.

Pickens landed this morning from his short vacation in Haiti, full of Haitian politics and declaring he is going to write an article on the doings down there.

Received word that three Negroes in Mississippi were sentenced to die February 3 from their lawyer, who wants to appeal to the U.S. Supreme Court, citing dissenting opinion of Judge Anderson of Mississippi supreme court. Hope we can help, as it looks like a bad case, but we have so little money.

January 15

No proofs back for *The Crisis* today. To the movies at night to see a musical, leaving Minnie working on book review for her Columbia class. Back home early, and we went over it together.

January 16

Spent the whole day marking up the dummy for the February *Crisis.* It turned out that I had estimated new copy and leftover material too close. Hardly believed it myself. Used every scrap of usable leftover and every line of fresh copy except two 2-inch boxes advertising coming article on domestic servants in Bronx. The editorials were about ten lines short, so wrote one on new Unemployment Insurance Bill—H.R. 2829.

Worked straight through dinner hour in office until 7:50. Took package to main post office to be sure it got off to Albany. To dinner at Pennsylvania Station, as Minnie long ago went to her class at Columbia. Was too tired to enjoy good meal. Home by 9 to catch that marvelous woman Lily Pons on radio. What a voice! Read in bed until Minnie arrived about 10.

January 17

Up late and still tired. Fairly heavy, very wet snow outside. Felt better after bath and breakfast on the way to the office. Arrived a little after 10, and when I consider I was out for the race until after 8 last night, I think the race is still far ahead of me.

Caught up a little on back correspondence at both offices. George Schuyler started out today on a swell idea of preparing a series of feature stories on famous N.A.A.C.P. cases, patterned after the study done each week in the Hearst paper magazine *The American Weekly*. His first story, "The Mule That Caused Three Murders," deals with the Jerome Wilson case of Franklinton, Louisiana.

George and I know the usual N.A.A.C.P. publicity is too intellectual, not only for Negroes, but for the American mass mind. This new stuff should go over—if they give it a chance.

January 18

Proofs finally back for *The Crisis* and read. Decided to change editorial on H.R. 2829 to general language in support of unemployment insurance legislation, as Senator Robert F. Wagner, coauthor of antilynching bill, had introduced President Roosevelt's unemployment bill.

Mediocre press release out—mostly antilynching material. Sent out story on Huey Long interview to papers.

Home and to movies to see *Broadway Bill* with Minnie; we both were delighted by delectable Myrna Loy.

A bowl of chili apiece, some beer, and to bed.

January 19

Why do the mornings at the office on Saturday get so crowded? Invariably as I arrive of a Saturday hoping that everything will be wound up at 12:30, something happens.

Today a lot of little things had to be looked after. The Ted Rowes came in about 12:30. They are so nice. Had hoped to make matinee of a musical show but they stayed and talked until 2:40. So I stayed and did column for K.C. *Call*.

Then to Forty-second Street to Whitehouse & Hardy for tan shoes, but could not get what I wanted. So to Edwin Clapp. They were out of size 12AA.

Home, dinner, and out afterward by myself to the Harlem Opera House to see and hear Earl Hines, the Chicago maestro.

January 20

Rain. Minnie up and to mass at 9, leaving me without waking up. After breakfast went down to the Museum of Natural History to see the Soviet educational exhibit and then across to the Metropolitan Museum to revel in Hearn gallery pictures and one or two other things.

Home, dinner, and a little reading.

January 21

Nothing of much importance in the day. Ran into Eddie Morrow in the evening at a barbershop and had, as always, quite a talk. Later, passed a saloon and ran into Elmer Carter, who regaled us with talk. Jesse Wayne, one of the owners of the place, and later Marsh Rivers, sat at his feet with me—rounds of drinks until nearly 1 A.M. I was drinking only ale and so arrived home in excellent condition.

January 22

Began snowing today, and it looks as though it might be a real storm. We need one here.

Down to Louis T. Wright's to see Trevor Bowen and say goodbye to him, as he is leaving Sunday for China. Elmer Carter and his wife there. Another long talk with Louis on his favorite subject—hospitals.

January 23

The Crisis was delivered this afternoon in the midst of the snowstorm. It looks pretty good.

Snowed all day—practically a blizzard. We closed the office at 4:30 to let everyone make it home.

Out tonight to see Caroline Hall at the Y.W. She is going to do an article for *The Crisis* on domestic servants in the Bronx. But she wasn't home. I waited an hour after our engagement and she hadn't showed up. Probably held up by the snow.

January 24

The city is digging out today. They say this is the heaviest snow in fifteen years: 17.5 inches. It's only three inches less than the snow of the famous Blizzard of '88.

Home, a little reading, and to bed.

January 25

Can't seem to get *The Crisis* distributed. Our man is Shaw, who lives in Jamaica out in Queens. He was snowed in nearly all day Thursday, slid into a ditch on Sunrise Highway, and stayed all night. Today he is working on *The Amsterdam News,* and his wife said she thought he might get around to us Monday. I hollered and she then thought he might get here tomorrow.

At the office late, going over publicity for the lynching art exhibit with a woman from the gallery.

A little huff with Minnie and off to the movies by myself to hear Dick Powell singing in *Flirtation Walk.*

Telephoned Hubert Delany about midnight and found he has the checks for the damages we won in lawsuit.

January 26

Finally got *The Crisis* off today, to be distributed in New York City. Not much else doing except the inevitable routine. Lunch with Schuyler and then back to office to write my piece for the *Call.* Away about 3 and to Times Square to hear Bing Crosby singing in *Here Is My Heart,* to say nothing of seeing Cab Calloway and his ensemble in person in the stage show. Cab is, as usual, an unbelievably entertaining clown. The crowd went crazy about him.

By the Y.W. after dinner, as Minnie went to her club, and saw Caroline Hall, who has consented to write the article on domestics for *The Crisis.*

A couple of Scotches-and-soda and home to bed.

January 27

A lazy day with breakfast about 11 and not out of pajamas until 4:45, after calling Hubert Delany and promising him to run down at once for a cocktail and a chat about the money from our suit. Met Max Yergan, the South African Y.M.C.A. man there, and was impressed once again with him.

Hubert insisted Minnie join us for dinner at Craig's. We stopped by the house for her and all went to a jolly dinner around the corner. Minnie entertained with her sly argument about the place of women in American life. Home about 9. Hearing Judge and Mrs. Toney had called only ten minutes before, went up to their apartment and visited for an hour.

January 28

The radio announced at 7:30 that it was 2 degrees above zero. The office as usual on Monday was colder than a Frigidaire. Never warmed up until 2 P.M. Walter is in Washington today on the Costigan-Wagner antilynching bill and will not be back until Wednesday.

Home and to sleep over a book; and finally persuaded to bed by the good wife.

January 29

An average day at the office without anything to disturb the routine. Sent my memo on reorganization of the N.A.A.C.P.'s branch structure and finances to Walter, Joel and Arthur Spingarn, Mary White Ovington, and Louis Wright.

Hubert Delany sent check today for $120 as my share of the damages on the restaurant discrimination case we won on January 8. Feels good, I can tell you. Two daiquiri cocktails to celebrate the café victory, then home.

January 30

Walter back from Washington with news H. L. Mencken will testify at the Costigan-Wagner bill hearings February 14. The antilynching exhibition is coming along okay.

Home and quiet evening, falling asleep in chair and listening to good frau's complaints that she is about to get a cold and why don't I do something about it. Finally, she betook herself, thoroughly greased, to bed, following my admonition to gulp a glass of whiskey.

January 31

The morning papers report 7,500 birthday balls held over the country for President Roosevelt and aid to infantile paralysis. I could not help but think of the good Negroes could do themselves by holding some such simultaneous celebration on one night for one of their causes— say antilynching. The N.A.A.C.P. has overlooked many chances to make money.

13 THE RADICAL
THIRTIES

On gloomy days during the Depression it sometimes seemed as if a dam had burst somewhere just upriver from me. The times were awash in revolutionary talk, fantastic dreams, and visions and radical formulas for restoring the country's shattered economy and national will. If it was a bad time for everyone, it was a terrible time for Negroes. Pushed to the very bottom of the heap, most black people were too hard-pressed getting from one day to the next to waste much time on revolution, but there was a constant temptation to dabble in outlandish ideologies—or simply to break and run.

I believed then as I believe now that the Constitution and the Bill of Rights are strong enough to see the country through even the worst of times, that socialists, Communists, and radicals of other stripes have no lasting message to offer Negroes. Still, it wasn't always easy to stand pat on America back in those days. Many people seemed more than willing to fold their hands.

One day I was walking with head bowed down Lenox Avenue in Harlem through a tropical downpour. My mind was rather absently sorting through a tangle of business at the office, and I wasn't paying much attention to my navigation. Suddenly I bumped into a tall man carrying an umbrella. In a resonant voice, he said, "Excuse me," and when I looked up, there was Paul Robeson, big as life and wetter than a seaside walrus. A dark cloud of irritation lifted from his face as he recognized me. For a few moments we stood there on the sidewalk talking, the rain dripping from our noses, the traffic splashing noisily up and down the broad avenue. "I'm bound for freedom," Robeson said. He was moving to London permanently, putting Jim Crow behind him for good. My heart sank as I listened to him. Throwing the baby of one's country out with the dirty bathwater of discrimination didn't look like wisdom to me. I tried rather weakly to talk him out of it, but of course I got nowhere. He grinned, we shook hands, and he hurried on down Lenox Avenue, disappearing behind gray sheets of rain.

On another bleak day I went down to a pier on the Hudson River to see off a ship carrying Langston Hughes and a small crowd of black writers and artists who were bound for the Soviet Union. They were going to make a movie on the condition of black people in America. The Russians were paying the passage. The trip was more of a lark than anything else to Langston and the others; I don't believe there was a card-carrying Communist in the lot of them, but they, too, were out to put an ocean between them and the United States, hoping that the leap would somehow make things better for them. I confess that as the ship pulled away from the pier I felt a sneaking desire to be aboard. As it turned out, the movie was never made. The Russians were astonished to discover that their guests were colored so many different hues of black. I suppose the Kremlin had been expecting a band of uniformly ebony puppets. The Red line on race didn't fit black realities in the United States, and it wasn't long before Langston and the others were back, fulminating against Russian idiots across the seas. Staying dockside and Stateside had been the right choice—I had missed no ticket to the promised land.

The thirties were a difficult time for the N.A.A.C.P. We were always short of money, but an even more serious problem was to devise and advance a program that could meet the severe challenge of the Depression. In my first years as Walter White's assistant, I tried hard and without much success to talk the N.A.A.C.P. into expanding its programs. Right after I returned from my expedition to the Mississippi delta, I sent a letter to Arthur Spingarn, chairman of the N.A.A.C.P.'s national committee and our chief volunteer lawyer, arguing that it would be an extraordinarily fine thing for the N.A.A.C.P. to hold itself up as a defender of the rights of Negroes everywhere and under all circumstances. As things were, I pointed out, we tended to be isolated in New York and out of touch with the very people we needed most to serve. I knew very well that the N.A.A.C.P.'s strategy of carefully selecting lawsuits and political issues and working from on high in Congress and the Supreme Court had produced many tangible benefits, but from the vantage of those muddy camps on the Mississippi, such tactics looked less meaningful than they did from the snug offices at 69 Fifth Avenue.

Counselor Spingarn was a good man, but he was first and foremost a practical lawyer. "I agree with you," he told me. "But this is a huge undertaking and would require an enormous amount of money." He pointed out that there were literally hundreds of cases coming to our office. "Your experience must have taught you how expensive each single case is if good attorneys are retained." I detected a note of condescension in what he said, but I let it pass; my job required a thick skin as well as a black one. Mostly I felt disappointed. But Spingarn did offer one suggestion that was encouraging. "Perhaps you are right that we ought to broaden our program," he said. "Perhaps it could be started if we got up a considerable volunteer group throughout the country, with ultimately a first-class lawyer retained full-time at the national office."

Here was at least a hint of progress. Strange though it seems now, the N.A.A.C.P. didn't have a staff lawyer in 1933. For our general, week-by-week legal problems we relied on Spingarn's advice; when big cases came up, we scrambled as best we could to find lawyers willing to take them on. In the twenties, Clarence Darrow had handled such large matters as the Sweet case. By the thirties, it seemed clear that the association had grown enough to fight its own battles. About a year after my exchange with Spingarn, the board did agree to retain Charles Houston to handle its most important legal work.

I wasn't always so successful with the N.A.A.C.P. brass. One year I had the unpleasant experience of colliding with Joel Spingarn over the seemingly innocent issue of whether he would address the annual N.A.A.C.P. convention in Chicago that summer. I released word to the Negro press that he would indeed be one of our speakers. A few days later I received a withering letter:

> When you wrote me about speaking at the Annual Conference in Chicago, I informed you that it was hardly likely that I should be able to attend, but that if it turned out to be possible it would give me great pleasure to address the Conference. Last Monday you informed me that you had sent out notices to the colored press announcing that I was to be one of the principal speakers at the opening session of the Conference. I have been thinking over this matter, and feel that this action is not in keeping with the high standards of conduct that have been characteristic of the Association for over twenty years. I do not feel you were justified in sending out such an announcement without my permission. But wholly aside from this less important phase of the matter, I do not wish to be put in the position of disappointing the Conference and so jeopardizing the confidence which the colored people have given me for so many years. I repeat that it is hardly likely that I shall be able to attend, but if I can, I shall be glad to speak; and I insist that words to this effect be stated in any announcement you may make in regard to me, in the press, in conversation or on the Conference programme. I should hate to have to make a statement to the colored press explaining this circumstance.

> Sincerely yours,

> J. E. Spingarn

I was astonished. Such a flap over a simple misunderstanding. All those "hardly likelies" and "I insists," and the implication that somehow twenty years of work on the color line was about to fly out the window—all over a press release. I mollified Spingarn, the sky did not fall in, and I learned an important lesson from the teapot tempest: the higher one rises in circles of power, the more touchy are the egos one has to endure.

I do not mean to give the wrong impression of Spingarn. He was a passionate believer in civil rights and in the N.A.A.C.P.'s cause, a highly praised literary critic, poet, soldier, and social critic—a thinker who longed to be a man of action. He had joined the N.A.A.C.P. soon after it was founded, and he served as the association's chairman of the board from 1913 to 1919, as its treasurer from 1919 to 1930, and as president from 1930 until his death in 1939. The second grand passion of his life was advancing the cause of the clematis, a clinging vine. Spingarn was fond of saying that the humble plant was "incomparably suited to drape a trellis or to hide the bareness of a new house." On the grounds of Troutbeck, his estate near Amenia, New York, he collected 250 species; his greenhouses were better stocked with clematis than those of the Royal Garden at Kew in England. Nothing irritated him faster than the clumsy efforts of non-botanists to pronounce the name of his pet vine. The right way to say it was to stress the first syllable, as if one were about to say clementine; stressing the second syllable was a sure way of winning a dunce cap from the N.A.A.C.P.'s most militant gardener.

Spingarn was quite aware that the N.A.A.C.P. needed to deepen its program. Not long after I went to work in New York, he began to mull over the idea of holding a second Amenia Conference at Troutbeck. The first Amenia Conference, held on the grounds at Troutbeck in 1916, had been an important turning point for Negro leadership. It took place shortly after the death of Booker T. Washington, and it produced a truce in the fierce quarreling between Washington's conservative followers and the impatient, brilliant, and upward-bound leadership of Dr. Du Bois. With James Weldon Johnson in retirement, with Dr. Du Bois frequently at odds with Walter White—and with the Depression lying so heavily upon the country—Spingarn found the times once again auspicious for a new get-together at Troutbeck.

When the idea first came up in 1932, I thought it was a good one. I suggested that no white people be invited to the conference, making me a black-power militant thirty years before my time. My reason was simple: since the purpose of the conference was to determine the reactions of young black leaders to conditions in the United States and abroad, it hardly seemed necessary to include whites. My no-whites proposal jarred Walter. He wanted to invite a number of young white firebrands like John Hammond, Jr., a rich kid from the Ivy League who was friendly to the N.A.A.C.P. and on good terms with left-wingers as well. To my satisfaction, Spingarn agreed that a conference on black aspirations needed no white aspirers, although he stipulated that a few white guests should be welcome at Troutbeck for a brief visit during the meeting.

When the invitations went out, Spingarn informed us that he would need ten sleeping tents, each to hold four army cots, and one large tent capable of accommodating fifty to sixty people. He had enough cots. Somewhat apologetically, he wrote to ask if it would really be necessary to furnish mattresses for them. ("Could the conferees sleep right on the army cot without mattresses as soldiers do?") Since the guests included several women, the bare cots were vetoed. We needed thirty-five double blankets. "Could they be hired for three or four or five days, or bought cheaply?" Spingarn inquired, adding that Macy's had "recently advertised real British Army blankets at 80 cents each—or possibly it was Gimbels."

In the end we scratched up enough tents, blankets, mattresses, and cots and headed for Troutbeck. There was no shortage of topics for the agenda. For over twenty years the N.A.A.C.P. had been working to secure for Negroes, by all lawful means at our disposal, the rights and privileges guaranteed to American citizens under the Constitution and by the laws of the several states. We were still working hard in Congress—though without much success—for a federal antilynching law. We were out to put an end to peonage and debt slavery among sharecroppers and tenant farmers. We sought to abolish the disfranchisement of Negro voters practiced throughout the Deep South. We hoped to wipe out wretched inequities in schools and in teachers' salaries that had gone unchallenged under separate-but-equal doctrines that ran long on separateness and very short on equality. Our main purpose then, as it is today, was to crush all segregation, discrimination, insult, and humiliation based upon race or color.

The Depression added a new level of complexity to this task. By tradition, the N.A.A.C.P. was a political organization preoccupied with civil rights; but the times were full of radical new economic theories, and it was obvious that we had to take up issues like unemployment. I was no Communist or rabble-rouser; but I had felt for a long time that the N.A.A.C.P. needed to pay less attention to brokers of power and more to its own people down where poverty and discrimination were the most severe. Officially, we informed the conferees that the object of the meeting was to discuss the present situation of the Negro in America with perfect freedom and without publicity. There were to be no limits set on opinions or expressions. The meeting was not to be an N.A.A.C.P. forum. No attempt to limit the discussion to the ideals or program of the N.A.A.C.P. was to be tolerated. Our hope was that a new view of the Negro's future and new programs would emerge from the discussions. In a preliminary invitation, Dr. Du Bois told the guests that there would also be "an opportunity to indulge in simple country pleasures, such as swimming, rowing, fishing, snake-hunting, and the like." That last diversion may have hinted at Dr. Du Bois's own view of the conference. In later correspondence we dropped the snakes in favor of woodland walks.

We met over a long weekend, arguing late into the afternoons and evenings; rowed, swam, and walked in Spingarn's woodland. We didn't solve any problems of the race, but the conference did generate a good deal of heat and excitement. In a final communiqué, we noted that individual ownership, expressing itself through the control and exploitation of natural resources and industrial machinery, had failed to equalize consumption with production and that the whole system of private property and profit had been called into question. We also pointed out that Negro labor and Negro leaders didn't seem to recognize the exploitation of Negroes by the existing economic order. This economic jargon sounded radical enough, but no one argued seriously that Negroes should throw in their lot with the Communists or attempt to bring down the government. So long as white workers clung to their own virulent racism, Communism seemed to offer no hope of relief to Negroes. We rejected fascism as an alternative form of government for the obvious reason that fascist racists would simply grind down black people even farther. We were also very leery of the paternalism of democratic reformers, those people who were so fond of telling Negroes what was best for them—without ever bothering to represent them in councils of real power.

The conference ended with no clear resolution or idea about the kind of governance that would do best by us. We tried to explain away this omission by arguing that our purpose was to analyze the present situation, not to lead colored people into the promised land. Still, at least a few good ideas came up before the conference was over. Franklin Frazier, then a very young sociologist, argued that black nationalism was something Negores would have to come to terms with honestly, and that the performance of charlatans didn't discredit the idea or explain away its appeal. Abraham Harris, an angry young economist, said we should prod the government into providing social insurance for Negroes. Charles Houston contended that black voters should scatter themselves among all political parties and work for reform from within. Emmet Dorsey, a political scientist, cautioned everyone that the long-range goal of integration should always be kept in view no matter what the other changes we pushed for. I raised the idea of forming a Negro bloc of informed, influential leaders, highly organized, national in scope, and with a franchise to tackle all the problems of Negroes—not just civil rights. My proposal was a small slap at Arthur Spingarn and the N.A.A.C.P. board for dismissing the expansive ideas I had brought back from the Mississippi delta as too expensive for the times.

If the Second Amenia Conference was not quite the watershed the first had been, it did prod the N.A.A.C.P. to begin seriously rethinking its program. But just as we were starting to grope for alternatives, Dr. Du Bois upstaged everyone with a surprise agenda of his own. When the January 1934 issue of *The Crisis* came out, it contained an editorial announcing that "the thinking colored people of the United States must stop being stampeded by the word segregation." Dr. Du Bois urged black people to form communities and farms of their own, to stick to themselves and lobby for their fair share of the capital F.D.R. was redistributing under the New Deal. "It is the race conscious black man co-operating together in his own institutions and movements who will eventually emancipate the colored race," he said. "The great step ahead today is for the American Negro to accomplish his economic emancipation through voluntary, determined co-operative effort."

The editorial touched off an uproar around 69 Fifth Avenue. There was Dr. Du Bois, the most uncompromising intellectual leader of the race, retreating to the philosophy of Booker T. Washington, the very philosophy Dr. Du Bois and the N.A.A.C.P. had fought so hard in the early days of the association. So the answer to our problems was to be voluntary segregation; we were to embrace Jim Crow. I was shocked. The newspapers coming into the office that month were full of criticism. In Washington, William H. Hastie, a young lawyer who later joined the N.A.A.C.P.'s legal team and ultimately became a federal judge, was the angriest critic of Dr. Du Bois's new line. "For fifty years," he exploded, "prejudiced white men and abject, boot-licking, gut-lacking, knee-bending, favor-seeking Negroes have been insulting our intelligence with a tale that goes like this: 'Segregation is not an evil. Negroes are better off by themselves. They can get equal treatment and be happy, too, if they live and move and have their being off by themselves, except, of course, as they are needed by the white community to do the heavy and dirty work.' " So far as Hastie was concerned, the answer to Dr. Du Bois was plain: "In theory there can be segregation without discrimination, segregation without unequal treatment. But any Negro who uses this theoretical possibility as a justification for segregation is either dumb, mentally dishonest, or else he has, like Esau, chosen a mess of potage." Hastie's words were even harsher than the criticism Dr. Du Bois had leveled at Booker T. Washington thirty years earlier—but I found it hard to disagree with him.

The puzzle was why Dr. Du Bois had adopted the voluntary segregation line. Obviously he had picked up a brick and tossed it through the biggest plate-glass window he could see. He vowed to make segregation—its positive aspects as well as its negative face—the subject of a year-long airing in *The Crisis*. To a degree this was a bold, iconoclastic, and even worthwhile enterprise. While the N.A.A.C.P. had always opposed segregation, it had never really defined the practice precisely; there was a good deal of vagueness in the association's working policy. As a practical matter of trafficking with necessary evil, it had approved isolated instances of voluntary segregation such as the all-black veterans' hospital at Tuskegee, established during the Harding Administration, and, later, a separate Negro officers' training camp during World War II. The acceptance of black universities, churches, and lodges was a variation on this theme. Even so, the very body and soul of the N.A.A.C.P. had always been devoted to eliminating segregation and discrimination. One could split hairs over when segregation was voluntary and when it was enforced, when it was a necessary evil and when it might look like a positive good, but all of us knew that, at root, segregation was a curse that had to be extirpated.

Why, then, had Dr. Du Bois introduced his startling break with tradition? I have always suspected that his motives were as much personal as philosophical and could be traced back to the resignation of James Weldon Johnson and the subsequent changing of the guard at the top of the N.A.A.C.P., a new state of affairs that transformed the comfortable old organization that Dr. Du Bois had loved, nurtured, and dominated for so many years. He made no secret of his belief that Walter White did not represent a change for the better. Walter's direction was toward high-pressure salesmanship in Washington and around the country, an approach that mixed poorly with Dr. Du Bois's highbrow intellectual orientation. Even before the row over segregation, Dr. Du Bois had argued that the N.A.A.C.P. needed to be reorganized from top to bottom, an argument aimed at getting rid of Walter. Against this backdrop, I suspect, Dr. Du Bois's sudden interest in segregation was a declaration of independence, a test of Walter's power, and an assertion of Dr. Du Bois's claim to be intellectual leader of the race—a line in the dust.

Unfortunately, neither Dr. Du Bois, the aging thinker, nor Walter, the talented young salesman, could come to terms. All winter, through the spring, and into the summer of 1934, I watched as the fight was waged in the pages of *The Crisis* and at the meetings of the N.A.A.C.P.'s board of directors. President Spingarn attempted to cool both combatants down, but he got nowhere. Walter believed firmly that Dr. Du Bois was raising havoc with the traditions, prestige, and future of the N.A.A.C.P.; Dr. Du Bois believed just as passionately that Walter was leading a cabal to censor and silence him. In June, Dr. Du Bois sent up a terrible indictment from Atlanta University, where he was teaching:

> Today this organization, which has been great and effective for nearly a quarter of a century, finds itself in a time of crisis and change, without a program, without effective organization, without executive officers who have the ability or the disposition to guide the National Association for the Advancement of Colored People in the right direction. These are harsh and arresting charges. I make them deliberately and after long thought, earnest effort and with infinite writhing of spirit. To the best of my ability and every ounce of my strength, I have, since the beginning of the Great Depression, tried to work inside the organization for its realignment and readjustment to new duties. I have been almost absolutely unsuccessful. My program for economic adjustment has been totally ignored. My demand for a change in personnel has been considered as merely petty jealousy, and my protest against our mistakes and blunders has been looked upon as disloyalty to the organization. So long as I sit by quietly I share responsibility. If I criticize from within, my words fall on deaf ears. If I criticize openly, I seem to be washing dirty linen in public. There is but one recourse, complete and final withdrawal, not because all is hopeless nor because there are no signs of realization of the possibility of reform and of the imperative demand for men and vision, but because evidently I can do no more.

With that blast of anger, sorrow, and self-pity, Dr. Du Bois left us. For a few weeks I waited with considerable trepidation to see what would happen, but to my surprise, the roof did not fall in. Dr. Du Bois had been a hero to me since my high school days, and his departure left an intellectual hole in the N.A.A.C.P. I felt a terrible pang at seeing him go. Later I found out that as part of his reorganization plans he had wanted to fire me along with Walter. This was a painful discovery at the time, but these things all happened long ago, and nothing is colder than a burnt-out crisis. The passions that seemed so crucial then were simply human, and if there is a lesson to the affair, I suppose it is simple and obvious: in office politics, blacks can be just as rough as whites.

The abrupt exit of Dr. Du Bois left *The Crisis* without an editor. As a temporary stopgap, the N.A.A.C.P.'s board of directors appointed me to edit the magazine for several months. My days on the *Call* had made a newsman for life out of me, and the prospect of editing my own magazine was intriguing, but I approached the job with caution. Dr. Du Bois was a very hard act to follow. No matter what I did with *The Crisis,* traditionalists were sure to complain. In addition, the N.A.A.C.P. board, in its inimitable way, simply dropped the job atop all my other regular duties at the office. For two years I had done the office work and publicity chores of two employees who had been lost to Depression austerity. Between them, they had earned $3,300 a year. Delighted with this savings, the board voted to pay me $20 a month to do their work. There were days when I felt like Bob Cratchit in thrall to Scrooge.

I took on *The Crisis* job anyway. Dr. Du Bois had founded the magazine in 1910, approaching Joel Spingarn with a request for $100 to start a "little bulletin." By the end of World War I, it had reached a circulation of 106,000, but by the time I stepped in, the circulation had plummeted. For several years prior to Dr. Du Bois's resignation I had worked as a consultant to the magazine and though I had taken care to leave its direction entirely in the hands of its sensitive editor, I had stored away a number of ideas for putting the ailing magazine back on its feet. I believe we were limping along at slightly less than 10,000 copies a month, and when I examined the books for the first time, I discovered that our creditors were after us for $1,600 in debts.

Since our own circulation was so anemic, we could not increase ad rates and revenues. For the moment there didn't seem to be anything I could do except to put out the most interesting and serviceable magazine possible within the meager resources available to me. If *The Crisis* survived, I thought, it might be possible to expand it later. In the meantime, I would try inexpensive ways of increasing circulation. One approach was to improve the distribution system. In Baltimore, for example, there were 162,000 Negroes and only two agents for *The Crisis,* a vacuum that clearly had to be filled.

The August issue was all but locked up when Dr. Du Bois left the N.A.A.C.P., so I was able to make no changes until the September and October issues. With page after page of white space staring relentlessly at me, I resolved to fill some of it myself. One evening I went down to the ninth floor of the Paramount Building in Times Square, where Fats Waller and his Rhythm Club played every Saturday on the Columbia Broadcasting System's radio network. I found Fats sitting behind the great Columbia organ. He was a huge man with a wicked grin. Although his fingers looked like bundles of knockwurst, they raced over the keys of the organ as lightly as any safecracker's. Fats told me that his father had been a preacher like mine and that he had to step lively to avoid winding up in the preaching business himself. At fifteen he wangled a job playing piano in a cabaret. A few years later he met Arnold Rothstein, the notorious gambler, who asked him if he ever wrote music. "Sure," Fats replied, though he had never written a tune in his life. Rothstein hired Waller to work on a Broadway show he was backing called *Keep Shufflin'*. Fats composed "Willow Tree," "How Jazz Was Born," and "Chocolate Bar," three of the show's hottest songs, and did well enough to land a grand tour of movie palaces in the Midwest. When he got back he wrote "Ain't Misbehavin' " for *Hot Chocolates,* another musical comedy and a smash hit. Then he moved on to the Kit Kat Club in London with Sophie Tucker and the Moulin Rouge in Paris. As he marshaled these facts, I wrote as furiously as my fingers would fly. Then, at 7:40, the big man looked up at a giant clock on the wall and stubbed out his cigarette. "Isn't that enough?" he asked with a smile as wide as Broadway. I had the first of a series of entertainment features that rescued me when all other contributors failed. Dark had fallen as I stepped from the Paramount Building into Times Square. The lights were on all up and down the Great White Way. I went home that night humming to myself.

A few weeks later I made a second expedition. This time my subject was Richmond Barthé, a young black sculptor from Mississippi who was just beginning to make a name for himself in the galleries of Chicago and Manhattan. He was an intense man with long, tapering fingers and a haunted expression. Barthé had been born in Mississippi and was the same age as I. He told me that a white family for whom he worked as a butler and office clerk had given him his first set of oil paints. He painted a head of Christ that caught the eye of a Catholic priest who managed to get him into art school in Chicago. When he reached the Second City, he had $100 in his pocket, $70 of which he spent on tuition. After he turned to sculpting, his fortunes improved. The Whitney Museum bought three of his pieces—"The Blackberry Woman," "Comedian," and "African Dancer"—and by the time I met him, his career was well launched. But he still shuddered over those hungry days when he had to borrow the carfare to get to his own first exhibition at the Women's City Club in Chicago. "For a while everyone persisted in giving me teas," he said. "What I craved was *meals.*"

The October issue of *The Crisis* was a great success, although it did have one bleak note. Walter had talked H. L. Mencken into contributing a short piece on Negro strategy in the thirties, and Mencken was his usual sour self. "The general feeling in the country, unless I misjudge it," he wrote, "is that the Negro has gone far enough, that he already has as much as he deserves and should be comfortable for a while . . . the majority of the American people are hunting for cover, not for freedom." The one group that wasn't hunting for cover was the Communist Party, which was looking for trouble under every stone. Their pet issue at the time was the Scottsboro affair, which had begun several years earlier aboard a freight train bound from the Southern Railroad's yards in Chattanooga to Memphis. A number of black and white hoboes had hopped the freight, and just before it reached Stevenson, a little village up the line, there had been a fight and the Negroes had tossed the white hoboes off the train. Swearing vengeance, the losers turned up at the station in Stevenson looking for the police. The stationmaster sent a report on the fight on to the sheriff of Jackson County, Alabama, who formed a posse and set out to arrest every Negro aboard the train. At Paint Rock, Arkansas, the posse stopped the freight and rounded up nine young Negroes— Charley Weems, Ozzie Powell, Clarence Norris, Olen Montgomery, and Willie Roberson, hard-luck cases from Georgia, and Haywood Patterson, Eugene Williams, Andrew and LeRoy Wright, all from Chattanooga. At twenty, Weems was the oldest of the boys; the youngest, LeRoy Wright and Eugene Williams, were thirteen.

The astonished posse also found two young white girls named Nancy Bates and Victoria Price dressed as workingmen. Seeing quickly enough that it didn't look proper to be traveling on the same train with so many black men, Nancy Bates claimed that the boys had raped her and Victoria. Instantly the girls became victims of a hideous crime, and the boys wound up in jail in Scottsboro, the nearest sizable town. I thought it was a miracle that all nine weren't lynched on the spot.

As I have mentioned, the story broke right after the N.A.A.C.P. had offered me a job, and I had waited eagerly for Walter to grab the case, but to my surprise, the New York office seemed inclined to let it go by. The Communists, however, scrambled aboard. At *The Crisis* we were bombarded with press releases on behalf of the Scottsboro Boys from the International Labor Defense, a front of fellow travelers. I wrote Walter warning him that the N.A.A.C.P.'s silence was hurting it with the black press: the *Black Dispatch* in Oklahoma City and the *Chicago Defender* were both supporting the I.L.D.; the Baltimore *Afro-American, The Amsterdam News,* and the *Atlanta World* were souring on the N.A.A.C.P.; and the *Pittsburgh Courier* and the *St. Louis Liberator* didn't know what to make of the situation.

Under my prodding, Walter organized some publicity and helped drum up legal counsel for the defendants. When I reached New York and took my new job he told me, "Roy, the Scottsboro Case is your baby." By that time, however, the Communists had beaten us out of the starting gates, something I have always regretted more than I can say. For the next few years there was little I could do for my baby but protest what was going on.

There was no question in my mind that a terrible perversion of American justice was taking place. Nancy Bates and Victoria Price had played the old police game of getting off a sharp hook by helping the law put someone else on it. When the posse first hauled the boys off the freight, they were only charged with vagrancy and inciting a riot. It wasn't until Nancy got together with the law that the rape charges were added. A brave medical examiner testified in court that neither of the girls showed signs of being raped. Nancy eventually retracted the lie, but Victoria Price clung to it, and the white juries of Alabama believed her. The Scottsboro Boys wound up in jail cells next to Alabama's execution chamber; every time a condemned man was dragged to the electric chair, the guards would laugh and yell at them, "You niggers are next."

Until the Scottsboro Case came along, the Communists had not had much success talking to American Negroes. The Communists offered a separate "black belt" to be carved out of the Deep South—a catchy idea, but so preposterous that only the worst dunderheads paid any attention to it. In the Scottsboro Case, however, the Reds found a drum they could thump with might and main, attacking the N.A.A.C.P., savaging the black bourgeoisie, raising money for other causes—doing everything, in short, but getting the Scottsboro Boys out of jail. I suppose the Party tried, but it looked to me as if the group was far more valuable to them as martyrs than as free men. From the point of view of those nine boys staring at the execution chamber, working out dialectics and the future of communism and capitalism wasn't the real issue. Their lives were the important thing, not abstract issues of Marxism, historical determinism, or even race, and I wanted to see them safe and free.

By the winter of 1935, the I.L.D. had disgraced itself thoroughly enough to allow the N.A.A.C.P. and other civil rights groups to re-enter the case. At precisely this time Joseph Stalin ordered his international outriders to form united fronts with liberal groups. Overnight we capitalist tools became potential comrades-in-arms. I was disgusted, but the chance was there to help the Scottsboro Boys, so I grabbed it. I became the N.A.A.C.P.'s representative on a new Scottsboro Defense Committee, made up of the N.A.A.C.P., the American Civil Liberties Union, and the Methodist Federation for Social Service, as well as the International Labor Defense and the League for Industrial Democracy. Dr. Allan Knight Chalmers, chairman and pastor of the Broadway Tabernacle of New York City, became head of the new committee, and we set out as quickly as we could to save the boys from the Communists and the white juries of Alabama.

The first problem was to do something about Samuel S. Liebowitz, the flamboyant attorney who had been defending the group for years. Liebowitz was one of the best criminal lawyers in the country, a sort of poor man's Clarence Darrow, but he treated Southern white folks and juries the same way he treated a lawyer from New York. Against heavy odds he kept the boys from the electric chair; but every time he swatted down a case against one or the other of the boys, Alabama would throw up another one. Finally, it became hard to tell whether the innocence of the nine boys, the honor of Alabama, or the craft of Sam Liebowitz was standing trial in the Scottsboro courthouse.

Putting Liebowitz in the back seat was not easy. At one point we managed to raise $3,000 for the defense, a large sum during the Depression, and we took the check down to Liebowitz's office. He had a suite paneled in wood with photographs of notorious murder suspects hanging from the walls. Those faces stared down impassively at us as we handed him the check. "This is chicken feed," he snapped—and tossed it right back.

In the end, however, he agreed to assume a lower profile in the case, and Clarence Watts, a white lawyer from Alabama, took over. About a month after our reorganizing, Watts persuaded an Alabama judge to sentence Haywood Patterson to seventy-five years instead of the electric chair. Patterson would have been on the far side of ninety after serving the term, so the sentence didn't look like much of a blessing to him. He said, "I'd rather die than spend my life in jail for something I didn't do," and I didn't blame him. But we suddenly had hope that if the case was pushed long enough and carefully enough, we might get the boys free. Late in 1937, Alabama agreed to turn loose Eugene Williams, Willie Roberson, LeRoy Wright, and Olen Montgomery, conceding that the evidence against them had been insufficient. To my anger, the state then turned around and argued that the same evidence was good enough to justify holding the other five. It took years to obtain their release. Andrew Wright, the last, wasn't freed until 1950, nineteen years after that miserable Chattanooga-Memphis freight train pulled into Paint Rock.

For a time, Olen Montgomery became more or less my ward. Olen didn't look like much: tall, rangy, he was blind in one eye and nearly blind in the other. Peering out at the world from behind thick glasses, he had the look of a man about to be hit by a safe that he didn't see dropping toward him. He could barely read and he had no skills, but we gave him an allowance of $35 a month and did the best we could to keep him in work. Every month or so he would turn up at the N.A.A.C.P.'s office, fired, lost, or looking for help. My phone would ring and the secretary would say, "Mr. Wilkins, your son Olen is out here again." I felt very sorry for him. Toward the end of 1939 he decided to go back South. After a few days in Atlanta he had a brush with a white policeman who recognized him and asked whether he was "one of those goddamned Scottsboro niggers." Guileless, Olen said yes, and the cop warned him that the good white folks might find him yet. Fortunately, Walter White's brother-in-law Eugene Martin, who lived in Atlanta, heard about the scrape and got Olen out of town fast.

Olen then lived with an aunt in Detroit, and it didn't take long for trouble to strike there, too. One night he took a girl named Tillie Faulner out drinking; they went home together and passed out in each other's arms. When Olen came to, he found himself looking at a roomful of policemen and a screaming landlady yelling that he had raped her roomer. He was arrested, and it looked for a minute as if the scandal might keep the other Scottsboro Boys in jail for good. I managed to keep the case out of the newspapers, and when Tillie emerged from her whiskey anesthesia, she allowed that she couldn't really remember what had happened, and the police let Olen go.

Olen knew he was a marked man, and it got harder and harder to help him. We got him a job on a tobacco farm near Hartford, Connecticut, a far safer place than anywhere below the Mason-Dixon Line, but he lost that job, too, and he finally decided to go back home to Monroe, Georgia. Before he left, he told me, "Mr. Wilkins, you has been a mother and father to me." A few days later I got a letter from him. Inside was a pawn ticket. I took it uptown to Harlem, redeemed a pitiful little bundle of clothes, and sent them down South. I didn't hear from him again.

The hard times and sad fate of the Scottsboro Boys didn't deter the Communists for long. No sooner did they lose their grip on the boys than they started looking for new causes elsewhere. I next saw them at work in 1936 at the first Negro National Congress in Chicago. The congress started as a simple federation of Negro groups committed to alleviating the distress of black Americans during the Depression, but it made a tempting united-front target for the Communists. I agreed to speak to the congress about lynching, as I wanted to see for myself what possibilities the congress had to offer and how the Communists intended to exploit it. On the opening night there were nearly 3,000 delegates and observers in the Eighth Regiment Armory. John Davis, a bright young radical and fierce critic of the New Deal who was in charge of the arrangements, was scurrying around looking as if he had been drawn through a knothole. The participation of the Communists had been well advertised in advance, and before the opening session a red-faced colonel named Warfield, a commander of the 8th Regiment, came storming in. The colonel had found a few scruffy Communists passing out Marxist leaflets. He was also angry on another score: the congress had failed to pay its $100-a-night rental fee. He threatened to throw John and the congress out of the armory bag and baggage.

Somehow John managed to persuade him that the delegates were devoted to the U.S. Constitution and had no intention of overthrowing the government, a fib as applied to some of them, and paid the fee. Colonel Warfield relented, the congress opened, and the Communists soon popped up in all the discussion groups, not actually leading, but with their fingers in the jam all the same. After the meeting, John took me aside and predicted confidently that the Negro National Congress would soon replace the N.A.A.C.P. as the country's leading race and civil rights group. It was only a matter of time, he said. Then he told me conspiratorially, "You don't have to worry, Roy. You're one of the smart ones over there. We'll have a job for you."

Nearly fifty years later it makes me smile to think back on his promise. Within a few years the congress, riddled with internal disputes among liberals, socialists, and Communists, sank into the hands of the Communist Party—only to vanish. John Davis was wrong—the N.A.A.C.P. survived.

Its survival and continuing resilience were due in part to the new program it finally began to develop during the middle 1930s. The thrust of this program was legal; its goal was to put an end to discrimination in the schools; its first champions were Charlie Houston and Thurgood Marshall, Houston's former student, who became his assistant. In those days, Thurgood was lean, hard, and Hollywood-handsome, a black Ronald Colman. He wore natty, double-breasted suits with immaculate white handkerchiefs sticking out of the breast pocket; he had a neatly trimmed mustache and a way of wrinkling his brow that made him look like a skeptical house detective listening to the alibi of a philandering husband caught *in flagrante* with a lady of the night. He came from Baltimore, and his tactics combined a shrewd Southern way of leaving white foes enough rope to hang themselves with a Northern spare-me-the-sorghum style. I first met him one evening in the middle 1930s in Baltimore, where I was to address the local N.A.A.C.P. branch. After the meeting Thurgood and I adjourned to have a few drinks and to talk politics. We stayed up half the evening. When Mrs. Lillie Jackson, head of the Baltimore branch, got word of our carousing, she was horrified. She fired off a prim note to Walter White in New York saying that, in the future, Mr. Wilkins would do well to give his speeches and go straight home without corrupting Baltimore. I forgave her. She was a warm, wonderful woman who ruled the Baltimore branch with an iron hand. During another trip, she offered to drive me to a meeting in her car. It was a hair-raising journey at high speed. As we whizzed by slower vehicles, I finally said to her, "Mrs. Jackson, please be careful." She looked at me balefully and replied, "Don't you worry, Roy Wilkins. Jesus is riding with me." Perspiring, I said, "Yes, ma'am, but so am I—for heaven's sake, slow down."

The N.A.A.C.P.'s new educational campaign had greater long-range consequences than the antilynching drive. To attack segregation and discrimination at the level of the schools was to get to the root of the problem in other areas: jobs and voting rights in particular. Our initial goals were fairly simple. We wanted to make sure that black children would have the same length school terms as white children: the standard practice through much of the South was to close the black schools, feeble as they were, whenever crops needed planting or harvesting. There was also a drive to eliminate the great gap in pay between white and black teachers of equal qualifications. In Maryland, for example, a grammar school teacher might be paid $600 a year if he or she was black, $1,100 a year if white. We also wanted to see to it that black students had buses, paid for at public expense, as the white students did. As things stood, the white kids rode to school while all too often black kids were left to trudge back and forth long distances. We wanted to eliminate the shocking discrepancy between the ramshackle shanties that so often served as black schoolhouses and the neat brick schoolhouses of the white school systems. We intended to equalize the per capita funds that the separate states spent on their white and black students. And we meant to see that talented Negro students could go on from college to postgraduate work and professional training. All these things involved forcing a Jim Crow educational system to live up to its own, pious, separate-but-equal promises until we could strike down the Plessy-Ferguson doctrine itself.

In the fall of 1935, Thurgood and Charlie started off successfully by taking up the suit of a bright young man named Donald Gaines Murray, who was suing the University of Maryland for entrance to its law school. The university registrar had refused to accept his application. University authorities argued that Maryland provided education for Negroes at the grammar school and secondary school level and scholarships for Negroes to take their higher ambitions beyond the state's borders; that, they felt, was enough. After steady pushing, the courts ordered the university to admit Murray. Three years later he graduated in the top third of his class, and on graduation day, Herbert O'Connor, Maryland's attorney general—and the man who had argued the case against admitting Murray—was there on the platform to hand him his law degree.

As the 1936 election drew near, I felt more and more optimistic about the potential of the N.A.A.C.P. The political skill we had shown during the Parker fight continued to grow. Our main victim in 1936 was Senator William E. Borah of Idaho, a decent senator and distinguished internationalist who had developed a blind spot about the Fourteenth Amendment and the rights of Negroes and who for years had opposed our campaign for a federal antilynching law. When he decided to run for the Republican nomination for President in 1936, we moved to settle the score. Borah had said that if he became President, he would veto any antilynching bill that crossed his desk, and then he made the mistake of opening his campaign in Brooklyn, right in our own back yard. Aaron Douglas and Romare Bearden painted a batch of pickets for us, and the N.A.A.C.P.'s Brooklyn and Harlem junior branches, the Holy Trinity Church of Harlem, and the Brooklyn Young People's Socialist League marched on Borah, badly embarrassing his maiden campaign appearance. Later, Negro Republicans voted heavily against him in the Ohio primary. He lost, and his presidential ambitions went a-glimmering. I was quite satisfied. The Republicans settled on Alf Landon—and the country got Franklin D. Roosevelt for a second term.

What I remember most about the thirties were days like those, times that produced faith that black people were making their way forward to equality. Sometimes inspiration arrived from long distances: the way Jesse Owens gave the lie to Hitler's Aryan bigots during the 1936 Olympics in Berlin, for example. Sometimes it came closer to home, like the day the Pullman Company, after a contract wrangle that had lasted more than a decade, summoned in A. Philip Randolph and the leaders of the Brotherhood of Sleeping Car Porters and said, "Gentlemen, the Pullman Company is ready to sign." Sometimes the exhilaration came with a rush. On the morning of the second fight between Joe Louis and Max Schmeling, I was in Albany putting *The Crisis* to bed at the printers. I had tickets to the fight in Yankee Stadium, and I didn't want to miss it. I had given Minnie one of the tickets, promising to meet her somehow. All that morning I rushed furiously to square away the magazine, but it was midafternoon when I hopped the train back to New York. As we pulled out of Albany, the conductor told me that the trip would take a little over three hours—I asked him to step on it. When the train finally pulled into 125th Street, three minutes ahead of schedule, the conductor asked with a wink, "That good enough for you?" I grabbed my hat, rushed for a cab, and reached my seat just after the bell for round 1 had sounded. Louis decked Schmeling less than one minute later; I didn't even have time to get my coat off. I think that must have been the shortest, sweetest minute of the entire thirties.

ABOVE LEFT AND RIGHT: Uncle Sam and Aunt Elizabeth Williams
BELOW: 906 Galtier Street, the house in which Roy Wilkins grew up in St. Paul

For Mama and
Papa
With Love,
"Minnie"

Roy,
Walter White,
and Thurgood
Marshall
outside
N.A.A.C.P.
headquarters
at Freedom
House, 20 West
Fortieth Street,
New York City

Roy among black
G.I.s in Louisi-
ana during
World War II
(*Courtesy U.S.
Army Signal
Corps*)

ABOVE: Roy in his office at Freedom House during the 1960s
BELOW: The March on Washington, 1963. Identifiable in the front row are Martin
Luther King, Jr. (far left), Joseph Rauh (fourth from left), Whitney Young,
Roy Wilkins, A. Philip Randolph, and Walter Reuther

Roy in the 1960s (*Courtesy the White House*)

ABOVE LEFT: Bishop Stephen Spottswood, President John Kennedy, Arthur Spingarn and Roy Wilkins at the White House, June 1964 (*Courtesy the White House*)
ABOVE RIGHT: Roy and President Lyndon Johnson (*Courtesy the White House*)
BELOW LEFT: Roy and President Richard Nixon (*Courtesy the White House*)
BELOW RIGHT: Roy and President Gerald Ford (*Courtesy the White House*)

Roy in his office on Broadway in the 1970s (*Courtesy the White House*)

14   A PRELUDE TO WAR

The apartment building at 409 Edgecombe Avenue was one of the few in Manhattan that dared to have a thirteenth floor; nearly all the others went from 12 to 14, skipping the bad luck in between. By the end of the thirties, Walter White was living in an apartment on 13, giving the lie to racist caricatures of the Negro, paralyzed by superstition and scared to death of haunts. Walter gave unforgettable parties in that apartment. At one of them, a great buffalo of a white fellow was talking passionately with a knot of guests. He had a wild tussle of hair and a suit that looked as if a train on the Sixth Avenue El had ridden over it. He was also holding a tall tumbler of water-clear liquid in his hand. The tumbler was full of gin, and the impassioned speaker was Heywood Broun.

Not long afterward, Broun helped organize the city's newspapermen into the New York Newspaper Guild. At the time I was writing for both the *Call* and *The Amsterdam News,* and when Broun invited me to join I accepted quickly. One of the first things we did was to set up a picket line at *The Amsterdam News,* and Broun became a faithful picketer at our demonstrations. The *News* was the largest weekly in Harlem, and it refused to recognize the guild. It amused me later when the publisher of the *News* asked Dr. Louis Wright, the first Negro to become chairman of the board of directors of the N.A.A.C.P., and me if we would arbitrate in a subsequent tiff between him and the staff of the *News.* The publisher had been a little careless in his choice—we found for the employees.

Louis Wright was one of the most impressive, most feisty doctors I have ever met. On Sunday afternoons before board meetings, he'd come to Walter's apartment at the Edgecombe, and we would thrash out ideas and strategy for the next day. Louis came from Atlanta. Like Walter, he had been through the Atlanta race riot of 1906, and like Walter, he had watched through the darkened windows of his home, gun in hand.

There the similarity between the two men ended. Louis had gone to Harvard Medical School, and when the school authorities tried to prevent him from studying obstetrics with the rest of his class at Boston Lying-in Hospital, he told them he had paid his tuition and meant to get precisely what Harvard had offered in its catalogue: obstetrics at Boston Lying-in. He won his point. During World War I he served as a medical officer. He used to tell a story about the white colonel who sent him up to the front lines hoping a German bullet would get rid of him. The Germans didn't shoot straight enough, and when Louis got back, the colonel looked at him and said, "Well, I sent you up there thinking you might be killed, but since you are here, you can take charge of the hospital; you're the best surgeon in the outfit." Louis didn't say thanks. He just walked out and took over the hospital. Later he became police surgeon for New York City and an expert on skull fractures.

I'm sure there were plenty of times during the thirties when he would have liked to have inflicted a few. The three of us used to sit at Walter's thrashing out Roosevelt's policies, the doings of the alphabet agencies—the N.R.A., W.P.A., A.A.A., C.W.A., P.W.A., and all the others—the antilynching bills in Washington, and Thurgood Marshall's legal wars. I remember the time we received an appeal for help from a white lawyer in Mississippi who was representing Ed Brown, Yank Ellington, and Henry Shields, three cotton-field workers who had been sentenced to death for the ax murder of a white farmer named Raymond Stewart.

There wasn't a shred of evidence linking the three suspects to the crime. Bloodhounds at the scene hadn't turned up a scent or any clues, so the law had been forced to become more imaginative. Someone remembered that Shields had had a fight with Stewart some months before, and that was all it took. The sheriff arrested him and charged him with the murder, claiming that a bloody ax and some bloodstained clothing had been found in Shields's house.

The prosecution wasn't able to produce that evidence in court, but it did produce a "confession." To obtain it, interrogators had beaten Shields within an inch of his life, and under the grilling, he had implicated Brown and Ellington. After some similar third-degree work they, too, confessed. Shields was so badly beaten that on the day of the trial he couldn't sit up in court. Ellington had been hung; his neck was cracked, his eyes were hollow, and it looked as if he might not live. It took one day to indict the three men, one day to try them and condemn them to death.

Luckily, the court made the mistake of assigning John A. Clark to their defense. Clark was one of those brave white Mississippians willing to stand up against local prejudice for the sake of the law. He knew a frame when he saw one, and he took the case to the Mississippi supreme court. A majority on the court upheld the convictions, but Judge W. A. Anderson, an honest jurist, wrote a dissent that encouraged Clark to push ahead with the case. "In some quarters," the judge observed, "there appears to be very little regard for that provision of the Bill of Rights guaranteeing persons charged with crimes from being forced to give evidence against themselves. The pincers, the rack, the hose, the third degree, or their equivalent are still in use."

Clark finally wrote us saying that it was becoming dangerous for him to continue the appeal: "I believe these men have been tortured to make them confess and that confession is the only evidence against them, but I cannot carry this case any further. It's so bad that I think it would be well if your organization would come in and help them." When we asked Louis what he thought about the case, he said, "Anytime a white lawyer in Mississippi says things are bad and he needs help, then we have to help."

We went in and got a stay thirty-six hours before the three men were to be executed. Thurgood and his people then took the case to the Supreme Court of the United States, and to the immense anger of Mississippi, we won a reversal of the convictions. Chief Justice Charles Evans Hughes wrote the Court's opinion, saying, "It would be difficult to conceive of methods more revolting to the sense of justice than those taken to procure the confessions. The rack and the torture chamber may not be substituted for the witness stand."

I thought we had won the day—but I was wrong. Mississippi decided to retry Ellington, Shields, and Brown. They were kept in jail; the chief justice of Mississippi's supreme court superseded a *habeas corpus* writ for their release while state prosecutors busily set about turning up "new evidence" against them. Fearing that a second trial would indeed railroad them where the first had failed, the three men agreed to plead guilty in return for reduced sentences. Ellington was sentenced to six months, Shields received two and a half years, Brown accepted a seven-and-a-half-year term. As far as Mississippi was concerned, liberal justice had been meted out. The three field hands were innocent, of course, but then, they hadn't been lynched or electrocuted, had they? To the Magnolia State, jail terms seemed a small price to exact in return for upholding the honor of Mississippi courts against a meddling Supreme Court in Washington. That was the way things were done down South.

In those days you never quite knew where or in what form Jim Crow would turn up next. In the spring of 1939, those honorable ladies, the Daughters of the American Revolution, refused to let Marian Anderson rent Constitution Hall in Washington, D.C., for an Easter concert. She was told that the hall was already taken for that afternoon. When her impresario, Sol Hurok, sought an evening booking, the D.A.R. told him that it was against their policy to rent the hall twice during the same day. Finally, dropping the subterfuge, the group conceded that it was also not D.A.R. policy to rent the hall to Negroes. Roosevelt's Secretary of the Interior, Harold Ickes, an old friend of the N.A.A.C.P., stepped forward and offered Miss Anderson the Lincoln Memorial for the concert. I still remember how black people from all over descended on Washington to hear her sing. For twenty-four hours before the concert they came, arriving by car, bus, train—just about everything but a mule. Every hotel room open to Negroes was filled; the Y.M.C.A. and the Y.W.C.A. had to turn people away. On the afternoon Miss Anderson was to sing, more than 100,000 people gathered at the Lincoln Memorial, spilling down the marble steps and spreading along the sides of the reflecting pool. Cameramen from Fox Movietone News, Pathé, and News of the Day jostled with reporters to get the best view. A little before 5 P.M., Miss Anderson came out before the crowd dressed in a black velvet skirt and a Russian blouse of orange velvet, with an orchid pinned to her coat. Secretary Ickes stepped forward to meet her. He said, "In *this* great auditorium, under the sky, all of us are free."

There was a tremendous roar of applause. Then Miss Anderson began to sing. She started with two verses of "America," and she finished thirty minutes later with "Nobody Knows the Trouble I've Seen." As her haunting contralto floated down from the Lincoln Memorial, across the reflecting pool and on to the Washington Monument, I remember asking myself, "Can any country hear that voice and stay as ugly as before?"

The answer, of course, was yes. When summer came that year, Minnie and I decided to drive to California. It seemed like a good time to take in San Francisco's version of the World's Fair and to see what the rest of the country had to offer. We had a new Pontiac, and the trip presented a chance to try it out on something more adventuresome than Riverside Drive. The course I laid out took us from Manhattan to Detroit, Chicago, and Omaha, on to Cheyenne, Salt Lake City, and Reno, through San Francisco and Los Angeles to Denver and Kansas City, on to St. Louis and Pittsburgh, and back home. I could see those miles of open road unfolding in front of the Pontiac: quiet, peaceful places away from the buzz of 69 Fifth Avenue. At the last minute, Sarah Dunstan, a social worker and friend of Minnie's, asked if she might come along with us. Sarah was an older woman with few opportunities to break away from the city; she would provide someone for Minnie to talk to while I concentrated on the driving, so I agreed to take her. In early September we tossed our suitcases in the trunk, crossed the Hudson, made our way through the industrial wastelands of New Jersey, turned right at the Pennsylvania Turnpike—and headed west.

The war in Europe followed us every mile. At first I was encouraged by the early, optimistic—and totally unreliable—reports that the French Army had cracked the German lines in a dozen places and would be able to protect France adequately. As we drove into Detroit, I reflected that if France and Britain could defend themselves, America should not enter the war. But this dalliance with isolationism, common enough at the time, didn't last very long. The blitzkrieg put an end to all such wishful thinking, and I knew we were sure to be drawn in sooner or later. As I studied the newspapers in Detroit, the first question in my mind was whether Negroes in the armed services were to be put through the same hell they had suffered during World War I. It had been only twenty years since black men were herded into the army, filling the few colored units, relegated to being laborers, deprived of the glory due them. The Negroes who reached France had to fight slander and servitude as coolies to get into the trenches. When they succeeded, they won glory more often than not fighting side by side with Frenchmen rather than their own countrymen. That had been a war to save the world for democracy, but of what little was saved, less went to the Negro. My own feeling was that if the armed services wanted to play the same game all over again, the white folks could fight their own war, clean up their own latrines, and tote their own baggage to the front.

As we left Detroit, I tried to put these cankered worries out of my mind. We drove through cities and factory towns, spent a night in Chicago, then left industrial America behind us, entering long, peaceful expanses of farmland and prairie. It was 102 degrees as we drove through Iowa, the farms slipping past through shimmering waves of heat. When we reached Omaha it was 103 degrees at dusk. The city had 220,000 sweltering Nebraskans, and its black people were almost the last we were to see until we reached the West Coast. From Omaha we crossed the Nebraska plains and entered Wyoming, following the path of the Union Pacific Railroad. The threat of war, the ways of the South, and my responsibilities at the N.A.A.C.P. all seemed to fall far behind us—until we reached Cheyenne.

Cheyenne was a quiet little place with no streetcars to dodge, no crowds elbowing in on every side. The few local blacks got by some-how, doing the usual jobs open to them in small towns. At the railroad station a porter told me he had gone through New York City once on his way home from France and had never gone back. After trying Chicago, Kansas City, and Denver, he had settled on Cheyenne. "It's a good place," he said, "if your hell-raising days are behind you."

From my bundle of tour materials I dredged up the name of a tour-ist home run by a colored woman. After some poking around we lo-cated the place. To my disgust, it looked like a corner of Tobacco Road. The wallpaper was peeling off in the bathroom; dirt had taken over in the bedroom. For staying in this squalor, the bill was $2.50 a night. Minnie took one look and said she would rather sleep in the car than spend a minute in a dump like that.

We got back in the Pontiac and drove to the finest tourist camp in town. When I went into the office to ask for rooms for the night, I found myself face to face with a Wyoming Snopes, a sour little white clerk who stared a moment before saying anything.

"How many in your party?" he finally asked me.

"Three," I replied. "Wife and a friend."

"We're all full up," he snapped—and looked away.

He was obviously lying. As I left the office I noticed that the parking lot was nowhere near full. I climbed back into the Pontiac steaming mad. He had clearly taken me for a chauffeur. The only reason he hadn't slammed the door on me the moment I walked in was that he had wanted to find out whether there was a white boss and family waiting outside behind me. "Wife and friend"— those innocent words had been enough to clear the picture up for him, and he threw us out. Here we were more than two thousand miles out in the free-and-easy West, and we might as well have been seeking a room in Montgomery, Alabama.

It was dark by then, and for a while it looked as if we might indeed have to sleep in the Pontiac. Finally, I found a small tourist camp on the edge of town. It, too, had a white clerk, but to my relief, he wel-comed me like a brother. He showed us a tidy, steam-heated cabin with hardwood floors, a tiled bathroom, two bedrooms, a breakfast nook and kitchen, and a locked garage. For all this luxury, the bill was four dollars a night. Minnie and Sarah brightened. We took the ac-commodations and spent a very comfortable evening. The next day, as I paid up, the owner told me he had just opened for business. He thanked me for stopping, gave me a few directions, and told me to send all my friends his way when I got back home. I drove off for Salt Lake City feeling much better about the common decency and good business sense of at least a few white people.

We were all looking forward to seeing Salt Lake City. For years Minnie and I had listened to the Mormon Tabernacle Choir on the radio. As we drove through the arid hills of southern Wyoming and down into the City of the Saints, a garden spot created in a desert valley where sagebrush and salt flats had once been the dominant landscape, I was innocent of the racial theories the Mormons had also cultivated in that valley—but I found out about them soon enough.

We stayed overnight in the home of some friends. Before sunup the next morning we rose and set off, intent on getting across the Bonneville Salt Flats and into Nevada before the main heat of the day. Blinking the sleep from our eyes, we climbed into the Pontiac and drove downtown in search of a cup of coffee and some breakfast before braving the desert. I drove down South Temple, a broad boulevard running westward, past the statue of Brigham Young that commands the intersection with Main Street, and pulled up in front of an all-night coffee shop within a stone's throw of the granite spires of the Mormon Temple. As Minnie, Sarah, and I got out of the car and entered the coffee shop, we were greeted by a manager who looked at us with all the good fellowship of a Grand Kleagle in Tallahatchie.

"We don't serve colored," he sneered.

The three of us were so taken aback that we retreated without putting up a fight. A few blocks farther on I found a second coffee shop, this one run by a Chinese family, some third-generation yellow brother up from the railroad-building days. Here, I thought, we would surely get breakfast in peace. But when we walked in, the Chinese short-order cook looked even more stricken than his white colleague up the street.

"No serve colored, no serve colored," he babbled frantically.

That was too much for me. There we were in a small Christian theocracy, a town soaked in religion, a place that had Brigham Young's statue on Main Street and his grave not far away, the temple and that tabernacle from which the celestial voices of four hundred well-tuned Mormons rolled out across the airwaves every week—and we couldn't get a cup of coffee because we were black.

"What kind of goddamn town is this?" I exploded.

The Chinese cook cowered. "Mo'mon town, Mo'mon town," he said in pidgin, a pleading look in his eyes.

If his accent hadn't been so comic, I might have opened a tong war right on the spot. Instead, I ushered the ladies back into the car and roared out of town, hurtling across the desert at top speed for the Nevada line. Just at sunrise, we reached Wendover, a railhead, gambling, and sporting town perched on the state line. Once again we got out of the car and walked into a coffee shop. This one was full of gamblers and ladies of the night preparing to go off shift. They nodded pleasantly as we came in, and without a second glance the counterman served breakfast. For years afterward, I would have taken the lowest-life Nevada gambler over a Mormon bishop any day. Minnie and I stopped listening to the Mormon Tabernacle Choir.

The nearer we drew to California, the more decent people seemed to become. A friendly woman who put us up for a night told Minnie that if she ever wanted to "take the cure" (get rid of me), she would always have a place to wait out a Reno divorce. In improved spirits, we made our way up the winding road over the Donner Pass and down the far side of the Sierra Nevada Mountains to San Francisco. After a few days with friends in Berkeley and a visit to the World's Fair, we drove down Highway 1 to Los Angeles. It was an unforgettable trip, the blue Pacific shimmering on our right and the Coast Range Mountains looming up on the left.

Los Angeles still had separate hotels for black people, many of which were excellent. We stayed at the old Dunbar Hotel, a stopping place that topped anything I had seen elsewhere. We arrived well after midnight on a Saturday, but the night clerk was all smiles, the bellboy was bright and alert, and we soon had a plateful of sandwiches from the grill downstairs. An all-night valet took our wrinkled clothes and returned neatly pressed pants, coats, and dresses next morning, along with a Sunday paper. The bathroom was immaculately clean, the curtains spotless.

Los Angeles was very hot—104 degrees—but we enjoyed ourselves. Clarence Muse, a Negro star who had made his way to the edge of Hollywood's film industry, took us out to a lot to watch Bobby Breen make a movie. We also went on a tour of Max Factor's Beauty Salon on Hollywood Boulevard, where they gave Minnie a free "glamorization" in their celebrated Brunette Room. Tom Griffin, the president of the Los Angeles N.A.A.C.P. chapter, held a splendid garden party in our honor, and Charles Matthews, a young assistant district attorney, took us on a full day of sightseeing.

We stayed in Los Angeles several days, then rose at 2:20 one morning and slipped across the desert by 9 A.M. to Las Vegas and Boulder Dam, missing the heat. Harold Ickes knew of our trip and had wired ahead, ordering a tour of the dam, which had been a controversial project among Negroes because of the lily-white employment policies that had gone into it along with all that steel, cement, and imagination. The same evening we drove to the Grand Canyon, arriving shortly after seven o'clock. We listened to the Louis–Pastor fight on the radio as we ate dinner in the Bright Angel Lodge on the rim of the canyon.

The next day the superintendent of the park met us and conducted us on a tour of the canyon, much to the disbelief of a crowd of tourists from South Carolina, Georgia, and Texas. We drove on to Albuquerque, where a fine colored lady put us up in her tourist home. Then we made our way up Pikes Peak in Colorado and to the Garden of the Gods, stopped in Denver, and pushed on to Kansas City for a visit with my brother, Earl, and his wife.

By 1939, Earl and Helen had been married nearly ten years, and I've never seen two people more in love. Helen had known Earl since she was twelve years old. She was a shy and bright-eyed child, a fierce reader and a natural student. The term before she showed up on the University of Minnesota campus, Earl had bumped into a group of friends on a street corner in Minneapolis talking excitedly about Helen's impending arrival. "That need be of no concern to any of you," Earl told the boys. That was that. Earl was Helen's beau all through college.

Courting her took plenty of finesse. Helen's father was terribly strict. He didn't allow his daughters to go out dating until they were eighteen years old, and he gave all their young callers a ferocious going-over. "I wouldn't encourage that young man," he told Helen when a lad failed to match his high standards. If the boy looked more promising, he would say, "That young man will make his mark." Earl was one of the young men whom Mr. Jackson sized up as a maker of marks. He allowed the two young people to go out and about, but on a very tight tether—they went canoeing and on picnics. Mrs. Jackson policed the fruit punch during parties at home, keeping a lookout for those foolhardy enough to try to spike the punch bowl from their pocket flasks.

By the time Earl went to work for the *Call,* he was obsessed with marrying Helen. While Mr. and Mrs. Jackson worried about Earl's finances, Earl worried about something more disturbing. He remembered all too clearly the way Armeda and our mother had died of tuberculosis. He lived in dread that the disease might strike him after he and Helen were married. He told Helen nothing of his fears, but years later, after they were married and Helen was pregnant with their first child, her doctor said to her, "I hope you appreciate what a fine young man you've married." "I think I do," Helen replied. The doctor then told her that before the marriage Earl had gone to him seeking every test known to man to check himself for tuberculosis. The tests had all been negative. Only then did Earl go ahead with the wedding. About a year and a half later they had a healthy little boy, whom they called Roger.

Earl was a great success at the *Call,* and life seemed to stretch gloriously ahead for them. Then Earl developed a bad cold, and he went quickly to the family doctor to check an ominous cough. Laughing, the doctor said to him, "Earl, you just keep scaring yourself because of your mother and sister."

"No, I want a sputum analysis," Earl told him.

They took the test—and this time the results were positive. Earl spent the next three years in the Missouri State Sanitarium. Helen's father had died by then, so her mother came down from Minneapolis to help take care of Roger while Helen went to work for the Y.W.C.A. After two years the doctors collapsed one of Earl's lungs; the other took hold—and he improved.

When we arrived, Earl was a semi-invalid, but he still managed to run his family honorably and well. Helen never thought of him as weak or dependent, because his mind remained so keen and full of energy. Roger still remembers the day Earl took him down to the railroad station in Kansas City to see a new streamlined locomotive come in. Looking at the gleaming streamliner, Roger blurted out that he would like to drive such a machine when he grew up. Earl believed in telling the truth. He looked sadly at Roger and warned him that such jobs were only for white boys. "But that's unfair!" Roger said. He had received his first lesson in race.

After we left, Earl's health weakened, and he spent more and more time in the upstairs bedroom of the family's neat little house on Mersington Avenue. His frail health depressed me, and after Minnie and I got back to New York, I tried to bury myself in work.

There was always more than enough to do. Thurgood Marshall was so successful with his legal campaigns that he set up a new wing of the organization. He did a little poking around with the Internal Revenue Service, studying the tax advantages of incorporating a separate, nonpartisan, educational and legal defense fund for the N.A.A.C.P. The result was the I.N.C. Fund, a wonderfully successful pool that offered tax breaks to N.A.A.C.P. contributors. It also offered Thurgood a bailiwick of his own, and from then on he handled the N.A.A.C.P.'s legal work, leaving the lobbying and politicking to Walter and me.

The work was often as frustrating as it was exhausting. One of my keenest disappointments was the steadfast refusal of Congress to pass a federal antilynching law. The more we lobbied, the more we publicized the hangings, shootings, burnings, and mutilations that took place in the South, the less respectable the lynch spirit became in Dixie. We had a giant banner inscribed with the words "A man was lynched today," and on the days we learned of lynchings we put the flag up outside the window of the office alongside the American flags that flew so cheerfully up and down Fifth Avenue. The owner of our building became so alarmed over the banner that he threatened to cancel our lease. We had to stop flying it, but we had made our point. The body count finally began to drop. While a federal antilynch law would have been of direct benefit to fewer and fewer victims each year, the broader effect of the legislation would have been to lift 13 million Negroes to the rank of free-and-equal Americans, fully protected in life and limb under the Constitution. But that particular improvement seemed to be more than the Southern bloc in the Senate could accept. In 1937 the House passed the Gavagan antilynching bill, but the Senate balked. In the 1938 filibuster, Senator Pat Harrison of Mississippi argued that to pass it would lead to granting Negroes in the Deep South the right to vote. There was the real nub of the matter. The full guarantee of citizenship, the promises of the Constitution, the basic rights of democracy—all these things the gallant South could not tolerate.

Every time you flicked on the radio or opened the newspaper that last year of the thirties, you heard about defending democracy. For black Americans, there was an unmistakable irony behind the headlines: a country that denied democracy to millions of its citizens in the South was suddenly rousing itself to defend democracy thousands of miles away across the Atlantic; a country that placidly countenanced lynch ropes and faggots for Negroes was suddenly expressing horror over the persecution of minorities in Europe; a country that abominated Nazis still winked at the Ku Klux Klan and the white master race ideology of Southern Democrats. Obviously Hitler had to be dealt with—black Americans felt the need to fight him as passionately as whites—but anyone with eyes, ears, and a sense of justice knew that segregation at home was also an evil that had to wiped out. Yet the country seemed oblivious to this obvious truth. We all know about the "good Germans" who were unaware of what was going on in their country during the Hitler years; unpleasant as it is to say, the United States was also full of good Americans who didn't see our own racial problems much more clearly.

The truth was that a black person could not escape the stain of race anywhere in America. I was bleakly amused when a German theorist named Hans Habe drew up his plan of how life would be for American Negroes under a global Third Reich. According to Habe, people of color were an inferior race, a nuisance that the white master race would have to keep in check. Germany would control their jobs and all forms of association that might lead to assimilation. Intermarriage would be *verboten* and sexual intercourse between races subject to the death penalty. Only whites would be able to vote; Negroes would be barred from roads, streetcars, motion pictures, and all public accommodations. They would never be allowed to become Nazis or to serve in the army, except in labor battalions.

This little scenario sounded very familiar to me. It could have been a page from Cole Blease, not *Mein Kampf*. At the time, Negroes were being kept in their "place" from one end of the United States to the other. Federal, state, and local governments and the American Federation of Labor effectively curbed assimilation by restricting upwardly mobile jobs to white workers, creating generation on generation of unskilled black laborers and domestics. Twenty-seven states and the District of Columbia banned intermarriage. White primary laws kept Negroes out of the political system in the Deep South; Jim Crow laws governed everything from railroad berths to drinking fountains. And with World War II coming on fast, the U.S. Army had restricted Negro fighting men to two regiments of infantry and two of cavalry. Negroes were not being sent to any concentration camps, of course, but what a thing that was to have to be thankful for.

Despite the anger I felt over these realities, as political conditions deteriorated in Europe I knew that Negro Americans could not and would not refuse to serve their country when hostilities finally broke out. In September 1940, after Roosevelt signed the Selective Service Act, Mayor La Guardia named a number of black citizens to local draft boards and asked me to serve. I was thirty-nine, and by the army's standards a little long in the tooth for boot camp, so I accepted the invitation gladly.

I've never had a harder job. The draft board was located up in Washington Heights, a Jewish neighborhood on the outskirts of Harlem. A Jewish dentist was chairman of the board, and he was a very tough man. When Jewish kids applied for deferments on the basis of health or as supporters of their mother, he would look at them stonily and pronounce them fit as fiddles. "Every Jew in New York City has a mother," he would say—and send them off to war. The black kids went, too. Only wealthy and well-placed whites had success in finagling deferments. I remember one case when I served on an appeals board. The son of a prominent newspaper publisher in New York City was working as a correspondent in the Soviet Union and claimed a deferment on the ground that he was supplementing American intelligence. After a local board drafted him, we on the appeals board upheld his 1-A classification. Then someone pulled strings with General Louis Hershey, head of the Selective Service, and we were all overturned. It was a fine little lesson in the way rich folks can be just a little more equal—and a lot safer—than everyone else in our country.

At about this time I received word from Kansas City that Earl was sick again. He had come down with pleurisy, and no longer had strength left to fight back. In January 1941 he died.

The funeral was held at his home. I hurried out to help with the arrangements. Roger still remembers hearing me order the grownups to compose themselves as he came downstairs on the day of the funeral. A single tear trickled down his cheek. I think he was braver than all the rest of us.

When the funeral was over, we had to bury my brother in a segregated cemetery. First Grandfather Asberry, then my mother in the red dirt of Mississippi, and now Earl in the clay of Missouri. From across the Atlantic and Pacific, World War II was blowing closer and closer, but white America was not yet ready to accept a Wilkins or any other Negro as an equal—not even in death.

15   THE WAR YEARS

On the morning of December 7, 1941, Minnie and I got up early and packed for a short trip to Washington. The War Department had invited me to attend a conference of black editors and newspapermen on how Negro manpower could be best put to use if war came. The War Department's own preferences ran toward drafting Negroes as dray horses, not soldiers, so I was eager to offer a few more positive ideas. Minnie ordinarily didn't like to go to Washington—she hated its Southern exposure—but I wanted some company, and she agreed to come along. Her plan was to visit a few friends and do some sightseeing.

When we reached Pennsylvania Station we found the platforms jammed with soldiers in fresh uniforms, gear at their feet. The men were laughing and joking with relatives who had come to see them on their way. We didn't pay much attention as we settled into our seats. In Trenton we looked out the window and saw more sunny scenes of parting like those we had witnessed in New York: apple-cheeked soldiers hugging mothers, gripping the hands of beaming fathers, stealing a few kisses from proud sweethearts—a sight for the cover of *The Saturday Evening Post*.

When the train pulled into Wilmington, Delaware, the sunshine suddenly disappeared. Grim young men stood next to weeping families; tearful young women clutched their young men. As the train creaked into motion, I stopped one of the soldiers hurrying down the aisle.

"What's going on?" I asked him.

"Haven't you heard?" he snapped. "The Japs just bombed Pearl Harbor."

I sank back into my seat. Minnie looked at me, but there wasn't much to say. The train chugged through Baltimore and on to Washington, picking up more soldiers along the way. I could feel an anger hard as the steel we were riding on settling over the train.

When we reached Washington, the capital was still in shock from the sneak attack. The next day I went to the manpower conference, while Minnie went to the House of Representatives. Congressman Joe Gavagan had wangled a seat for her, and she was there when the President took the rostrum and told a joint session of Congress: "Yesterday, December 7, 1941—a date which will live in infamy . . ." Roosevelt spoke for a little over six minutes, just long enough to call for a declaration of war. "We will gain the inevitable triumph, so help us God," he said, and Minnie listened as the Congress roared its approval. The vote for war was 82–0 in the Senate and 388–1 in the House. Jeannette Rankin of Montana, a woman of pacifist views and unswervable conscience who had been the only nay vote in 1917, voted once again against the declaration of war. As the joint session broke up, Minnie passed Miss Rankin in the corridor: she was weeping.

Across town at the War Department's conference, I was having problems maintaining my own composure. Sitting around the table were twenty of the country's leading black editors, flanked by a small army of military brass and public-relations experts. The War Department wanted us to buy the idea that a little cheerleading was all it would take to keep black men in fighting trim. Changing the military was the last thing the War Department wanted to think about. There were no plans to take Jim Crow out of uniform.

The arguments the War Department offered put all of us on the spot; no one wanted to spoil morale or undermine the war effort. The more timid editors in attendance that day argued only that segregation was a factor that worked against the effective use of black soldiers. "Fine," the War Department men said. "But it's only one factor, a factor that cannot be changed. The army has always been segregated; it will always be segregated; there is nothing that can be done about *that* particular problem." Faced with the stonewall, most of the editors fell silent. Three of us—the editor of the *Chicago Whip*, Claude Barnett of the Negro Associated Press, and I—didn't back down. We argued that so long as segregation existed in the armed forces the military would never be able to put black fighting men to good use; morale would always be rotten. Segregation wasn't just a factor; it was as deadly as nerve gas. Jim Crow had to go. That's where we stood after breakfast that morning—and we were still there after dinner.

I didn't intend to compromise with those brass hats. For over two years I had been watching the country moving toward war, and just about everything that had been done in the way of national defense indicated that Negroes would be subjected to the same shabby treatment they had received during World War I. The only exception had come after A. Philip Randolph organized his March on Washington movement to keep American factories that were turning out military hardware for U.S. allies abroad from turning black workers away from their gates. Randolph's idea was to have 10,000 people march down Pennsylvania Avenue for defense jobs and dignity. Where all the marchers were to come from was a puzzle. Randolph's union, the Brotherhood of Sleeping Car Porters, had about 10,000 members, but they were scattered far and wide across the country. The N.A.A.C.P. thought the march was a good idea, so we decided to give the Brotherhood a hand. Randolph supplied the impetus and organization backbone for the march; we tried to provide the manpower. In many places, the movement's branches had overlapped those of the N.A.A.C.P., and for a time I worried that competition might work to our disadvantage. But Randolph had insisted all along that a march was just what the word meant—something temporary—and that a permanent organization wasn't what he had in mind. If I remember correctly, the Jersey City branch of the N.A.A.C.P. used to adjourn, reconstitute itself as the local March on Washington movement, and get back to business. So it had gone. F.D.R. had talked Eleanor Roosevelt and Fiorello La Guardia into calling Walter White to get Walter to dissuade Randolph from the march. The President's argument was that violence might erupt in Washington, that the marchers would simply defeat their own purposes.

Walter couldn't have talked Randolph out of that march even if he had wanted to—which he didn't—but he was too deft a politician himself to let the President and the First Lady know that. Instead, he angled for a meeting at the White House, and the President agreed, summoning Randolph and Walter to the Oval Office. Randolph held his ground, and F.D.R. surrendered. On June 25, 1941, the President issued Executive Order 8802 barring discrimination by race, color, creed, or national origin in any defense plant receiving contracts from the government for war production or for training workers for war industries. Only then did Randolph call off the march. To this day I don't know if he would have been able to turn out enough marchers to make his point stick. Walter always suspected that he was bluffing, but what a bluff it was. A tall, courtly black man with Shakespearean diction and the stare of an eagle had looked the patrician Roosevelt in the eye—and made him back down.

The War Department was not ready to make similar compromises. The U.S. Army wanted as few black soldiers as possible—and it intended to use them as hostlers, not fighting men. The army's new air corps didn't want them at all, and the navy was only in the market for mess attendants. As time went by, the Red Cross would even try to segregate the black and white blood in its blood banks. And at one point, someone seriously suggested that Washington ought to build Jim Crow bomb shelters against the threat of enemy air raids. I had to laugh at that proposal. So far as I was concerned, if the time ever came, any white folks who thought they were too good to jump into a shelter alongside their black neighbors deserved to be blown to hell.

No matter what the generals and War Department argued, the truth was that segregation was the evil behind all the race problems in the military. Segregation meant inferiority, pure and simple; there was no way to duck it. No matter what the army pretended, there had never been segregation with equality in the United States. Here we were about to fight a war against racial bigotry and barbarism, to depend heavily on nations of color elsewhere, yet the War Department proposed to shame our own black soldiers. Once drafted, they were to wait months for induction, ostensibly because the government had not had enough time to build Jim Crow facilities for them. At training camps they would find themselves set apart from their white comrades-in-arms. There would be separate buses for them, separate counters for cigarettes and candy, separate movie theaters on base, and a Jim Crow roost in the theaters in town.

I didn't convert the War Department. All I could do was keep from throwing in with them, go home mad, and start fighting. The most flagrant example of discrimination came not long afterward in the army air force. From New York, we sent a wire to Washington asking if Negroes were to be trained as pilots. We received a one-sentence reply saying the War Department didn't think so. Then an intrepid, twenty-four-year-old engineering student from Howard University sought our help in breaking this color line in the sky. His name was Yancey Williams, he had a private pilot's license, and when the army turned him down he sued. Thurgood Marshall did what he could to help in the case, and under pressure, the army made a small concession. It agreed to train thirty-three black pilots for a pursuit squadron of twenty-seven planes, the crack 99th Pursuit Squadron, an outfit that subsequently attracted some of the most promising young leaders of the race. The scale of that breakthrough could be measured by a small bit of arithmetic. At the time the army begrudgingly agreed to form the black squadron, which trained in a Jim Crow base at Tuskegee, it was calling for 30,000 pilots a year. Though blacks comprised one-tenth of the population at that time, they would only be one one-thousandth of its air force.

Even in the face of such humiliation, the will of Negroes to fight did not die. One day I was on a train from Denver to Chicago when a young porter stopped by my seat for a talk. He was a good-looking kid, twenty-three years old, with clear eyes and a quick smile. He was making his last run on the railroad before joining the 100th Pursuit Squadron, the group which was formed after the 99th surprised the military with its competency. He put a beer down in front of me, shifted anxiously, and said, "Do you think there will be any chance of us flying bombers? That's what I would like to do—but they are sending me to Tuskegee."

I told him that the army seemed intent on segregating not only its airfields but the kind of flying it taught.

"But I have had some experience with flying big ships," he said. "In Minnesota I used to fly with a man who had a four-engine Stimson. He let me at the controls sometimes when we were up together. I'd sure like to fly an army bomber."

A bell rang somewhere in the car, and he headed off to find another passenger a cold bottle of beer. "Maybe by the time I go in, they'll have a place for us," he said as he left.

Had the army seen his straight shoulders, heard his firm voice? Here was a brown-eyed young man who wanted to fight as surely as any blue-eyed kid. The army should have been ashamed of itself.

I knew it would not take long for the racial strains created by the draft and by segregation in the armed forces to spill over into civilian life. Before the war was well under way, black folks at home had heard horror story after horror story about the treatment of their boys in uniform. Nerves tautened, poisons spread. The result was inevitable—in 1943 an ugly series of riots scarred Los Angeles, Mobile, Beaumont, Detroit, and Harlem.

In June 1943 there was a wildcat strike at the Packard plant in Detroit, which made engines for bombers and P.T. boats. After bigots at the plant went on strike to protest the promotion of three Negro workers, Walter went to see what was going on. He reported that he had heard one of the strikers say, "I'd rather see Hitler and Hirohito win the war than work beside a nigger on the assembly line."

I thought that cracker was fighting for Hirohito and Hitler already. His remark and the strike revolted me: 25,000 good Americans were willing to threaten the nation's defense because three of their countrymen had won promotions. The strike stoked racial tempers around Detroit to the kindling point. Toward the end of June, the riot that had been smoldering flared into life at Belle Isle, a park owned by the city. The incident that triggered the violence was minor. On the bridge linking Belle Isle to the rest of Detroit, a white driver collided with a black driver, and there was a scuffle that ended as quickly as it had started. But terrible rumors quickly began rippling through the city. In the white neighborhoods, fools said that a black man had raped a white woman out at Belle Isle; in the black part of town, fools said the whites had thrown a black lady and her baby into the lake. There was rioting for thirty hours, and when it was over, thirty-four people were dead: twenty-five were Negroes—seventeen killed by policemen. Not one of those killed by the police was white. The police said they had simply shot looters, but Thurgood went out to Detroit, did some investigating, and found that there had been plenty of random shooting.

Only a month after the Detroit riot, Harlem erupted. This time the trouble began at a hotel uptown when a policeman shot a soldier in the shoulder while clumsily trying to calm a drunken fracas. Once again the rumor mills began churning. Before they had finished, the cop had shot a black soldier to death in cold blood at the hotel. It wasn't long before the bricks started flying along 125th Street and Lenox Avenue.

The evening the riot broke out, Minnie and I were coming home from downtown on the bus. At 116th Street and Seventh Avenue a brick came hurtling through the window. "Get down on the floor," I yelled at Minnie, who was too curious to leave the window.

In the barrage, a woman was badly cut. The bus driver stepped on the gas and took off for Sydenham Hospital. He dropped the casualty at the emergency room, then drove uptown as if nothing had happened. When we got home we were shaken; but we didn't know at all what was going on.

A short while later, the telephone rang. It was Walter. He told me that Harlem was up in arms and that Mayor La Guardia had just telephoned from City Hall asking for help. He was headed for the police precinct on West 123rd Street.

I grabbed my hat and coat and headed for the lobby to intercept him. Walter was as white as La Guardia; how long either of them could last on the streets of Harlem was anyone's guess. I caught Walter in the lobby; we took a cab and made it safely through all the bricks and bottles to the police station. We took La Guardia out for a tour of the battle zone. He had his Italian up. He rushed on bands of rioters, ordering them to cease and desist, and most were too startled by the sight of the red-faced mayor to do anything but obey. It was a miracle nothing happened to him. Walter finally suggested a small tactical retreat. He persuaded the perspiring mayor to send for sound trucks. We divided, climbed into the relative security of the trucks, and began cruising the streets, urging everyone to cool off.

Shortly after we set off, the phone rang back at 409 Edgecombe. Minnie picked it up. The caller was a lady who helped her around the house and who lived in central Harlem on Seventh Avenue.

"Mrs. Wilkins," she said anxiously, "it's awful! I recognize Mr. Wilkins's voice in a truck. He's begging everyone to go home—but they won't."

Minnie told her to calm down and take another look. A few minutes later she came back from the window with a more reassuring report. The sound truck had disappeared up the avenue. Out on the curb an old man had plunked down his loot: a gallon can of vanilla ice cream, which he was polishing off as I rode on my rounds.

The riots in Harlem and Detroit inevitably led white folks to cluck their tongues, shake their heads, and ask in pained bewilderment what the black folks thought they were up to. The answer was obvious, though it didn't seem to register with those who disapproved.

America was so accustomed to setting the Negro outside any moral and ethical consideration that the country had been going about its business as if no conflict existed between its high pronouncements and its practices. Our leading statesmen, our radio stations, our newspapers were denouncing dictators, racial and religious bigotry, and brutality; they were extolling democracy, humanitarianism, equality of peoples; they were wringing their hands and tearing their hair over the Austrians, the Czechs, the Danes, the Norwegians, and the rest. Black America listened to the radio, read the newspaper. But if it was cause for international distress that Jews were beaten in Berlin and scourged in a loathsome ghetto in Warsaw, what about a tear for black ghettoes in America? If aggressors in Central Europe and Asia could be quarantined, what about aggressors on the racial front here?

Black people wanted nothing new or startling. They were asking nothing they had not asked for before Hitler came to power, nothing inconsistent with the declared war aims of the United States, nothing inconsistent with the Constitution and the Bill of Rights. They were asking quite simply for complete equality: equality before the law, equality in security of person, equality in human dignity. Negroes did not need us at the N.A.A.C.P. to tell them that it sounded pretty foolish to be against park benches marked JUDE in Berlin, but to be *for* park benches marked COLORED in Tallahassee, Florida. It was grim, not foolish, to have a young black man in uniform get an orientation in the morning on wiping out Nazi bigotry and that same evening be told he could buy a soft drink only in the "colored" post exchange. We pointed these things out, and we continued to attack Jim Crow in the military. Negro servicemen responded with overwhelming support, and the N.A.A.C.P. grew during the war as it had never done before.

During these years the N.A.A.C.P. and the Urban League engaged in a friendly but rather stiff competition stimulated by the strong egos of Walter White and Lester Granger, the Urban League's director. This situation made me uncomfortable because both organizations, though different in structure, program, and constituencies, were working for black equality. I felt their operations should have been complementary. I became the subject of much teasing around the office one year when Granger invited me to be one of the speakers at the Urban League's annual dinner. At the time, our fight against segregation in the armed forces was at a high pitch, and a few days before the dinner Granger called and asked if I planned to talk about segregation in the armed forces. I said that I could not discuss the position of the Negro in America during the war without talking about Jim Crow. Lester told me that Colonel Ned Gourdin, a handsome, Harvard-trained Negro who commanded black soldiers guarding strategic points in and around New York City, would be a guest of honor and such a discussion would embarrass him. I said there would be no hard feelings if the Urban League wished to withdraw its invitation, but Lester declined.

At the dinner I decided to speak off the cuff on segregation in the armed forces and its effect on black people and the image of the United States abroad. The members of the audience were mostly white—and mostly secure in social and financial position. They felt a moral obligation to do something about the problems of black people—but not too much. To my great surprise I received a standing ovation at the end of my remarks, followed by Colonel Gourdin's congratulations and thanks. The injustice of Jim Crow in the service was beginning to penetrate the conscience of the nation far more deeply than I had expected. It was a good sign for the future.

I have to confess that a few of the people around the Urban League could have given me some lessons in making money. One day in the early forties, a bright and eager young man named John Johnson came to the office to talk to me about an idea he had for starting a new magazine, a pocket-sized publication that would summarize newspaper and magazine articles about Negro life. I knew the almost continuous financial difficulties *The Crisis* had had, and I told him that in my opinion the time was not right to venture into the field. Fortunately, Johnson ignored me and began publishing *Negro Digest* in November 1943. He followed that with *Ebony*. Between 1945 and 1972 he produced *Tan Confessions, Proper Romance, Jet, Hue, Beauty Salon,* and *Jet Jr.,* giving Negroes an uplifting view of their progress in the United States.

As the Second World War dragged on, the N.A.A.C.P. grew stronger and stronger. The financial drought of the Depression years began to ease, our membership rose, and our influence began to expand. Dr. Du Bois rejoined us for a second spirited tenure. When the war came to a close, he, Walter, and I were invited to attend the United Nations charter conference in San Francisco as observers. Walter and Dr. Du Bois took the train out to the Coast for the opening of the meeting. Walter said that traveling with Dr. Du Bois was always quite a trip.

When Walter had to return to New York, I served in his place. I spent a great deal of time with Mary McLeod Bethune, the articulate and dedicated president of the National Council of Negro Women and an advisor to President Roosevelt. She had come to San Francisco as a consultant to the United Nations, but her organization had not been able to give her enough money to cover transportation and living expenses. She solved part of the problem by staying in the home of a friend across the Bay, but when I arrived she was desperately in need of money to get back home. She told me she had presented her problem to Walter and asked the help of the N.A.A.C.P., and she felt that Walter had studiously avoided her after that. My immediate reaction was that the N.A.A.C.P. should not hesitate to assist its twenty-first Spingarn Medalist in an emergency, and I told Walter so over the phone. He agreed, and I passed the needed funds on to Mrs. Bethune. After that she always said I had rescued her from a time of peril. She never forgot that small incident.

After the jubilation of V-E Day and V-J Day had passed, I began to brace myself for the harder days I knew lay just ahead. Black soldiers had returned home after World War I to find—particularly in the South—that the whites were scared to death of them. They had learned how to use guns—and they would no longer stay in their "place." Black soldiers still in uniform had been lynched back then, and it looked to me as if the same thing would happen again. We might have licked the master race in Europe, but our own master race pretenders down South had not begun to fight.

Toward the end of February 1946, my worst fears proved founded when Mrs. Gladys Stephenson and her son James walked into the Castner-Knott Electric Company in Columbia, Tennessee. James

Stephenson was nineteen years old. He had spent nearly three years in the navy during the war, and he had accompanied his mother that day to help her register a complaint about the stiff price of repairs on a radio that didn't work when she got it home. When Mrs. Stephenson complained about the slipshod work, the white repairman hit her.

James Stephenson had not gone to war for three years to watch a white man slap his mother. He stepped forward and slugged the repairman, sending him crashing through a plate-glass window. The sound of the fracas quickly drew a crowd. In the usual course of Southern justice, a policeman set about arresting the Stephensons. When Mrs. Stephenson protested, the policeman hit her above the eye and trundled both her and her son off to jail. Fortunately, the sheriff in Columbia had enough presence of mind to get the Stephensons out of town fast. Unaware of this development, seventy-five white men kicked the jailhouse door, demanding that the Stephensons be handed over to them. The sheriff threw open the door, leveled a tommy gun at them, and ordered them to disperse, telling them that their prey was gone. The mob withdrew, casting about for a new plan of action.

Columbia had a black ghetto that the local white folks called Mink Slide. It consisted of a small business district and a residential neighborhood. As night fell, the blacks in the ghetto retreated to their darkened homes expecting a mob. When four white policemen wandered into the neighborhood that night, the local blacks mistook the police for the advance guard of the mob. Someone shouted, "Here they come," and there was a volley of shots. No one was quite sure who had fired first, but the four policemen were wounded. They retreated on the run.

I could hardly believe what happened next. With military efficiency, the local police, State Highway Patrol, and State Guard cordoned off the business district. Shortly before dawn, a small army of lawmen, backed by furious white residents toting rifles and shotguns, moved in and shot up the ghetto, vandalizing whatever their bullets missed. They scattered the instruments of the local black doctor, tore up the files at the insurance office, shot out the mirrors and cut up the four chairs in the barbershop, broke the tables and threw away the balls in the pool parlor. The mob signed the carnage by painting the letters KKK on a coffin at the Morton Funeral Home.

Once the havoc in the business district was complete, the forces of white law and order invaded every Negro home in the ghetto, ostensibly in search of weapons. The marauding police, State Guard, and State Highway Patrol shot into houses and herded the residents into the open with hands aloft—a scene right out of the newsreels from Germany. In all, the police arrested 106 black Columbians that day, slapping them in jail without bail or formal charges. To justify this miscarriage of justice, the law asserted that there was an insurrection afoot in Maury County, a plot by blacks to topple the powers that were. The man they charged with leading the dark cabal turned out to be the chairman of the local Red Cross and War Loan drives.

We got word of the Columbia disaster and entered the case immediately. Maurice Weaver, a white lawyer from Chattanooga, Z. Alexander Looby, a lawyer of West Indian descent who worked in Nashville and who was a member of the National Legal Committee of the N.A.A.C.P., and Thurgood Marshall went to Columbia to put things back together. They succeeded in getting a change of venue for the trials to Lawrenceburg, Tennessee, about fifty miles away, a little backwater with a sign posted at its city limits saying NIGGER, READ AND RUN. DON'T LET THE SUN GO DOWN ON YOU HERE. IF YOU CAN'T READ, RUN ANYWAY. It was not safe for Marshall, Weaver, and Looby to spend the night in Lawrenceburg or Columbia. They had to drive more than 200 miles round trip from Nashville every day. As the trial went on, local crackers threatened to take all three to the nearby Duck River for a little lesson in Southern manners, a sure invitation to a lynching.

The judge and prosecuting attorney in the case lost no chance to humiliate the defendants; but the jury's sense of fair play was outraged and the jurors acquitted all but two of the defendants. Later in the year, Marshall, Looby, and Weaver went back and won freedom for the last two Columbians on appeal.

The evening after the verdict, the three lawyers set off for Nashville. No sooner had they crossed the bridge leading out of Columbia than they found their way blocked by a gray automobile parked in the middle of the highway. Thurgood was driving. He blew the horn, but the car stayed put. When he pulled off on the shoulder and passed the car, a highway patrol car parked nearby drove up, siren wailing, and stopped him. The law announced that it had warrants to search for whiskey. Finding none—Thurgood kept a close eye out to make sure none was planted—the police let the three lawyers go. But a few miles down the road the cop car wheeled up behind them and stopped them again. This time Marshall was charged with being drunk, and was invited into the other car. The white lawmen then told Looby and Weaver they could go on their way to Nashville.

Looby and Weaver watched as the car carrying Marshall set off down a side road toward the Duck River, but instead of going on to

Nashville, they took off in hot pursuit of Thurgood's escort. The chase discouraged the crackers, who returned to Columbia, hauling Thurgood before the local magistrate, a man named Pough. He smelled Thurgood's breath.

"This man isn't drunk, he hasn't even had a drink," Pough announced after the nose test, and he let Thurgood go. Marshall, Looby, and Weaver borrowed another car and slipped unnoticed out of Columbia. This time they reached Nashville safely. If Looby and Weaver had not had the presence of mind and plain courage to tail those crackers down the road, Marshall might have wound up in the Duck River—and the Supreme Court would have lost a champion of civil rights.

Life in the northern reaches of Manhattan was a good deal safer. After the war, the main problem we had at the N.A.A.C.P. was coping with success and booming growth. As time passed, Walter spent more and more of his energies on visible lobbying, leaving me to run the store. We outgrew our quarters at 69 Fifth Avenue and moved into a larger office in Freedom House, a building at 20 West Fortieth Street overlooking Bryant Park and the Fifth Avenue Public Library.

Those were busy years. I'm afraid I became something of a martinet around the office, but the people who worked for the N.A.A.C.P. were wonderful and I loved all of them. One of my favorites was Bobby Branche, a young woman who worked as the office manager and who provided everything from sane conversation on civil rights to a needle and thread when I lost a button.

The war was a great watershed for the N.A.A.C.P. We had become far more powerful, and now the challenge was to keep our momentum. Everyone knew the N.A.A.C.P. stood against discrimination and segregation, but what was our postwar program to be? Beyond opposing discrimination and segregation, where would we stand on veterans, housing, labor-management relations, strikes, the Fair Employment Practices Commission, organizations at state levels, education? What would we do to advance the fight for the vote in the South? We were badly in need of a program, something fresher than our traditional lobbying and public-relations campaigns. I used to wince when old friends walked up to me, jabbed me in the ribs, and said, "What letter of protest did you write today?" We had a big membership—500,000 members and 1,200 branches—and a large income, but we didn't know how to use them.

What made this state of affairs all the more troubling was the continuing activity of the Communists, who had reverted to their prewar tactics and program. For a while they tried to turn the Columbia trial into another Scottsboro, and though we were able to keep them at bay, throughout the late forties and into the early fifties, we had to keep on our toes to stay ahead of them. They worked fast, and they intended to make the N.A.A.C.P. leadership look slow and foolish and to confuse our branches as much as possible. I knew we could denounce them but I felt the better way was to organize and lead our membership more effectively.

My view at the time was that the great weakness of the organization lay in its branch structure—New York didn't pay enough attention to the branches. The wartime boom came because enough people had been aroused and wanted to join—and they had the money to join. We had picked up a large membership with relatively small effort, but the situation in the future was bound to be different. Unless we took care of the membership, it was sure to melt away. When the war ended we had only two field workers and a director of branches to handle half a million members; we had four or five major administrative departments and two offices outside New York City, but no real planning or coordination of the N.A.A.C.P.'s policy and program. It was virtually impossible to lay down coherent policy lines and enforce discipline. Walter White was the only man who could be spared for extracurricular work, long-range projects, and the like. The rest of us had to stick to our desks and the work at hand.

I was extremely anxious that we not fumble the opportunity the war had passed into our hands. The Communists posed a hostile threat, and the Urban League presented a friendlier one. The league was quietly hiring better-prepared staffers than we were, opening new offices, and expanding in other ways, which meant we could not rest on past performances or content ourselves with quoting statistics on our size. We had to organize a militant membership or run the risk of waking up one morning to discover that we had become a shell with only a few thousand faithful dues-paying members.

Throughout the spring of 1946, these accumulating anxieties built up around me, but in May, a larger fear swept up out of nowhere. That month I took a long trip to visit some N.A.A.C.P. branches down South. The work was hard, and when I got back to Harlem I had a bad chest cold and a high fever. Dr. Farrow Allen, a fine young Negro doctor from Harvard Medical School, who was my physician, came to see me. I confessed to him that in addition to the cold symptoms I had some others that didn't seem like a cold. Dr. Allen insisted on a set of X-rays immediately. They showed what the doctors initially thought was a small polyp on the colon. A week later I was in the hospital for what I thought would be a minor operation, but the growth turned out to be malignant. Dr. Allen steered me to Dr. Russell, a well-known gastrointestinal surgeon who told me as gently as he could that I would have to have a colostomy.

The news shocked and frightened me. For the first time in my life I felt helpless and hopeless, and I couldn't help wondering if I wouldn't be better off dead. I had never heard of this particular operation, and the details seemed horrible. I was forty-five at the time, I had been married seventeen years, and I wondered what Minnie would think about having a freak for a husband. I postponed telling her for as long as I could—only to find that she knew much more about the operation than I did. As a social worker she had had considerable experience with medical problems, and among her cases there had been a client who had had a similar operation. She knew what to expect, and as usual, she was optimistic and encouraging. Without her, I would have been lost.

In the middle of June 1946, I entered Post Graduate Hospital in New York City. I was badly frightened. The operation took place on the afternoon of June 20, 1946, and that morning I called Walter. He wasn't in, so I left him a message.

> I guess you know that the Dodgers are badly in need of a catcher and that the Billy Herman deal raised hell in Flatbush. I don't suppose you noticed in the papers a day or two ago that when the reporters were after the Brooklyn management on the Billy Herman deal, somebody told them that Branch Rickey was still the old master and that he probably would have a statement to make when he came back from Nashua.
>
> I don't suppose you remember that Nashua is a farm team of the Dodgers and that Roy Campanella is catching for Nashua and is rated as a better than fair hitter and has been so hitting.
>
> Wouldn't it be something if Rickey came back with Campanella as a catcher for the Dodgers? Last year when there was so much talk of Negro players getting a try-out for the majors, it was said, by those who know, that Campanella was the best all-around Negro player. However Rickey picked Jackie Robinson because he is good and because he was a four-letter athlete, a college man, and a lieutenant in the army, all of which could help the publicity.
>
> Just as I am getting ready to go downstairs, this little thought came to me because you are such a baseball fan, and I wanted to pass on the thought in case you had not seen that Rickey was in Nashua.

I suppose it's only human for people to prepare to meet their maker on such days. I would like history to record that what I thought about was the Brooklyn Dodgers.

16   OUR NATIONAL GOVERNMENT MUST SHOW THE WAY

The summer of 1946 was a terrible time to be laid up. I spent day after day in my hospital room, a lump in the bedclothes, staring at the ceiling. Outside, Harry Truman was in the White House, and great changes seemed possible. Some days I was certain I would never live to see those changes take place, other days I didn't even care. It was the lowest time of my life.

When Truman took office, there had been a raft of worries among Negroes—he was an untested haberdasher from Klan country. But I had known him when he was a judge back in Kansas City, and one of the things he had done back then was to save a home for Negro boys that the white folks thought was too good for colored children. I had been watching him for a long time, and I was inclined to give him enough room to show what he was really made of. I wrote an editorial in *The Crisis* pointing out that he had compiled a reasonable record on many matters affecting race and that he was entitled to a chance to add to that record as President. As pressing as the problems of black people were, we still had to remember that race was only one of the crises facing the country after World War II. We had to share time with the postwar economic reconstruction of Europe, negotiations with the Soviet Union, and the demobilization and reintegration of our armed forces into American life—more problems than any one man could solve by himself.

There was, nonetheless, enough evidence to support hope that Truman might surprise everyone, Southerners and black people alike, when he got down to the business of race. Anyone who mistook Harry Truman for a pint-sized Bilbo was making a big mistake. As Jackson County judge in Kansas City and as senator from Missouri, Truman had not kept company with the Southern race baiters of the 1920s and 1930s. It was true that he had been a creature of Tom Pendergast's Democratic machine in Kansas City, and also true that some of Pendergast's men had been crooked enough to hide behind a bedspring, but I knew that as judge and then senator, Truman had learned to count the 20,000 black voters in Kansas City and the 110,000 black voters in Missouri. In 1935 he had backed the Costigan-Wagner antilynching bill; he had voted against poll taxes; he had given modest support to Roosevelt's Fair Employment Practices Committee; and during the months after F.D.R.'s death, he had been willing to edge far out on the limb on behalf of the F.E.P.C. I remembered what he had said on Labor Day, 1945: "The bigots of race and class and creed shall not be permitted to warp the souls of men." I had to admit that some of his early appointments were a mark against him—the worst was James Byrnes, a shameless white supremacist, as Secretary of State—but I also knew that Truman's own views on race were border state, not Deep Dixie: he didn't believe in social equality, but he did believe in fair play. No one had ever convinced him that the Bill of Rights was a document for white folks only.

In early September, while I was still convalescing, Walter led a delegation from the National Emergency Committee against Violence to the White House for an audience with Truman. During the meeting, Walter briefed the President on the mayhem in Columbia, Tennessee, and gave Truman a rundown on other eruptions around the country. The one I recall best was the case of Isaac Woodward, a young black soldier who mustered out of uniform down South only to have his eyes gouged out three hours later by a white sheriff. Walter returned and told us that Truman had listened, fists clenched on the arms of his chair, as the delegation told its horror stories. Finally, the President stood up and said, "My God, I had no idea that things were as terrible as that. We've got to do something."

So we had the President's ear, a good beginning; but from my hospital bed, I watched these developments listlessly. The truth is that I was feeling very sorry for myself. There were days when I would have welcomed death.

Thank God for Minnie. She was with me every moment, sympathizing but prodding me every day to pick up the pieces of my life. Without her, I don't know how I would have pulled through. Slowly I began to recover, and by the latter part of September, I felt better physically. Minnie organized a short vacation to Phoenix. She argued that a train trip, a little fresh air, and a change of scenery would do me good. She said she would act as the travel agent and nurse; all I had to do was pick up my feet and move. I was dubious, but finally I gave in.

I'll never forget that trip. On the train between New York and Chicago, Minnie fell ill, and suddenly I had to take over. In my alarm over

Minnie, I forgot my operation and the gloom that had been paralyzing me. We had a five-hour layover in Chicago before catching the Santa Fe for Phoenix, and I managed to get in touch with Dr. Ned Beasley, an old friend, who prescribed some medication for Minnie. Then I trundled her off to the railroad depot, and we traveled on to Phoenix. In Arizona, Dr. Lowell Wormley, another old friend, met us at the station. Dr. Wormley was driving a Packard roadster, which he turned over to us. As I took the wheel, all the confidence I had lost in the hospital returned with a rush. Wherever we went during the following days, I insisted on driving, and as the miles dropped behind that roadster, I forgot about my handicap. From Phoenix we went on to Los Angeles to spend some time with Charles and Clarissa Matthews, a couple we had known for years. I had a splendid time and came back a mended man. From then on, what I had once considered a crippling physical handicap never interfered with any aspect of my life.

At the beginning of October I returned to the office and work. In December that year, Walter's visit to Truman paid off. The White House issued Executive Order 9808, setting up the President's Commission on Civil Rights. The commission's mandate was to "inquire into and determine whether and in what respect current law enforcement measures and the authority and means possesed by the federal, state and local governments may be strengthened and improved to safeguard the civil rights of the people." I didn't think much of the bureaucratic language, but the intent seemed very encouraging. When Truman had told Walter, "We've got to do something," he had meant it.

While Walter was working on the President, Thurgood Marshall was working on the courts. Thurgood is a very modest man, and I don't think our country really knows how much it owes him. All through those years he was there, tall, calm, implacable, briefcase in hand, arguments ready. During the war the Supreme Court had struck down the all-white primary in Texas in the *Smith vs. Allwright* case. As a result, a few Negroes had succeeded in voting during the 1944 Democratic primaries in Texas and Arkansas. South Carolina, however, had responded by doing away with all its laws on primaries, apparently calculating that the Supreme Court would no longer have anything to rule on, and Alabama, Georgia, Mississippi, and Florida continued to deny Negroes the right to vote in Democratic primaries. The Deep South was very well dug in for a twenty-one-year battle that did not end until the Voting Rights Act of 1965.

Through *Smith vs. Allwright,* Thurgood opened an early and very serious breach in the South's defenses. I mention this as another small reminder that the great legislative victories of the 1960s can be traced back to legal fights begun in the 1940s and even earlier: the first Texas primary case had come in the 1920s. If the leaders of the civil rights movement in the 1960s had a clear view of the finish line on many issues, it was because they were standing on the shoulders of others who had been fighting long before them.

The broadest shoulders of all belonged to Thurgood. By the late forties, the N.A.A.C.P. was participating in hundreds of legal suits. When Governor Olin D. Johnston of South Carolina defied the *Smith vs. Allwright* ruling—what he said in effect was, "White supremacy will be maintained, let the chips fall where they may"—George Elmore, a black voter from Richland County, was courageous enough to challenge him. The N.A.A.C.P. helped Elmore sue South Carolina, and in Federal District Court we encountered one of the bravest Southern judges I can recall—J. Waties Waring. Judge Waring issued an injunction against Ward 9 Precinct and the Democratic Executive Committee of South Carolina, warning that Negroes could not be flimflammed out of the American right to register and vote. His order said, "It's time for South Carolina to rejoin the Union. It's time for South Carolina to fall in step with other states and to adopt the American way of elections." South Carolina appealed, of course, and the appeal went to old friend, Judge John J. Parker, who had become a Federal Circuit Court judge. Judge Parker threw the appeal out, saying, "No election machinery can be upheld if its purpose or effect is to deny the Negro on account of his race or color, any effective voice in the government of his country or the state of community wherein he lives." If we had Judge Parker on our side, we were obviously getting somewhere.

While Thurgood was in the vanguard of the fight for voting rights, he also broadened our campaign for equal education. For a time after the *Gaines vs. University of Missouri* victory in 1938, the N.A.A.C.P. strategy was to hold the South to the strict letter of the separate-but-equal doctrine until we could bring Plessy-Ferguson down. If Southerners were going to talk separate but equal, then we meant to make sure they provided equal schools, teachers' salaries, and such. But in 1947 Thurgood shifted the strategy, and the N.A.A.C.P. opened a direct assault on segregation itself, starting at the graduate and professional school level. That year we helped a young woman named Ada Sipuel sue the University of Oklahoma for admission to its law school. We also helped an intense, balding student named Herman Marion Sweatt sue the Board of Regents of the University of Texas for admission to the only law school in the Lone Star state. It took several years to win these cases, but they broke the ground for the attack on segregation at the secondary and primary school levels that came in *Brown vs. Board of Education.*

I still remember one of the nice things that happened when we began the Sweatt case. In a desperate attempt to buffalo us, the Board of Regents of the University of Texas offered to fix Sweatt up with some teachers in a basement in Houston. The Regents tried to sell us on the proposition that such facilities were equal to those in the white law school. The pitch was so ridiculous that a group of indignant white students got together and organized an N.A.A.C.P. chapter. It was the first chapter at a lily-white college in the South. Those white kids stuck together and raised the roof on Sweatt's behalf, and the Regents got just what they had coming to them.

Thurgood and his troops opened a third important front in 1947. He invited a group of lawyers and sociologists to New York City and organized a campaign against restrictive covenants, those rotten contracts white real estate operators and home owners used to pen blacks into the ghetto. Orsel McGhee of Detroit, an outraged victim of one of the covenants, sought our help. McGhee had bought a house in a white neighborhood. When he moved in, the neighbors took him to court on a restrictive covenant, and the Michigan supreme court upheld the covenant. We went to the United States Supreme Court to argue that such contracts were in violation of the Constitution. Everyone from the American Jewish Committee to the American Civil Liberties Union to the A.F.L. and C.I.O. joined us in filing *amicus curiae* briefs, and in the end the Supreme Court ruled that the covenants could not be enforced. The fight for a permanent F.E.P.C., the National Emergency Committee against Violence, and the restrictive covenant battle drew together the constituents of the powerful coalition that fought so sturdily and successfully for civil rights throughout the 1950s and 1960s.

All these developments happened in 1947. It was an exhilarating year for the N.A.A.C.P., but in the midst of all the action, I received an alarming letter from Walter.

March 8, 1947

AIR MAIL SPECIAL DELIVERY

Dear Roy:

Very Confidentially, I had a rather severe heart attack in St. Croix, my blood pressure going to 194/120. They kept me in bed for six days which, incidentally, was not a smart way to spend that much of a 14-

day vacation. The treatment, however, brought the blood pressure down to 100/60 from which it rose to normal. An electro-cardiogram was made yesterday which, fortunately, shows that there is as yet nothing organically wrong with my heart. But Louis Wright has ordered me to go to a hospital as soon as possible for a complete check-up and wants me to cancel all speaking engagements and to stay away from the office as much as is humanly possible until this check-up is complete. His first recommendation was that I go to a sanitarium for six weeks but I think I have talked him out of that. It appears to be a situation created by lack of rest and not having taken any vacation for several years.

Cordially,

Walter

This was disastrous news. I was still banged up, Thurgood had also suffered a serious illness the year before, and now Walter was against the ropes. For a time it looked as if the grim reaper was going to cut down all three of us just as we were making real progress. Walter's letter reached me in Los Angeles, where I had gone for a regional N.A.A.C.P. meeting. I quickly wrote back to him.

Los Angeles, Calif.
March 11, 1947

Dear Walter:

I was shocked to have your letter, although I had been prepared for it in a measure by a letter written to me and to Thurgood by Bill Hastie which reached us just before we left San Francisco.

I guess, now, you will believe those of us, including Louis, who have been begging you to take a rest and slow down your many activities. You *must* check your darting hither and yon. You are too valuable, you have too rich and necessary an experience to be lost to the cause. I thought that at this stage you realized this, and yet when I telephoned your home (expecting to find you in bed where you should have been) Gladys told me you had gone to the office! That routine down there is the very thing you should not be exposed to. Please!

See you Saturday,

Roy

Fortunately, Walter listened to us. He recovered—and the N.A.A.C.P. kept up its steam.

Those postwar years were a time of sowing for the N.A.A.C.P. To our constitutional fight for civil rights we added other objectives—fair housing, the minimum wage, and aid to education—and we lobbied against the Taft-Hartley Labor Act. Dr. Du Bois worked up a petition that placed the grievances of American Negroes before the United Nations. His idea was very provocative, and he succeeded in making it plain that if the United States wanted to assume a role of international political, economic, and moral leadership, it was going to have to deal much more honestly with its own moral problems at home.

During this time Truman kept an eye on us from the White House. In June 1947 he agreed to address our thirty-eighth convention in Washington, and became the first President to do so. A great crowd gathered at the Lincoln Memorial to hear him. Eleanor Roosevelt was there to warm up the audience before Truman spoke. "Now is the time for the people of the United States to be as great as their great men," she said. "If they are, there is no question in my mind that we will lead the world and our people and have unity, and our people and the people of the world will be brothers." Truman listened to her, then rose to a loud ovation. We all craned forward. Truman was no F.D.R.: he wasn't an aristocrat; he wasn't slick; he couldn't wrap Congress around his finger or get people to love him. But he was direct where Roosevelt had been slippery, open where Roosevelt had always kept his flanks protected. He spoke with a Midwestern twang, a plain-spoken, no frills delivery. He said that it was his deep conviction that the country had reached a turning point in its long history of efforts to guarantee freedom and equality to all citizens. "Recent events in the United States and abroad have made us realize that it is more important today than ever before to ensure that all Americans enjoy these rights," he observed. Then he paused, and said: "When I say all Americans, I mean *all* Americans."

There was a great roll of applause and shouts of approval that echoed from the monument to Lincoln to far beyond Washington. All the radio networks were carrying Truman's speech that day, and the State Department was recording it for broadcast overseas.

"We must make the federal government a friendly, vigilant defender of the rights and equalities of all Americans. And again, I mean *all* Americans," Truman said. He added that every man should have the right to a decent home, to an education, to adequate medical care, to a worthwhile job, to an equal share in making public decisions through the ballot, to a fair trial in a fair court. Those rights, of course, were the very ones that had disappeared when Plessy-Ferguson became the law of the land. For half a century the South and many parts of the North had been hiding behind the Plessy-Ferguson doctrine and the older one of states rights, cheating black people of their political birthright. Truman said the cheating had to stop.

"We can no longer afford the luxury of a leisurely attack on prejudice and discrimination," he told the delegates that day. "There is much that state and local governments can do in providing positive safeguards for civil rights. But we cannot, any longer, await the growth of a will to action in the slowest state or the most backward community—our national government must show the way."

There it was—an unequivocal pledge. For the first time, the President was putting himself and the government where they should have been all along: at the head of the parade, not on the sidelines.

After the convention, I left for a trip to the Middle West feeling more certain than ever that we would beat segregation. I felt fit and ready for the next round, but as I flew into Kansas City searing pains in the abdomen struck me down. When I got off the plane, I went to the home of some friends and collapsed. A doctor patched me back together and put me on a plane for home. Back in New York I found myself right where I had started the year before: in the hospital staring at the ceiling. The doctors were sure that I had a recurrence of cancer. They took Minnie aside one evening and told her that they thought my condition was hopeless. She told them, "*I* don't believe it."

Somehow I made it through that first night, and the next, then through a full week. The doctors were still convinced I was a goner. They told Minnie that at the outside I had only a few months left and to let me do whatever I wanted. Minnie followed their orders. As the summer moved into fall I went to more baseball and football games than I had ever seen in my life. Every time I turned around, Minnie was there pushing me out the door toward Yankee Stadium or Ebbets Field. I remember going off to a football game one crisp afternoon equipped with an overcoat, a raincoat, and a flask of bourbon as protective antifreeze. When I got home that evening, the antifreeze was gone, my head was spinning, and I was wearing my overcoat over the raincoat. Minnie took a sniff of my breath and looked at me suspiciously. "Roy Wilkins, why are you wearing your overcoat *over* your raincoat?" she said, fixing me with a cool eye.

"To keep my raincoat dry," I said slyly—and I wobbled safely off to bed.

To the surprise of everyone but Minnie, I made a complete recovery. They said it was a miracle remission; whatever the case, I was spared. The N.A.A.C.P. was approaching a time of great fruition, and I thank God I lived to see it.

The first good thing to happen came at the end of October 1947, when Truman's Commission on Civil Rights released its final report. The document was called "To Secure These Rights," and it contained more than I had dreamed possible. The commission said that the four basic rights that needed securing most were the safety and security of the person, citizenship and its privileges, freedom of conscience and expression, and equality of opportunity. It conceded that a giant gap loomed between the promises the nation made to its citizens and the miserable realities it handed out to its minorities. The states had refused to close this gap. The federal government had defaulted on its obligation to do the job when the states would not. As a result, the commission said it had found "a kind of moral dry rot" at the very foundations of the republic.

To get at that rot the commission set down thirty-five recommendations, ranging from reorganizing the Civil Rights Section of the Justice Department to banning discrimination in the armed services, establishing voters' rights legislation and a Fair Employment Practices Act, encouraging state action banning segregation in the schools, passing statutes outlawing Jim Crow in public services, transportation, and places of public accommodation. The commission also said that Congress should make federal grants-in-aid or other forms of assistance to public or private agencies for any purpose conditional on the absence of discrimination and segregation based on race, color, creed, or national origin.

The report was a blueprint that we used for the next two decades, and I watched as Truman carried it rolled up under his arm in the 1948 elections. In January 1948, he made civil rights part of the cutting edge of his State of the Union message, then sent message after message to Congress on the issue. In the industrial states of the North that year, black and Jewish voters looked like the vital, swing voters in any close election. Truman knew he needed our votes—and so did we. The N.A.A.C.P.'s capable publicist Henry Lee Moon had just written a book called *Balance of Power: The Negro Vote*. In the spring of 1948, Walter sent a copy to Truman with a little note saying, "You will enjoy and profit from it."

Truman didn't need hints from us, of course; he could count. But the President did need help to keep Negroes from wandering off toward Henry Wallace, who was traveling around the South that year with Paul Robeson, talking to integrated audiences and lambasting segregation. The work of the Commission on Civil Rights did much to offset Wallace's appeal among general Negro voters, but Truman took no chances. He came up with his own ten-point civil rights program, which included everything from getting rid of the poll tax, setting up a permanent federal commission on civil rights, passing a federal antilynch law to turning the civil rights section of the Justice Department into a full division.

The program was more than enough to send the South into the Democratic National Convention at Philadelphia that summer howling for blood. When Walter and I reached the city, the Dixiecrats were already talking war, so we did some strong talking ourselves. Walter went before the platform committee, took a seat, and nailed a few hides to the door. What he said was, "The day of reckoning has come when the Democratic Party must decide whether it is going to permit bigots to dictate its philosophy and policy or whether the party can rise to the height of Americanism that alone can justify its continued existence." I was proud of him that day: a few months back from a heart attack, he was more than ready to fight.

The Southerners on the committee listened and bit their lips. When talk of rebellion and bolting the party reached its height, Walter and I went to *The Philadelphia Bulletin* and bought a large ad to let everyone know how the N.A.A.C.P. felt about things. We asked for the largest typeface we could afford, and the message we sent took just three words: LET 'EM WALK.

I watched fascinated as Truman tried to navigate his way between the Southerners, who wanted no significant civil rights plank, and a crew of liberals, who were pushing hard for a plank of real substance. The hardest pusher was Hubert Humphrey, then the pink-cheeked mayor of Minneapolis, who was running for the U.S. Senate. His constituents were Northerners, and I knew folks saw race a bit differently up there. The Dixiecrats were seething on the convention floor when Humphrey took the podium and congratulated Truman for the courage he had shown on civil rights. I listened as Hubert lit into the South. "There are those who say to you—we are rushing this issue of civil rights," he said. "I say we are 172 years late. There are those who say this issue of civil rights is an infringement of states rights." He paused, then said, "The time has arrived for the Democratic Party to get out of the shadow of states rights and walk forthrightly into the bright sunshine of human rights."

There was a wild demonstration. The Southern civil rights plank was voted down, and the Northern plank—supported by big-city bosses who didn't think Truman had a prayer in 1948 anyway and who were looking to score what consolation points they could with their minority home folks—carried the day. When the Dixiecrats bolted the party, I thought to myself, That's just fine; white Democrats are finally ready to lay it on the line. The Democratic Party may wind up with a conscience after all.

Two weeks later Truman issued Executive Orders 9980 and 9981 abolishing discrimination in the federal civil service and calling for "equality of treatment and opportunity regardless of race, color or creed in the armed forces." He stopped short of saying that he meant to do away with segregation in the military, but a few days later, when a reporter asked him in a news conference if that was his intent, he snapped, "Yes."

Those orders got Truman off the hook with Phil Randolph, who had threatened to lead a campaign of open draft resistance if the country returned to a peacetime draft without abolishing segregation in the military. We had taken a survey showing that 71 percent of Negroes were in sympathy with Randolph, though how many would actually have bucked the draft is hard to say. With Truman on the record against Jim Crow in the services, Randolph called off his campaign, as he had done with the first March on Washington. There is no question in my mind that he helped push Truman toward doing the right thing, just as he had helped F.D.R. along on the eve of the war. The draft resisters of the Vietnam era may not have known it, but Randolph was their spiritual and historical father.

The election in November vindicated our confidence in the power of black voters. Truman's electoral college victory over Governor Thomas Dewey of New York depended upon California, Illinois, and Ohio, which he won by a margin of 58,584 votes. He won by 17,865 votes in California; the Negro precincts in Los Angeles gave him 25,028 votes more than Dewey. He carried Illinois by 33,612 votes— and the black wards in Chicago gave him 128,541. He won Ohio by 7,107—and the Negroes in Cleveland gave him 14,713. The message was plain: white power in the South could be balanced by black power at the Northern polls. Civil rights were squarely at the heart of national politics—if we could keep them there.

17 THE WALLS COME TUMBLING DOWN

nyone who expected Harry Truman to take us by the hand and lead us right into Canaan was mistaken. The inauguration passed, winter turned into spring, and the heart of Congress remained as cold as ever to the cause of civil rights. The high spirits I had felt in November turned to gloom: black people might be able to swing a presidential election, but their leverage would mean nothing as long as the Senate could use the filibuster to stymie the man in the White House.

The N.A.A.C.P. made a monumental effort to do away with the filibuster in 1949, but the Senate responded by making it harder than ever to impose cloture in civil rights debates. By a vote of 63–23 it passed a new set of rules stipulating that only upon a vote of two-thirds of the entire body could a filibuster be stopped. When all but eight Republicans joined the Southern Democrats in the vote, Walter White shook his head and began calling the G.O.P. the "Gone Old Party."

Losing that campaign was a terrible defeat: it kept meaningful civil rights legislation bottled up for years. Whenever a President showed the slightest sign of favor toward civil rights, the Senate could tie his hands. Of the three branches of government, the Supreme Court became our best hope for justice. For a time, I thought it was our *only* hope.

In the spring of 1949, I received a bad jolt. Walter requested a year's leave of absence, and I became the acting executive secretary of the N.A.A.C.P. My first job was to preside over the annual convention in Los Angeles. On the day Minnie and I were to take the train to the West Coast, I spent the morning in Washington at a civil rights conference. The meeting ended early, and I was back in New York by mid-afternoon. I planned to meet Minnie at Grand Central Station, but on the way I stopped by our headquarters and found Walter there. He called me into his office, and, looking a bit uneasy, he motioned me to sit down.

"Roy," he said, "there's something I've been meaning to tell you." I braced myself.

"Gladys and I are divorced," he said. "We haven't been getting along for some time. Gladys went down to Mexico, and the divorce has gone through."

I had been expecting a political crisis. This personal difficulty stunned me. I had spent my first evening with the N.A.A.C.P. at the Whites' apartment, with Gladys's restorative cooking and Walter's conversation. They had seemed a perfect match to me: a wonderful homebody and a wonderful busybody working in tandem. When I blurted out how sorry I was to hear the bad news, Walter shrugged. "I thought you should know," he said. Then he lapsed into silence.

As I got up to leave, Walter shot me a rather odd glance. The look puzzled me, but by that time I was late for the train, so I paid no attention to it. Minnie was waiting at the station with our bags. We caught the train safely and set off for the West Coast.

As we rolled up the Hudson, I told Minnie about Walter's news. She was quite distressed as she was very fond of Gladys. From a woman's point of view, Walter had been a difficult man to live with. Gladys had been a superb hostess; she had gone along with all of Walter's exhausting entertaining. And Walter wasn't always grateful.

Because of the divorce, the ride out to Los Angeles was cheerless. For three days we were cut off from New York. When we stepped off the train and onto the platform at the depot in Los Angeles, I found out why Walter had given me that odd look back at the office. As we walked down the platform, a throng of reporters pushed forward. It turned out that Walter hadn't just gotten a divorce: he had married a woman who had been divorced three times—and who also happened to be white. That was the small detail Walter had neglected to tell me before I had set off for the convention. I arrived to find the delegates in an uproar.

Walter's new wife was Poppy Cannon, a handsome, intelligent woman whose previous three husbands had each been different one from the next. For some reason she had fastened upon Walter as her fourth. He was lovable enough, I suppose, and he did keep company with people like Eleanor Roosevelt and Harry Truman. As I thought back, it struck me that Poppy had been interested in Walter for years. At one point, several years before, the switchboard operator at the N.A.A.C.P. had taken me aside to complain bitterly about Poppy's constant phone calls. "If that Mrs. Cannon calls Mr. White once more, I'll go crazy," the operator had said. "She always wants to know where he is, where she can leave a message. She never takes 'Mr. White is not in' without trying to track him down." At the time I had just laughed at the complaint. I have never been a very close observer of other people's affairs, and I certainly missed that one.

In Los Angeles half the delegates wanted to lynch Walter for leaving Gladys, and the other half wanted to string him up for marrying a white woman. Just about everyone thought he should get out of the N.A.A.C.P. for good. Luckily there were enough level-neaded people on the board of directors to handle the situation more rationally. We had a very heated fight, but in the end the cooler heads won. Our argument was simple: how could an organization committed to integration fire its chief executive for marrying a white woman? It didn't make sense, and it wouldn't look good—not at all.

Once that crisis was out of the way, I settled down to running my first convention. I felt a little nervous as I tackled the job: filling the role that Walter and James Weldon Johnson had played was no small order, but there were so many details to attend to that I didn't have time to fret my way into any serious trouble.

The opening night mass meeting took place at a church in the black community. The delegates jammed every pew and flowed onto a stone porch outside. The mayor of Los Angeles welcomed us to the city and promptly left. Then Dr. Claude Hudson, a veteran of N.A.A.C.P. work, spoke on some of the achievements of the organization and nearly stole a couple of pages from my speech. I had to do some fast improvising on the political climate and racial atmosphere we were up against, but the delegates seemed to like what I had to say, and the house was visibly excited when I finished.

Over the next few days, I had to deal with a contingent of comrades who had turned up among us. Their main objective was to get the N.A.A.C.P. to repudiate its endorsement of the Marshall Plan and to condemn the Atlantic Pact. At every opportunity, they moved their applause section into the auditorium and clapped whenever their lines were touched upon. I suppose they hoped to make it look as if the N.A.A.C.P. was going pink even if they couldn't win the votes they were after—every time an issue came to a vote, they were soundly drubbed.

Behind the scenes, I did all I could to keep them down. One of the smaller matters they were up in arms against was an editorial in *The Crisis* rebuking Paul Robeson, who had said hotly that if the United States chose to go to war with the Soviet Union, black folks just might not choose to fight. It was a wrongheaded thing for Paul to say, and I had called him on it. Anyone with any sense at all knew that the feeling among ordinary black Americans was, "I ain't got a quarter in Russia but I got a home and a job here." Black people would fight anyone who was an enemy of their country. I held a conference with the leading members of the Robeson front. I told them that I had had fourteen letters of protest over the Robeson editorial: nine had come from members of the Progressive Party, three from miscellaneous left-leaners, and one from Benjamin Davis, the radical city councilman from Manhattan. I told the hotheads that the mail didn't look like a very representative sample of support, adding that if they wanted to make an issue of it, I would simply cite the letters, which I had with me in my briefcase.

The Robeson matter died right there. The comrades then turned to the more sensitive issue of Dr. Du Bois, who had rejoined the N.A.A.C.P. during the war and then broken with us once again afterward. The issue was complicated. There had been considerable friction between Dr. Du Bois and Walter and plenty of other angles that the radicals simply didn't know about. I told them that no good could be done by washing Dr. Du Bois's linen in public, but if they wanted to talk half a day, I could probably talk three days. That put a stop to the Du Bois fight. We finished by passing a resolution congratulating him on his birthday.

The finest moment of that convention came at a Sunday meeting in the Hollywood Bowl, where Madame Pandit, India's ambassador to the United States, presented the Spingarn Medal to Dr. Ralph Bunche for his good work in Palestine. For days Los Angeles had been preparing for the ceremony. The Chamber of Commerce had helped string pennants and banners, not only across Central Avenue and the other Negro districts, but all over the main shopping and retail districts and across the main boulevards and intersections in Hollywood. Everywhere one looked, there seemed to be signs calling out: WELCOME N.A.A.C.P. and DR. BUNCHE DAY, JULY 17, HOLLYWOOD BOWL.

Ordinarily a meeting like ours drew only about 7,500 people to the Bowl, so the police assigned only a dozen extra officers instead of the usual twenty-six. I believe 15,000 people turned out for the affair. Highland Avenue leading to the Bowl reminded me of the 155th Street viaduct when the Yankees were playing a doubleheader with the Boston Red Sox. Traffic moved forward an inch at a time. People began arriving as early as noon, and jammed into the lower sections of the Bowl, and stood on the ramp even farther down, leaving only the bleachers at the top of the Bowl empty. I had never seen anything quite like it.

At two o'clock we opened the festivities with two bands and a magnificent choir of 300 voices. The music ran for a full hour before the platform guests filled in and took their seats on the stage. There was an announcement that the Amalgamated Clothing Workers Union had contributed $5,000 and the United Auto Workers $2,500 to the cause. When we took up a collection from the crowd, we received $3,400 in cash and another $3,000 in pledges. When Edward Dudley, a prosperous member of the platform committee who had once worked for the N.A.A.C.P., stood up and pledged $250, the wife of one of our staffers leaned forward and whispered loudly, "Only *former* employees of the N.A.A.C.P. can afford pledges like that."

Madame Pandit introduced Ralph Bunche, who rose to a tremendous ovation and accepted the Spingarn Medal. The police and the Bowl's security men had to politely shove aside nearly a hundred photographers before he could start his speech. When it was over, six husky Los Angeles policemen had to battle their way to his side to protect him from people who wanted to tear at his coat sleeve or touch him on the shoulder or yell something about his school days in Los Angeles.

We had planned for the meeting to be over at 5:30, and it was 5:28 when we sang "God Be with You Till We Meet Again." Afterward Minnie and I spent a few days in Yosemite with some friends, then moved on to Seattle for a branch meeting of the N.A.A.C.P., took the day boat to Vancouver, and came home across Canada through the Canadian Rockies. I was at my desk as scheduled on Monday, August 1, ready for work.

There I had plenty of first-rate help. As the years went by, the N.A.A.C.P. began to attract more and more talented people. In 1949, Mrs. Constance Baker Motley, who later became a federal judge, and Jack Greenberg, a brilliant young white lawyer, both served under Thurgood Marshall. Clarence Mitchell was working for us on labor problems. A year later he went down to Washington and opened the office that served us so well through the big legislative campaigns of the 1950s and 1960s. Walter Reuther, one of the best friends black folks ever had in the labor movement, joined the N.A.A.C.P. board of directors.

A number of pressing issues fell on us in 1949: the omnibus civil rights bill; legislation on lynching, poll taxes, and equal rights in Washington, D.C.; prodding the F.H.A. and the Veterans Administration to accept antisegregation amendments to their programs; fighting restrictive covenants; and expanding health care and social security benefits. There were so many issues that it wasn't easy to decide which should take top priority.

That fall we decided to put F.E.P.C. at the top of the list, and in November, we organized the National Emergency Civil Rights Mobilization. The idea was to assemble all the separate lobbying groups that had an interest in F.E.P.C. and to take on Congress and Harry Truman together. We hoped to build on Phil Randolph's March on Washington idea, adding more troops and a little more lobbying sophistication. The thinking was that if we could revive F.E.P.C. legislation we might get Congress to act on other pressing civil rights bills later. We set January 15 as the date for our campaign.

As January approached I was scared to death that the mobilization wouldn't work. A poor showing would have been worse than a humiliation for the N.A.A.C.P.; it would have encouraged Congress to cling to its do-nothing ways on civil rights. When Minnie and I took the train to Washington, I felt really nervous. We had made reservations at a colored hotel, but when we got into town, what we found was a room with beaverboard walls, dust, and spiderwebs. Minnie took one look and said it was the worst place she had ever seen.

"I'm not going to sleep here, that's all," she said. The way she looked, I knew there was no point in trying to change her mind. She phoned George Johnson, an old friend, who came over and picked her up while I went off to an organizational meeting for the mobilization.

When Minnie reached the Johnson home, she decided to strike a blow for freedom herself. She phoned the Willard Hotel, an old white palace downtown, and asked for a room. She said nothing about color.

"Yes, we've got a double room available," the room clerk told her.

"All right," Minnie said, "I'll be down about ten o'clock, and my husband will be in later."

She went back to the colored hotel and picked up our bags. Then she set off for the Willard, where the room clerk quickly checked her in. He had seen the same thing in her eyes that I had. When I came in later, I broke the Jim Crow line, too. It was the first time either of us had stayed in a white hotel in Washington.

The Willard was one of the first hotels to lift the color bar, and opened to Negroes shortly thereafter, thanks to Mary Church Terrell, a grand old lady in her eighties. She organized pickets all over town and shamed Washington into living up to its responsibilities as a capital for all Americans.

My anxieties over the mobilization turned out to be misplaced. We mustered 4,000 people: delegates from thirty-five states. The Anti-Defamation League of B'nai B'rith sent 350 people; the American Jewish Congress 185; the C.I.O. produced 386 people, and the A.F.L. 119. In all, sixty groups, including unions, trade associations, churches, and race organizations showed up, with the N.A.A.C.P. in the forefront. It was a glorious day. Out of this lobby the Leadership Conference on Civil Rights, a group of organizations, developed. Arnold Aronson was chosen as its secretary and I as its chairman. Arnold is a quiet man, brilliant, humane, and completely dedicated to the idea of a democratic society. Through the years, working with him was always stimulating.

We deployed across Washington, catching congressmen and senators in their offices, buttonholing them in the corridors of the Capitol, pushing F.E.P.C. harder than it had ever been pushed before. There were a few rough patches. At one point Minnie heard one of the N.A.A.C.P.'s brave Southern workers giving a little Southern-fried hell to a white-faced group of politicians. Our man was saying, "I told that Jew this and those niggers that." "My God," Minnie asked the leader of that particular wing of the mobilization, "why didn't you cool him off?"

"We did," the chairman replied. "You should have heard what he was saying *before* we talked to him."

After some sharp needling, President Truman agreed to invite a delegation from the mobilization to the White House. I led the group on my first trip to the Oval Office. I thought I could get action out of the White House simply by the force of good argument. Politics is a little more complicated than that. When we got settled in, I pulled out a statement and began to read it to Truman, who looked at me like a Missouri mule that has just been kicked by a mule skinner.

"You don't need to make that speech to me," he said. "It needs to be made to senators and congressmen."

I was taken aback, but Truman gave ground quickly. He said he knew that if the United States hoped to lay any claim to world leadership it was going to have to pass a more honest program of civil rights, and he promised us that he would keep the feet of Congress to the fire "even if it takes all summer."

After we left the White House, there was a huge press conference. I had never seen such a large, integrated group of reporters. In the middle of the conference, a true believer from *The Daily Worker* stood up and ragged me about why his newspaper hadn't been invited to cover the mobilization. "You know very well why *The Daily Worker* wasn't invited," I told him, and the room broke into laughter.

The next day the newspapers reported that the mobilization had been the largest mass lobby ever to fall upon Washington.

By 1950 the comrades were a problem that the N.A.A.C.P. had to face squarely. At the 1949 convention they had provided the only sour notes, and I had not let them horn in on the mobilization. Part of my reasons were personal—I just didn't like the way Communists did business—but political considerations also dictated that they be shut out. We were having enough trouble getting Congress to consider even the most elementary civil rights legislation; the last thing we needed was to give ammunition to red-baiting Southern congressmen and senators, who would have loved nothing better than to paint us pink. If we had accepted help from the Communists, or had ducked the issue of keeping them out of the mobilization, Gabriel would have blown his horn for a long time before Congress did right by black Americans.

During the mobilization I had laid down a formal statement of policy barring the Communists, and other political groups as well: Young Progressives, Young Republicans, Socialists, Democrats, and the members of the American Labor Party or the Communist Party were not to be given credentials as members of those groups. We wanted a non-partisan, non-left movement. That stopgap approach had gotten us safely through the mobilization, but by the time we reached the N.A.A.C.P.'s own convention in Boston that summer, I knew we would have to get far tougher. In Boston we put forward a motion that condemned attacks by Communists and fellow travelers on the association and its officers, and directed the board of directors to take the necessary steps to eradicate Communist infiltration and, if necessary, to suspend, reorganize, lift the charter of, or expel any branches that came under Communist control. After the delegates passed the resolution by a 6–1 margin, our more radical friends rose in high dudgeon and stormed out of the room.

I was happy to see them go. Ever since the twenties the Communists had been in a lather over ways to seduce Negroes. God knows it was hard enough being black, we certainly didn't need to be red, too. Over the years the comrades tried one group after another: the American Negro Congress, the League of Struggle for Negro Rights, the International Labor Defense, and the National Negro Congress in its later phases. Each time they failed because their positions were self-serving and contradictory. When they concocted the idea of the Black Belt Republic in the Deep South, Doxey Wilkerson warned them that they couldn't put the hammer and sickle in the hand of Jim Crow and expect black people to cry, "Hallelujah!" The deep thinkers ignored Wilkerson—and the Black Belt Republic flopped. Negroes saw through the I.L.D.'s manipulation of the Scottsboro Boys: the Communists wanted to score propaganda points; Negroes wanted the boys to go free. A. Philip Randolph, the most successful black labor leader of the time, had agreed to head the National Negro Congress for a while, but Randolph wound up leaving when the congress degenerated into an expanded radical cell. He warned the delegates exactly what was happening before he stepped down—and was booed for his honesty.

By the time the mobilization and the Boston convention rolled around, the Party knew it had done poorly whenever it tried to go into the race business on its own, so it set out to infiltrate other groups that had a legitimate claim to the hearts and minds of black people. But all along, the comrades made a fundamental mistake: Negroes were oppressed, but they were first and foremost Americans. No amount of Marxist flattery could turn them away from the United States toward the Soviet Union.

As an example, I have often wondered how the Communists ever thought they would crack the black churches. There were 15 million Negroes in the United States in 1950, and of these, nearly 6 million were Baptists. Any comrade who thought he was going to turn those folks away from Jesus and on to Joseph Stalin had to be smoking his own opium. Negroes wanted good jobs and good homes, the opportunity to raise children and educate them, room to love and grow old. These things could all be had if the Constitution was honestly applied. *Das Kapital* didn't have a chance of competing with the Declaration of Independence or the Bill of Rights.

The problem was to get those documents off the supine page and change the laws of the land. Thurgood Marshall led that particular crusade for us. As I look back now, I can still see him scowling over his briefs, smoking too many cigarettes, jamming papers into his briefcase, and dashing out of the office to catch the train for Washington and the Supreme Court. After the N.A.A.C.P. won the Sweatt Case, and Oklahoma admitted Ada Sipuel to its law school, Thurgood kept right on hammering. At the 1951 convention in Atlanta he got together a team of civil rights lawyers and laid plans for the final rush on Jim Crow. The team drew up a campaign aimed at breaking the color line in transportation, employment, places of public recreation and assembly, the last holdouts in the military—and the elementary schools. I could feel momentum building.

You could see small signs of progress everywhere. During the 1951 convention, Ralph Bunche came to Atlanta to speak to us. We were meeting in the Deep South, but the white mayor of Atlanta did his best to make us welcome. He sent a motorcade of police to escort Ralph into town. Ralph couldn't get a room in the city's white hotels, but there he was, roaring into town with all the massed force of the white city fathers in front of him. Later, someone told me he had overheard two black men discussing the motorcade as it passed by.

"Well, will you look at that," said the first man. "That's Dr. Ralph Bunche. He's a big man at the United Nations."

"What about it," said the second. "He gets his hair cut the same place you do."

It was a depressing little story. Where was the praise due Ralph? How could the impulse to strive and rise survive such barbershop bitterness? It was a feeling that had to be resisted, rooted out.

By 1951, Walter had returned from his leave of absence. There was still plenty of lingering anger over what he had done. A faction in the N.A.A.C.P. tried to keep him from coming back, but Eleanor Roosevelt, who had become a powerful board member, did some talking for him and he was accepted once more into the fold.

As Walter's health was still delicate, Thurgood kept up the N.A.A.C.P.'s legal campaign while I kept an eye on the politicians; it was an intelligent, productive division of labor. Every now and then Thurgood would invite me to his strategy sessions.

"Thurgood," I asked him one day, "why do you invite me to these meetings? I'm no lawyer."

"That's true," he said. "But you sure know English."

Whenever Walter was feeling ill, I took over ceremonial assignments and interviews for him. In 1952, I went to Springfield, Illinois, to size up Governor Adlai Stevenson before the election. Averell Harriman was with him the day I arrived, and the three of us sat and talked for two hours. The lessons of 1948 had registered with Stevenson; he knew the importance of the black vote, and he didn't take it for granted. He put his feet up on his desk, sat back, and talked comfortably about black issues. He was more relaxed than Roosevelt, more in tune with racial issues; he was also a good deal more subtle than Harry Truman. "What a President he would make," I told Minnie when I got back home.

Not long afterward, Dwight Eisenhower invited me to have a little talk with him at his suite at the Commodore Hotel in Manhattan. The atmosphere when I walked into his room couldn't have been more different from the one in Springfield. Eisenhower was tense, and sat surrounded by aides. I could see right away that he knew very little about racial matters in the United States, and whenever I asked a question, he turned to the squadron of aides at his side for the answers. He gave me fifteen minutes of his time.

I have to admit I was not eager to see him become President, but only a year later it was Eisenhower who appointed Earl Warren Chief

Justice of the Supreme Court. Warren represented the best strain of California Republicanism. In 1942, when he was running for governor, he had come to an N.A.A.C.P. convention in Los Angeles and made a strong impression on me. Whether Eisenhower knew where Warren stood on race or not, I will never know, but Eisenhower managed through Warren to make history.

May 17, 1954, was the last day the Warren Court handed down decisions that spring. In the New York office it was an ordinary enough day. Thurgood and Bob Carter, one of his assistants, had gone to Washington on the off chance that the Supreme Court might rule on the *Brown vs. Board of Education* school cases. Jack Greenberg was minding the store for him. When Warren handed down the *Brown vs. Board* decision, Thurgood grabbed his hat and bolted from the room. He found a telephone and called Greenberg, who relayed the news to Walter and me just as the switchboard began to light up with calls from everywhere.

After other victories we had broken out a quart of Scotch and celebrated. This time the decision was so overwhelming that for a while we forgot the toasts. We all just sat there looking at one another. The only emotion we felt at that moment was awe—every one of us felt it.

Later in the day Thurgood came back from Washington. I heard a commotion in the corridors outside my office—laughing and cheering—then the door flew open and Thurgood walked in with a grin as wide as Fifth Avenue. He walked right over and kissed me. Later that afternoon we held a press conference, and Walter did the talking while Thurgood sat quietly in the background. I can still see him sitting there, smiling slightly. Plessy-Ferguson was through. An American Joshua in the person of Thurgood Marshall fit the battle of Jericho—and the walls came tumbling down.

18   EXECUTIVE SECRETARY

May 17, 1954, was one of life's sweetest days. We had won a second Emancipation Proclamation. For fifty-eight miserable years—from the day the Supreme Court had handed down Plessy-Ferguson—black Americans could defend themselves with little more than the moral certainty that segregation was wrong. Over those six decades we had preached and persuaded and won converts, but we could not enforce our convictions. Without the law, we were helpless. Plessy-Ferguson had made us subject to the every whim and fancy of whites.

It had been in the South, of course, where those whims and fancies were the most ugly. There we had been squeezed into the hollows, alleys, and back streets across the tracks; there we sat in the back of the bus; there for every white man, no matter how low, who passed by, we had to step off the sidewalk, remove our hat, and say, "Sir." White children had been provided with good schools; our children got shanties. We were robbed of the vote. In war we were called on to serve, then degraded and mistreated even as we fought to defend the same flag that flew over every American. Through all those miseries we had known that moral justice and the country's political principles were on our side. Now the law was on our side, too. The Constitution was behind us. Our children were to have a chance in life without being penalized before they were born.

At the risk of belaboring the obvious, I want to point out that the school cases were a legal victory, a fitting reward for the N.A.A.C.P.'s faith in the basic institutions of the country and for its patient strategy of correcting injustices by taking them to the courts. Within ten years, many impatient folks would find it easy to criticize the N.A.A.C.P. for that very faith. I can still hear their epithets—from "babe in the woods" to "Uncle Tom"—ringing in my ears. No matter what was said later, the real point is that without the N.A.A.C.P. there would have been no fight against lynching, no victory over the white primary, no defeat for restrictive covenants, no triumph over Jim Crow in the military, no liberating action for the schools. The N.A.A.C.P. had been fighting the good fight for a very long time. It cleared the underbrush and opened the way for the civil rights movement in the fifties and sixties. Nat Turner and Mahatma Gandhi may have provided some new models as the years went on, but the N.A.A.C.P. was the granddaddy of us all.

When I got home on Decision Day, I took down a bottle of Scotch and Minnie and I held a small celebration. From where we sat, Thurgood was the hero of the hour, but credit also had to go to a long line of lawyers: to Charlie Houston, William Hastie, Loren Miller, and Robert Carter, black lawyers who had pressed our issues home, and to Moorfield Storey, Clarence Darrow, Nathan Margold, Arthur Garfield Hays, Arthur Spingarn, and Jack Greenberg, white counselors who had stuck by the N.A.A.C.P. over the decades. I still give the greatest credit of all to the N.A.A.C.P.'s branches, the plain folks under fire who had had courage enough to take their grievances to the courts. Because of them, America had turned a corner from partial to full freedom for its black citizens. Just as the country could not exist half-slave and half-free in Lincoln's day, so in Earl Warren's era it would not stand for full citizenship for whites and cut-rate citizenship for blacks.

My sense of euphoria that evening was a bit naïve. Swept away, elevated, exalted, I failed to anticipate the ferocity of the resistance that quickly grew up in the Deep South. As Minnie and I drank to Earl Warren, another fifteen years of tribulation was just beginning.

The N.A.A.C.P. did not become overconfident or lax. Within a week after the Supreme Court's ruling, Thurgood and his legal team were fanning out on six separate fronts: education, employment, health, housing, transportation, and recreation. The immediate problem was to consolidate our gains and to lay plans for the future. To get things organized, Thurgood held a conference of his troops in Atlanta. There was no crowing. Channing Tobias, the chairman of our board of directors, set forth the official posture of the N.A.A.C.P. "It is important," he said, "that calm reasonableness prevail, that the difficulties of adjustment be realized, and that without any sacrifice of basic principles the spirit of give-and-take characterize the discussions. Let it not be said of us that we took advantage of a sweeping victory to drive hard bargains, or to impose unnecessary hardships upon those responsible for the working out of the details of adjustment." The working group reported back to us that it would insist that the Supreme Court's decision be upheld to the letter. Its final report said: "Having canvassed the situation in each of the states, we approach the future with utmost confidence. We look upon this memorable decision not as a victory for Negroes alone, but for the whole American people, and as vindication of America's leadership of the free world."

Light and sweetness. How good they felt at the time—and how misguided they were. At first, Thurgood hoped to have desegregation well underway by September 1955. I believe it was Ralph Bunche who said around this time that the country's prejudice against black people was "more veneer than deep grain"; that "it could be peeled off with little damage or pain." Well, we were all wrong.

Up to the time of the school cases, seventeen Southern and border states and the District of Columbia required segregation in the public schools. Wyoming, Arizona, New Mexico, and Kansas had "permissive" systems allowing Jim Crow to operate but not requiring segregation. Those four states quickly dropped this "permissiveness," turning to sounder virtues. Farther to the South, Delaware, Maryland, West Virginia, and Missouri, along with a few scattered towns of good souls in Texas and Arkansas, were the first to comply with the Court. But the Deep South, led by Virginia and Mississippi, battened down its hatches and shouted, "Never!"

I still remember picking up the newspaper and reading an interview with a fourteen-year-old Dixie belle who said, "I'd rather grow up to be an idiot than go to a school with a nigger in it." Anyone could see that she was well on the way to becoming that idiot; a little integrated schooling might have saved her from her fate. This attitude and stance spoke for a generation of die-hard bigots, young and old.

In Mississippi a similar sense of misplaced outrage would spawn the White Citizens' Councils. Too shrewd for bedsheets and burning crosses, the councils still breathed the spirit of the Ku Klux Klan. One of the council organizers said very early on, "We intend to see that no Negro who believes in equality has a job, gets credit, or is able to exist in our communities." His warning couldn't have been much clearer to black people: Bow your head, get gone—or die.

Starting in Mississippi, the White Citizens' Councils spread like a plague to Alabama, Georgia, and beyond. Negroes who petitioned to get their school boards to desegregate, Negroes who tried to register and vote, Negroes who were members of the N.A.A.C.P. all became the targets of the councils. Farmers who had been friendly to us found that the local bank wouldn't give them crop loans at planting time. Banks suddenly foreclosed mortgages that they had carried for years; stores cut off credit and supplies; landlords jacked up rents;

bosses fired Negroes all over the South for seeking their rights within the new climate that the Supreme Court had created in the country.

I don't want to argue that the South was universally set in the mold of bigotry, but it did cling desperately to segregation. The purpose of segregation had never been to separate the races physically. As W. J. Cash pointed out in his classic study *The Mind of the South,* whites and blacks on the plantations had lived side by side in a relationship that was "nothing less than organic." The real function of segregation was to maintain a caste system under which the hardest-working, most talented, cultured, or prosperous black person was lower in standing than the lowest of whites. The meanest white sharecropper could sit out on his porch scratching his fleas, kicking his dogs, and feeling superior to any Negro down the road. The system made life more tolerable for Southern whites, who have always been given to complaining about the injuries their own excesses have so often heaped upon the region.

The South did have one asset: a vestigial sense of fair play that survived despite everything else. The worst white bigots found themselves up against that sense as surely as they were up against the Court and the N.A.A.C.P. Unfortunately, such voices were not the rule in the days after the *Brown vs. Board* decision as the South confronted the reality of doing without Jim Crow. When public officials did their duty and the press backed them up, integration was able to proceed, slowly, painfully, but forward; where there was wavering or outright hostility, the law of the land did not function.

The quality of the arguments put forth by our opponents was plain awful. Some said that integration would lower the general standard of education, thus conceding what we had argued all along: that while the separate but equal system was undeniably separate, it was in no sense equal. The solution advanced by the diehards was to keep separation. Who could accept that?

More cunning voices contended that Negro teachers would be the first victims of the school cases and wept great crocodile tears over them. I did not share those fears, nor did the majority of Negro teachers. The race had produced thousands of excellent teachers qualified by professional training, experience, temperament, and family background to teach any children in any school anywhere. I suppose, like the white folks, we had some teachers who were incompetent, but as far as I was concerned, they and their white counterparts would be the unmourned casualties of integration.

Hypocrites argued that a minority of Negro children would suffer damage in predominantly white schools; others feared for the whites in predominantly Negro schools. There was an uproar over things like cafeterias, restrooms, playgrounds, and athletics. And the usual morons raised their terrible howl over the threat of intermarriage.

Such fears could not be laughed away; long-standing racial myths and traditions made them too powerful. But I believed they could and would be dealt with and solved as black and white alike went about the business of making the law work. The resisters argued that society could not be changed by a law, which was baloney: obviously Plessy-Ferguson had had a dramatic effect on changing the lives of black Americans. There was no question in my mind that *Brown vs. Board of Education* would also change society—the difference was that this time the change would be for the better.

The hollowest and most maddening argument of all was that black people wanted too much too fast, that they were pushing too hard too soon. This self-serving line had no real basis in fact or history, but everyone from the local school-board president to William Faulkner in the pages of *Life* magazine suddenly started yelling at us, "Go slow!"

What the Go Slowers really meant was "Go nowhere." The truth was that we had been moving very slowly and very patiently for the better part of a century. By 1954, it had been nineteen years since Donald Gaines had sued the University of Maryland Law School to admit him. By the time Texas and Oklahoma came around to desegregating their graduate schools, it should have been obvious that change in the high school and grade schools was coming next. The South knew this very well. How else could one explain the way it scrambled to upgrade black school shanties in the vain hope of heading off pressure to do away with them entirely? By any fair calculation, governors and school boards had had nearly twenty years to see the train coming down the track. It didn't just roll up to them overnight.

Faced with such arguments, I had to work hard to keep my temper. For decades Negroes had been deeply wronged. They had gone to the courts; they had kept faith with the American system; they had been moderate, dignified, and very, *very* patient. Still, the South bleated that we wanted to move too swiftly. And too many white folks said all the N.A.A.C.P. had to do was shut up and leave the working out of the Court's ruling in the hands of the South. It was obvious to me that change had never come in the South without pressure, that delay would only enable the worst bigots to regroup and figure out how to raise even more hell. If black people and the N.A.A.C.P. had gone slowly, the South, quite cheerfully, would have traveled even slower. We didn't want to go too fast; what we were afraid of was standing still. The only way to begin was to begin. The real question was, "Where first?"

That fall, I went to California to attend a conference at Asilomar. Minnie came with me, for we hoped to sneak in a short vacation. She stayed with friends up in Berkeley, and on the last day of the conference they drove down to Monterey to pick me up. The next morning we were back in Berkeley sitting at the breakfast table when the phone rang. Channing Tobias was on the other end of the line.

"It's Walter," he said. "He's as sick as he can be. The office is falling to pieces. Get back here right away."

We took the first train east that afternoon. I wasn't quite sure what to make of the phone call. Perhaps Tobias had been too alarmed, I thought to myself. In Nevada the train made a brief stop. I got off, found a phone, called New York, and raised Thurgood. "How bad is he?" I asked. "It's very bad," Thurgood said quietly. "I'm glad you're coming back."

Walter's heart was acting up on him again. As soon as I returned, it was clear to me that he would not be able to keep pace with the killing grind of running the N.A.A.C.P. The South was buckling up to run us out of existence. Walter didn't want to miss a good fight, but we talked him into taking a long sick leave. He was sixty-one years old, and there was no point in taking any chances.

The leave seemed to pick him up. He spent the early winter resting and gaining strength. Then, early in 1955, he and Poppy took a vacation in the Caribbean. On the afternoon of March 21, he stopped by at the office, back from the white beaches and sunshine, tanned and in good spirits. He spent some time with Tobias, then chatted with me. He told me he was feeling a world better, than headed home. I was relieved to see him looking so bullish. After he left I stayed late at the office straightening up a few administrative tangles. At about seven the telephone rang. Poppy Cannon was calling. "Walter's dead," she said. "Can you come over here right away?"

I put down the phone and stared at it. I could still see Walter walking jauntily out of the office, animated, bustling with plans, full of life. Finally, I called Minnie, telling her I needed some moral support. I grabbed a cab, picked up Minnie, and went to White's town house at 242 East Sixty-eighth Street.

We didn't know what to expect. When we arrived, Poppy opened the door, her eyes red from weeping. She showed us into the living room, and we all stood there a moment looking at one another helplessly, not knowing what to say. Poppy told us what had happened. Walter had collapsed with an acute coronary thrombosis not long after returning from the office. His body was still lying in the bedroom; the undertaker had not yet arrived. Who but Walter would make a point of stopping by the office before going home to die? I thought to myself. After ten or fifteen pained minutes, other friends began to arrive and Minnie and I left. There was nothing we could do.

The funeral took place three days later at St. Martin's Protestant Episcopal Church on Lenox at 122nd Street in Harlem. Channing Tobias delivered a eulogy. From Walter's young days investigating lynching in the South to his missionary work on the Presidents of the United States, his record was one of brave service. Tobias told the story of how he and Walter had sat side by side in the White House briefing Harry Truman on mob violence in Columbia, Tennessee, and how Truman had agreed to do something about it. He also described the visit he and Walter had paid to Eisenhower before Ike set off to keep his "I shall go to Korea" pledge. Eisenhower had let a fifteen-minute appointment run on for an hour; later, one of his first acts as President was to direct the District of Columbia to set an example for the rest of the country in tackling segregation. Walter had had his say in that matter, too. "Looking this way today," Tobias told the mourners, "are sharecroppers of the Deep South who are now privileged to serve their own people as do other people without discrimination, public school teachers whose salaries are no longer determined by the color of their skin, servicemen in every department of our defense forces who have been liberated from Jim Crowism, workers of all kinds who now enjoy union protection, children who have been lifted to a plane of self-respect by the Supreme Court decision in the school cases, and thousands of white people who have been lifted from the blighting evil of race prejudice." Then he read James Weldon Johnson's poem "Lift Every Voice and Sing." The words rolled out across the packed church:

> Sing a song full of faith that the dark past has taught us,
> Sing a song full of the hope that the present has brought us,
> Facing the rising sun of our new day begun,
> Let us march on till the victory is won.

The old words had new power with the Supreme Court's action. Walter had lived to see a second emancipation begin, and now he was gone. In April the board of directors picked me as the N.A.A.C.P.'s new executive secretary.

19 A SMALL CRUMB FROM CONGRESS

It was a wonderful time to lead the N.A.A.C.P.—we had become the oldest, wiliest, and best-organized civil rights group in the country. I had no illusions about my power: the days of Frederick Douglass and Booker T. Washington were gone forever; no one man could lead all black Americans. No one man could even handle all the work around the N.A.A.C.P. The old-fashioned, aristocratic style of James Weldon Johnson and Walter White's one-man band had been effective in their time, but I wanted the N.A.A.C.P. to function as a team, and over the years, it did so wonderfully. Thurgood Marshall ran his legal operation to devastating effect, and Clarence Mitchell became so resourceful around Washington that people started calling him the honorary senator. Gloster Current, our director of branches, was everywhere in those days. I hired John Morsell, a brilliant young sociologist and excellent administrator, who became my assistant. We had brave field people like Medgar Evers and Ruby Hurley down South and talented young men like Franklin Williams out West. Herbert Hill, our labor secretary, grabbed hold of Jim Crow in the A.F.L.–C.I.O. and squeezed so hard you could hear George Meany's splutters all the way to New York. Henry Lee Moon, our publicist, kept the press releases flowing out in a torrent. If I wanted a team, I couldn't have had a better one.

In the weeks after Walter's death, I had plenty of time to map my new line of attack. The main objective seemed obvious to me: the N.A.A.C.P. had to get all three branches of government pulling together for civil rights. The Supreme Court had helped and heartened us, but the Supreme Court could not accomplish everything by itself. Congress and the White House had to come around, too.

How to get them to was the rub. Congress hadn't passed a meaningful piece of civil rights legislation since Reconstruction. In the Senate, the filibuster and the seniority system enabled the South to lynch every civil rights bill that survived the House Rules Committee. At the White House, Dwight Eisenhower was doing as little as he could to help us. President Eisenhower was a fine general and a good, decent man, but if he had fought World War II the way he fought for civil rights, we would all be speaking German today. In the first two years after the Supreme Court ruling in the school cases, he said only a few timid words on behalf of desegregation, and those had to be dragged out of him at a press conference. I felt certain that he could do better. He had to stand up, be President of the United States, use the vast and varied powers of his office to set up and maintain obedience to the Constitution and Supreme Court. Harry Truman had split his party over civil rights—he was courageous. During the 1950s, I could detect no such similar grit around the White House. There was a constant threat that the impetus Truman had given to civil rights would dribble away.

If the President had put his personal prestige and the influence of the White House solidly behind the Supreme Court right after the school-cases decision, it might have been possible to blunt massive resistance more quickly. As it was, the President's early actions were at best equivocations and at worst derelictions. They gave a false sense of legitimacy to obstructionists and nullifiers. I'm sure the President didn't mean to have this effect, but it worked out that way all the same.

There was nothing abstract about the South's hatred for the N.A.A.C.P. at that time. One of our bravest people was the Reverend George W. Lee of Humphreys County, Mississippi. He and a grocer named Gus Courts, who was president of the N.A.A.C.P. branch in Belzoni, Mississippi, managed to talk 400 black people in Humphreys County into registering to vote. The situation in Humphreys County may be judged by some simple math: while there were 16,012 Negroes eligible to register, only those 400, inspired by the Reverend Lee and Courts, dared to try. On the night of May 7, 1955, just a few weeks after I became executive secretary of the N.A.A.C.P., Reverend Lee was walking down Church Street in Belzoni. Some coward with a shotgun shot him down in cold blood.

It was clearly a political assassination, but the local lawmen practically pretended that nothing had happened. A scattering of lead pellets was found in Reverend Lee's mouth. Confronted with them, one local sheriff said placidly, "Maybe they're fillings from his teeth." No one was ever arrested or prosecuted for the murder.

By November, Gus Courts was about the only black man left on the voter registration rolls in Humphreys County; others had dropped off. A landlord tripled the rent on Courts's grocery store. He moved. Then no one would give him credit on goods. Finally, around Thanksgiving time, someone shot Gus, too. Luckily, he survived. I have a picture of him in the hospital, all swathed in bandages, his eyes shut, his hands folded over his chest. A young black man stands next to him, gripping the hospital bed with one hand, jamming his other hand deep into the pocket of his overcoat. The young man in the picture is studying Courts carefully. His brow is wrinkled, his lips tight. It is Medgar Evers, who had become the N.A.A.C.P.'s field secretary in Mississippi. Anyone looking at that photograph could see that he was not a man to be toyed with. And anyone looking at that face should have known that no race that had produced the Reverend Lee, Gus Courts, and Medgar Evers was going to back down before white bigots. Economic blackmail couldn't do the job. Nor could murder.

Several weeks after Reverend Lee's murder the Supreme Court ruled that Jim Crow would have to be liquidated "with all deliberate speed." On the day of the decision, Thurgood grabbed a copy of the ruling and flew back to New York City. That same afternoon we sat down, thrashed over the Court's language, and considered our response to it. What was missing was any fixed deadline for compliance. The Court's strategy was to insist on prompt action and to reaffirm the basic principles it had laid out on May 17, 1954; in effect, substituting positive legal language for a specific date. I was disappointed, but since the decision couldn't be undone, I decided to make the best of it.

We called a press conference, and I said that the N.A.A.C.P. thought the Supreme Court had acted positively. Thurgood then stepped forward to say that his legal team was "ready, willing, and able" to keep the South honest in carrying out the law. At the time, Governor Herman Talmadge of Georgia and his attorney general had promised to buck the Court in every one of Georgia's 159 counties. Thurgood said calmly that if Georgia pursued such a renegade course, he would go into every county in the state to make sure the law was obeyed. As I recall, one of the reporters asked him how long the fight might take if the entire South behaved as Georgia had promised to. Thurgood thought a moment and said, "It will not take one hundred years—*that* I can guarantee."

After the assassination of Reverend Lee and the shooting of Gus Courts that spring, the field reports that reached me during the summer of 1955 were more and more frightening. With the White Citizens' Councils stirring up the whole state of Mississippi and self-appointed race purifiers concocting plots everywhere, it was only a matter of time before someone else was killed. The bloodshed came in Brookhaven, Mississippi, a town in the southern part of the delta, where Lamar Smith, a brave man who had been urging Negroes to use absentee ballots to vote against local white politicians, was shot to death on the courthouse lawn. The murder took place in midday and plenty of white witnesses saw it, but a local grand jury said there was not enough evidence to indict anybody. Two weeks later, Emmet Till, a crippled fourteen-year-old boy from Chicago who was visiting relatives in Money, Mississippi, was kidnapped from his house and lynched at the Tallahatchie River, ostensibly for "wolf-whistling" at a white woman. No one was ever convicted of Till's murder either.

For me massive resistance was no longer a matter of principle, an honest difference of opinion on the meaning of the Constitution and the rights of the several states; it had become a blood issue. As I read the papers, I worried for our people in the South, for Medgar Evers, for Ruby Hurley, for all of them. The Smith and Till murders revolted decent people, shocked the White House, and angered the Justice Department, creating a backlash of sorts against massive resistance. Where there were martyrs there was pressure for change, but what a terrible price it was to pay, what an indictment against the forces of the status quo. If I had known at the time how many more martyrs were to come, I don't know whether I would have had the heart to go on.

The best Southerners were as dismayed as everyone else by what had happened. They did not want to see a renaissance of night riders or the Ku Klux Klan. There was a deep pool of decency within the region, but I was never sure whether the South's best instincts or worst emotions would run the show. White Southerners had a knack of turning aside the real issues of race. First during slavery, then during Reconstruction, they always deflected the simple issue of injustice to Negroes to the more comfortable, but essentially false, issue of whether or not the North was unreasonably pushing the South around. No one would fight quicker than a Southerner at such a provocation, and no one would forget more quickly the suffering of Negroes. I knew that one of the most difficult tasks ahead of me would be to keep the old runaround from taking place all over again.

Until then we had been fighting mostly alone, but some help was on the way. In November 1956, the Interstate Commerce Commission, acting on a suit in which we were the main plaintiff, banned segregation in railroad depots, bus stations, airports, and other places involved in interstate travel. The reaction in some corners of the South was reasonably positive. Even before the end of the year the separate COLORED signs began to come down in waiting rooms. It was a small but very important psychological advance. Where the outer signs of Jim Crow were falling, I felt sure that the deeper constraints Negroes carried within themselves would fall away as well. And when ordinary black people felt confident enough to stand up to Jim Crow, they were sure to bring him down. That is just what happened, a revolution that started in the aisle of a Cleveland Avenue bus, in Montgomery, Alabama.

At that time, about 50,000 black people lived in Montgomery. To understand what took place there, you have to know what went on in the city's buses every day. White Montgomery bus drivers called their black passengers "niggers," "coons," and "apes." Blacks had to pay their fare at the front door of the bus, then trudge around to the back door to get aboard; as often as not, by the time they got there the bus driver would have gunned his motor and pulled away. Only white passengers could sit in the first four rows of seats in the buses, and when that white preserve was filled, Negroes sitting in the rows behind had to give up their seats to any white man or woman who came along. Anyone who refused to do so could be arrested.

The black riders of Montgomery had been enduring such insults for years, but on the afternoon of December 1, 1955, Rosa Parks, a seamstress who had been secretary of the N.A.A.C.P., decided she had had enough. I remember her very well. She was a quiet but spirited and very determined lady who knew how to stand up for her rights. On that particular December afternoon she boarded the Cleveland Avenue bus and took the only open seat immediately behind the seats reserved for white passengers. At the third stop, the bus driver turned around and saw a white man standing in the aisle. Mrs. Parks and three other black passengers were still sitting. The driver told the black passengers to give up their seats, but no one moved. When the driver warned them that they were asking for trouble, three of the four passengers reluctantly stood up. But Mrs. Parks held her ground.

She told us later that after she refused to give up her seat, the driver got off the bus, found two policemen, and came back to scare the daylights out of her. When the two officers asked why she had not moved, she answered that she had paid her fare and was entitled to a seat. The explanation was simple and sound, but it was too much for the law in Montgomery. The police arrested Mrs. Parks and took her to jail, fingerprinting her like a common criminal. They left her in a cell to think things over for a while.

One of the first people to get word of the arrest was E. D. Nixon, an old friend of mine who had served several times as head of the

N.A.A.C.P. in Montgomery, and who had also been an organizer for the Brotherhood of Sleeping Car Porters. He was straight as a ramrod, tough as a mule, and braver than a squad of marines. When he took up the case, the white establishment of Montgomery didn't have a chance.

Mrs. Parks had worked for Nixon. She ran a small office for him, keeping in touch with Alabama's black community and staying close to the city's politics. When the police arrested Mrs. Parks, Nixon told me later, he thought to himself, Jim Crow has put something in my hands.

The first thing he did was rush down to the jailhouse, where a desk sergeant told him to mind his own business. Fred Gray, the attorney who handled most of the N.A.A.C.P.'s business in Montgomery, was out of town, so Nixon enlisted the help of Clifford Durr, a courageous white lawyer, who got Mrs. Parks out of jail. She had used her one call to get in touch with her mother, and her husband arrived on the run just as Nixon and Durr completed the job of bailing her out. As the Parkses drove off, Nixon jumped in his car and followed them home, where he persuaded Mrs. Parks to fight the arrest in court. When he got home himself, he quickly calculated that virtually all the black people in Montgomery could reach their jobs by walking—if they wanted badly enough to stay off the buses.

In that moment, the Montgomery bus boycott was born. Nixon tried the idea on his wife, who pointed out that it was December and cold outdoors, and predicted that people would not walk in such weather. She also laughed and told him that if headaches were on sale he was the sort of man who would march into the drugstore and buy a dozen.

Nixon went ahead anyway. He told me later that under normal circumstances he would have organized the boycott under the auspices of the N.A.A.C.P., but since at the time he did not hold an N.A.A.C.P. office, he had to improvise. He soon discovered the Reverend Martin Luther King, Jr., pushing the Reverend King out of obscurity and to the forefront of the civil rights movement. So Nixon was the true godfather of the boycott; through him all the years of fighting and organizing done by the Brotherhood of Sleeping Car Porters and the N.A.A.C.P. came to fruition in Montgomery.

Nixon had been in touch with the local N.A.A.C.P. president and broached the idea of a bus boycott, but was told that the local branch would have to check first with New York. Nixon was no man to put up with delay. He felt that the time for action would have come and gone long before an exchange of letters with New York could take place.

Thus, Nixon decided on an alternative course of action: he turned to the city's black churches for help. He got on the phone and started calling every minister in town. Reverend King was the third name on his list; he listened politely to Nixon's plan and said, "Brother Nixon, let me think about it for a while." Nixon called a dozen more ministers before ringing Reverend King back. This time Dr. King told him that he was interested in the boycott. "I'm glad to hear you say so," Nixon told him, "because I've talked to eighteen other people and told them to meet in *your* church tonight. It would have been kind of bad to be getting together there without you."

Nixon locked Reverend King into history. Nixon couldn't attend the first meeting at Reverend King's Dexter Avenue Baptist Church because he had to go on a weekend run on the railroad, but he arranged things so no officers would be chosen for the boycott until he got back. He also leaked word of the boycott to the *Montgomery Advertiser*. The newspaper stepped right into his trap, printing a story saying that the city's blacks were going to meet early in the week at the Holt Street Baptist Church to work out the final plans for a bus boycott. That story got the word out to blacks all over town. Nixon returned from his railroad run early on Sunday morning, called his list of ministers, and asked if they had read the newspaper that day—and then he told them to read the story to their congregations from the pulpit. By Monday, everyone in town knew that something big was about to happen.

The ministers met Monday afternoon to organize themselves for the mass meeting that evening. Nixon was sitting in the balcony of the church as the ministers began their deliberations—they were timid and fearful. Nixon sat there listening, feeling more disgusted every minute. Finally, he could stand it no longer. He told me afterward that he decided to take charge himself. "I got so mad, I forgot I was in church and jumped up and told them some things you don't hear in Sunday-school books," he said. "I asked if they were all little boys. Then I called them cowards. Reverend King jumped up and shouted *he* wasn't a coward. And you know, that was the very moment that he got nominated."

In that instant a powerful union of forces took place. The black churches were vitally important in the South, but for decades they had concentrated on otherworldly business. It had been the Brotherhood of Sleeping Car Porters and the N.A.A.C.P. that had spoken out the most boldly and taken the most risks for civil rights down South, and it was the voice of those groups that spoke through Nixon that day. But when Dr. King stepped forward in response to Nixon's taunt, the forces of the older civil rights organization and the great strength and numbers of the black churches finally joined together.

I received my first full field reports from Montgomery two weeks after Mrs. Parks and the people of Montgomery took their stand. W. C. Patton, one of our field secretaries, went to Montgomery and talked to Reverend King, Mrs. Parks, and Fred Gray. He wrote me that the boycott was so successful that the bus company had been forced to discontinue four lines in Negro neighborhoods. Almost no black riders were taking the bus, and the mass meetings in support of the boycott filled the churches to overflowing. Gray had offered to handle the legal work of the protest with the direction of the national legal staff of the N.A.A.C.P.

This was all good news, but it also put me in a difficult bind. In negotiations with the bus company and with Montgomery's city fathers, Dr. King and his people at first demanded only courtesy from white drivers, Negro drivers for Negro neighborhoods, and a first-come–first-served seating formula by which black riders would occupy the seats in the rear of the bus, moving forward as they were filled, while whites would take seats from the front rearward.

I wrote Patton that the N.A.A.C.P. could not enter the case or use its legal staff to support such a mild protest. The Montgomery Improvement Association seemed to be talking about improving segregation, making it more polite. The N.A.A.C.P. wanted to knock it out completely. At the time, we had a similar bus case in appeal in South Carolina. With our national program calling for the complete abolition of segregation, and with our lawyers arguing the South Carolina appeal on that basis, we could not go to Montgomery simply to ask Jim Crow to have better manners.

No matter how moderate the Montgomery Improvement Association's demands were, the whites in town failed to understand them. They responded with a crackdown. It began with minor harassments like a flood of traffic tickets and nuisance arrests. Those tactics didn't sway the Negroes of the city, so the White Citizens' Councils began to go to work. At the end of January bombs went off at the homes of Nixon and Reverend King. Fred Gray faced an indictment and the threat of disbarment for his work; then his draft board classified him 1-A, taking away his deferment as a part-time minister. When all of that was not enough to defeat the boycott, the police contrived to arrest nearly a hundred of the city's black leaders for supporting it.

I have seldom seen Thurgood Marshall so angry. He told me he had never encountered a more obvious case of white bigots using the machinery of the law to oppress a lawful enterprise organized by American citizens. The N.A.A.C.P. agreed to defend all the people the city had rounded up, and as the months passed by, N.A.A.C.P. branches around the country also contributed tens of thousands of dollars to the cause. In Washington, Clarence Mitchell intervened with General Louis Hershey of the Selective Service to overrule the punitive draft board action against Gray. The board had argued that since Gray was only a part-time minister, he was not entitled to the same deferment given full-time ministers. General Hershey knew the real score. He observed that Christ himself had been a full-time carpenter and a part-time minister—and gave Gray back his deferment.

The initial skepticism I had felt about the Montgomery Improvement Association gave way to real pleasure at its work. One of Reverend King's favorite stories was about a very old woman he met one day trudging to work with the younger protestors. He saw that she was footsore and weary, and out of compassion, he told her that no one would hold it against her if she rode the bus. She told him that her feet might be sore but that her soul was rested—and she meant to have freedom. It took nearly a year for the courts to rule in favor of the Montgomery Improvement Association, but those people would have kept walking if the case had run for ten years.

I knew that the Montgomery bus boycott had put all Alabama off balance. The state was eager to settle scores, and at the University of Alabama, the white extremists got their chance. Barely a week after the dynamite bombs went off at the houses of Dr. King and E. D. Nixon, Autherine Lucy appeared on campus to register for the spring term. The low way Alabama treated her rankles me to this day. All Lucy wanted was to become a fully qualified librarian, but the university had spent four years in the courts trying to thwart that modest goal. Earlier court rulings in the Texas and Oklahoma cases were clearly on her side, but after *Brown vs. Board of Education,* the University of Alabama resolved to keep itself white no matter what the cost.

Autherine Lucy was the one who had to pay the penalty. The day she arrived on campus, a mob of young white thugs pelted her with rocks and eggs. She found refuge in a classroom, her heart pounding, the crowd outside shouting, "Kill her, kill her." The university did not disperse the mob or punish its members. Instead, its board of trustees blamed Autherine Lucy for the trouble and suspended her.

I asked Herbert Brownell, Eisenhower's Attorney General, to help. He did what he could, but as usual, our best friends were the federal courts. Three weeks after the incident a Federal District Court judge in Birmingham ordered Lucy reinstated, but within a few hours the university permanently expelled her, arguing that she had treated the trustees with disrespect. Thurgood and Constance Baker Motley flew to Alabama and brought the crushed student back with them.

White Alabama leveled lie after lie at Lucy and the N.A.A.C.P. Some said we had recruited her for a cynical campaign to crack the color line at the university. In truth, the university had admitted her in 1952, the dean of women sent her a welcoming letter, and only after she tried to register and school officials took note of her complexion had she been rejected. Other people said she was too old to be a real student, ignoring the fact that she had been kept out of the school for four years by the university's illegal obstruction. Still others called her pushy. They sneered that she had worn matronly clothes, not bobby sox, to school and complained that she had arrived in a Cadillac. The facts were that she had been escorted to the front of the registration line for her own protection; that she was a dignified young woman, a former member of an N.A.A.C.P. youth chapter, no bobby soxer; and that friends drove her to school. What possible difference could it have made what car she arrived in?

The point was that since the Texas and Oklahoma court cases, Negro students had safely entered graduate schools in Tennessee, Kentucky, Missouri, North Carolina, Virginia, Delaware, Arkansas, Oklahoma, and Texas, all states that had once had laws enforcing segregation. In no sense could Autherine Lucy have been considered a "test case" in the South. All she and the N.A.A.C.P. were seeking was to get Alabama to match what other Southern states had already done. The real test at hand was far different: how far could Alabama go in flouting the law?

When Autherine Lucy came to New York, we held a press conference for her. She sat before the microphones and TV lights, wearing a plain, light-colored dress; her hair was neatly parted on one side, and she clutched her arms tightly as she spoke. She said she had been completely disheartened by what had happened to her, but that there was nothing Alabama could do to check her faith in the ultimate justice of democracy. "I shall maintain my faith in my country," she told everyone. If I had been a white Southerner that day, my face would have burned with shame.

One of the things that angered me most about the Lucy case was that so many who should have known better used it as an excuse for telling the N.A.A.C.P. to slow down. A few weeks after the violence on the campus of the University of Alabama, William Faulkner wrote in Life magazine: "Go slow now. Stop now for a time," he warned us. "You have shown the Southerner what you can do and what you will do if necessary. Give him a space to get his breath . . . to look about and see that (1) Nobody is going to force integration on him from the outside; (2) That he himself faces an obsolescence in his own land which only he can cure." Faulkner had worked himself into a righteous frenzy over the safety of Autherine Lucy, but later in the year admitted that if he had been born a Negro, he would probably have joined the N.A.A.C.P. himself.

More infuriating was the way so many whites in the North accepted the propaganda. Many of those people swallowed Faulkner's line whole. We were inundated with clippings from the editorial pages of ostensibly liberal Northern newspapers endorsing the go-slow line. Our staff members returned from speaking tours to report that they had been bombarded with questions about the "speed" of our operations. Both in Congress and in the major political parties—and among many liberals outside the political arena—the record usually could be summed up in one phrase: "We have met the enemy—and we are theirs."

In that particular election year, even Adlai Stevenson, a sincere liberal and rationalist, was not immune to such pressures. Two days after Autherine Lucy was mobbed in Tuscaloosa, I picked up my copy of *The New York Times* to read that Stevenson had given a speech before a Negro audience in Los Angeles that all but capitulated to the go-slow boys. The story reported that Stevenson had "emphasized a view that only 'gradual' means would satisfactorily settle the school crisis and other problems affecting equal rights for all Americans."

Was this the same Stevenson who had put his feet up and talked so affably with me about race and politics only four years earlier? If the White House was determined to dawdle on desegregation and if Stevenson promised to do no better, then Negroes were in a real fix. I sat down and wrote Stevenson one of the angriest letters of my life; three pages, single-spaced. I meant to draw a few points for him as plainly as I could. Among them was that to Negro Americans "gradual" meant no progress at all, or progress so slow as to be barely perceptible. It meant progress at the whim and pace decreed by whites without consultation with Negroes. It meant progress without relation to laws or the Constitution or the interpretation of the courts. And to vast numbers of Southerners, gradual meant never at all. "They don't mean go slow," Thurgood used to say. "They mean don't go."

The South and the North suddenly seemed to be filled with disciples of gradualism. None were willing to establish a timetable for doing away with segregation; no two-, five-, or even ten-year plans were offered. No concrete goals were set, no standards outlined, no rewards posted. Gradualism meant whimsical, spotty, paternalistic gifts ladled out now and then by the master to the peasant. Every improvement in the status of the Negro as a citizen had resulted from outside pressure, and at every step the white Southerner had shouted, "Too fast." Until those same white Southerners began to move under their own steam to solve their own racial problems—in a manner acceptable to both races—they could expect outside pressure. I certainly meant to keep it on, and even increase it, however I could.

If Adlai Stevenson fell in with the gradualists, I asked myself, how many more liberals would he draw with him? The danger had to be faced squarely, so I told Stevenson that when he lectured a Negro audience to be patient and to abide by a gradual approach to Negro problems nearly two years after *Brown vs. Board of Education,* he was scraping a raw nerve. It was like asking the peoples in the satellite countries behind the Iron Curtain to accept gradualism in their struggle for liberation. In the minds of every Negro in that audience were the murder of Emmet Till and the bloody suppression of the Negro vote in Mississippi, the cowardly economic pressures and vicious racial propaganda of the White Citizens' Councils, the savage attacks upon Negroes by Southern politicians like Senator James O. Eastland, the open defiance of the government and the U.S. Supreme Court by Southern legislatures and state officials out to intimidate Negro citizens and to sink the Bill of Rights. That audience was also thinking of the terrible scene at the University of Alabama, where a thousand young white men had thrown rocks and eggs at a lone Negro woman, threatening to kill her for daring to become a librarian.

Whether he meant to or not, Stevenson had told those Negroes that if he were President he would allow states that had been stealing their rights for scores of years to continue doing so without interference on the part of the federal government. The real question before liberals and everyone else was not how fast we were going but whether the federal law was supreme or not.

Five days passed before I received a telegram from a wounded Stevenson. He told me that he was surprised that anything he could say on civil rights could still be news, and he said he had been disturbed by my letter because it had distorted his public statements on the issue. Then he trotted out the very arguments I had attacked him for. He told me as politely as he could that he believed the question before us was not what the country was trying to accomplish in civil rights but how it was going about it, that the solution would require time, and that he opposed cutting off federal aid to segregated schools. I remember in particular one line in that telegram: "We must recognize that it is reason alone that will determine our rate of progress." Olympian liberalism, so far above the fray, so fatuous. It was political pressure, pushing and shoving, that was going to determine the rate of progress. Reason alone was the last thing we could count on to do the job. Stevenson also told me that he still thought it would be possible to keep civil rights out of the presidential campaign in 1956. As much as I liked him, I couldn't let him get away with it.

I apparently struck a liberal nerve in taking Stevenson to task. Shortly afterward Eleanor Roosevelt, one of Stevenson's staunchest backers, wrote Channing Tobias that I was setting a reckless political course and hinting that she might have to resign from the board of directors of the N.A.A.C.P. Although she pleaded as her reason that she was not able to attend regular meetings, the real thrust of her letter was lost on no one around the office. After Tobias told me about the letter, I asked her if we could get together. I laid before her the same argument I had put before Stevenson, and I managed to talk her out of resigning.

Stevenson soon began to talk straighter, pressing the idea that the President had a responsibility, if not to solve the race problem, at least to insist on action toward solutions, but for years afterward, he never quite forgave me.

It took constant lobbying to keep the Democrats and the Republicans from sweeping civil rights under the carpet in 1956. To make sure that the issue was aired fully, the N.A.A.C.P. helped sponsor a second great visitation on Washington. The idea was to repeat the mass mobilization that had worked so well a few years earlier. In all, we got about 2,000 people from fifty-two national religious, labor, fraternal, and veterans groups together for what we called a National Delegate Assembly for Civil Rights. With those members, the House and Senate could not ignore us.

There were times in those days when going to Washington felt like slipping into a Ku Klux Klan rally. The week before we met, Senator Harley M. Kilgore, a decent Democrat from West Virginia, died, and Senator James O. Eastland of Mississippi, an altogether different kind of politician, assumed the chairmanship of the Senate Judiciary Committee. Senator Eastland was no friend of the N.A.A.C.P. Over the years he had said in the South and on the floor of Congress that the Fourteenth Amendment "was fraudulently procured and illegal"; that the Supreme Court had been "indoctrinated and brainwashed by left-wing pressure groups"; that "the Negro race is an inferior race." His philosophy was rooted in the promise "We will protect and maintain white supremacy throughout eternity." That such views could hold sway in the Senate's highest committee on justice is one measure of what the N.A.A.C.P. was up against.

At the beginning of March, the National Delegate Assembly for Civil Rights descended on Washington. We stayed at the Willard Hotel down Pennsylvania Avenue from the White House, and our first meeting took place at the Metropolitan Baptist Church. I told the delegates that evening that Congress had sold civil rights legislation down the river time and time again, and that the sellout had to stop. We had had hearing after hearing, promise after promise—the time had come for action, and the responsibility for that action lay squarely with the Congress of the United States. Everyone nodded in agreement, but they got up and cheered when Clarence Mitchell took the podium. He told them that Senator Eastland was a stinking albatross around the neck of the Democratic Party—and that the Democrats might just have to kiss our votes goodbye come November.

Clarence had been doing some work on the Republicans, and they had come up with one enticement in 1956 that went beyond anything the Democratic Party had to offer—a civil rights bill. The legislation was in part the result of Clarence Mitchell's efforts to convert the Justice Department to the cause of civil rights. He began by making obvious all the machinations the South was using to subvert the right to vote, a basic right of all Americans. One of his favorite examples was a case in Deep Dixie where a voter registrar had refused to enroll a black voter who couldn't answer the question "How many bubbles are there in a cake of soap?"

Clarence enlisted the help of Attorney General Herbert Brownell, one of the more enlightened men in the Eisenhower Administration, and the Justice Department and White House together came up with a package of civil rights proposals. The Justice Department would ask Congress to authorize a new assistant attorney general to deal with civil rights violations, the White House would name a bipartisan commission to look into flagrant abuses of civil rights, and Congress would be urged to strengthen the United States Code to punish anyone intimidating voters.

These were the ideas from which the 1957 Civil Rights Act later grew. I thought they were modest in the extreme, and that the White House should use its full powers to curb civil rights abuses. The President, for example, could have withheld federal funds from states defying the Supreme Court. The delegate assembly in Washington put together an eight-point program improving on the Administration's civil rights package. We called for equality in employment, a real

F.E.P.C., abolishing the poll tax, protecting the right to vote, establishing a civil rights division within the Justice Department—with genuine authority to protect civil rights in all sections of the country—setting up a federal commission on civil rights, eliminating segregation in interstate travel, and changing the rules that gave the House Rules Committee and Southern Democrats in the Senate the power to choke off meaningful civil rights legislation.

Our strategy was to emphasize laws protecting individuals against violence. The delegates spent their time cornering representatives and senators on behalf of our program, and Congress responded warily. In the following weeks, the House did pass a civil rights bill embodying most of Eisenhower's proposals, but the Senate waited until almost the end of its session before scheduling hearings on the measure. As had happened so often before, the bill died without a whimper when Congress adjourned for the election season.

Keeping faith with the democratic process in light of such constant reversals was difficult. I had to tell myself a dozen times a week to stay calm and keep on plugging. Some days it seemed as if talking was all we could do. At the end of May, we got together with the Brotherhood of Sleeping Car Porters, the A.F.L.–C.I.O., and some church groups for a civil rights rally in Madison Square Garden. There were 16,000 people in the Garden that evening, and on the platform, Eleanor Roosevelt, A. Philip Randolph, and Tallulah Bankhead sat side by side with Reverend King, Adam Clayton Powell, Jr., and E. D. Nixon. Mrs. Roosevelt stood and said New Yorkers as well as Southerners had a race problem, and they could start solving it by integrating housing in the city. Miss Bankhead, who was born in Alabama, told the crowd that "bigoted, stupid people who had outraged democracy" had made the rally necessary. And Adam Powell said the Eisenhower Administration was doing all it could to nullify the Supreme Court and put Jim Crow back between the people and equality. That was probably laying it on a little thick, but there were dozens of things President Eisenhower could have done short of using federal troops to enforce the Supreme Court's ruling. As it was, he hadn't even called a conference to discuss the possibilities.

That spring President Eisenhower had managed to goad me beyond what patience could bear over the National Reserve Training Program Bill, a piece of legislation aimed at building up the National Guard. Coming so soon after the Korean War, the bill looked like a sensible national security project that permitted young men to satisfy their military obligation by serving in state guard units instead of the army's regular reserve units. The difficulty was that since the National Guard remained under the command of state governors, it had also remained segregated in the Deep South. To attack this flaw, Adam Powell had introduced an amendment in the House of Representatives requiring the desegregation of the guard. The amendment got further than anyone thought possible, and the Southern Democrats threatened to kill the entire bill.

President Eisenhower was outraged. I think what galled him more than any threat to the national security was Adam's effrontery. Adam was the best weapon we had in Congress in those days, our Great Amender. Since his constituents returned him to Congress year after year, the seniority system had pushed him upward as surely as any Southern Democrat. From his vantage, he fixed desegregation riders to every piece of legislation he could get his hands on.

The South usually managed to gang up on Adam's amendments, but somehow the National Guard amendment slipped by them. I believe President Eisenhower's response was, "This is not the place to have any extraneous legislation." It was hardly extraneous to try to desegregate the National Guard, since Jim Crow had already been banned in the regular armed forces, but the President's complaint encouraged segregationists and much of the press to attack Adam and the N.A.A.C.P. for backing him up.

I did not intend to start out as executive secretary of the N.A.A.C.P. by knuckling under to that kind of pressure. I informed the President that I didn't relish having my patriotism called into question in this way. Black people loved their country, had fought for it, and would do so again, but we would not be insulted simply for seeking to bring the National Guard into the modern world. In the end, Congress disposed of Adam's amendment, and for a time the guard went on white, but President Eisenhower knew that raising his voice would not intimidate the N.A.A.C.P.

The last speaker in Madison Square Garden that night was E. D. Nixon. He told me later that he had been sitting on the edge of his seat for so long that he was all but numb, and didn't think anyone would pay much attention to him after so many celebrities. It was shortly before midnight when Nixon stood up and said, "I'm E. D. Nixon from Montgomery, Alabama, a city that is known as the Cradle of the Confederacy and the city that stood still for more than ninety-three years until Rosa Parks was arrested and thrown in jail like a common criminal, and 50,000 Negroes rose up and caught hold of the cradle and began to rock it till the Jim Crow rocker began to reel and the segregated slats began to fall. I'm from *that* city." People began to shout and yell and thump one another on the back, and the Garden resonated with enough joy and hope to keep all of us going for months afterward.

Ironically, the Montgomery bus boycott, which did so much to sustain all of us in those years, also became a source of friction over strategy and tactics. Dr. King and his foot soldiers showed the great possibilities of direct action and nonviolent resistance in fighting Jim Crow. The common people of Montgomery marched to freedom innocent of what E. D. Nixon, the Brotherhood of Sleeping Car Porters, and the N.A.A.C.P. had done to break ground for them. The legal battle would have been won in the courts without a day's marching, but the marching offered another kind of victory. In its steadfastness, in its solidarity, in its soul power, the Montgomery bus boycott provided an inspiring model. The way ordinary black people had risen behind Reverend King no longer let Southern whites who "knew their Negroes" get away with the old lie that everything would be all right if outside agitators would just mind their own business.

There were, however, limitations to what the tactics of Montgomery could achieve. My own view was that the particular form of direct action used in Montgomery was effective only for certain kinds of local problems and could not be applied safely on a national scale. Although there was a great deal of excited talk about adapting the tactics of Gandhi to the South, the fact remained that the America of the Eisenhower era and the Silent Generation was not the India of Gandhi and the Salt March. When Gandhi led his people against the British, Indians made up the vast majority of the population; noncooperation could wreck a national economy. Such tactics could work in the South, but only in cities like Montgomery, where Negroes were in the majority or in sufficient numbers to make their weight felt. In San Francisco that summer, for example, the city's black population tried to organize a boycott against the Yellow Cab Company, which refused to hire Negro drivers. Everyone's heart was in the right place, but the blacks of San Francisco could not accomplish what their brothers and sisters in Montgomery had. When one subtracted from their total numbers those who drove their own automobiles, the boycotting group was of such small proportions that the cab company could safely ignore it. The danger I feared was that the Montgomery model would lead to a string of unsuccessful boycotts where conditions were not so favorable at a time when defeats could only encourage white supremacists to fight all the harder.

During the summer of 1956, we took up this problem at the N.A.A.C.P.'s forty-seventh annual convention. The delegates voted to broaden the N.A.A.C.P.'s program by all lawful means and to recommend that the board of directors give careful consideration to the Montgomery model. I remained convinced that the best division of labor was for us to support Reverend King and direct action down South while devoting our own resources to keeping the White House and Congress honest on desegregation. The benefits of what we could attain through our legal campaign in the courts and our lobbying with the executive and legislative branches would ultimately come down to Negroes in the South and the rest of the country. Reverend King could do his work, we could do ours, and all black Americans would be better off for it. Some folks, however, were so overwhelmed by Montgomery that they didn't see the subtle problems lying behind the model. They criticized us loudly for not hopping aboard the Montgomery bandwagon then and there, and the seeds for harmful future rivalry were planted.

Even so, I have a fond spot in my memory for that convention: it was my twenty-fifth anniversary with the N.A.A.C.P. The delegates gave me a silver bowl, which I still have on a sideboard just beyond my dining table. At the closing meeting that year, I outlined for the delegates the campaign that lay ahead of us. Both political parties had been so busy scratching each other's back that year that Negroes had been left out in the cold. In a few weeks the bands would begin playing and the speeches would begin ringing out, but I didn't want the noise to impress us. I expected each of the two political parties to advance far beyond its 1952 platform on civil rights. It would not be enough for Republicans or Democrats to state that the Supreme Court had spoken, that its decision was the law of the land. There had to be action. They had to pledge to ensure that the Court's decision was made effective, that *prompt* beginnings were made toward school desegregation where the South was in rebellion. We were tired of crawling forward only to have people yell that we were going too fast. We were sick to death of it, and we weren't going to settle for it anymore.

I had hoped to spend the early part of 1956 thinking through a new approach to the South, but events did not allow for such leisurely plotting. Those who opposed integration had been doing their own calculating, and soon they were attacking the N.A.A.C.P. on every side. The first serious battle came in Louisiana, where local lawmen poking through their legal codes came up with an old law requiring activist organizations to file membership lists with the state. They informed us that we had to comply with the law. The insult atop the injury was that the law had been aimed originally at the Ku Klux Klan. I had seen what ruin the White Citizens' Councils could heap upon N.A.A.C.P. members whose names got in the papers, and I would not expose every N.A.A.C.P. member in Louisiana to such extortion. When we refused to hand over our membership lists, Louisiana applied for and got an injunction that prevented us from holding any meetings in the state. While we fought the injunction on appeal, we had no choice but to comply with it. In no time at all, we were effectively out of business in Louisiana.

Alabama struck next. A circuit court judge granted the state a restraining order that prohibited us from organizing any new branches or maintaining an office in the state or from raising funds or collecting membership dues. The state's attorney general also warned us that we had violated laws requiring us to register with Alabama. We explored the possibility of complying, only to be told that we would not be allowed to proceed. Alabama obtained a court order requiring us to submit all our records, including membership lists. When we refused to submit the lists, the court found us guilty of contempt and fined us $100,000. We had to fight the contempt citation all the way to the Supreme Court before it was overturned. In the meantime, we could not operate openly in Alabama or Louisiana, and you could hear the White Citizens' Councils from Baton Rouge to Birmingham cheering.

My ears were still ringing with those setbacks as the political conventions approached. The Democrats met in Chicago that year, the Republicans in San Francisco. A week before the Democratic National Convention, Lawrence Spivak of NBC invited me to appear on *Meet the Press*. I was the first black leader to appear on the network, and I looked forward eagerly to the broadcast. On the morning of the program, I settled into my chair and squinted through the bright lights at the news panel that was there to interrogate me. What I got was a home-fried going-over. The first question was why the N.A.A.C.P., an organization that had been around for nearly fifty years, had never received much attention until the Supreme Court ruling on segregation in the schools. The snide intent of the question, I suppose, was to make us out as a band of latter-day *agents provocateurs*. Thomas Waring of the Charleston, South Carolina, *News and Courier* then asked whether the N.A.A.C.P. was out to sacrifice the old reservoir of goodwill between white and black folks in the South by "forcing association" against the will of the whites. Spivak asked if I hadn't been unfair in saying that both political parties had left the Negro out in the cold. And so it went.

The line of questioning reflected the terrible ignorance of the press, which was simply revealing its own stupidity to the public. It was not difficult to refute such rhetorical inquiries—the fact and merits of civil rights were all on my side—but I felt irritated as I left the studio that day.

My irritation lifted in the weeks following as hundreds of letters came in from all around the country criticizing the level of the questions I had faced. Later that summer I was vacationing in Grand Teton National Park when a man and woman from San Bernardino, California, stopped me and insisted that I use their car for a tour of Jackson Hole and a side trip to Yellowstone. They made the offer, they said, solely because they liked what they had seen on *Meet the Press*. I remember thinking that as an old newspaperman I might have looked down on television for too long and that I would do well to make better use of the medium in the future. As the years went by, with relentless focus television was to show the ugly face of Jim Crow to the rest of the country and the world. It was a wonderful new ally until it turned on us so abruptly during the urban riots of the mid-1960s.

The *Meet the Press* interview provided a good warm-up for the political conventions. In Chicago, the strategy of the Southern Democrats was to hold out against any mention of the Supreme Court ruling or against any plank committing the Democratic Party to action on civil rights. By taking such an extreme position, the South could then give in a little and make a passing reference to the Supreme Court, while holding to the objective of barring any promises of enforcing the Court's decision.

In reply, I had a six-point plank ready for the platform committee. It called for ending racial segregation by pledging the federal government to act specifically to implement the Supreme Court's ruling, to strengthen federal civil rights laws and increase the enforcement capabilities of the Justice Department, and to see some protection for the right to vote, fair employment practices legislation, and new rules in the House and Senate against the filibuster and other forms of parliamentary obstructionism.

It was a long list. On the morning of my appearance before the platform committee, I pondered how best to dramatize my case. As I was shaving, I got an idea. I reached down, picked up a small bar of hotel soap lying on the washbasin, and slipped it into my pocket. During my presentation to the platform committee, I stopped, reached into my pocket, and pulled out the soap. "I have here a small bar of soap borrowed from a Chicago hotel," I told the startled committee members, asking *them* to answer how many bubbles were in it, as the Southern registrar had done down South. They got the point. I kept that little bar of soap and took it to San Francisco to use on the Republicans.

I wish I could say that I converted both parties, but both refused to be budged. Not only did the Democratic platform avoid any promise to enforce the Supreme Court's desegregation orders, it also managed to refer to the Court's action as "part" of the law of the land, an infuriating concession to the South. Although the Republicans met a week after the Democrats and had a chance to improve on the Democratic platform, they lost the opportunity. They did manage to say that the G.O.P. would "accept" and "concur" in the Supreme Court's action, but the plank also said that school desegregation would have to be accomplished "progressively," an endorsement of gradualism. The Republicans promised to reintroduce the Eisenhower Administration's civil rights bill again in the 85th Congress, but since they made no effort to strike out Rule 22 in the Senate, the President's bill was left to the mercy of the filibuster.

On balance, the Republican platform was a shade better than that of the Democrats—but only a thin shade. For my money, both parties gave the Negro the royal runaround on civil rights. The Democratic plank smelled to heaven; the Republican plank just smelled. If the final judgment were to have been made on those two planks alone, black voters would all have done better going fishing that November.

I didn't get much time to brood over the disgust I felt after the conventions. In September, the Virginia state assembly held a special session and passed no less than seven separate laws against the N.A.A.C.P. We were prohibited from soliciting funds to defray the cost of litigation in antidiscrimination cases, barred from advocating desegregation of the public schools in compliance with the Supreme Court, and threatened with barratry suits. Other statutes restrained organizations from encouraging citizens to seek their rights, forbade us to give financial help to anyone involved in lawsuits against the State of Virginia, and required that we post our membership lists in public. The intent of this legislation was clear: to destroy the N.A.A.C.P. in Virginia.

No sooner did Virginia craft its laws than Texas jumped into the fray. With no warning, the state's attorney general appeared at our office in Dallas demanding to inspect documents and records. Not long after that, an assistant attorney general from Texas turned up in New York City on the same errand. After we refused to disclose our membership lists, those gentlemen obtained an injunction charging us with violating laws governing corporations in Texas and banning us from operating there.

Thurgood and I flew to Tyler, Texas, to fight the injunction. At the injunction hearings, the attorney general produced 493 exhibits, ranging from letters, memoranda, financial statements, and canceled checks to branch minutes, constitutions, and bylaws, which were supposed to convict us as an outlaw organization. We told the judge that many of the exhibits had been collected through intimidation, and several assistant attorneys admitted that when they had interrogated our branch members, they had taken armed Texas Rangers or state highway patrolmen with them. One local N.A.A.C.P. official testified that he had not been permitted to drive his own car from home to the place where the branch records were kept, but instead was forced to ride in a police car. Other squads had rounded up schoolchildren and their parents, forcing them to appear before a justice of the peace who was supposed to be conducting "a court of inquiry." The obvious purpose of the strong-arm tactics was to intimidate the victims into denying that they had authorized school suits in segregated school districts. Predictably enough, we lost the argument. Texas had thrown a rope around us.

Shortly thereafter, Georgia accused us of failing to pay proper taxes—even though we were a tax-exempt organization—and dragged us into court. Eventually we were able to cut through all these legal entanglements, but the fight took time, money, and energy that might otherwise have gone into more fruitful enterprises. In one sense, however, the harassment was rather flattering: it showed how pervasive our influence was—and how desperate the South was to stamp us out.

The results of the election that November didn't surprise me. Negro voters in the South, who in 1952 had voted more strongly for Stevenson than Negro voters elsewhere in the nation had done, switched sharply toward the Republicans, more sharply than Northern Negro voters. Resentment against the pernicious role of Southern Democrats in hamstringing all civil rights legislation was one of the main reasons for the switch. We were stuck with President Eisenhower for another term, but I thought it was just possible that when the new Congress convened in January we might have our best chance in years of passing a civil rights bill.

As always, the main obstacle was the Senate filibuster, but toward the end of November I received an encouraging letter from Hubert Humphrey. "The filibuster is an undemocratic practice unworthy of our traditions of constitutional government," he wrote, saying that he and other Senate liberals were studying ideas for changing the rule. On this matter, Humphrey was always with us. He knew as well as I that unrestricted debate in the Senate was never employed as a means of ensuring adequate discussion of vital issues. It was simply a means of giving a minority power to dictate to the majority. In theory, such a device could be beneficial against tyrannical majorities, but the irony was that this so-called protection of the minority was almost invariably invoked as a means of preventing the Senate from enacting legislation to protect the nation's most persistently abused minority.

Under the rules of the Senate, a filibuster could be closed only by a vote of two-thirds of the membership—sixty-four senators. There was no provision for closing debate on a change in the rules, so a filibuster in that quarter could go on forever. All we had to work with was one small loophole. On the opening day of Congress, business proceeded under ordinary parliamentary rules and a motion to alter the Senate's standing rules could be passed by a simple majority. Any attempt to filibuster at that point could be squelched simply by moving the previous question and securing a majority vote for the motion. Thus, the only chance we had to get rid of the filibuster was on the first day of Congress. We had tried for years to pull off this parliamentary maneuver, and at the opening of the new Congress we tried once again. We lost, but we managed to get thirty-eight senators to support us, far more than had ever backed us before. As things turned out, this show of strength helped considerably to move things along. All through the next eight months, the most important figure in the struggle for the 1957 Civil Rights Bill was Lyndon Baines Johnson, the old Br'er Fox of the Senate—and the most capable politician I have ever met. In those days, Johnson was just beginning to get religion on civil rights. The historical, irreversible impact of the Supreme Court's ruling in *Brown vs. Board* was not lost on him, and he had noticed the drift of Negro voters away from the Democratic Party in the 1954 and 1956 elections. He dreamed of becoming President himself, and knew that so long as he had Jim Crow wrapped around him, the rest of the country would see him only as a Southerner, a corn-pone Southerner at that, rather than a man of national stature. So around 1957 he began to change his course on civil rights.

With Johnson, you never quite knew if he was out to lift your heart or your wallet. In 1957, the House once again passed its Civil Rights Bill and sent it to the Senate. The bill had four titles: the first set up a commission on civil rights, the second established a civil rights division under an assistant attorney general in the Justice Department, the third gave the Attorney General power to correct abuses of any constitutional rights, and the fourth specifically protected voting rights.

We had a number of meetings with Johnson during the spring and early summer of that year. He told us frankly that all he cared about was voting rights, that the bill couldn't pass with Title III, and that he was going to take it out. Title III allowed the Attorney General to bring suit on a wide variety of civil rights violations, including segregation of schools. Thus he could put the force of the Justice Department behind the Supreme Court decision—and that was too much for Dixie.

Johnson did want a bill—but only a watered-down measure—so he talked the Southern Democrats out of filibustering the bill by promising to knock out Title III. To sweeten the pot for them even more, he added a jury trial amendment stipulating that civil rights violators could be cited for contempt of court only after a trial by jury, not on the orders of a judge alone. No Southern jury would have convicted a voter registrar for refusing to enroll Negroes. The jury trial amendment was simply a device to defend segregation, not to defend the sanctity of the jury system in the South. There was no clear right to a trial by jury in such contempt cases. The long-standing rule of law was that when a person violated a valid court order, whether it was a matter of paying alimony, a labor relations decree, or an antitrust order, he laid himself open to conviction of contempt of court and punishment without a jury trial. Southerners had never protested the fines and jail sentences meted out to the N.A.A.C.P. and its people without jury trials—they were only trying to protect civil rights violators *from* the federal courts.

Senators Richard Russell of Georgia and Sam Ervin of North Carolina led the South against the legislation—and they got some help from President Eisenhower. Toward the beginning of July, Russell bellowed that he would not stand by idly while the government forced the Supreme Court's ruling on the South with bayonets. The image of bayonets, a throwback to Reconstruction, was one of Southern making, but President Eisenhower was so moved by this false bleat that he invited Senator Russell to the White House and spent the better part of an hour talking to him about it. A few weeks later, when a reporter asked the President about Title III during a news conference, Eisenhower said "he didn't understand it." Didn't understand the strongest title in his own bill? Ridiculous. The President's remark appeared to give substance to Russell's complaint that Title III had been slipped into the bill surreptitiously, another false claim. Southern senators used the development to bring around Northern and Western Democrats and to lean on wavering Republicans. There is no question in my mind that, wittingly or unwittingly, Eisenhower contributed mightily to the confusion with which Title III was eliminated. Not long afterward, we lost the fight on the jury amendment, too.

The night the jury trial amendment went through, Vice President Nixon and William Rogers, who succeeded Brownell as Attorney General, bumped into Joe Rauh, the head of Americans for Democratic Action, and Paul Sifton, the legislative representative for the United Auto Workers. "Boys," Nixon said, "I think the best thing to do is to let the bill die. We'll get you a better bill next year, or after the '58 election."

Joe Rauh is one of the shrewdest liberals I know. He thought things over for a while, then came to me with the story. Vice President Nixon had been with us through much of the fight that year, as had the more liberal Republicans, but they were now saying that no bill was better than what we had before us. Liberal Democrats like Wayne Morse of Oregon were even more angry, and within the N.A.A.C.P. tempers were so hot that I won't repeat what people were saying. Could I go on with such a bill?

Joe suggested we assemble the top leaders of the Leadership Conference on Civil Rights and thrash the problem out. We had the meeting in the library of an office building on K Street in Washington. It was a difficult session. Joe argued that after eighty-seven years the time had finally come for a civil rights bill, even a watered-down one, and that once Congress had lost its virginity on civil rights, it would go on to make up for what had been lost. From a dry-eyed point of view, I thought it was impossible to argue that the bill was worse than nothing. It did have a Civil Rights Commission, however tame it might be; it did get civil rights out of the broom closet and into the front office of the Justice Department; and it did do something about voting rights.

The arguments took all morning. We broke for lunch, then returned to the conference table for the rest of the afternoon. I had never felt quite so on the spot. I had not asked for the bill that ad taken shape; I had wanted somethiOf much stronger. I had opposed the jury trial amendment. I had winced at the arguments of old friends who said that since the South had not filibu tered to kill the bill, it had to be too weak to be worth anything. In the end I concluded that at phe very least the measure would expand Negro registration, a significant improvement. I also hoped that if the bill passed we would be able to demonstrate its weaknesses by the 1960 election and get much stronger legislation. With the bill passed we were in a better position to campaign than we would have been without it. A start toward our goal, I believed, would be better than standing still. At the end of that long afternoon, I decided to buck the prevailing sentiments against the bill and support it.

If I had gone against the bill, I think it would have collapsed. The Republicans, as Nixon had shown, were for letting it die. The liberals would not have gone on against me. But I said I would see the miserable thing through—and it passed the Senate.

The decision was one of the hardest I have ever made. The House toned down the jury trial amendment a bit before sending the modified bill back to the Senate, where it passed once and for all toward the end of August. But there wasn't much comfort in that. Richard Russell went back to Georgia and claimed that by dropping Title III, Congress had repudiated *Brown vs. Board,* and in a misguided way, he was partially right. Hot heads around the N.A.A.C.P. and the black press wondered what on earth I had been up to.

I still think I did the right thing. In the middle of the battle, Hubert Humphrey took me aside and said, "Roy, if there's one thing I have learned in politics, it's never to turn your back on a crumb." He knew what he was talking about. The crumb of 1957 had to come first before the civil rights acts that followed later. If I had spurned it, we might have been waiting outside the bakery for a much longer time.

20   FROM LITTLE ROCK
TO THE SIT-INS

A few days after the Civil Rights Bill passed Congress, I received an urgent message from Little Rock, Arkansas. Mrs. L. C. Bates, the Arkansas president of the N.A.A.C.P., wrote: "There is a real campaign of terror going on down here. A cross was burned in front of my house on Sunday. They broke my picture window on Tuesday night. We have set up floodlights in front of my home, and it is being guarded around the clock."

This dispatch signaled that Little Rock was to become our next pitched battleground over desegregation. I knew at the time that the people who were trying to terrorize Mrs. Bates were underestimating her. She knew the White Citizens' Councils, understood them— and refused to knuckle under to them. Her friends called her Daisy; what her enemies called her was usually unprintable. For years, she and her husband had run the *Arkansas State Press,* a brave and outspoken black newspaper. The *State Press* had supported the Supreme Court ruling in the school cases, so the enemies of desegregation in Little Rock did all they could to put the newspaper out of business. The local gas company dropped a large advertising contract; so did the telephone company. Political candidates who usually bought ads at election time told the Bateses that they no longer dared to appear in the *State Press.* A paper company that had supplied their newsprint since 1941 suddenly refused to honor their credit. The Arkansas State Department of Internal Revenue reviewed their tax returns, announced that they owed $1,200 in back taxes, and demanded immediate payment, threatening to take a lien on their presses and equipment if they couldn't come up with the money right away. Somehow, Mrs. Bates managed to survive all those pressures, but each time her enemies failed, they redoubled their efforts to get her out of the way. It shocked me that so much trouble was afoot in Little Rock. Compared to Mississippi, Georgia, and Alabama, Arkansas had seemed relatively progressive. After the Texas and Oklahoma cases, the University of Arkansas had admitted black students, and after May 17, 1954, the cities of Fayetteville, Charlestown, and Hoxie had worked out voluntary plans for desegregating their schools. There had been some troubles, but I believe Arkansas might have made its way safely into compliance, except for the views, ambitions, willfulness, and machinations of one man: Governor Orval M. Faubus.

The same day Daisy Bates told us about the state of siege around her house, Governor Faubus went to the Pulaski County chancery court to get a petition restraining the Little Rock school board from carrying out its plan for integrating the city's schools. I found it hard to see how the Little Rock plan could offend anyone. The timetable was so slow and the scope of the plan so limited that we had gone to court to oppose it. Despite all our arguments, a United States District Court had approved it, so reluctantly, we had withdrawn our opposition. We decided to let the schools open and see how things worked out.

Governor Faubus chose to sabotage us. He claimed that violence would break out if the school board proceeded with integration. I'm not sure where he got his information, but I don't believe he was talking about what was going on at the Bates house. Together with community leaders, the school board had carried out a sensible program of educating and preparing the community for desegregation. City officials said they were mystified by the governor's stories about violence. The police chief and sheriff both said they could deal with trouble if it arose, but they made no impression on Governor Faubus. He got his court order and later sent the Arkansas National Guard to Central High School, where the forces of revolution he meant to quell consisted of nine Negro schoolchildren: six girls and three boys.

Faubus was cunning. He knew better than to say that the orders of the guardsmen were to prevent those children from entering school. Instead, he said piously that the soldiers were simply there to suppress violence. A good federal judge named Ronald Davies said if Governor Faubus wanted to act as a "preservateur of the peace," that was just fine—and he ordered the school board to go ahead with the integration plan immediately.

I remember the gratitude I felt, but I was deeply worried for those children. As any parent knows, the first day of school can be a harrowing time for a child, but what those nine Negro schoolchildren faced was not a simple matter of making new friends or adjusting to new teachers: in the more benighted reaches of Little Rock, self-righteous bigots were threatening to kill them. The innocence and bravery of those children was heartrending. The night before setting off for school, Elizabeth Eckford, one of the six girls, took out her Bible, turned to Psalms, and found these verses: "The Lord is my light and my salvation; whom shall I fear? the Lord is the strength of my life; of whom shall I be afraid?" With no more than that cloak of protection wrapped around her, she went to sleep, got up the next morning, and set off for Central High School, where Governor Faubus showed his true colors. As soon as Elizabeth and the other black schoolchildren appeared, 270 armed soldiers turned them away.

Never before in the course of massive resistance had troops been called out to defy a federal court order admitting black children to school. It looked to me as if Governor Faubus was up to nullification pure and simple, nullification in deed, not just in the abstract. Central High School was no Fort Sumter, but Governor Faubus was doing just about everything he could to secede from the Union.

I knew that if the N.A.A.C.P. let him get away with his insurrection, all we had accomplished would be swept away. After work that day, I went home, had a drink, poked a little at my supper, and fell into bed. When I got to the office the next morning, I sent President Eisenhower a message warning him that Governor Faubus was deliberately provoking a test of the authority of the federal government and challenging him to put the rebellion down. What worried me most was that if Governor Faubus were allowed to move ahead unchallenged, any state or region of the country would be free to decide whether or not to abide by the Constitution as it saw fit.

I am sure that the President didn't need me to tell him these things; he had to be aware of the danger. But in spite of it, he moved very slowly in bringing Governor Faubus to heel. Three weeks of negotiating and maneuvering followed, during which all the work that had been done to prepare Little Rock for desegregation was frittered away. The F.B.I. arrived in force to investigate Governor Faubus's talk of violence, and Herbert Brownell complied with Judge Davies's order that the Attorney General seek an injunction against Governor Faubus. In the meantime, President Eisenhower invited the governor to the summer White House in Newport, Rhode Island, for a talk. Afterward, Governor Faubus left, promising to obey "valid court orders," and President Eisenhower said he was "gratified." I was not. I did not believe that the governor would change his spots, nor did the board of directors of the N.A.A.C.P., so we urged the President to do something more than chat with him. We asked Eisenhower to take direct command of the Arkansas National Guard and to instruct the

Attorney General to begin whatever legal steps were necessary to put down the Arkansas rebellion.

After the N.A.A.C.P. board made its position known, I took a few steps on my own. Two days before Governor Faubus was to have his day in court, I got in touch with the White House and asked the President to meet with a number of Negro leaders to consider the unrelenting persecution of Negro citizens in areas of the South. I was boiling mad. Before the voting on Title III of the 1957 Civil Rights Act the President had invited Senator Russell to the White House and listened to all that Georgian nonsense about bayonets in the South. The only bayonets I could see were those planted by a Southern governor against nine black children and the Supreme Court of the United States. Then the President had invited Governor Faubus to Newport for an audience. The leaders of the Southern resistance to the Supreme Court seemed to be welcome any time, but the President had shut his door on Negro leaders. I told him that we did not relish having our destiny debated by others while we sat in the anteroom, that we were entitled to be heard.

The next day, Sherman Adams, keeper of the President's door, telephoned me. He said the President would agree to see a delegation of less than ten leaders, "six if possible." The date set for the meeting was October 15, but over the next forty-eight hours events ran out of control in Little Rock, and I didn't get into the Oval Office until the following summer.

With Little Rock coming to a boil, Adam Clayton Powell sent me a cable inquiring about my views on the crisis. I sent him a letter, which gives a sense of how I felt at the time.

September 19, 1957

Dear Adam:

I have your wire asking for comment on Arkansas. I cannot comment in language suitable either for the stationery of the N.A.A.C.P. or the ears of a Baptist clergyman.

All unbiased observers agree that there was no incipient violence in Little Rock when the Governor called out the troops, allegedly to preserve peace and order.

It must be remembered that the school desegregation plan developed by Little Rock school officials was challenged in the courts as being too slow by N.A.A.C.P. attorneys acting for parents, but was approved twice by the Federal court. We accepted the court's ruling and prepared the people to go along with it, even though we were not satisfied.

The hysterical opponents now charge that a judge from North Dakota has come down to Arkansas and forced a plan on Little Rock without knowing anything about the local situation. Ridiculous.

We shall see by tomorrow whether the conference Governor Faubus had with President Eisenhower had any meaning or whether it was just one of those things.

I have great difficulty in speaking calmly about the role of President Eisenhower in this whole mess. He has been absolutely and thoroughly disappointing and disillusioning from beginning to end. I am willing to grant that perhaps he did not want to get into a fight on behalf of the Negro but he didn't do anything when the authority of his own Federal Government was challenged.

I have tried very hard to be fair and objective about Mr. Eisenhower. I have tried to make allowances for the pressures under which he works. I have made allowances for the need of Southern votes in Congress to pass some of the legislation necessary for the well-being of our country. Yet with all these allowances, I still believe that any President of all the people would at least have issued a strong statement on the individual cases of violence that have occurred since the desegregation opinion, even if he did not issue a statement calling for overall observance of that opinion.

I just cannot for the life of me understand how a President could have allowed the mistrust to develop that presently exists in the South.

Firm words and resolute action by him and his Administration would have rallied public opinion in 1955 when there was ample evidence that things were going badly. The white people in the South who could be called moderate were begging for some encouragement from the Chief Executive. The wobbly liberal white opinion in the North that knew what was right but hesitated was looking to Washington for a word. The President kept silent. His Administration wore kid gloves publicly and did nothing privately (that we know of) in the Roosevelt manner so that the White Citizens' Councils, the ignoramuses (and many in the North) felt that they had a green light to do as they pleased.

The situation has hardened not because the N.A.A.C.P. is insisting on obedience to the Supreme Court, but because the White House had abandoned its own Supreme Court and has abdicated leadership in a great moral crisis.

I cannot help but believe that even Calvin Coolidge would not have turned in such a performance.

Very sincerely yours,

/s/   Roy Wilkins

P.S. When Senator Russell made his "bayonet" speech on July 2, the President promptly invited him to the White House, where they chatted for 50 minutes. What was agreed upon, nobody knows, but Russell emerged seemingly reassured. On July 16, in the late afternoon, the

White House released a statement on behalf of the President (he was on the golf course) saying he was demanding his full, four-point civil rights bill. At his press conference on the morning of July 17, Mr. Eisenhower calmly announced that he "did not know" about Part III of the bill, and that he "never intended" that thus and so should happen. At that moment he pulled the rug out from under Brownell and gave the signal for the elimination of Part III from the bill. His attitude encouraged further chopping of the bill, which might not have taken place if he had stood firm.

My view was not very diplomatic but I'm afraid it was accurate. President Eisenhower had done what he had done—and the chickens had come home to roost in Little Rock.

The day after I wrote to Adam, Judge Davies knocked the last legal pretense out from under Governor Faubus. "Now begins the crucifixion," the governor said dolefully. What baloney, I thought to myself. The governor was not Jesus. Defying the Supreme Court was no ministry; it was disgusting. Judge Davies enjoined Governor Faubus and the National Guard from obstructing integration at Central High School. Within three hours, the governor called off his troops. The city and state police took over through the weekend.

I knew that we had won only the easiest part of the battle. The following Monday, the nine Negro children succeeded in entering Central High School—through a side door. A mob of about 800 angry whites then surrounded the school. The police did not break up the crowd. After three hours, Daisy Bates decided to get the children out of there. When they were safe, she told President Eisenhower that they would not return until she had his word that they would be protected.

It was an inspired challenge. Mrs. Bates was a direct and independent-minded woman. No one could tell her what to do; she acted by her own light and vision. Those particular strengths of character squared well with the N.A.A.C.P.'s working strategy, which was to keep the national office out of Little Rock, leaving the leadership of the fight in the hands of state and local officers. We did not want to provide Governor Faubus with the pretext that "outside agitators" were responsible for the fight. Mrs. Bates handled things her own way. To show her contempt for the bigots, she didn't mend the broken picture window at her home or replant the scorches left on her front lawn by burning crosses. She left those scars as symbols of the disgraceful conduct of her foes. Her challenge to President Eisenhower came from the same impulse. The next day he federalized the Arkansas National Guard and ordered a group of 1,200 paratroopers from the 101st Airborne, one of the toughest units in the U.S. Army, to Little Rock. I suppose he would have done what he did anyway, but Mrs. Bates certainly prodded him on his way.

I didn't expect Governor Faubus to draw in his horns, even though he had retreated. One of the more persistent misconceptions about those times is that once President Eisenhower bit the bullet and sent the troops to Little Rock everything worked itself out. The reality was far more complex. By the beginning of October, it was clear that most of the white children at Central High School were willing to make desegregation work, but the adults just wouldn't leave them alone. Once President Eisenhower withdrew the paratroopers, leaving federalized National Guardsmen in their place, life for the nine Negroes became a daily misery. A small band of white students—I don't believe there were more than thirty or forty in all among the 1,990 students in the school—set itself the job of running the black youngsters out. White adults egged the young thugs on, and school officials were either too lax or too frightened to do much about the problem.

The reports I received were infuriating. The favorite target of the white kids was Minnie Jean Brown, a sixteen-year-old girl in the eleventh grade. She was a friendly, outgoing student who wanted to major in English. She was also tall and strong, the most imposing of the nine Negro schoolchildren. In no time the renegade white students singled her out for elimination. For weeks she was jeered, blocked from entering her classroom, kicked, threatened, kept away from her table in the cafeteria, hit with bowls of soup, bombarded with racist epithets. Until December she held her temper; then two white boys baited her beyond endurance and she spilled her cafeteria tray on them. For this retaliation, she was suspended. After some reconsideration, the school authorities readmitted her, but they exacted a promise that she would not strike back at her tormentors no matter what the provocation.

The attacks grew worse. "Any day upon entrance to school I may be welcomed with a lotion or water shower from the second-floor stairway," she told us. "Walking down the hall I am insulted countless times. When I enter classrooms, I hear phrases like, 'Here comes that nigger, Minnie Jean.' I can be kicked, hit with rocks and candy, smeared with ink, souped in the cafeteria. Scores of things can and usually do happen to me in the course of a day." Finally, in February, a white girl trailed Minnie Jean from the first to the third floor of Central High, calling her a "nigger bitch." Minnie Jean turned on the girl and called her "white trash." For those two words of reprisal the board of education expelled Minnie Jean for the remainder of the school term.

It was a familiar, shabby story. Rather than protect and stand by the target of racial injustice, the authorities chose to solve their "problem" by getting rid of the victim. I had seen such things happen hundreds of times. Unconscious or conscious, the motive behind such actions was to leave black people so numb with injustice that they would give up in despair.

When I looked a little more deeply into the situation, I discovered that in the months leading up to Minnie Jean's expulsion there had been no fewer than forty-two separate attacks on the Negro students at Central High. I am sure that the actual total was much higher—it was a matter of pride among the nine not to complain. Gloria Ray, one of Minnie Jean's classmates, refused even to talk to school authorities about what she had suffered until a white boy who tried to push her down the steps snarled, "I'm going to get you out of this school if I have to kill you."

The worst problem was that the National Guardsmen appeared to have orders to do nothing about these attacks except observe them. This was something more than benign neglect. Obviously, in ordering the admittance of the Negro students, the court had been thinking not merely about their physical entry to the premises of Central High but also of protecting their right to obtain an education. Just as obviously, they could not get that education if the troops on the scene did nothing about the malevolence of young white hoodlums. The default of the guard left the tiny minority of white troublemakers in charge. When Minnie Jean was expelled, the same young punks turned up with labels on their lapels reading, *One down—eight to go.*

When I told Wilber M. Brucker, Secretary of the Army, what was going on, I received only a bland assurance from one of his aides that everything possible was being done, that I had to understand that school authorities were responsible for control and discipline, and that the troops would not "usurp" that authority. Thus we were confronted with the incredible spectacle of the government of the United States placing the burden of enforcing the orders of its high courts upon the slender shoulders and young hearts of the eight teenagers who were left after Minnie Jean was expelled. That summer the N.A.A.C.P. awarded the schoolchildren and Mrs. Bates the Spingarn Medal in honor of and gratitude for what they had done.

Beyond Little Rock, the summer of 1958 was a perilous time for civil rights. Baffled by the Supreme Court, our enemies were faring much better in Congress, where their main goal was to destroy the Court's power. Senator William E. Jenner of Indiana, a conservative Republican, introduced a bill to deny the Court the authority to review cases involving the right to practice law before the state courts, which, together with the new barratry statutes in places such as Virginia, could have crippled N.A.A.C.P. lawyers in the South. The bill would have made it a crime under the Smith Act to teach or advocate the violent overthrow of the government. Under its provision, any Negro who pressed for his rights could face prosecution in the state courts of the South as a traitor to his country. It also permitted the states to prosecute for "subversion"—unless Congress specifically banned them from doing so.

That was just the beginning. Other legislation before Congress made it virtually impossible for anyone in a state's custody to invoke *habeas corpus* to test the constitutionality of his detention. Free from "interference" by the federal courts and the doctrine of *habeas corpus,* state judges could have locked up black citizens and thrown away the key.

At the same time, the House passed a states rights bill offered by Representative Howard Smith of Virginia, a Democrat and leader of the massive resistance. It stipulated that in any conflict between federal and state laws, the state law would hold sway unless Congress had specifically directed the federal government to preempt the field. Those bills sound preposterous today, but they were taken very seriously at the time: Senator Jenner's bill failed of approval by only one vote.

With so much at risk in the legislative branch, it became more important than ever to get help from President Eisenhower. Since April 1953, I had been trying unsuccessfully to get a word with him. Until Sherman Adams called me during the Little Rock crisis, all my requests had been shunted to aides. Winter and spring passed, and nothing came of the Adams call. Since early 1956, A. Philip Randolph and Reverend King had also been trying to win an audience with the President. Reverend King had attempted to lure him down South to make a speech on behalf of integration. The President had left us all out in the cold.

In the middle of June that summer, I got a telephone call from the White House. The President was willing to see me the following week. He was also inviting Randolph, Reverend King, and Lester Granger, head of the Urban League. We didn't have much time to plan, but when we walked into the Oval Office we had a nine-point program to place on the President's desk.

There was a round of introductions. The President was polite, but he seemed quite stiff. He was no more at ease among Negro leaders than he had been as a candidate. Randolph opened the meeting for our side. He thanked the President for the work he had done on behalf of Negroes; he said we all respected his courage and integrity; he commended him for what he had done at Little Rock. At that, the President seemed to relax and brighten a bit. That's laying it on, I thought, keeping a straight face. Randolph then took out the statement we had prepared. The preamble warned the Administration that the course of peaceful advance toward equal citizenship had reached a critical turn. The nation could honestly and forthrightly move through inevitable tension to a democratic solution to the desegregation problem, or it could depend on evasion and compromise, which purported to avoid tension but which in reality would lead the entire society toward economic, racial, and moral frustration. We knew something had to be done soon. We could not combat pneumonia by prescribing a tablet of aspirin and a goblet of goodwill.

I rather liked the last line, but Randolph, ever practical, skipped the whole preamble and turned right to our nine recommendations. In his mellow voice, he read them all. Before school started that fall, he told the President, we wanted him to declare in no uncertain terms that he would uphold the Supreme Court with all the strength of his office. We suggested that he call a White House conference of constructive race leaders to restore communications between white and black Southerners and to discuss means of complying peacefully with the Court's rulings. We felt a need for the agencies of the federal government to supply more information and support to state and local officials, and community groups working on educational and action programs furthering integration. We wanted the White House to prod both political parties to lay aside partisan biases and to pass a new civil rights law that would include Title III. We asked him to file an *amicus curiae* suit opposing the order of Judge Harry Lemley, who the preceding week had delayed Little Rock's integration plan until 1961. We told him that he had to act more strongly to protect the right to vote. We wanted to investigate a murderous wave of bombings of churches, synagogues, homes, and community centers, and to extend the life of his new Civil Rights Commission for at least a year. Finally, we thought the time had come for the President to make it clear that federal money would not be used to subsidize schools, hospitals, housing, or any other project where the color line was still up. In short, what we were after was for President Eisenhower to enunciate a clear national policy on desegregation—and to act on it.

When Randolph finished reading, Eisenhower looked stonily back at him. Then Reverend King took up the case. He told the President that a successful White House conference would offer the chance for the executive branch to mobilize the country's emotions and faith and that the President could offer moral leadership as no other man in the country could. He also believed that a conference would provide an invaluable forum within which the goodwill of the best white Southerners could be expressed, free of the economic and political reprisals that kept the lid on them down South. If the federal government offered local governments more help and support, he said, it would not be possible for the local white folks to use delaying tactics so successfully. As politely as he could, Reverend King also told the President that while morals could not be legislated—Eisenhower's favorite argument—*action* could keep the immoral under control.

At that point, I spoke up. The thing most important to me was restoring Title III to the Civil Rights Act, giving the Attorney General the power to act against all violations of the rights of black Americans. I told the President frankly that Little Rock and the Lemley decision had dismayed, distressed, and angered me, that as I had been on the way to the White House that morning, a porter at Pennsylvania Station had told me the Lemley ruling had "given the segregationists a map" showing all they needed to know to overturn school integration. I reminded him that the previous fall he had gone to Oklahoma City to bestow some science scholarships on a group of high school students, one of whom had been a young black girl. She would never had stood before him that day if it had not been for the progress of integration in Oklahoma City.

I yielded the floor to Lester Granger, who spoke for a few minutes. Attorney General William Rogers, the man Eisenhower picked to replace Herbert Brownell that year, was also in the room, as were Rocco Siciliano, an assistant on minority groups, and E. Frederick Morrow, an old friend of mine who had given up his work with the N.A.A.C.P. to go into politics. As Lester talked, I could see that the Eisenhower team was getting ready to defend itself. At first the President left all the talking to the Attorney General, who pointed out that progress *was* being made, that setbacks could be regarded as temporary, that lawsuits might not be wise in every situation. He also grumped a little that our statement had not been equipped with the sort of friendly written preface that Phil Randolph had delivered orally. Before I had time to laugh, the Attorney General turned on me and argued that *I* had been willing to drop Title III during the fight for the Civil Rights Act. That was a very low blow. To attribute to me the Administration's own cowardice simply because I had chosen to let the President get away with it in the interests of future progress was more than I could take.

Before I could protest, the President spoke. He said that it dismayed *him* to hear that after five and a half years of progress under his Administration there was still so deep a sense of bitterness among Negroes—perhaps more action would only produce greater bitterness. It was a touchy moment. Lester Granger, Randolph, and I assured him that the grievance was not directed at him personally; that it came because of the constant obstacles that Negroes faced when they sought to win their most basic rights.

The President thought for a few seconds, then agreed that there was a need for forceful action from Washington. To my disappointment, he said nothing about the Lemley decision or about Little Rock. "I don't propose to comment on these recommendations," he said. "I know you do not expect me to. But I will be glad to consider them. There may be some value to your idea of a conference. But I don't think anything much would really come of one."

Randolph said quickly that a conference would give the President a chance to set a high moral tone for future action. "There's only so much any President can do at those meetings," the President replied. And that was that.

I am still surprised when white politicians, memories foreshortened by the passing of time, tell me that things began to go our way once President Eisenhower acted at Little Rock. The truth is that the crisis stretched out for months, the patience of black citizens wearing thinner and thinner with every passing day. The Supreme Court did strike down Judge Lemley's decision later that summer, and President Eisenhower said he was pleased. The President also incorporated some of our ideas in the civil rights legislation that he proposed to Congress the following year. In the meantime, however, Little Rock didn't go away. Having lost in the courts time and time again, Governor Faubus got together with the Arkansas state legislature and closed the Little Rock schools. Once again it took long months of legal work to undo that unconstitutional action, and while the struggle went on, black children in Little Rock were without school altogether. White parents sent their children to private academies, but we had no such recourse.

One of the most painful jobs I had that fall was to go to Little Rock in November to ask Negro parents for forbearance while the lawyers reopened the schools through the courts. When I arrived, there was a mass meeting. Looking about the room, I pulled myself together and said, "Some of you have wondered whether colored people should set up schools of their own, but this we cannot do. We cannot deliberately set up a system that the federal courts have ruled illegal and unconstitutional. If we do, we will play right into the hands of the segregationists, selling out the youngsters who have endured so many hard days at Central High School, and all other Negro children who are trying to move ahead to full opportunity, not to second-class citizenship." I wasn't quite sure how the group would take my arguments, but the parents cheered—and stayed the course.

Ultimately the schools were reopened. Governor Faubus had lost. Sometimes I wonder if he realized how much his action would cost him. During the worst days of the struggle I received a copy of a letter that the Reverend Abbot Book, a clergyman in California, had sent to Governor Faubus. Reverend Book wrote that he was a native of Virginia and the grandson of a Dixie rebel who had died on the Confederate side at Gettysburg. But he told Governor Faubus: "When history is written for the generations which lie ahead, you will not be honored for the un-Christian manner of the un-American stand that you have taken. Free Americans will think of you as a hiss and a byword."

By the summer of 1958, young black people were angry at the betrayal of the promise of *Brown vs. Board of Education,* fed up with President Eisenhower's dawdling, and disgusted with the South's lock on Congress. They were restless, eager for action. But what form of action would they adopt? That summer I got the answer. In Oklahoma City, members of the N.A.A.C.P. youth council sat down at a series of segregated lunch counters, politely demanded service, and stayed put when the nonplused management refused.

The Oklahoma City sit-ins were the forerunners of the sit-ins that captured the attention of the country eighteen months later in Greensboro, North Carolina. They were enormously successful, and by the end of the year, our young people had integrated thirty-nine stores in Oklahoma City. We held workshops and seminars on tactics. The stage was well set for what was to happen later.

The tactics themselves were not new. Adam Clayton Powell and the *Chicago Whip* had used economic boycotts in the early 1930s to lend sting to their don't-buy-where-you-can't-work campaigns, and members of the Congress of Racial Equality had used the sit-in during the 1940s. The "new" methods were old methods which in one form or another had been used by people everywhere in their fight for better wages and working conditions, for women's suffrage, and for human dignity. The N.A.A.C.P. had been using them for decades, through times when the national climate of opinion was even more hostile than it was in the waning years of Dwight Eisenhower.

What was new was the mood of black people, a sense of deep grievance coupled with the willingness to adopt direct action and apply it on a broad scale. The success of the Montgomery bus boycott had stimulated this mood, but neither the Southern Christian Leadership Conference, which grew out of the boycott, nor the N.A.A.C.P., with all its experience and organizational strength, really gave birth to the sit-ins. They were the work of our young people, acting on their own impulses. A great wave of feeling was welling up within them, something more powerful than anything I had seen before.

To understand it, you must consider some of the events that took place between 1958, when President Eisenhower tardily invited a few black leaders to the White House, and February 1960, when the Greensboro sit-ins invited the entire country to look again at the slow pace of desegregation.

The first incident was a demented crime. On the afternoon of September 19, 1958, I was working in my office at the N.A.A.C.P. when one of the staff rushed in with some terrible news. In Harlem that day, Reverend King had been standing in the shoe department at Blumstein's Department Store signing copies of his new book *Stride Toward Freedom* when out of the crowd stepped an insane black woman, who stabbed him in the chest with a razor-sharp Japanese letter opener. I rushed down to the street, grabbed a cab, and got to Harlem Hospital as fast as I could. I stayed until a three-man team of doctors finished a delicate operation to remove the letter opener. The point had lodged against Reverend King's aorta—even a sneeze would have killed him. Only his unshakable faith and calm had carried him through.

I rode home that night feeling deeply shaken. A few more millimeters and black Americans would have lost the most brilliant voice they had. Millions of black people must have felt the same way I did that evening. But in addition to the horror they felt at the crime and the sympathy they felt for Reverend King, another heavy thought had to have fallen on them: it was foolish to believe that any one leader could bring us out of the wilderness. Deliverance would come only if everyone took part, if everyone found a new strength within.

Reverend King recovered, and as fall turned into winter, he rose from his bed and marched forward, a scar in the shape of a cross over his heart. At the same time, the young people were stirring. The N.A.A.C.P. had never seemed so full of life and energy. On all fronts, we began to move in tandem, not behind one leader, but behind an idea. It took some time to formulate that idea, but in the end it came to be expressed in two words: Freedom now.

The emphasis fell on the last word. The political parties and the Congress of the United States, however, went about their business as if they had all the time in the world to act. This slowness of white politicians to perceive what was going on further heightened all the pent-up frustrations.

The off-year elections took place in the fall of 1958. I tried to get Congress to stir, but most days it felt as if I were wading through mud. We instructed all N.A.A.C.P. branches to step up their voter registration campaigns and to press all candidates to come clean on whether they favored full civil rights, obedience to the courts, and wiping out racial segregation, or whether they planned to go the way of Governor Faubus in Arkansas and Senator Byrd in Virginia. We needed to get black voters beyond the South to exert the maximum counterpressure on the Dixiecrats. This meant that we had to force non-Southern senators and congressmen to stay out of bed with the Southerners. It was not enough for non-Southern politicians to make rhetorical speeches separating themselves from Faubusism. If they wanted our support, they had to vote down Jenner-Butler bills, states' rights bills, and other attempts to wreck the Supreme Court.

When the elections were over, the results were mildly encouraging. Some of the Court wreckers lost their seats, and a new class of liberals entered the Senate: Kenneth B. Keating of New York, Hugh Scott of Pennsylvania, Harrison Williams of New Jersey, Eugene McCarthy of Minnesota, and Jennings Randolph of West Virginia. In New York I was sorry to see Averell Harriman lose the governor's mansion in Albany, but in Nelson Rockefeller we found a supporter who was also committed to improving race relations and securing basic civil rights for black Americans.

Governor Rockefeller had been a friend of the N.A.A.C.P. for years. He was a great, bluff politician with the grip of a jackhammer operator and a grin as broad as the stage at Radio City Music Hall. The only man I ever saw get the better of him on the banquet circuit was Kivie Kaplan, a member of the N.A.A.C.P. board of directors who ran our life membership campaign. One night Kivie turned up at an N.A.A.C.P. dinner when Governor Rockefeller was sitting on the dais. Taking the rostrum, Kivie told the audience what pleasure it gave him to see that all the honored guests on the platform were life members of the N.A.A.C.P. The audience burst into applause, and Rockefeller beamed like a schoolboy. Afterward, Kivie whispered to Rockefeller, "By the way, Governor, you *are* a life member, aren't you?" "I'd better look," Rockefeller whispered back. We had his check in the mail the following week.

Rockefeller was an exception to the general run of top political leaders we had to work with at the time, and Lyndon Johnson's full conversion was still several years in the future. When Congress convened in January 1959, I organized sixteen civil rights groups and the N.A.A.C.P. for another attempt to attack the filibuster on the opening day of the 86th Congress. As usual, however, L.B.J. had ideas of his own; he wanted to have his cake and let the South eat it, too. With some help from Senator Everett Dirksen, the minority leader, he passed a compromise cloture rule that required a two-thirds vote by all senators present, rather than by the entire membership of the Senate. Since nearly everyone voted on civil rights bills, and since we had never managed to get more than fifty-five votes on cloture, the South remained safely insulated against real progress on civil rights. At the same time, L.B.J. proposed his own four-point civil rights program, including a conciliation bureau to be funded by the federal government, subpoena rights for the Attorney General in voting cases, letting the F.B.I. investigate bombings of churches, synagogues, and schools, and extending the Civil Rights Commission until January 1961.

Johnson was still offering liniment to cure a tumor. He was trying his mightiest to cast himself as a national leader, positioning himself to run for President, but for all practical purposes his concessions to the South meant that any effective civil rights legislation would be blocked. I wasn't going to endure the frustrations of 1957 all over again; I attacked the Johnson package.

Its most blatant weakness was that Johnson had entirely left out mention of the desegregation of public schools. The courts were full of the issue. State legislatures were doing all they could to reverse the courts; troops had been called out in Little Rock; the prestige and power of the Supreme Court and the human dignity and citizenship of 17 million Negro Americans was at stake. The Senate majority leader had ignored all these facts. The other critical failure was that the package made no attempt to restore Title III of the 1957 bill and to give the federal government the power to enter all civil rights cases. Without Title III, the best that could be said was that L.B.J.'s plan was a sugar-coated pacifier.

President Eisenhower did a little better, but not much. He sent the Hill a package of ideas that adopted some of the proposals we had presented to him at the White House the previous summer. Among them, he wanted legislation giving the government power to act when court orders were defied. But he, too, failed to reintroduce Title III.

The real work of keeping civil rights alive was taken up by men like Senator Paul Douglas and Representative Emanuel Celler, both of whom tried mightily to restore Title III. For the rest of the term, as black Americans watched intently, Congress occupied itself at leisure with cutting the liver and lights out of the Douglas and Celler bills.

While all this was going on, the media, which were to come to life on the civil rights issue in the 1960s, seemed blindly ignorant much of the time. In early February 1959, I flipped on my television set one evening to see Chet Huntley, one of the better broadcast journalists, criticizing us. He said, "I'm not sure this is fair, but I suggest that there would be more chance for desegregating schools if there were less reliance on the courts and federal power. The N.A.A.C.P. may have outlived itself, because the white Southerners, who must prevail if anyone will, consider it an unacceptable symbol." What Huntley had to offer next was even more extraordinary. "Nor is it fair that militant Negro leadership must be abandoned while white leadership can continue," he said. "But just as Negroes have the most to gain, it is they who must make the unfairest sacrifice to achieve it. I suggest that if militant Negro leadership is removed, militant white leadership will in turn atrophy and disappear. I hope I'm right."

Such arguments were too fatuous to take seriously, except that they had been broadcast to millions of viewers. To carry Huntley's line of thought to its logical conclusion, all that black Americans had to do was put on leg irons, deck themselves in chains, and shuffle up to Senators Eastland, Russell, and Byrd, asking those kind old massas to put everything right for them.

I demanded equal time to reply. NBC was obviously embarrassed—its phones had started ringing within twenty seconds after the broadcast. In all, 225 viewers had called to complain; 25 had phoned in support. Even so, the network couldn't quite bring itself to a square deal. It offered me a half hour, some of which would be taken up by a recap of Huntley's position, some by Thomas Waring, a journalistic spokesman for the South. I could count on ten minutes.

It wasn't much of an offer, but since it was the best I could get, I took it. With so much on the line, I had to measure my every sentence, my every word for image arousal, related associations, color, accuracy, impact, collateral connotations, and all the other bizarre new angles of the medium. I worked on my answer feverishly, praying that all the hopping and skipping I had done would be accurate enough to keep me from delivering my last words at breakneck speed or being cut off.

The evening of the broadcast I put on my blue TV shirt and went to the studio. Huntley opened the program with a self-serving little quote from John Milton's *Areopagitica:* "Where there is much desire to learn, there of necessity will be much arguing, much writing, many opinions; for opinion in good men is but knowledge in the making." Waring then served up the usual home-fried homilies for the South.

I was so mad I barely heard them. When my turn came, I told Huntley that the difficulties he had complained of did not come from black Americans but from Southern state legislators and governors, from wrongheaded newsmen, and from the dynamiters. That loud noise he had heard was the rending of the Constitution. If Huntley's moderates were so eager to act, I asked, why hadn't they done so in those hundreds of school districts where no lawsuits had been filed, in those hundreds of towns where there was no N.A.A.C.P. branch? Were they peacefully going about desegregation in those places? In a pig's eye, they were. The good white folks down South were not afraid of the N.A.A.C.P.; they were afraid of white extremists. If the haters and bomb throwers were not held to account, they would only grow more powerful. For the N.A.A.C.P. to withdraw or to stand idly by would have been to forfeit our rights as Americans. As for violence, we had been the victims, not the perpetrators. We rejected violence; we placed our faith in law.

In Harlem, friends told me later, the TV sets were blazing. In the barbershops and saloons people were shouting, "Get him, Roy. Tell them. Amen." I won the evening hands down. A few days later I got another message, this one on the letterhead of the United States Senate. It said rather primly, "Dear Roy, the moral and legal arguments upon which you relied tended always to cement goodwill." It was signed John F. Kennedy. Another one running for President, I thought to myself—and forgot about it.

Almost as if to prove the point I had made on the broadcast, a few months later a white mob in Poplarville, Mississippi, staged the first lynching since 1955. This time the victim was a black man named Mack Charles Parker, who had been accused of an assault on a white woman. Forty-eight hours before his trial, a lynch mob seized him in the jail, dragged him by the heels down three flights of stairs—his head bumping each step along the way—threw him into a getaway car, and shot him. His body was dumped from a bridge into the Mississippi River. The F.B.I. went to Poplarville, conducted a thorough investigation, and turned the results over to Mississippi authorities. The governor agreed to give the report to the Pearl River County grand jury, which chose not to act on it until the following November. The mob had not been willing to wait forty-eight hours to let Parker get a fair trial, but Mississippi saw nothing wrong in waiting six months, letting evidence fritter away, before acting on Parker's murder. In the end, of course, the grand jury refused to indict anyone. It was one more affront to decent black citizens. The miracle was that the overwhelming majority of them kept faith with the fundamental laws and institutions of the country despite such things.

Those Poplarville murderers were the folks Huntley had said would melt away if the N.A.A.C.P. only left them alone. And there were the House and Senate, emasculating civil rights legislation while the Poplarville mob did Parker to death. These things were not lost on black Americans. Yet when their pain drove them to civil disobedience in the 1960s, many white politicians expressed surprise. "How can they be surprised?" I used to ask myself.

There were limits to how much could be endured. As President Eisenhower's second term neared its end, I found it harder and harder to keep feelings in some of our branches from boiling over. A few weeks after the Parker lynching, a jury in Union County, North Carolina, acquitted a white man of an attack on a black woman. After the jury rendered its verdict, Robert Williams, the local N.A.A.C.P. president, angrily told a wire-service reporter, "We can get no justice under the present system." William was a hot-tempered man. I could understand his hard feelings, but I couldn't condone what he said next: "Since the federal government will not bring a halt to lynching in the South, and since so-called courts lynch our people legally, it is necessary to stop lynching with lynching."

It was obvious that I could not urge Congress to pass an antilynching law while allowing one of the N.A.A.C.P.'s own presidents to advocate the rope. I telephoned Williams, who told me he had been more or less accurately quoted. He explained that he had been expressing his personal feelings, not the policy of the N.A.A.C.P., but he said he didn't intend to be silent. We suspended him. He later made his way to Cuba and China, driven into a radical exile by what he had seen down South, furious, I am sure, at me. Like Williams, I believe in self-defense. While I admire Reverend King's theories of overwhelming enemies with love, I don't think I could have put those theories into practice myself. But there is a difference between self-defense and murder, and I had no intention of getting the N.A.A.C.P. into the lynching business. So I made our principle stick—and lost a passionate member. Years later he would come back to haunt me. On days like that my job was a sad one.

Several weeks later, I had a close brush with those good white militants Chet Huntley had told me about. On May 17, 1959, I flew to Jackson, Mississippi, to celebrate the fifth anniversary of *Brown vs. Board of Education* with Medgar Evers and the branches of the Mississippi N.A.A.C.P. There were 2,000 people from forty Mississippi counties in Jackson, courageous people every one. They all knew about the Poplarville lynching; they had all counted the years since the Supreme Court's decision in the school cases. There didn't seem to be much to celebrate that day except their own steadfastness. Since the Supreme Court's ruling, 400,000 Negro children had been admitted to previously all-white schools, but two million were still in segregated systems. I told the crowd that with such numbers against us, we had to keep on fighting harder than ever. I talked a little about the Parker lynching. One of the more incredible arguments offered by some white Mississippians in defense of the crime was that the Supreme Court would have struck down any jury's verdict of guilty because Poplarville didn't allow black people to serve on juries; it had been necessary for the mob to do the job itself. There was Catch-22 with a Mississippi vengeance.

While I was speaking, eight plainclothes deputies were ready with arrest warrants for Medgar Evers and me. We were charged with violating Mississippi laws against advocating integration. A local member of the White Citizens' Council who was running for the state legislature had sworn out the complaint against us, but the deputies lost their nerve and failed to serve the warrants. It turned out that the chairman of Mississippi's State Sovereignty Commission, which was responsible for enforcing the state's color line, had talked them out of it. "This is just what the N.A.A.C.P. would have wanted—to have Wilkins arrested in Mississippi," he reportedly told them. "They would have paid $1,000 to have that happen." The truth was that I would not have paid two cents for the privilege. Mississippi had shown too clearly how its jails could be holding pens for lynch mobs.

All the while, Congress paid little attention to what was going on. That summer, the House Judiciary Committee voted 18–13 to strip the Civil Rights Bill of anything that even smacked of Title III. The Southern Democrats had only nine seats on the committee, so they had obviously secured plenty of outside help in gutting the bill. President Eisenhower had not put civil rights on his "must list" of legislation, so Republicans felt free to walk away from it, returning the party to where it had stood before 1956. I asked Congressman Celler to try to restore Title III on the floor, but he did not succeed. In the Senate, the Douglas bill was similarly ravaged by the Judiciary Committee.

Congress rushed to adjourn before Nikita Khrushchev arrived from the Soviet Union on a state visit. All we had to show for the year was a token extension of the Civil Rights Commission and a promise from L.B.J. to take up what was left of the Civil Rights Bill by February 15 of the following year.

It was a dismal performance. No human being can endure such feelings of helpless frustration forever, and two weeks before L.B.J.'s promise fell due, the pot boiled over—in Greensboro, North Carolina.

On February 1, 1960, four young students from North Carolina A&T State University—Ezell Blair, Jr., David Richmond, Joseph McNeil, and Franklin McCain—went into Woolworth's, bought school supplies, then walked over to the Jim Crow lunch counter and ordered coffee and doughnuts. The white waitress behind the counter refused them, waving them to the stand-up hot-dog counter in the basement for black people. When they stayed put, a black woman who was washing dishes called them the sort of riffraff who held back the race. Finally, the manager came over and tried unsuccessfully to soft-soap them into leaving. They stayed until closing time. By the time they got back to campus, everyone from their fellow students to the governor of North Carolina knew what was going on.

It was an electrifying moment. The resistance of local white merchants, the emasculation of civil rights legislation in Congress, the tortuous pace of the courts, the unfriendliness of the White House had all pushed a new generation to fall back on its own resources and to step up the moral, political, and economic pressure for change. Ezell Blair and Joseph McNeil had been officers of the Greensboro youth council of the N.A.A.C.P. I don't know whether or not the 1958 sit-ins in Oklahoma City influenced them directly. The Greensboro sit-ins seemed to be spontaneous, a brave action that threw open the gates to an idea whose time had more than come. Within a few weeks the sit-ins spread to South Carolina, Virginia, Florida, Tennessee, Alabama, and Texas.

I bearded the management of Woolworth's and S. H. Kress and Company. Through the national office and our local branches we raised money to make bail and pay fines for as many student demonstrators as we could help. We also tried to find new schools and scholarships for those who were expelled.

Herbert Wright, our youth secretary, was all over the South that spring, organizing, training, helping wherever he could, and sending dispatches back to New York. By mid-March, when the sit-ins were sweeping across the South, he was in Orangeburg, South Carolina, where black students from South Carolina State College and Claflin

College had tried to hold a rally against segregation in the town square. The local police had arrested nearly 500 of these peaceful demonstrators, and Herbert was standing near an officer named Captain Whetstone, who intercepted the students on the way to the square. In his report he sent back a snatch of dialogue that captured the spirit of those days.

> CAPTAIN WHETSTONE: Why don't you go back to the campus? I don't want to shoot a single drop of water on you.
> STUDENTS: We are going through. Proceed. Forward. Let's go forward.
> CAPTAIN WHETSTONE: Who is your leader?
> STUDENTS: I am (*in a chorus of hundreds*).
> CAPTAIN WHETSTONE: (*Grabbing a radio and calling the jail*) There are 200 of them here under me, 115 on Lower Russell Street.
> CITY JAIL: Hold 'em! Hold 'em!
> CAPTAIN WHETSTONE: We can't stop 'em!
> CITY JAIL: Use your water on 'em!
> CAPTAIN WHETSTONE: They've been through the damn water!
> CITY JAIL: Use your gas!
> CAPTAIN WHETSTONE: We ain't got no more!
> CITY JAIL: Oh, my Lawd. What are we going to do with these niggers?

What a pitiful cry. To hear it you would have thought that the sit-ins and the demonstrations of 1960 came out of nowhere, that they were a surprise attack, a dirty trick. Nothing could have been further from the truth. For years the pressures had been building, and when they finally exploded, all Southern police could do was claim one more stab in the back and reach for their water cannons, tear gas, and dogs. As the Orangeburg students were herded off to jail, one young black girl pulled out her Bible and began reading. "Nigger, stop that damn praying," one of the officers yelled at her. "Father, forgive them," she replied. "For they know not what they do."

The faith of the Montgomery bus boycott had joined with the sheer energy of youth. I directed our national branches to support the sit-ins, and at the end of March I rounded up the entire staff of the national office and went around the corner to Fifth Avenue, where Woolworth's and Kress had two large dime stores face to face. We pounded the pavement and picketed the devil out of those stores. A placard had never felt lighter on my shoulder.

As the sit-ins gained momentum, L.B.J. kept his promise and returned to the issue of civil rights, but in my view, and the view of the board of directors of the N.A.A.C.P., the skeletonized proposals that Congress debated that year had been brutalized by so much sneaky ditching, dumping, chopping, and trimming that what remained was hardly worth reading. After some filibustering the Senate did vote 71–18 to pass what was left, but it was clear that both parties had produced the very least that they could give civil rights with a straight face. As far as I was concerned, both parties were welcome to whatever dubious credit they could claim for their part in tearing down what had been Eisenhower's timid proposals. The President himself made no serious effort to save his ideas from the pruning hook. In fact, he was pictured as being "happy" with the wretched remnant that Congress passed, and at no time did L.B.J. intervene to stay the hacking done by the Southern Democrats. The only section of the 1960 bill that made any real pretense of meaning business was Title VI, in which the Justice Department had come up with a plan for federal "referees" to oversee voting rights challenges. But even that safeguard was so hedged that most disenfranchised Negro citizens still had to run the same hopeless obstacle courses that local registrars always set up between them and the vote.

The exuberance and success of the sit-ins led some people to believe that direct action alone would quickly change injustices that had lasted for years, injustices that were reflected in the poor showing of Congress in civil rights. I was shocked that spring to hear the N.A.A.C.P. criticized at a conference called by the S.C.L.C. in Raleigh. When I picked up my newspaper, I read that Reverend King had said that the sit-in demonstrators were "moving away from tactics which are suitable merely for gradual and long-term change."

His remark could easily have been interpreted as a rebuke to the N.A.A.C.P. and its procedures, although no one (not even the Communists) had described us officially and openly as disciples of gradualism. We were usually pictured by Southern segregationists and Northern temporizers as extremists. We did work through the courts, and the courts did their job at an agonizingly slow pace. But that pace was beyond our control, and to equate our faith in law with gradualism, the South's main device for resisting change, was a very low blow. It was one of the few times I felt called upon to respond harshly to Dr. King. The problems of race relations were many, varied, and complex. There was plenty of work for many hands and hearts. But precisely because there was so much work to be done and because our opponents had so many resources, including the free use of state power, any division between those who were working to advance our cause would have been disastrous. Historically, it also would have been the cause for shame among those who had the greatest stake in the security of untrammeled opportunity—our young people—if division had occurred between the N.A.A.C.P. and S.C.L.C.

I sent word to Reverend King of the pain I had felt after the Raleigh conference, which had given birth to the Student Nonviolent Coordinating Committee. I told him that the N.A.A.C.P. was interested exclusively in securing first-class citizenship for Negro Americans as speedily as possible. We realized that the attainment of this object required the astute and unselfish use of a variety of methods, and we would continue to use all of them. But we believed that citizenship had to be firmly secured in law, or it would become a whimsical thing, dependent on local or regional happenstance. One could serve whatever vegetables, salads, or frothy desserts were attractive or attention-getting, but the meat and potatoes had to be citizenship protected by law. I also told him that what was needed was collateral and cooperative support, not derisive criticism. The pioneers in the N.A.A.C.P. had suffered too much for me to fail to defend their record. The air cleared afterward, and my admiration for Dr. King remained as great as ever, but from then on, whenever we had disagreements among ourselves, we tried very hard to keep them in the family.

Such wrangles were extremely unpleasant, but I knew it was essential to keep the sit-ins and the prospect of direct action within proportion. The students were young, committed, and valiant, but they were not organized. They would have no staying power beyond a few short years' time. My own experiences had taught me that the struggle would still be going on long after they were out of college and immersed in other concerns. Only a strong organization like the N.A.A.C.P. could survive the wear that went on year after year after year.

As we approached our national convention in St. Paul that summer, these views of mine worried some of my friends. I suppose they were afraid that our own young delegates might run off with us. I was curious to see what would happen. More than 500 representatives from the youth councils came to St. Paul, full of inspiration from the sit-ins, and when they got together for their caucus, I went over to see how they were doing. Some of my friends advised me not to go—they worried that too much hostility had built up across the generation gap. Once in the room, I announced that the latest run of sit-ins had just integrated a number of stores in northern Virginia. A great whoop filled the hall, and before I knew it, two husky students had reached up, grabbed me, and hoisted me to their shoulders. Together we bobbed through the room shouting, laughing, and crying in triumph. I've never known a moment like it before or since.

Finally, the room fell silent. And there was Arthur Spingarn, the president of the N.A.A.C.P., an old white liberal who recognized the changing of the guard when he saw it. "I thank God for what I have lived to see just now," he said. He had to blink back tears. "In my fifty years with the N.A.A.C.P. nothing has moved my heart more than the intelligence, the courage, and the resolution you have shown. Don't stop," he continued. "Don't delay. The time for advance is always now." The kids put me down—and side by side we headed into the sixties.

21 THE KENNEDY YEARS

When John F. Kennedy became President later that year, everyone expected him to come in and tear up the pea patch for civil rights. But it didn't happen that way. Through all the years I knew and watched Kennedy, I did not for a moment doubt his moral fervor, and his sympathy for black Americans was real enough as well, but getting him to turn those emotions into tangible political action was a matter of an entirely different order. Until the last six months of his life he moved forward very, very cautiously on civil rights. One of the hardest problems the N.A.A.C.P. faced in those years was to complete his education on race and to keep his feet to the fire on Capitol Hill.

The task was made all the more difficult because it was so easy to like Kennedy, to fall under his charm. He had a quick, athletic mind; he was neither smug nor orotund; and he had a gift for making just about anyone feel comfortable in his company. He first caught our eye at the N.A.A.C.P. in the very early 1950s. One day Clarence Mitchell was on the Hill making his rounds and bumped into Adam Clayton Powell, who was talking to a thin young man with a broad Boston accent. Powell waved Clarence over and introduced him to the young congressman from the Eleventh District of Massachusetts. After Powell's lean colleague left, Powell nodded toward the receding politician and said to Clarence, "You know, you ought to keep an eye on Jack Kennedy. He's going to be somebody very important one of these days."

We did keep an eye on him, and for the most part he was very helpful to the N.A.A.C.P. As a freshman congressman, one of his first votes was in favor of a bill to outlaw the poll tax, and in 1950 he cast nine separate roll-call votes for a strong F.E.P.C. In the Senate he voted regularly to change Rule 22, though as a liberal he was overshadowed by people like Hubert Humphrey and Paul Douglas. In

1956, I watched his maneuvers to become Vice President with curiosity more than anything else.

I didn't meet Kennedy until 1957. Then one day during the lobbying for the 1957 Civil Rights Act, I had lunch with him in the Senate dining room. We smoked a lot of cigars and sipped a lot of cold coffee. He was pleasant enough, and he backed Title III, which was quite important to me, but our relations got off on the wrong foot when he also agreed rather surreptitiously, I thought, to help Lyndon Johnson pass the jury trial amendment. At one point in the maneuvering, Johnson counted his votes and came up short of support for the amendment, so he prevailed on Kennedy and a number of other non-Southern senators to put the amendment over the top, arguing that the bill would be filibustered to death if they didn't join him.

Kennedy bought that argument, although we didn't know it at the time. One morning Clarence brought some friends down from Boston to put a bit of pressure on Kennedy. Kennedy turned on all his charm, and it wasn't until the end of the meeting that one of the visitors said, "What about the jury trial amendment? How do you stand on that?" Kennedy stood up, laughed, and said, "You don't have to worry about me on that. I'm all right."

That was all he said. Then he went out and voted Lyndon Johnson's way. He may have been all right with the Senate majority leader, but it was a long time before he was all right with me. Kennedy prided himself on his *realpolitik,* but the reality behind all the politicking was his own future. I guess it is not fair to be too harsh; I've never met a politician who didn't share the same quality to one degree or another.

For more than a year, Kennedy's vote on the jury trial amendment strained his relations with us at the N.A.A.C.P., though he did his best to smooth things over. In the fall of 1957 he came to one of our banquets in New York. Minnie was talking to me that evening when Kennedy walked up. As the photographers closed in on us, she moved to get out of the way. "Oh, no, Mrs. Wilkins," Kennedy said with a broad grin. "You get in here with us, too." It was a nice thing to do, and politic. Minnie never forgot that handsome face and those good manners. She liked Kennedy, and that didn't hurt him with me.

The jury trial amendment, however, continued to rankle me. I was also offended by the way Kennedy started rubbing elbows with the South as he began looking up the road to 1960. During the spring of 1958, when he was running for re-election to the Senate, I gave a speech in Pittsfield, Massachusetts, calling him on these Southern connections. The South would never have gotten away with its defi-

ance of the Supreme Court in those years without the help of Northern and Western senators, Republicans and Democrats. Since Kennedy clearly had presidential ambitions, his fraternization with
Southern senators and governors alarmed me a good deal. I believe I
said in Pittsfield that Negroes could not help being offended by the
picture of Kennedy with his arm around Governor Griffin of Georgia.

I meant the complaint figuratively. Kennedy took it literally and
sent me a letter saying he had never been photographed with his arm
around Griffin. Obviously my crack had stung him; it threatened to
hurt him among the black voters of Massachusetts and among black
voters nationally in 1960. He added a prim little postscript to the first
of the barrage of letters he sent me that summer ("I am somewhat
saddened that when speaking of pictures you emphasized one which
did not exist instead of the picture of you and me which does exist,
taken at the N.A.A.C.P. banquet last fall"). Before the summer was
out, he was accusing me of singling him out for retribution and
Clarence Mitchell of being a crony of Richard Nixon.

It was a nasty, destructive interlude, but we finally patched things
up. In mid-October, several weeks before the election, I sent a letter
to the Massachusetts Citizens Committee for Minority Rights praising Kennedy's help in the fight against the filibuster in the Senate.
The headlines next day were predictably favorable, and Kennedy's
letters once again became friendly. In 1959 he sent his congratulations after my fight with Chet Huntley and NBC. As he made his way
through the 1960 primaries to the Democratic National Convention
in Los Angeles I studied his progress carefully.

The political conventions were very important to the N.A.A.C.P.
that year. I wanted to hold both parties to a more honest platform
than the shameful effort they had made on civil rights in 1956. A.
Philip Randolph and Reverend King were both thinking the same
thing. During the spring of 1960, at the height of the sit-ins, the
N.A.A.C.P.'s board of directors authorized us to hold large civil rights
rallies in Los Angeles and later in Chicago. Not long afterward, Randolph and Reverend King proposed marches on both conventions. We
got together and combined our efforts.

In June I was startled when I picked up the newspaper and saw a
story saying that the N.A.A.C.P. planned to have 5,000 pickets in Los
Angeles. I wrote Randolph pointing out that state and municipal ordi-
nances might ban mass picketing and that such a large undertaking
on such short notice could allow irresponsible and politically undesir-
able people with ulterior motives to enlist. I also argued that the demonstration had to be one that would state the civil rights case and try

to win friends for it. I did not believe that a mass picket line that would clog up entrances, irritate delegates and officials, and possibly erupt into a name-calling disorder would advance the cause. Randolph wrote back that my logic compelled him to agree. In the end we had a march, but with no confrontations.

A week before the convention was to open, I flew to Los Angeles to make our case before the Democratic platform committee. The Leadership Conference had worked up a seven-point program covering education, housing, employment, voting, congressional rules, a permanent civil rights commission, and support for the citizenship of all Americans. That same summer the winds of change were blowing through the former colonial nations of Africa, and I pointed out to the committee that while independence days were being worked out in London, Paris, and Brussels, Negro children in Jackson, Birmingham, and Prince Edward County, Virginia, were still waiting for their government to enforce the school orders of its own Supreme Court. I wanted to see the Attorney General given power to use civil action to desegregate the schools, I wanted school boards to submit desegregation plans no later than the 1961–62 school year, and I wanted the federal government to cut off their funds if they failed to comply.

The platform committee had 104 members, and for the first time in my memory the pro-civil rights groups seemed to have the upper hand. The Democrats came up with a strong civil rights plank, far stronger than in 1956. I believe that we succeeded that year because of a number of new factors: the independence movements in Africa and the growing awareness they produced of the devastating effect that segregation was having on U.S. foreign policy, the sit-in demonstrations, and the strategic distribution of the Negro vote in the Northern industrial states.

Our rally also helped. We had rented the Shrine Auditorium, and on Sunday afternoon at 1:30, Reverend King and I led a march from the auditorium to the Los Angeles Arena, where the Democrats were to meet. By the time we reached the arena, 2,500 people were marching behind us. Paul Butler, chairman of the Democratic National Committee, was there to meet us. Looking out over the marchers, he said he was glad to see real people coming to let a little hot air out of the delegates. Everyone laughed. But then he said, "We dedicate ourselves to the elimination of all discriminatory practices at the earliest possible moment without violence." The marchers roared, "No, no. Now—not later." "I mean now," Butler said, correcting himself. That small victory in hand, we turned around and marched back to our own hall.

There were thousands of people waiting for us—a full house. Hubert Humphrey, Stuart Symington, and John Kennedy had agreed to speak to the rally; Adlai Stevenson and Lyndon Johnson sent emissaries. Of all the candidates that year, Humphrey probably had the strongest claim on our loyalty, but he was not in contention. Kennedy had done away with him during the primaries, and when Clarence Mitchell introduced Kennedy that evening, there were loud boos.

Kennedy rose, grinned, and plunged ahead with his speech. "The next President of the United States cannot stand above the battle engaging in vague little sermons on brotherhood," he said, adding that the immense moral authority of the White House had to be used to offer leadership and inspiration to those of every race and section who recognized their responsibilities. He promised to use the legal authority of the White House to protect the right to vote, fulfill the requirements of the Supreme Court on school desegregation, and put an end to discrimination in federal contracts, employment, and housing. "My friends," he said in closing, "if you are sober-minded enough to believe—then to the extent that these tasks require the support, the guidance, and the leadership of the American Presidency—I am bold enough to try."

It was a good speech. Then, to nearly everyone's dismay, Kennedy picked Lyndon Johnson as his running mate. To choose a Texan who had voted against every important civil rights measure until the 1957 and 1960 Civil Rights Acts was a shock. I can still see Joe Rauh down on the convention floor leaning into a TV microphone, imploring Kennedy not to make such an awful mistake.

I was inclined to give Johnson time to prove himself. I felt that he was not a visceral segregationist, that his behavior and votes appeared to have been dictated more by Texas political considerations than by any ingrained racial hatred. As minority leader, then majority leader, he had not often seen eye to eye with us, but he had been honest, telling us what he intended to do and keeping his word when deals were possible. He was the shrewdest legislative fox I had ever seen. As Vice President he would undoubtedly try to follow Kennedy into the White House, and that meant he would have to broaden his sectional connections, since he could never become President as a Southern segregationist. It also seemed clear that he could provide the legislative experience Kennedy so obviously lacked. After weighing all these considerations, I decided to take a gamble on Johnson. When I told people that we ought to him give a chance, I received plenty of shocked looks, but as time went on, Johnson didn't disappoint me.

The day before the 1960 Republican National Convention opened, we met at the Liberty Baptist Church on South Parkway in Chicago. More than 2,200 people filled the church, and the police set up barricades outside, where another 3,000 people jammed the street. Nelson Rockefeller spoke; so did Jacob Javits, Kenneth Keating, and Hugh Scott. But Richard Nixon, making the first of a number of costly mistakes with black voters that year, decided not to talk to us. The Republicans did manage to come up with a relatively strong civil rights plank, but only, I suspect, because Rockefeller forced Nixon into it. Nixon himself had his eye on winning some Southern states, and he wanted a much softer plank.

The selection of L.B.J. as Kennedy's vice presidential candidate also forced Nixon to consider a stronger civil rights stand. With a Southerner like Johnson on the ticket pledging to support a strong Democratic plank, the Republicans had to come up with something attractive on civil rights to stay in contention for the Northern independents they had to add to their own conservative base to win the election. At the time of the convention, the Republicans did not anticipate that the South would respond so negatively to Kennedy's religion and the Democratic Party's plank—or they might have gone along with Nixon's views.

As the convention closed and the general election campaign neared, I felt a bit frightened by the forces lining up behind Nixon and by the way some among his followers were manipulating the religious issue. If Nixon had been elected by a coalition of Northern and Southern conservatives, with the latter including both Negro haters and Catholic haters, we could not have expected much on civil rights. Against those forces, Kennedy and Lyndon Johnson looked like shining liberals.

At first Kennedy showed every sign of carrying out the Democratic platform. There was a rump session of Congress that August, and the Leadership Conference called on the politicians to make a down payment on their platforms by passing a significant piece of civil rights legislation before the election. The result was an exercise in cynicism. In the Senate, Everett Dirksen reintroduced a few measures left over from the 1960 Civil Rights Act. The Democrats voted to table the proposals, as Dirksen knew they would; he himself had voted to table the same ideas earlier in the year. His goal all along was to make the Democrats look bad on civil rights before Election Day, and he succeeded. Kennedy then pointed out that Eisenhower could eliminate discrimination in federally funded housing "with a stroke of the pen." As things turned out, of course, it took Kennedy himself nearly two years to make that stroke after the election.

When the campaign opened that September, Kennedy clearly did not have the black vote in his pocket—many Negroes had abandoned Stevenson in 1956 to vote for Eisenhower. If Nixon had played his hand better in 1960, he might have picked up another dozen or so percentage points of the black vote and won the election. Robert Kennedy was acute enough as a political manager to realize his brother's vulnerability, and Louis Martin, an old newspaper friend of mine who was counseling the Kennedys on black issues, also told them that they needed to be in closer touch with the N.A.A.C.P. Kennedy knew very little about Negroes; he had a few black friends, but they were not civil rights leaders. He knew he had to begin educating himself quickly.

Not long after Labor Day, Kennedy invited Robert Weaver, the chairman of the board of the N.A.A.C.P., and me to his home in Georgetown for a little seminar. Kennedy met us in his living room, then ushered us into the dining room, where the cook had fixed him a late supper. He ate as we talked. We covered the aspirations of black Americans, what they expected of the government, and what they expected of him; what he could do to respond to their hopes and demands; the programs of the N.A.A.C.P.; the immediate need for enforcing school desegregation. Kennedy listened closely. I am sure he was sizing up Bob Weaver, an expert on housing, for future use. Kennedy was at ease with us, as Stevenson had been in 1952. Negroes did not make him uncomfortable. After about an hour he ushered us to the door. As we left, I noticed Mayor Robert Wagner of New York waiting in the hall to give Kennedy a briefing on the problems of the cities. I was impressed with the candidate I had seen that evening. In the three years since our difference over the jury trial amendment he seemed to have grown a great deal.

As the campaign picked up speed, black voters came to admire Kennedy's youth, his grace, and his apparent willingness to break with the past. To most of them his Yankee background and fresh, hell-raising side outweighed any nervousness over his Catholicism or flirtations with the South. I remember being particularly struck by his performance in the first television debate with Nixon. Minnie and I were in Quebec City on a short vacation, and we stayed at our hotel to watch the tussle. Minnie disliked Nixon's politics and was curious to see whether Kennedy, a fellow Catholic, could handle the Vice President. I had no inkling of how important the debates would be; the notion of televised campaign talk still looked like a worthless spectacle to me. But as the civil rights question came up, I found myself leaning forward, fascinated. Kennedy's ideas on the problems of the Negro were not new, but his formulation of the bleak expectations of black Americans, their terrible problems in the fields of education, employment, and health, were fresher and far bolder than anything Stevenson had been willing to say. Minnie turned from the TV set and said to me, "This is what we have been looking for."

Later that month, when Kennedy telephoned Coretta King to show his concern over the jailing of Dr. King in Georgia—and when Robert Kennedy gave hell to the judge who had sentenced Dr. King to four months at hard labor for violating probation on a trumped-up traffic charge—Negro voters were won over in droves. I believe Reverend King's father said that if he had a suitcase full of votes he would put it at Kennedy's feet. Millions of other black people felt the same way. A few weeks later Kennedy won 70 percent of the black vote, crucial to his victories in Illinois, New Jersey, Michigan, Delaware, and South Carolina. Since Kennedy won the election by less than 100,000 votes, to have lost any of those particular states would have been disastrous. Had Richard Nixon been a little more generous, or just quicker on his feet in helping Reverend King, he, not Kennedy, might have become President.

The outcome of the election pleased me greatly. Not since the New Deal had such a surge of electricity run through Washington. I remembered the Democratic Party's strong civil rights platform and the promises Kennedy had made to us in Los Angeles—and I hoped for great things from him.

My illusions faded very quickly. Within ten days of the election, Clarence Mitchell had taken careful readings around Washington and found that Kennedy had no intention of beginning his new Administration with a full-scale legislative program for civil rights. Kennedy argued that the issue would divide the Democratic Party and cost him his chance of passing legislation in other fields. It was the same rationale we had been hearing for twenty-five years, but to make matters worse, Kennedy was giving away his game even before it started. The South couldn't be wangled into the slightest crumb if Kennedy said from the start that legislation was out. We were not after sops from Kennedy. We wanted Congress and the White House to come out of hiding and line up alongside the Supreme Court on segregation. We thought we had had a clear promise from the Democrats and from Kennedy himself to do just that, but now he was backing down.

In December, I made a speech attacking this excessive caution, pointing out that black people who had contributed so significantly to Kennedy's election had a right to expect better of him. The speech registered. After Harris Wofford, a Kennedy civil rights advisor, and Louis Martin passed word to the President-elect that he had some problems on his hands, Kennedy invited me to the Carlyle Hotel in New York to talk things over.

The meeting took place two weeks before the inauguration, at a time when many black Americans had not detected his waffling on civil rights legislation. Minnie and a friend of hers saw Kennedy in a car at City Hall Park. Minnie's friend was a staid old maiden lady, but when Kennedy's limousine pulled up, she suddenly jumped up on an iron fence, waved wildly, and shouted, "Jack, Jack—over here, Jack." Later, looking rather sheepishly at Minnie, she said, "I don't know what came over me. But isn't he wonderful!"

It was the Kennedy charisma that the newspapers were so fond of writing about, and I intended to resist it when we talked. Arnold Aaronson, secretary of the Leadership Conference, and I met beforehand and went to the Carlyle. Kennedy was ready for us. I believe the Parke-Bernet Gallery across the street used to supply paintings for the President-elect's suite at the Carlyle. The day we arrived an impressionistic work by Romare Bearden was on the wall, a great, cheerful blob looking down at me as I prepared to hear the new President. I'd known Romie Bearden since he was a little boy, and it augured well.

We told Kennedy that we knew he planned to use executive orders instead of legislation in the civil rights field—and that we felt the approach was inadequate. If that was really what he had in mind, we said, then why didn't he consider one monumental executive order to cover everything—a second Emancipation Proclamation. Kennedy looked up from his soup and shook his head. He said he didn't know whether he had the power to tackle education, housing, travel, public accommodations, and employment with a single executive order. He was adamantly opposed to taking any such risk. "Why don't you call Ted Sorensen," he said, stalling diplomatically. "Write him a memo. We'll see what comes of it."

We were also unsuccessful that day in trying to talk him into helping us with the Rule 22 fight at the opening of Congress. We had lined up a fair amount of support—by our count, we were perhaps three to five votes short of winning—and we wanted Kennedy to use his influence to secure those extra votes. Our idea was to convince him to persuade Mike Mansfield, the new Senate majority leader, to lobby for the rules change. Mansfield's support, we believed, would be enough to bring the other votes around. After we made our pitch, Kennedy stood up and chuckled. "I don't know if Mike wants anything," he said with a shrug.

What he meant was that Mansfield was so stiff-necked and incorruptible that Kennedy could think of no *quid pro quo* that might bring him to our side. It was a politic way of ducking the issue. The interview came to an end with the President-elect assuring us that he would do all he could and that he had every intention of sticking by the Democratic platform. Within a month, the Senate voted 50–46 to bury any rules change. That left the filibuster intact at least through the beginning of the 88th Congress in 1963. We were off to a very bad start with Kennedy.

In the following months, Kennedy kept his word to apply executive action where he could. As I recall, it was on Inauguration Day, just at dusk, that the coast guard unit passed the President's reviewing stand. Kennedy craned forward and noticed that there were no Negroes in the unit. The next day he called the coast guard commandant on the carpet. Assured that the coast guard did not make a practice of Jim Crowing its marching units, Kennedy said, "Well, I didn't see any yesterday in the parade." After that, the coast guard did better. It was a small idea, but I thought it was a surprising one to occur to Kennedy on what was perhaps the most important day of his political career.

I was also pleased by the effort he made to place Negroes in top government jobs. He appointed Bob Weaver Chairman of the Housing and Home Finance Agency, a subcabinet job and the highest any Negro had ever held, which put Weaver in place for a full Cabinet post later. Carl Rowan became Deputy Assistant Secretary of State for Public Affairs; Andrew Hatcher was named Assistant White House Press Secretary; Cecil Poole became U.S. Attorney for Northern California; and later that fall Thurgood Marshall was named to the U.S. Circuit Court of Appeals. Kennedy also took a count at the State Department, and discovered 15 blacks among 3,674 foreign service officers. The figures were just as dismal in other government departments, and during the next few years Kennedy exerted real pressure to improve the arithmetic.

All these gestures could not make up for defaulting on a legislative program. It looked very much like a holding action. Joe Rauh used to joke that Kennedy had adopted a new version of Harry Hopkins's old political formula for F.D.R.: "Spend, spend, spend—elect, elect, elect." Kennedy's version seemed to be "Appoint, appoint, appoint—elect, elect, elect."

If we were to be reduced to executive action, I meant to get Kennedy to do more than he was doing. As he had suggested at the Carlyle, we prepared a long memo for Theodore Sorensen, whom I met at the White House in February. Among other things, we suggested that Kennedy should consider executive action to withhold federal funds from school districts defying the Supreme Court and to sign the order on housing that he had used to taunt Eisenhower. Sorensen accepted our memo and promised to consider it, but his own opinion seemed to be that there was no immediate pressure in the country for civil rights. To push ahead too rapidly on housing might put Bob Weaver's nomination at risk in Congress, and to push on the other fronts might provoke a national controversy just as the new Administration was getting started. As I left the White House that day, I thought to myself, It's nice to be able to get through the door again. But I began to wonder how much good it was going to do.

A few weeks later I wrote a letter to Harris Wofford summing up my general sense of frustration with Kennedy during those first months in office.

> Dear Mr. Wofford:
>
> The Kennedy Administration has done with Negro citizens what it has done with a vast number of Americans; it has charmed them. It has intrigued them. Every seventy-two hours it has delighted them. On the Negro question it has smoothed Unguentine on a sting burn, even though, for a moment (or perhaps a year), it cannot do anything about a broken pelvis. It has patted a head even though it could not bind up a joint.
>
> The point is not so much whether we have come out thus far with what we were due (we have not) but whether the lines have been set in such a way that we cannot later recall our proper share. It is plain why the civil rights legislative line was abandoned, but nothing was accomplished by the maneuver. It did not save the Minimum Wage Bill from gutting, and it will not save other legislation. The Southerners and their Northern satellites function whether a civil rights bill is proposed or not.
>
> An Administration gets as much by whacking them as by wooing them. J.F.K. might as well have had a civil rights bill in the hopper; he might have won the Senate Rules fight (he could have) as he would have had a procedure open when he does decide to get behind a civil rights bill.

It was to take Kennedy more than two years to get behind a civil rights bill of the sort I was talking about. Only a month after I wrote to Wofford, Pierre Salinger, Kennedy's White House press secretary, wandered into the briefing room one day and said, "The President has made it clear that he does not think it is necessary at this time to enact civil rights legislation." The South had nothing to worry about;

it was a cactus bouquet for Negroes. If I'm not mistaken, Salinger's remark came just five days before the Freedom Riders rolled into Anniston, Alabama, where a Mother's Day mob burned the first bus.

The Freedom Rides were the work of C.O.R.E., which had been around since the 1940s, mostly in the background. The year before the rides, James Farmer, a great burly man who led C.O.R.E., had been program director for the N.A.A.C.P. for a short time. He was not naïve enough to consider the Freedom Rides a test of Irene Morgan or *Boynton vs. Virginia,* the relevant Supreme Court ruling striking down segregation in interstate bus travel and in depot facilities, and he knew what to expect when the buses reached the heart of Dixie. The real test he was setting was for the White House and Justice Department: how far would the Kennedys go to protect the riders when the inevitable violence occurred? It was a desperately brave, reckless strategy, one that made those touch-football games played by the Kennedys look like macho patty-cake.

The day after the first bus was burned, Clarence Mitchell and I met Robert Kennedy at the Justice Department. The President's brother was shocked by the violence, but he didn't really seem to understand it. The Administration's first reaction to the rides was that they were a destructive form of grandstanding that could only embarrass President Kennedy at his summit meeting with Khrushchev two weeks hence. I told the Attorney General that dictatorship in Alabama was as great a menace to the United States as any tyranny abroad, that he had to come up with federal protection for the riders. He agreed to have the F.B.I. investigate the bus burning, which wasn't much, and then sent federal marshals, who arrived late but helped a good deal when they did get down South.

The violence surrounding the Freedom Rides provided a clearer demonstration of our arguments for the need to grant the Attorney General broad Title III powers to step into civil rights cases. After John Seigenthaler, the young assistant Kennedy sent down to investigate, was savagely beaten by a mob of thugs in Montgomery, the Justice Department knew exactly what was going on.

To a degree, C.O.R.E. had succeeded in drawing the Administration into action: the Kennedys began to see that it would be impossible for them to avoid more direct engagement. But still they held back. A few weeks after the first Freedom Rides, the President named Harold Cox, Senator Eastland's old college roommate, as a federal district judge in Mississippi. For 986,000 Negro Mississippians, Judge Cox was another strand in their barbed-wire fence, another cross over their shoulders, and another boulder in the road up which their young people had to struggle. It took the Senate one week to approve Judge Cox's nomination, one year to pass that of Thurgood Marshall. I remember Clarence said once that the White House was beginning to look like a dude ranch—with James O. Eastland as the general manager.

During the N.A.A.C.P. convention that summer, we chartered a twenty-two-car Freedom Train to take the delegates from Philadelphia to Washington to ask their representatives for more action on civil rights. When the President learned we were coming, he invited the members of the N.A.A.C.P. board and our state presidents to call on him at the White House. Before the meeting, he asked Arthur Spingarn, Bishop Stephen Gill Spottswood (the new N.A.A.C.P. chairman), and me to join him upstairs in his study for a short talk. We exchanged some pleasantries, and as we were walking downstairs for the general assembly, Jackie Kennedy came rushing up from the basement. She had smudges of dirt on her nose and chin, and she looked very excited. "Oh, Jack," she blurted out, "I've found the Lincoln china!"

The President said to her, "I'd like you to meet Bishop Spottswood, Mr. Spingarn, and Mr. Wilkins."

"How do you do, how do you do, how do you do," she said to each of us in turn; then turning radiantly to Kennedy, she repeated, "Jack, the Lincoln china."

Grinning at her, he leaned over and rubbed the smudges from her cheek. Then we went downstairs.

Once in the Oval Office, Kennedy was all grace and good manners. He pulled out chairs for the ladies and listened politely as Bishop Spottswood read a rather tough statement: "The absence of a clear call from you for enactment of civil rights legislation has become a source of dismay to the forces working for civil rights. In view of the specific pronouncements of the platform on which you were elected and in light of your own promise last fall to employ legislative action to attain civil rights, there is grave concern over the prospect that without support from the White House, there might be no congressional action on the various, urgently needed bills now in various stages of unpreparedness."

It took Bishop Spottswood several minutes to read the rest of the message. Kennedy listened impassively—his gaze didn't wander, he didn't fidget. When Bishop Spottswood finished, the President stood up, and as graciously as he could said he would not change his mind or his tactics. "We remain convinced that legislation is not the way," he said, adding quickly, "At least, it is not advisable at this time."

I was extremely disappointed. We still had achieved none of our major priorities, and we pointed out to Kennedy that Congress had savaged all his major bills that term, even though he had held back on civil rights. His strategy for winning friends obviously wasn't working. Kennedy nodded, but his response to changing his approach was a single word: "No."

It was one measure of Kennedy's political smoothness that just about everyone left the White House that day feeling charmed by the man. But when we reported back to the full delegation of the Freedom Train, the pain was obvious: we had heard plenty about the Lincoln china, nothing about a second Emancipation Proclamation—or a meaningful legislative program.

At the beginning of 1962, Kennedy did come up with a few voting-rights proposals, but in his State of the Union message that year, he left out Title III, the F.E.P.C., deadlines for complying with the Supreme Court on school desegregation, and any hint of withholding federal funds from states that clung to defiance of the Constitution. At the time there were still roughly 2,500,000 Negro children in segregated schools, and integration was proceeding at the rate of about 1 percent a year. At that deliberate speed, it would take until the year 2063—around about the two hundredth anniversary of the Emancipation Proclamation—to accomplish desegregation. You couldn't go very much more slowly than that.

I think 1962 was perhaps the lowest moment for the civil rights movement during the Kennedy years. In March we assembled the leaders of the major civil rights groups for a conference at Seabury House in Greenwich, Connecticut, to see what could be done. The N.A.A.C.P. was there, as were the Urban League, S.C.L.C., S.N.C.C., C.O.R.E., the American Friends Service Committee, and the Race Relations Department of the National Council of Churches. It depressed me to see that S.C.L.C., C.O.R.E., and S.N.C.C. were all in full-fledged competition with the N.A.A.C.P., when cooperation and solidarity were obviously needed. All had programs on housing, employment, voter education, public accommodations, travel, and recreation that were virtually identical with ours. We talked of the need to coordinate our work, not duplicate it or divide our forces, but except for some good results on voter education and registration in the South, we were not really pulling together.

It was also during the summer of 1962 that Dr. King ran into some very serious setbacks in Albany, Georgia. The S.N.C.C. kids had been there working on voter registration; when Dr. King arrived and the newspapers gave him all the ink, there was some angry muttering.

Some of the S.N.C.C. people were beginning to call King "De Lawd" behind his back. We paid some of the expenses of the Albany movement, only to be insulted for being on the wrong side of the generation gap.

The local police chief used to get down on his knees and pray with the demonstrators, then lock every one of them up. Direct action, for all the exhilaration it had produced in Montgomery, with the sit-ins and the Freedom Rides, had suddenly come up against a hard, unmoving rock. If the entire South had been as deft and devious as Albany in avoiding integration, we would have been in very serious trouble. As it was, the situation in Albany affirmed more than ever my own belief that we would gain our goals only when the White House and Congress, as well as the Supreme Court, were all acting on our side.

Against this backdrop a series of shocks finally jarred the Kennedy Administration out of its lethargy on civil rights legislation. The first came after Governor Ross Barnett of Mississippi went back on his word to keep order at the University of Mississippi when James Meredith registered. Bob Weaver was in Kennedy's office when word came that Barnett was reneging. Kennedy turned scarlet. "Why that goddamn son-of-a-bitch," he snapped. Bob told me that he had never seen Kennedy so mad.

It was the worst confrontation since Little Rock, and this time it cost several lives. Minnie and I were in Europe at the time, where we spent half our time in press conferences arranged by the American embassies in England, France, and Italy. At a dinner in Paris one evening, a young French woman with left-wing political views announced snidely, "President Kennedy has finally called out the troops, I see." Minnie glared at her, and I had to step in before we had an international incident on our hands. "We don't believe in calling out troops before they are needed," I said. Fortunately, that shut the young woman up. At the end of this working vacation, we sailed home from Genoa aboard the *Constitution,* an appropriate vessel for those turbulent days. What Governor Faubus had done to President Eisenhower, Governor Barnett had done to John Kennedy. The President knew he could no longer pet the South and count on it to purr.

I noticed some clear signs of change in the civil rights message that Kennedy sent to Congress the following February. The President acknowledged that the voting rights provisions of the 1957 and 1960 Civil Rights Acts had not been strong enough. He advocated an extension of the Civil Rights Commission for four years, and he called for federal help to school districts that were carrying out desegregation plans. However, he made no plans for a permanent F.E.P.C. and set no deadline for school desegregation. Kennedy had finally recognized the need for legislative action. I'm not sure whether we had reached him or whether all those inside agitators down South had gotten his Yankee dander up, but he was beginning to move.

During the spring and early summer two disasters forced Kennedy to pick up speed. The first was Birmingham. Day after day we watched Police Chief Bull Connor with his snarling dogs, fire hoses, and cattle prods attacking peaceful black demonstrators. Of all Reverend King's demonstrations and exercises in moral witness, Birmingham probably worked best on Kennedy. What the country saw in Birmingham was a moral outrage that could not be condoned. President Kennedy knew he could not ignore it—he felt the same anger that everyone else did.

The second disaster took place across the Alabama border in Jackson, Mississippi. In May 1963, as Birmingham was writhing from the toils of Bull Connor, Medgar Evers was leading a campaign to desegregate local stores, businesses, and public facilities in Jackson. When the mayor of Jackson denounced the campaign on two local television stations, Medgar demanded equal time to reply. His arguments were irrefutable. "If you suffered all our deprivations, if you were called by your first name, or 'boy,' 'girl,' 'auntie,' or 'uncle,' would you not be discontent?" he asked the whites of Jackson. He also told them that he had been born in Mississippi, lived there since 1918, and served his country in World War II. He was no outside agitator. His message was plain and reasonable: "The N.A.A.C.P. believes that Jackson can change if it wills to do so. If there should be resistance, how much better to have turbulence to effect improvement, rather than turbulence to maintain stand-pat policy. We believe there are white Mississippians who want to go forward on the race question. Their religion tells them there is something wrong with the old system. Their sense of justice and fair play sends them the same message."

After some scuffling at the meetings, the mayor agreed to hire Negro policemen and school-crossing guards, to take down the Jim Crow signs from gas stations and public buildings, and to declare all public facilities open to citizens regardless of race. But he then went back on the agreement, and the community organized sit-ins, picketing, and other forms of direct action. Anyone who thinks the N.A.A.C.P. worked through the courts alone would do well to review that campaign. The police got out their clubs; hundreds of demonstrators were arrested; a Molotov cocktail was thrown into Medgar's front yard.

What was going on in Birmingham and Jackson was more than I
could bear to watch from the safety of New York. I flew to Jackson on
May 31, 1963. Earlier that day the police had arrested more than five
hundred demonstrators, filling the jails to overflowing and setting up
improvised wire pens on the state fairgrounds. At the mass meeting
that night I told the crowd that Hitler had finally found his way to
Mississippi. In Birmingham the authorities had turned dogs and fire
hoses loose on peaceable demonstrators. In Jackson another touch
had been added to the Nazi imagery with the establishment of
hog-wired concentration camps. The only thing missing was the
ovens.

The next morning Medgar and I led a group of picketers to Capitol
Street and Woolworth's. It was a sweltering day. Medgar was wearing
a sign around his neck that read END POLICE BRUTALITY, when Deputy
Police Chief J. L. Ray stopped us. He ordered us to end the demonstration. When we refused, he pulled the sign off Medgar's neck and
arrested us, along with Mrs. Helen Wilcher, a brave lady who also
held her ground.

The police hustled us off to jail and charged us with restraint of
trade. Bail was set at $1,000. It was a familiar trip. I had made it
nearly thirty years before in Washington, and I knew that day I was
once again where I belonged.

In New York, Minnie was in her garden working when the phone
rang. She dropped her trowel and went inside to answer it. The caller
was a reporter from U.P.I.

"Mrs. Wilkins, have you heard from your husband recently?" he
asked.

"Not since about one o'clock this morning," she said, her heart
sinking. "He called me then."

"Well, it just came over the wire that he's been arrested in Jackson,
Mississippi."

The call scared the daylights out of Minnie. She had visions of the
Southern police beating and doing just about every other thing you
can imagine to me. She started calling the N.A.A.C.P. office in Jackson but all Mississippi seemed to be one busy signal. Finally she di-
aled Mrs. Evers—and the phone was answered.

"Yes, they were arrested," she said quietly. "They are at the jailhouse. The lawyers are over there now."

A few hours later the lawyers bailed us out. When I got back to
New York I discovered that just about everyone but Minnie was de-
lighted at what had happened. I still have a letter that Percy Sutton, a
Harlem lawyer and very canny politician, sent me at the time. It read:

Dear Mr. Wilkins:

Even on 125th Street here in Harlem, the Black Nationalists were saying on Sunday, *Sutton, your boy Wilkins was in the thick of it— Boy, that's the stuff.*

I think it might be accepted as truth that such is the drawing capacity power of national television today that in our larger cities the local N.A.A.C.P. might be diligently involved in a mass protest, picketing and boycott of a store on one street, while a block away, the Negro citizen, sitting in his house and watching Dr. Martin Luther King on television *2,000 miles away* says: "Go get 'em Rev. King—that's the boy—tell 'em off." Then, after a minute of reflection, he is likely to say: "By God, the N.A.A.C.P. ought to be doing something like this," completely unaware that the N.A.A.C.P. *is doing something like this*—and only a block away.

I had to laugh at the letter. Sutton had a point about the more mediagenic and distorting aspects of direct action. Still, what I wanted was a real legislative program from Kennedy, not a stretch in a Southern hoosegow. New laws would make a difference; nothing is deader than last week's newscast or headlines.

The police had taken care not to rough me up in Jackson. I remember kidding Minnie about her fears when I got back home, but she was not amused. To her mind, the South was still as dangerous as ever. As things turned out, she was right.

Several days later I watched Kennedy give his response on television to what was going on in Birmingham and Jackson. "We are confronted primarily with a moral issue," he said. "It is as old as the Scriptures and as clear as the American Constitution. The heart of the question is whether all Americans are to be afforded equal rights and equal opportunities; whether we are going to treat our fellow Americans as we want to be treated. If an American because his skin is dark cannot eat lunch in a restaurant open to the public, if he cannot send his children to the best public school available, if he cannot vote for the public officials who represent him, if in short he cannot enjoy the full and free life which all of us wants, then who among us would be content to have the color of his skin changed and stand in his place? Who among us would then be content with the counsels of patience and delay?"

This was the Kennedy who had spoken to us in Los Angeles. This was the message I had been waiting to hear from him. I fell asleep that night feeling new confidence. For the first time in years a real change seemed to be at hand. At about 2 A.M., the phone beside the bed rang. Minnie reached over and picked up the receiver. Robert

Ming, an N.A.A.C.P. attorney who was helping with the campaign down in Jackson, was on the other end of the line.

"Tell Roy that Medgar has been shot—murdered," he said.

"What?" Minnie murmured, not believing what she had just heard.

"Yes," Bob said. He couldn't bring himself to say much more.

Minnie hung up the phone, then shook my shoulder. "Medgar has been shot," she said. "He's dead."

Oh, my God, I thought to myself. Don't let it be true.

My eyes filled with tears. I had not felt such a rush of feeling since Earl's death. If there was one moment in my life when I hated whites, that was it. Medgar Evers was one of the bravest, most selfless men ever to throw in his lot with the N.A.A.C.P. He worked close to the earth, next to the people. He was always steady, even in the shadow of violence. The night when a white psychopath shot him down from cowardly ambush, Medgar was wearing a tie clasp in the shape of the scales of justice. And when the police sent his wallet back from the hospital, Mrs. Evers opened it to find a five-dollar bill. The face of Lincoln was stained with Medgar's blood.

I flew to Jackson for the funeral. I said that day that as surely as we were standing there the Southern political system had put the assassin behind the rifle that killed Medgar Evers. He was buried in Arlington Cemetery overlooking Washington. At that last, sad ceremony I said that Medgar Evers had believed in his country—it now remained to be seen if his country believed in him.

A week after Medgar's death, Kennedy proposed what was to become the 1964 Civil Rights Act to Congress. At about the same time, he invited the major civil rights leaders to the White House to discuss ways and means of working for the bill. We met in the Cabinet Room. Lyndon Johnson was there in the background. Robert Kennedy was over to one side; one of his little daughters ran into the room and he simply picked her up and put her on his lap, where she sat for ten minutes or so, putting her tiny fingers to his face. Finally, he lifted her gently and carried her out.

The President opened the meeting by telling us that the main problem was to decide how were we all going to function. In his own view, the trick would be to find enough Western and Northern senators to produce the votes for cloture when the South began to filibuster the proposed bill. L.B.J. estimated that the Administration could count on about fifty senators to support the legislation and about twenty-two to oppose it. Bringing around the remaining swing votes was the chore before us.

We were badly divided among ourselves on tactics. For most of the year A. Philip Randolph had been talking about an Emancipation March on the capital for jobs. Dr. King, who had no real legislative experience, was thinking of applying direct action and the tactics of Birmingham to the capital, a line of thought I considered disastrous. Walter Reuther of the United Automobile Workers wanted to set up a "Coalition for Conscience" to run the lobbying. I wanted the Leadership Conference to handle the job.

Both Kennedys were apprehensive about mass demonstrations in the capital. "We want success in Congress, not just a big show at the Capitol," the President said. "Some of these people are just looking for an excuse to oppose us. I don't want to give them the chance to say, 'Yes, I'm for the bill—but not at the point of a gun.'" Robert Kennedy was also afraid that we would try to enlarge the Administration's package and come up with a bill that could not pass. For a moment I was stricken with a sense of *déjà vu:* at last we had some real legislation to work on, but the strategic considerations of the Administration made it sound as if we were back in 1957.

The opposition of the Kennedys to demonstrations put us in an awkward bind. There had been so much talk about a march of some sort on Washington that we could not simply back down. If we called off the pressure and Congress worked its usual runaround on civil rights, the damage to all of us would be devastating. I remember Reverend King telling Kennedy as politely as he could that every direct-action movement he had been in had seemed ill timed at the moment, including Birmingham.

Kennedy chuckled. At another point he said, "You may be too hard on Bull Connor." When everyone gasped, he laughed again and added, "After all, Bull has probably done more for civil rights than anyone else." The joke broke the tension in the room. Kennedy told us he had a private poll that showed his popular support falling from 60 percent to 47 percent. The election was only a little over a year off. "This is a very serious fight," he said. "The Vice President and I know what it will mean if we fail." He said in closing that the main thing was to keep confidence and faith in one another. Then the meeting broke up.

Afterward we held a lunch and strategy session at Reuther's hotel suite near the White House. One purpose of the meeting was to talk Dr. King out of trying to apply the model of Birmingham to Washington. Obviously we had to offer an acceptable alternative, as he was under heavy pressure to assume an even more strident line. I favored the quiet, patient lobbying tactics that worked best on Congress. The disagreement put Reuther and me on one side, Dr. King on the other, and Randolph in the middle. Randolph's march for jobs offered us a perfect compromise. We all adopted it, broadening its purpose to back the civil rights bill. The March on Washington was on.

At the beginning of July, we held another organizational meeting in New York City. There were a few moments of tension. Randolph wanted to make Bayard Rustin head of the march, but I opposed the idea. I have always admired Rustin's organizational skill and brilliant mind, but I worried that some aspects of his radical past might provide ammunition for our enemies, who were doing all they could to attack the march. Randolph held his ground, so we worked out a compromise. Rustin did most of the work, but he had to stay in the background. History has attached the name of Reverend King to the march, but I suspect it would be more accurate to call it Randolph's march—and Rustin's.

We set up headquarters on West 130th Street in Harlem. Before long Rustin had 200 people at work with him, with more outriders all across the country. We set out to bring 100,000 marchers to Washington, and in the end we got a quarter of a million people in and out of town before dusk.

As August groaned through the dog days and the day of the march approached, the Kennedys grew more and more nervous. Louis Martin was on the phone all the time. There were times when Washington seemed paralyzed with fear. On march day, the business community closed shop. The apprehension spread to the government agencies. Behind these jitters lay a ridiculous, ignorant fear of black Americans. At the time, most of white Washington couldn't tell the difference between the talk of a stomping Baptist preacher and the words of the wildest black nationalist. Washington seemed to think it faced an assault by tens of thousands of radicals. Malcolm X, for example, was calling the demonstration "The Farce on Washington," but such fine distinctions were lost on the white folks. Louis told me later that the Administration had the army preparing for the march as if it were World War II.

There were a few small contretemps on the morning of the march. We wanted to meet the President, but Kenny O'Donnell, the keeper of Kennedy's schedule, opposed us. Since Kennedy was not sure what was going to happen that day, he wanted room to react. A bit reluctantly, we agreed to see him at the White House once the march was over. Then Archbishop Patrick O'Boyle, one of the march leaders, took a look at the speech that John Lewis of S.N.C.C. planned to deliver and said he wouldn't take part unless Lewis toned it down. I believe there was a sentence in the speech that read: "We will march through the South, through the heart of Dixie, the way Sherman did." Lewis was going to burn Jim Crow to the ground nonviolently, taking matters into S.N.C.C.'s hands and creating a source of power beyond the national structure. Bishop O'Boyle bridled at the fiery rhetoric. I thought the more important point was that Lewis was denouncing the legislative process at a demonstration called in large part to back the Civil Rights Bill—that seemed like a double cross. In the end, Lewis agreed to take out the remark, and the march was a great and moving day in the sun for everyone.

I can still see all those faces staring up toward the Lincoln Memorial, and I well remember the words Randolph spoke that day. He said, "Let the nation know the meaning of our numbers. We are not a pressure group, not an organization or a group of organizations. We are not a mob. We are the advance guard of a massive moral revolution for jobs and freedom." On this day word came that W. E. B. Du Bois had died in self-exile in Ghana, and in my speech I said, "Now, regardless of the fact that in his later years Dr. Du Bois chose another path, it is incontrovertible that at the dawn of the twentieth century his was the voice that was calling to you to gather here today in this cause." Then Dr. King enunciated his magnificent dream of integration, to close out the afternoon. No one who heard him speak that day will ever forget him.

When the speeches were over, we made our way through the crowds and over to the White House. Louis met us at the front gate and showed us in. Kennedy was waiting, relief written all over his face. "You did a superb job of making your case," he said. Then, discovering that we had not eaten since breakfast, he sent out for coffee and sandwiches. As we left, the buses were already taking the last of the marchers back home. Louis took a final tour of the city and found that everyone had left by 7 P.M. When I got back to New York I found a message from a lady in Toronto. She told me she had been ironing when the television switched to the march. Suddenly she found herself crying. "Those are God's people," she said. Black—and white.

After the march, pressure for the Civil Rights Bill picked up steadily. In September, a murderous madman put a bomb in the Sixteenth Street Baptist Church in Birmingham, killing four children. I sent word to Kennedy that he ought to cut off every nickel of federal aid to Alabama. The leaders of the march also got together and sent him a warning that when people couldn't look to their government to defend them, they would take steps to defend themselves. But as the momentum behind the bill continued to grow, the Administration began to backslide. At one stage, Emanuel Celler, who was chairman of the House Judiciary Committee, managed to add a strong F.E.P.C., Title III provisions for the Attorney General, permanent status for the Civil Rights Commission, and an anti-Jim Crow statute for businesses that held government licenses, but Robert Kennedy went before the committee with a request to tame down the bill. With the Republican leadership also at work, the committee passed a watered-down, compromise bill in late October. Kennedy called the result "a better bill than the Administration's," but I didn't think so. I took the compromise as a challenge to strengthen the bill again later. The House reported out the compromise on November 20, and that's where things stood when John Kennedy left for Dallas.

I was working in my office the day Kennedy was shot. When the first news bulletin came over the radio I scoffed at it. Hell, he's down in Texas now, I thought. Nothing can happen to him there. A few minutes later I picked up my hat and coat and headed out for lunch. When the elevator doors opened in the lobby, I saw people pressed against their radios; on Fifth Avenue, grown men were weeping.

It was a miserable moment. Kennedy had contributed significantly to changing the moral climate of the country, the first step before civil rights legislation could be passed. He believed that his package would have passed Congress by the following summer. I am not quite sure how much of it would have survived if Lee Harvey Oswald had not intruded so savagely into the country's history. Of all the memorials that were offered to Kennedy after his death, none was finer than the Civil Rights Act of 1964. But to raise that monument, it took the temperament and skill of quite a different President—Lyndon Baines Johnson.

22   L.B.J.

The day after John Kennedy's assassination I received a telephone call from one of Lyndon Johnson's harried staffers in Washington. It was the first of the dozens of messages I received from Johnson over the next few years. The aide didn't have much time to talk, and his tone was urgent. He said, "The President would like to talk to you next Friday."

I wondered what required such a prompt talk with me. The following Wednesday, L.B.J. addressed a joint session of Congress, and there was no longer any mystery. He meant to open his new Administration by completing the most important tasks of the old: Kennedy's tax bill and the Civil Rights Bill. I watched his speech on television. Speaking in homey Texas cadences, he told Congress, "We have talked long enough in this century about equal rights. We have talked for a hundred years or more. It is time now to write the next chapter—and to write it in the books of law."

The speech took some of the gloom off the grimmest Thanksgiving I had spent for some time. The next morning I got up early and flew to Washington. The bleak atmosphere of the assassination still hung heavily over the White House. An aide ushered me in, and I spent the next forty-five minutes with the new President. He had lost his air of gruff heartiness; he was more somber than I had ever seen him before.

When we sat down, he brought a chair within a few inches of my knees. He wanted to talk about the Civil Rights Bill and what the people in the civil rights movement needed to do to get the bill past Congress. He was making Hubert Humphrey his field captain in the Senate, and he expected a good deal of help from the Republican leadership of both houses; but he knew that the South would put up a fierce show of resistance. He said the outcome, the very future of the country, depended on how we all handled ourselves over the next few months. Johnson talked quickly, earnestly. It was the first time I had really felt those mesmerizing eyes of Texas on me. When Lyndon Johnson wanted to sell an idea, he put all his being into the task. Leaning forward, almost touching me, he poked his finger at me and said quietly, "I want that bill *passed.*"

I was struck by the enormous difference between Kennedy and Johnson. Where Kennedy had been polite and sympathetic on all matters of basic principle, more often than not he had been evasive on action. Kennedy was not naïve, but as a legislator he was very green. He saw himself as being dry-eyed, realistic. In retrospect, I think that for all his talk about the art of the possible, he didn't really know what was possible and what wasn't in Congress. He was always hesitating, weighing what he could and couldn't do. I don't believe he ever really understood the South. The real enemies of civil rights didn't give a tinker's damn if he introduced civil rights bills or suppressed them. If he did, they would fight him; if he didn't, they were not going to collapse in gratitude and let his other bills go through. They would fight those, too. When it came to dealing with Congress, Johnson knew exactly what was possible. I had feared that Kennedy would sacrifice several vital sections of the Civil Rights Bill to get the rest passed, but Johnson made it plain that he wanted the whole bill. If we could find the votes, we would win. If we didn't find those votes, we would lose, he said. The problem was as simple as that. "I'm going to help wherever the Constitution will let me," he promised as he brought the meeting to a close. "But I can't do the lobbying myself. I don't think you would expect me to do that."

I left the White House that day convinced that Johnson was willing to go much farther than he had ever gone before. As a young congressman he had won a good reputation as an F.D.R. liberal, but when he reached the Senate, the glow faded. He became one of the main obstacles to any change in the Senate rules. Even in those days, however, he had been different from most Southerners. It was always possible to talk to him. He didn't have much more experience with black people, but he had a sympathy for Mexican-Americans, who were treated like dirt in Texas, and he was not a classic race baiter. The main difficulty was that he served as a champion of the "you want too much too fast" school of thought on civil rights. Back in those early days he told Clarence Mitchell a story that typified his approach. An old friend from Texas had been talking to him about race, and said, "You know, there would have been a fight if I had gone into San Antonio with a Negro only ten years ago. Four years ago there would have been plenty of hate in everyone's eyes. Now—no one would pay any attention to it. That's progress."

I didn't put much faith in this particular kind of progress. The story took place a year before the Supreme Court handed down its decision in the school cases, and at the time, L.B.J. wasn't doing much that I could see to help the course of progress along. His excuse was that while he recognized the virtue of civil rights, he wasn't going to do anything that would split the Democratic Party.

Lyndon Johnson was always unpredictable, however, and he didn't keep to that course. I suppose he began to run for President when he was three, and he knew he had to make a break with his Southern roots at some point. By 1957 he seemed to have concluded that supporting voting rights was the safest way to start. He became Mr. Voting Rights in the Senate. He used to tell us that once Negroes had voting rights, everything else would follow. His argument was nonsense, of course, since Negroes remained an outvoted minority, but Johnson was so eloquent that he sold it to a good many people. In 1957 he turned the Civil Rights Bill into a voting rights bill. This was progress of the three steps forward, two steps back sort. You didn't find him praising school desegregation. In 1960 he succeeded in passing another Civil Rights Bill, mostly so he could run against John Kennedy. No one took that bill very seriously. But after Kennedy was killed, Johnson became the greatest civil rights President of our lifetime, and if he hadn't stumbed into Vietnam, he might have come out of the 1960s as a liberal hero on the scale of Franklin D. Roosevelt.

I began to see the first real changes in Johnson when he was Vice President. He had always been capable of a constructive personal response to race issues, but suddenly it became possible for his feelings and his future to coincide. As Senate majority leader he had thought mostly about himself and the voters of Texas; as Vice President he began to think about himself and the entire country—he no longer held back on civil rights.

President Kennedy did not leave his Vice President very much room for serious action, but Johnson made use of what little he had. During the spring of 1961, Kennedy made him head of the President's Commission on Equal Opportunity in Employment, a rusty old agency going back to Harry Truman's days in one form or another. Johnson took the job seriously. He was always on the telephone to businessmen, union leaders, and civil rights leaders. "This is the Vice President calling," he would begin. By the time he had hung up, we'd all be counting our fingers, checking our wallets, and shaking our heads at what he had talked us into.

In April 1961 I went to Washington to bring Johnson an N.A.A.C.P. complaint on job discrimination at the Marietta, Georgia, plant of the Lockheed Aircraft Corporation. The federal government had awarded

Lockheed a $1 billion contract in spite of blatant race discrimination at the Marietta plant—where even the time cards for workers had separate colors for black and white.

In those days, Johnson had an office across from the White House in the old Executive Office Building. When I paid my call, he had just come back from a diplomatic trip to Africa. A secretary showed me into his office, where a photograph album was lying on the coffee table. I picked it up and thumbed through it. It was full of 8 x 10 glossy photographs of Johnson on the road in Africa, a tall, smiling man surrounded by crowds of people, who all happened to be black. I still wonder whether Johnson put the album out to soften me up; I can't imagine him leaving such a collection out for Senator Eastland. As I was leafing through the book, Johnson came in. He sat down, sized me up, and said something I have never forgotten. "You know," he began, "in Senegal, when I looked into the eyes of the mothers there, they had the same look as the people in Texas, the mothers in Texas." He paused a moment to let the effect sink in, then added earnestly, "All mothers want the best for their children, and the mothers in Senegal were no different from the white mothers in Texas."

That was Lyndon Johnson: sentimental, old-fashioned, manipulating, but at bottom somehow sincere. He didn't *have* to talk that way. You could tell by his tone that behind all the soft soap there was genuine feeling.

I told him that it had been outrageous for the Administration to make him head of an antidiscrimination committee one week and to hand out a $1 billion Jim Crow contract to Lockheed the next. He nodded his head in agreement. "We're working on that," he said. He told me that his investigators were already looking into the case, and he said that the contractors had agreed to cooperate rather than resist him. "We mean business," he promised. He was as good as his word. By the end of the year the plant had hired 200 more Negro workers and given out 59 promotions. For the first time, 13 professional and clerical jobs went to Negroes.

The Lockheed case was just a small step, more important for its symbolic value than anything else, but it did show the way Johnson's thoughts were leaning. Not long afterward, Minnie and I gave a party in New York for Whitney Young, who had just come to town to take over the Urban League, and his wife. The day of the party I got a telephone call from Theodore Kheel, the New York labor arbitrator, who asked if he might bring the Vice President. That evening Johnson swept in and spent nearly an hour, even though the stop was only supposed to last fifteen minutes. He was in fine spirits, ribbing the

men and offering a flattering word or two to all the ladies. He wasn't
the handsome ladies' man that Kennedy had been, but I remember
thinking as he left that I had never seen a better man with a crowd.
His common touch—before he lost it because of Vietnam—was extraordinary. No politician understood better than he the necessity to
keep in touch with the people—or what it would cost him if he failed.
Much later, when he named Thurgood Marshall to the Supreme
Court, he told Clarence Mitchell, "You know, I wanted a Justice on
the Supreme Court who knew the law and was respected for his
knowledge of the law, but also had never lost touch with ordinary
people. *That* was the reason I appointed Justice Marshall."

Through the winter, spring, and early summer of 1964, I watched
with increasing pleasure as Johnson applied his own touch to the
Civil Rights Bill. After all those years of Eisenhower's aloofness and
Kennedy's evasiveness, it was a wonderful relief to be dealing with
him. Johnson was a voracious watcher of TV news. One evening as I
was sitting in front of my TV set, a correspondent for one of the networks reported that Johnson had cut a deal with Senator Russell to
drop fair employment protection from the Civil Rights Bill. No sooner
did the reporter sign off than my phone rang. It was the President.
Steaming with indignation, he said that the story was untrue, that no
such deal was in the offing. A few minutes later the phone rang again.
This time the caller was Clarence Mitchell, who had also seen the report and who said that he felt it had to be wrong. "Well, Clarence," I
told him, "you must be right, because the President just called from
Texas to say it wasn't true."

After that Johnson was on the phone constantly. He called me before each of his major speeches on civil rights and after each civil
rights crisis, and there were plenty. During one of those calls, he
dropped whatever issue it was that preoccupied him, practically in
mid-sentence, and said, "I'm always calling you. Why don't you call
me more often?" I was nonplused. From then on I had no trouble
getting through to him whenever I had to.

Johnson adopted a bold strategy for the Civil Rights Bill. As majority leader, he had argued that filibusters were not powerful enough to
kill legislation whose time had come. "All you've got to do is get the
votes, or run the Senate round the clock until you do get them," he
used to say. Then he would go out and compromise the bill in question until so little was left that there was no point in filibustering it
anyway. In 1964, he was not in a compromising mood. One day he
took Clarence and Joe Rauh aside and told them, "You tell Mike
Mansfield to put that bill on the floor, and tell everybody that it's

going to stay there until it passes. I don't care if it stays for four, six, or eight months. You can tell Mike Mansfield, and you can tell anybody else, that the President of the United States doesn't care if that bill is there forever. We are not going to have the Senate do anything else until that bill is passed. And it is *going* to pass."

The majority leader got the message. Mansfield was able to bypass the Senate Judiciary Committee and the hatchet of Senator Eastland; the bill went directly on the Senate calendar, and the inevitable filibuster began. Johnson then dropped the usual counterattack of round-the-clock debate. He didn't want to give the Southerners any chance to say that they had been cheated out of their fair say. He planned to let them talk until they ran out of wind and strength, which is just what happened.

The House got down to business much more quickly, beginning debate on February 3, 1964. To help things along, we arranged for N.A.A.C.P. delegates from ten key states, people who knew their congressman personally, to come to Washington. Clarence Mitchell organized our lobbying and kept at it tirelessly. The House bill had eleven sections and was the most expansive civil rights measure in modern times. Our enemies tried to hamstring it with no less than 140 separate amendments. A bipartisan committee of Northern Democrats and Republicans managed to knock out 103 of the worst amendments, leaving 37 comparatively minor revisions, which were accepted.

I was pleased with the bill that finally emerged. It strengthened the right to vote and banned discrimination in public accommodations as well as segregation in all public facilities. It gave the Attorney General power to begin school discrimination suits and provided help to local school boards struggling to devise desegregation plans. It also directed all federal agencies to eliminate discrimination in their operations and empowered the federal government to withhold funds from defiant states and school boards. It barred job discrimination, extended the life of the Civil Rights Commission, and established a community-relations service to calm racial tensions at the grassroots level.

After the House voted 290–130 to pass the bill, we had proof that the will of the people could be translated into sound legislation. On the day the bill passed, Clarence and Joe Rauh were standing in a House corridor congratulating themselves when a pay phone nearby rang. One of them picked it up. Lyndon Johnson was at the other end of the line. "All right, you fellows," he said. "Get over to the Senate. Get busy. We've won in the House, but there is a big job across the way." Joe and Clarence still tell that story. No lobbyist could ever outdo Lyndon Johnson. He even knew how to raise you on the pay phones.

About this time I got another of those phone calls myself. "When are you going to get down here and do some civil righting?" Johnson wanted to know. He told me that if we were to break the filibuster we would have to convince Everett Dirksen to see things our way, and he said the only way to do that was to persuade Dirksen that Negro voters in Illinois would scratch his back a little if he would scratch theirs. The job took lots of doing. Dirksen thought the Negro vote in Illinois was hopelessly down on him and that there would be no bene-fit for him in supporting the Civil Rights Bill. He started out by offer-ing a number of amendments that weakened the bill. "You'll have to take out Title II on accommodations and Title VII on employment be-fore I'll support you," he told us. But in the end we did nothing of the sort, and he chose not to go against us. He claimed later that he had made a hundred changes in the bill, but the only serious alterations were in some administrative procedures. He was simply breathing a little of the celebrated Dirksen fog into the air, telling Republicans that it would be safe for them to vote for a "Dirksen bill." At one point Hubert Humphrey called Joe Rauh into his office and showed him Dirksen's changes. Joe told me that he looked at the changes and thought, so what. The deal Dirksen was offering was so much better than anyone had expected that it wasn't very hard to go for it. We did not have to suffer through 1957 all over again.

The mood of the country ran very strongly in favor of the bill. In late May, as the filibuster was limping along, Dwight Eisenhower in-vited me to his farm in Gettysburg, Pennsylvania, to talk about it. Two days later he wrote the New York *Herald Tribune* that civil rights had become the nation's most critical domestic challenge and that the country had a profound obligation to each of its citizens. He was a late convert, but his support helped, as did Dirksen's. On June 10, the Senate voted for the first time in history to impose cloture on a civil rights measure.

I will never forget that moment. The vote came at eleven o'clock in the morning. Hubert Humphrey was in the Senate chamber, even though he had just learned that his son had developed cancer. Sena-tor Clair Engle of California, who was dying of cancer and could no longer speak, had himself wheeled in and cast his vote by pointing to his eye. The Senate voted 71–29 to impose cloture. Of the 33 Repub-licans, 27 voted with us: Senator Dirksen had done his job well. Once cloture was imposed, the rest was relatively easy. President Johnson signed the bill into law that year, just two days before the Fourth of July.

The victory represented decades of effort by the N.A.A.C.P., but we did not reach it without the help of many friends. Presidents Kennedy and Johnson, Senators Mansfield, Humphrey, Dirksen, and Thomas Kuchel of California, John McCormack, Carl Albert, Emanuel Celler, Charles Halleck, William McCulloch, Clarence Brown, and Richard Bolling in the House all helped enormously. As I recall, Senator Russell said a bit gloomily after his defeat that every time he looked up he seemed to be faced with someone from the A.F.L.–C.I.O., the women's groups, the fraternal or civil organizations—or a minister. But if one man deserved the credit, I think that man was Clarence Mitchell. Black Americans will always be in his debt for the extraordinary work he did in those long months of lobbying.

The Civil Rights Act was a measure by the people for the people. If Congress had not passed it, I don't think Negro Americans would ever have recovered from the injustice. Their faith in the Constitution and in orderly democratic processes had already been tested almost beyond endurance. The Civil Rights Act came just after the tenth anniversary of *Brown vs. Board of Education*. After an entire decade of unfulfilled promises, 90 percent of Negro children in the South and border states were still going to all-Negro schools, and in the North, *de facto* segregation was getting worse than ever each year. The Civil Rights Act became a Magna Carta for the race, a splendid monument for the cause of human rights.

Even as Johnson signed it and began handing out all those pens, I knew that we were not home free. The act would not implement itself. I hoped that the South would comply voluntarily with it, but I was sure that some communities would put up desperate resistance. I knew that we had to pull ourselves together and press on.

The first challenge that summer was to deal with Senator Barry Goldwater of Arizona. While the House and Senate were debating the Civil Rights Bill, the Goldwater people, intense in their own wrong-headed way and very skillful in political organizing, had been running off with the Republican Party's presidential nomination. During the spring, Goldwater had told the country that returning the G.O.P. to the White House would "cool the fires of racial strife." He had also complained that the Civil Rights Bill would force people to like folks they might not otherwise want to like. Morally, his arguments were absurd. Goldwater ignored the fact that the strife had grown out of the refusal of certain states to protect the rights of their black citizens or to allow the federal government to do the job for them. From the time of the Civil War to the assassination of Medgar Evers, the history of the issue was clear—and written in blood.

Goldwater had his eye on the South. He said over and over that he believed in leaving civil rights issues to the states; to the same states, it might be observed, that had violated civil rights every time they had the chance. No matter how much he rationalized his position, no matter how decent a man he might have been, he was still offering a grant of immunity to the South for its cattle prods and shotguns, for the armored tanks and police dogs of Birmingham, the bomb murders of little children in Alabama churches, and the death of Medgar Evers. Goldwater was playing a cynical game of politics with an issue in which the life and death of 20 million black Americans were involved. They were through with patience and paternalism. In 1964, they were not going to tip their hats and shuffle back to 1900.

I sent messages to Goldwater warning him that there might be violence in the streets if the legitimate grievances of Negroes were not attended to. I told him that sophistry and antebellum oratory were the last things we needed; I urged him to join the Republicans in the House and Senate who had lined up behind the Civil Rights Bill. But I didn't get anywhere; he wanted the South and he was willing to pay the price to get it. I did no better with the G.O.P. platform committee when I flew to San Francisco that summer. The Goldwater people owned the convention, shouting down the most liberal supporters of civil rights and adopting only the mildest of civil rights planks.

The trouble I feared erupted right after the G.O.P convention. Harlem went up in riot after an off-duty policeman shot James Powell, a black kid who got into a fight with an apartment superintendent on the Upper East Side of Manhattan. Then violence struck Rochester, New York, Elizabeth, Paterson, and Jersey City, New Jersey, Rexmoor, Illinois, and Philadelphia.

The riots upset Lyndon Johnson badly. He called the leaders of the major civil rights organizations and demanded to know what was going on. He said he was afraid that the violence would hurt the chances for implementing the Civil Rights Act and that it would hurt him in his fall campaign against Goldwater. He not only wanted to beat Goldwater, he wanted to crush him, and he didn't want anything to get in the way of that goal.

I shared some of his concern. After the Harlem riot, I sent cables to Dr. King, Whitney Young, A. Philip Randolph, James Farmer, and John Lewis arguing that we should all get together and talk over what needed to be done. I was deeply worried by the white backlash that had made itself felt so plainly in the campaign of Alabama's governor,

George Wallace, and in the hooting and catcalls at the Cow Palace in San Francisco. In my view, the tragic violence in Harlem, the Wallace campaign, and the Goldwater nomination were all linked. The danger was that if we didn't play our cards coolly and intelligently, the promise of the Civil Rights Act might be diminished or nullified and a new decade of violence ushered in. I believed that with the backlash at work, there could be no real safety in assuming, as many did, that Goldwater had no chance of winning the election. If we made the wrong moves, I thought he had a good chance to win.

We met in New York at the end of July. It was a difficult meeting. At first there was considerable disagreement on where we all stood and what we should do, but in the end, most of us agreed to a significant change of tactics for the rest of the political year. We called for a moratorium on mass marches, picketing, and demonstrations until Election Day. This was a major sacrifice, but our goal was to secure justice and equality as well as law and order. We made it plain that we did not approve of looting, vandalism, and any other type of criminal action, and drew a sharp line between those kinds of violence and the legitimate protests of citizens denied their rights. What appalled us most was the idea that white racists might succeed in equating the summer riots with the demonstrations that had been so vital to civil rights progress in the South.

To my surprise, we got some help from the F.B.I. in laying those fears to rest. The F.B.I. investigated the summer riots, ready to bay at the slightest hint of a conspiracy. But in the end, J. Edgar Hoover's people issued a report that cleared the civil rights movement completely. The report called the riots "a senseless attack on all constituted authority," but conceded that they had not been race riots "in any accepted sense of the term: Negroes had not rioted against whites; nor had whites rioted against Negroes." The F.B.I. also took pains to say that its investigation had determined that the riots had not grown out of the civil rights movement. The victims had been Negro storeowners as often as white, Negro police officers had been assaulted along with white officers, and most of the trouble had been the work of young people in their teens and early twenties, no revolutionary cadre. After the F.B.I. report there was no excuse for race to be drawn into the campaign. That year was the only time that the N.A.A.C.P. had broken a long tradition of nonpartisanship in election years to oppose Goldwater.

I ran into a few serious problems at the Democratic National Convention in Atlantic City. The hottest issue was whether the Mississippi Free Democrats should displace Mississippi's segregated delegation. The insurgents had tried to win seats through the regular channels, only to be ruthlessly shut out because of race; so they had set up a parallel party of their own, meeting the rules of the Democratic Party and pledging to support the nominee and platform. They were far more loyal than those white Democrats from Mississippi. I argued that they should be seated.

Joe Rauh was helping the Mississippi challenge. I agreed with his view that if the convention had to pick between two delegations, one loyal and one unreliable, it should pick the loyal one and reject the lily-whites. But L.B.J. didn't see things that way. He believed that the Civil Rights Act would win him the black vote in the fall, but he did not want to lose the South, so he enlisted Humphrey and Walter Reuther, Joe's main client and one of his oldest political heroes, to try to talk him out of the challenge.

I saw what the President was up to—it wasn't one of his finest hours. But Joe held out. He believed that if he could wangle eleven votes on the credentials committee, enough for a minority report, and get just eight state delegations to demand a roll-call vote on the minority report, the convention would support the Free Democrats: it would be 1948 all over again. That, of course, was the last thing Johnson wanted. Some people said that when Fannie Lou Hamer went before the credentials committee with her moving challenge to the lily-whites, Johnson called a press conference of his own in an attempt to gobble up her TV time. He was worried, all right.

I winced as he pushed Humphrey into the role of peacemaker and compromiser, leaving little doubt that Humphrey's chance to become Vice President depended on the outcome. The first compromise offer was that the insurgents would be given standing as "honored guests." All that added up to was a few seats in the galleries, and they turned it down. The second proposal was to seat two of their leaders—Aaron Henry, who was also a state officer of the N.A.A.C.P., and Reverend Edwin King—as at-large delegates; to exact a loyalty pledge from the white delegation; and to promise that at future conventions no segregated delegations would be seated. As far as I could see, Johnson's calculation was that the proposal would force the white Mississippi delegation to bolt, but would keep the rest of the South in line, avoiding a second Dixiecrat rebellion.

Aaron Henry was sympathetic to Johnson's idea, but Fannie Lou Hamer wasn't, and neither was Bob Moses, a brave young organizer for S.N.C.C. who had helped create the Mississippi Free Democratic Party. So Humphrey asked Bayard Rustin and me to talk to Moses. We did, but Moses believed that the challenge could succeed. He underestimated Johnson, who put irresistible pressure on the credentials committee and the state delegations, and squelched the challenge. The convention exacted the loyalty oath from the lily-whites, and as Johnson predicted, they stormed out of the hall. The insurgents held a sit-in in their seats. As psychologically satisfying as the moment was, it did not add up to being seated in place of the white delegation. If Johnson had been willing to let the Mississippi Free Democrats name the two at-large delegates offered them, and if Fannie Lou Hamer had been one of them, perhaps an understanding could have been worked out. But Fannie Lou Hamer and many of the other Free Democrats were a bit too radical for L.B.J. As it was, Mississippi wound up with no real delegation that year. Four years later, in Chicago, the Democrats kept their word and seated the Mississippi Free Democrats, but in the interim a lasting sense of grievance did terrible damage to relations between white liberals and black organizers in the South. Fannie Lou Hamer and Moses both thought they had been sold out. Moses took a vow never to talk to whites again. His fury was understandable, if extreme. I watched and worried for the future.

Despite the bad moments at the convention, Johnson's victory over Goldwater that November gave him the landslide that he so coveted. The returns ratified his decision to press strongly for the 1964 Civil Rights Act and repudiated Goldwater's cynical flirtation with the South. In January, Johnson invited me to Washington for the inauguration. I was not far from him during a prayer service at the National City Christian Church, and I have never seen a happier politician.

Our next major campaign was to strengthen voting rights. One reason the 1964 bill did not contain stronger protection for voting rights was our fear that if we gave the South such an opening it would do what it had done in 1957: agree to support voting provisions, then wreck everything else. I don't think Johnson expected to get a voting rights law right away. He seemed content to allow some time to see how the Civil Rights Act would work in practice.

The South gave us no time for a breather. That March, Governor Wallace turned loose his troopers on the peaceful demonstrators who were marching from Selma to Montgomery to demand their voting rights. Bloody Sunday in Selma came just as Johnson was sending the U.S. Marines to Vietnam in force. Here we are sending troops to fight the Communists ten thousand miles away and we can't even keep George Wallace in line down in Alabama, I thought at the time. It was not a pretty thought, but many others shared it.

Selma put Johnson on the spot just as Little Rock had President Eisenhower. At first Johnson moved cautiously. He took his time before sending troops to protect the marchers, but he also decided to take advantage of the moment to step up speed on the Voting Rights Bill. In mid-March he telephoned me to tell me what he had in mind: a voting rights law that would redeem the bloodshed of Selma—and make sure it didn't happen again.

I flew to Washington to be in the galleries on the evening of March 15, 1965, when Johnson took his plans before a joint session of Congress. I can still see him standing there, blinking in the bright light, looking up from his text. He said, "I speak tonight for the dignity of man and the destiny of democracy." In the galleries everyone leaned forward. "The command of the Constitution is plain," he continued. "There is no moral issue. It is wrong to deny any of your fellow Americans the right to vote. What happened in Selma is part of a far larger movement that reaches into every section and state in America. It is the effort of American Negroes to secure for themselves the full blessings of American life. Their cause must be our cause, too. Because it is not just Negroes, but really it is all of *us* who must overcome the crippling legacy of bigotry and injustice." He paused and looked up: "And we shall overcome."

I had waited all my life to hear a President of the United States talk that way. There was a great roar of applause. I looked to my left and I looked to my right and I saw men and women with their eyes full of tears. And at that moment, I confess, I loved L.B.J.

23 THE FIRE THIS TIME

Selma was the civil rights movement's last great parade of the 1960s, four days of tramping and bearing moral witness that wound across the Edmund Pettus Bridge and fifty miles on down U.S. 50 to Montgomery, where Jefferson Davis had taken his oath as President of the Confederacy and where George Wallace was still muttering defenses of white supremacy, an idea whose time had long come—and gone.

I joined the march on the fourth day. When I arrived, the marchers were camping at St. Jude's just outside Montgomery. There must have been 30,000 people on hand for the last four-mile walk to the State Capitol. The original marchers, those who had come through sun, rain, and mud, all the way from Selma, wore orange plastic jackets. I thought they had won the privilege of leading the parade right up to George Wallace's front door, so I walked behind them as we set off that morning.

We marched out of St. Jude's through the outskirts of Montgomery and up Dexter Avenue to the Capitol, where armed Alabama state police were waiting for us. Someone had put plywood down over the gold star marking the spot where Davis had taken his rebel oath; I suppose they didn't want us to desecrate a holy Confederate shrine by stepping on it. We had a voting rights petition ready for George Wallace. He didn't come out of the Capitol, but every now and then the venetian blinds on his office window parted and you could see him peering out at us through a set of binoculars—a banty segregationist who couldn't believe the crowd.

We gave him something to think about. I knew the Voting Rights Bill would pass Congress: the only real question was how tough it would be. Marches were not the tactics that would be needed to register Negroes once the bill became law, but the march worked gloriously in Selma. Early in the month, at the Edmund Pettus

Bridge, officials of the state of Alabama had used their clubs, bull-whips, and tear gas in a violent attempt to persuade Negroes that the First, Fourteenth, and Fifteenth amendments didn't apply to them. The crowd on the Capitol steps, black and white, spilling away as far as you could see, proved that Wallace and company were wrong. I can still see Andrew Young, who was then a thin young aide to Dr. King, standing up and calling out to the man hiding behind those venetian blinds in the governor's executive suite: "We come to warn that someday some of you in the statehouse are going to be in the cotton patch, and some of us in the cotton patch are going to be in that state-house. We come to love the hell out of the state of Alabama."

It was a warm spring day. Coretta King led the crowd in singing "The Star-Spangled Banner." As the anthem faded away, the Confederacy's stars and bars flew in limp defiance from the top of the Capitol. Reverend Ralph Abernathy stood to introduce Dr. King: "As God called Joshua to lead his people to Jordan, so also he called Martin Luther King to go to Montgomery and say to Pharaoh Wallace, 'Let my people go.' "

Smiling, Dr. King climbed up on a flatbed trailer and, taking a microphone, told Pharaoh Wallace exactly what the crowd had on its mind. "Today," he began, "I want to say to the people of America and the nations of the world: we are not about to turn around. We are on the move now. Yes, we are on the move, and no wave of racism can stop us. . . . We are on the move now, and not even the marching of mighty armies can halt us. Let us march on segregated schools . . . on poverty . . . on ballot boxes. We must keep going."

It was a fine moment, the best since the March on Washington. I flew back home feeling rejuvenated. Then word came that a group of murderous Ku Kluxers had shot and killed Viola Liuzzo, a white woman from Detroit who was driving demonstrators back to Selma after the march. Earlier that month another group of thugs had beaten to death the Reverend James Reeb, a white Unitarian minister. I had gone to Casper, Wyoming, to deliver a eulogy at a memorial service for him. Mrs. Liuzzo was a member of our Detroit branch. As I flew to Detroit for her funeral, the good feelings I had felt on march day soured into a poisonous anger.

The blood of those two innocent white friends dotted the final i's and crossed all the t's on the Voting Rights Act. With martyrs, Congress found the strength to move forward. The issue it faced couldn't have been much clearer. Negroes had been struggling for voting rights since the end of Reconstruction. At the N.A.A.C.P. we had been in the front of the battle since 1915, when, at our pushing, the

Supreme Court in *Guinn vs. the United States* had done away with the grandfather clause. Between 1927 and 1944, in *Nixon vs. Herndon* and *Smith vs. Allwright,* we had gotten rid of the all-white primary. The 1957 Civil Rights Act had empowered the U.S. Attorney General to take civil action on behalf of Negroes denied the right to vote. When it passed, I had believed in good faith that we had settled the matter. But legal technicalities, the slow pace of court decisions, and in some cases the complete hostility of the lower courts had combined to cheat Negroes of their voting rights all across the South. The efforts of Congress in 1960 and 1964 to strengthen the 1957 Act were well meant, but all three civil rights acts together had not yet made the Fifteenth Amendment a living document.

Negroes were still being registered in dribs and drabs, and only after long litigation. We needed to transform this retail process into a wholesale procedure, to register vast numbers of Negro voters quickly, once and for all. The bill offered by President Johnson and Attorney General Nicholas Katzenbach was a good one, but I wanted to see it strengthened to bar the poll tax everywhere, to increase the power of federal voting examiners, and to provide the maximum protection from physical and economic intimidation to all those who braved the wrath of the South to register and vote.

The poll tax issue was a difficult one. We had always argued that Congress could abolish poll taxes by statute; others had maintained that a constitutional amendment was necessary to do the job. We had supported the efforts to ratify the Twenty-fourth Amendment. As a result, the poll tax became an anachronism in federal elections, but many states kept it for state and local contests. In some parts of Virginia, for example, you could vote for President without paying the tax, but you had to cough it up before you could vote for a state legislator or local alderman. In Alabama, Georgia, Louisiana, Mississippi, South Carolina, and sections of North Carolina and Virginia, where the adult Negro population ran from one-fifth to one-third of the total adult population, the poll tax and other forms of harassment had held down registered Negro voters from a high of 46.8 percent in North Carolina to 6.7 percent in Mississippi. Obviously something had to be done.

The N.A.A.C.P. lobbied hard to get rid of the poll tax. President Johnson didn't agree with us at the time, and I also had some trouble keeping all the forces within the civil rights movement lined up behind us. Three groups seemed willing to sacrifice the poll tax ban to win quicker passage of the bill. The Mississippi Freedom Democratic Party and S.N.C.C. wanted to get the bill behind us quickly so publicity could focus on their campaign to purge the House of its white Mississippi congressmen. Dr. King was running a student project down South that summer; he believed that his work would be adversely affected if he didn't have the Voting Rights Act behind him by July. There were also the advocates of L.B.J.'s other Great Society programs who had hoped to put social welfare and labor legislation proposals to Congress before civil rights. When Selma switched the timetable on them, they argued that a long fight over the poll tax in a House-Senate conference would only threaten the rest of the Great Society. Against these diverse pressures, the N.A.A.C.P. had to hold firm. Senator Edward Kennedy and a number of other liberals gave us their help. The South organized a lame filibuster that got nowhere; the Senate voted to impose cloture. In a way, I think the cloture vote saved face for the Southerners. That year they had neither their old energy nor the sympathy of the country behind them.

During the spring and early summer of 1965, the civil rights movement seemed to be at the very apex of its power. That June President Johnson called me before his Howard commencement speech to tell me that he was ready for an all-fronts assault on the problems of race. I was astonished by his fervor and by his daring. He called the race crisis a "seamless web," he acknowledged the damage that had been done to the Negro family over the centuries, and he argued that it would not be enough to open the door of opportunity to Negroes. After three hundred years of slavery, then enforced second-class citizenship, he believed that the victims had to be helped through the door and on their way. No President before had ever been so enlightened or bold in facing up to these truths.

I came away from the conversations I had with L.B.J. feeling that he was not only with us but often ahead of us. At the beginning of August I went to Washington to talk with him about a White House conference on civil rights to be held that fall. When the obligatory business was out of the way, I took the opportunity to point out that only 9 of the 4,000 midshipmen at the U.S. Naval Academy in Annapolis were Negroes. He looked back at me in disbelief. "I'm going to get the Secretary of Defense to look into that right away," he promised. Robert McNamara and Paul Nitze, who was then Secretary of the Navy, did study the problem, and it was rectified. It was as easy as that in those years to do business with L.B.J.

A few days later, Congress passed the Voting Rights Act. L.B.J. invited the leaders of the civil rights movement to Washington for the signing. It was a great day, a wonderful coda to the Civil Rights Act of 1964. The President's sense of the dramatic was in full play. He arranged to sign the bill in the President's Room off the U.S. Senate, the same spot Abraham Lincoln had chosen early in the Civil War to sign a bill freeing slaves the Confederacy had mobilized for war service. As he signed the document, he took pens out of a battery in front of him that must have numbered one hundred. People used to kid him about the corny excess of all those souvenir pens. I suppose it was a little silly, but I confess that I still have the one the President gave me after the ceremony—and I'm old-fashioned enough to treasure it.

In the rotunda, with a statue of Abraham Lincoln brooding over his shoulder, L.B.J. then delivered a fervent speech, the culmination of a thesis he had been working on since 1957. Earnest, almost imploring, he said, "Let me now say to every Negro in the country: You *must* register. You *must* vote. And you must learn, so your choice advances your interests and the interests of the nation. [The] law is a challenge which cannot be met simply by protests and demonstrations. It means that dedicated leaders must work to teach people their rights and responsibilities and to lead them to exercise those rights. If you do this, then you will find . . . that the vote is the most powerful instrument ever devised by man for breaking down injustice and destroying the terrible walls that imprison men because they are different from other men."

"Terrible walls"—the phrase still comes back to me. As things turned out, the most terrible walls were not the ones President Johnson was thinking about. The ones that really counted were at the boundaries of America's ghettos. It was just a few days after L.B.J. signed the Voting Rights Act into law that the prison he had conjured up burst its seams in Watts.

The passion of Watts, the rage, the fires, the crackle of gunfire, the looting all took whites by surprise. I was not surprised in the slightest. We had had early warnings the year before in Harlem and elsewhere. Even so, California had blithely passed a statewide proposition rejecting fair housing, an injury that could only make California Negroes feel hopelessly penned in their ghettos. The chief of police in Los Angeles was the sort of fellow who could call Negroes "monkeys in a zoo." Mayor Sam Yorty was a law-and-order man—law for the white folks and plenty of orders for everyone else. Given this background, the riot was no surprise, but I was not prepared for the sheer scale of the violence: night after night of bloody spasms that turned fifty square miles of the city into a war zone.

I remember watching the carnage on television, praying for it to stop, to burn itself out. As the fires died down, I picked up *Newsweek* and found that one of its reporters had captured the desperate new mood. Standing outside a ravaged store, a young teenager said ruthlessly, "You jes' take an' run, an' you burn when they ain't nothin' to take. You burn whitey, man. You burn his tail up so he know what it's all about."

I don't know which was worse—the grief I felt or the anger. There was no real philosophy, no law, not even any easily comprehensible sociology behind the riot. It was fury flashing up and striking out. Those were frightening days. The country was on the edge of a very destructive time, with eruptions of violence on one side and a real threat of repression on the other.

There was no mystery to what was going on. In the civil rights movement, we had reached into the worst corners of oppression in the South; we had held the country to its principles and conscience and obtained the 1964 Civil Rights Act and the 1965 Voting Rights Act; but we had not even touched the misery and desperation of the urban ghettos outside the South. Nor had we come any nearer to correcting the economic sources of the race crisis. The day President Johnson signed the Voting Rights Act, it looked as if we were bringing to an end all the years of oppression. The truth was that we were just beginning a new ordeal.

At first, my greatest fear was that hostile whites would fail to distinguish rioters from real civil rights demonstrators, that they would simply blast us all. We in the movement could not, would not, and did not condone or in any fashion approve rioting and looting as weapons to secure citizenship rights. I called for a frank and fearless study of the cause of the riot, and Governor Pat Brown appointed John A. McCone, a former director of the Central Intelligence Agency, to head an eight-member commission of investigation, but I have to admit that these gestures did little to root out the problem.

I still remember how shocked President Johnson was by what had happened. I don't think he wanted to believe the first reports. He seemed to take the riot as a personal affront, a rejection of all he had done for black Americans. This was irrational, of course, and in the end he pulled himself together. Although he was shaken, he didn't cut and run, a temptation which many lesser politicians at the time succumbed to. He did not use the riot as a pretext for stopping or rolling back the progress that had been made. I watched him on television as he said, "We must not let anger drown understanding. . . . It is not enough to decry disorder; we must also strike at the unjust conditions from which disorder largely flows." In the years that were to come, I watched with greater and greater sadness as the anger L.B.J. warned us against rose and gained the upper hand.

Those first weeks after Watts were a miserable time for the civil rights movement. Dr. King was practically run out of Watts when he went to California to see what was going on. Those folks in the ghetto didn't need his dreams—they wanted jobs, a decent place to live. Dr. King and the rest of us suddenly found ourselves in the middle of a two-front war. In one direction we had to keep the South from making a Jim Crow comeback in Congress; in the other we had to do something about the ghettos in the cities. No one was really prepared with a strategy or workable program. We seemed more and more often to fall out among ourselves.

In the fall of 1965, though, I had one of the proudest days I had experienced when, at the invitation of Patricia Roberts Harris, L.B.J.'s newest ambassador, Minnie and I stopped in Luxembourg while in Europe. Pat had her first formal dinner as ambassador in our honor. This beautiful black woman of superior intellect presiding over an American embassy in Europe, albeit a small one, lifted my spirits from the depths to which Watts had taken me. It seemed also to be symbolic of Pat's commitment to the cause of black Americans that a person so identified with the civil rights movement as I should be her first guest of honor.

A year or so later, I opened my mail to find a letter from a young man who had considered the situation and wrote to convey his feelings; what he had to tell me was typical of the spirit of those times. Looking at that letter now, I still wince. "Dear Mr. Wilkins," he wrote. "You, Dr. M. L. King, and A. Philip Randolph and many others have done a marvelous and outstanding feat and I sincerely embrace you wholeheartedly for it, but there is a biblical connotation that I believe has pertinence to our revolution, that is, God replaced Moses when he couldn't communicate with his followers in the wilderness. He replaced him with Joshua, a young militant warrior, who led the children of Israel to the promised land. He was the same gentleman who made the sun stand still, destroyed the walls of Jericho. God Almighty knew he was a man, and indeed so was Malcolm X and most certainly is Stokely Carmichael."

The letter represented the new mood of the day. Between the beginning of August 1965 and the end of the following year, it sometimes seemed as if the roof had caved in and the floor was about to give way, too. A new generation short on history and long on spleen chased after me and the N.A.A.C.P. day and night. Some said we were just too old, others that we were playing Uncle Tom for white

America. If the attacks hadn't been so unfair, so divorced from the actual record, so patently one-sided, they would have hurt more; as it was, they still hurt plenty.

There had been friction within the movement before—it was inevitable—but after the summer of 1966 I began to worry that the squabbling might get out of hand. If there was a single turning point, it probably came about the time James Meredith took up his walking stick and struck off down Highway 50 for Jackson, Mississippi, marching against Jim Crow and fear. He was a brave and very difficult man. I believe he wrote in his memoirs that he felt a "divine responsibility" to advance human civilization. His goal was to inspire Negro Mississippians to register and vote and to help them (and himself) overcome the fear that pervaded their daily lives. These were all worthy goals, but after a miserable, bushwacking white man shot Meredith from ambush near Hernando, Mississippi, I thought the march turned into a disaster for the civil rights movement.

After the shooting, I caught the next plane for Memphis. I found Meredith in Room 511B of Bowld Hospital and spent half an hour talking to him. The would-be assassin had peppered him with several rounds of number-four birdshot, and he was badly banged up. Dr. King and Floyd McKissick of C.O.R.E. had already been there. They wanted to persuade Meredith to let the civil rights movement stand in for him, to make the march a national demonstration. I think Meredith, who was a loner, had some reservations about the plan, but in the end he agreed, and the march was on again.

In contrast to the marches on Washington and Montgomery, I think now that the march through Mississippi was snakebit from the first step. At the time, we thought we should mobilize revulsion over Meredith's shooting and turn it into support for the 1966 Civil Rights Bill. Along with a number of other things, the bill had provisions guaranteeing federal protection for civil rights workers. But S.N.C.C. and C.O.R.E. had a different idea. They wanted to turn the march into an attack on the Johnson Administration. I believe the way Stokely Carmichael put it was that the time had come to "put President Johnson on the spot."

I suspect Stokely also wanted to do the same thing to me. Away from the hospital, we had a strategy meeting. I argued that if we started to hate all white men we were going to waste our energy. But Stokely had the last word. He said, "We got to tell the federal government about all those lies they have been telling us. When they *needed* Meredith they sent in the troops, but when they don't need him, he was just a nigger in the cotton field. We need power."

It was a fateful word. Stokely and S.N.C.C. had drafted a "manifesto" which I considered a personal attack on President Johnson. Stampeding the crowd, Stokely accused me of selling out the people, and his S.N.C.C. claque shouted to back him up. I refused to sign the manifesto. I got nowhere with my idea of using the march to back the Civil Rights Bill. Finally, in disgust, I left the meeting to catch a 1:10 A.M. plane home.

The next morning I got a call from Memphis. The firebrands had made a few minor changes in the manifesto, hoping I would sign it. I still thought the document was tendentious and in virtually all respects as bad as the original. I refused to sign, and the march went on without me.

I still believe that the way S.N.C.C. and C.O.R.E. took over the Meredith march was a tragedy for the civil rights movement. Scores of organizations might otherwise have been encouraged to rally around the Civil Rights Bill. Instead, Stokely set off down the road for Jackson, with Dr. King in tow, to draw crowds and reporters. In Greenwood, Mississippi, Stokely got up and yelled, "The only way we gonna stop them white men from whuppin' us is to take over. We been sayin' freedom for six years and we got nothin'. What we gonna start saying now is 'Black Power.' "

Those two words—and what havoc they caused. If Stokely had not joined S.N.C.C. he would have made a wonderful Madison Avenue sloganeer. He had an absolute genius for the provocative phrase. Black power was just a slogan, loaded words, not a real program, but it crystallized resentments that had been building for years, the frustrations of black folks on one hand—and all the animosity of the white backlash on the other. The phrase couldn't have been more destructive if Senator Eastland had contrived it. I imagine he sat there saying to himself, "Now, why didn't I think of that?"

No sooner were the words out than Stokely and everyone else had to scramble to define them. Over the next few weeks and months they were defined, redefined, and defined all over again. No one ever seemed able to agree on just what black power really meant.

The issue was not new. There had been Negro banks and savings-and-loans for nearly seventy-five years. Obviously black people had been thinking of economic power for a long time. For sixty years the N.A.A.C.P. had asserted the right of Negroes to self-defense against the violence of white oppression. During the Parker affair in the thirties and the elections of 1948 and 1960, Negroes had amply shown how aware they were of their own political power. None of these things was new. The younger people were either ignorant of the long record or they chose to ignore it.

The real question, so far as I was concerned, was whether S.N.C.C. and Stokely were after a revolution. I had always believed that for American Negroes revolutionary fantasies were suicidal. To oppose revolution did not mean to fear whites; I knew that anyone who was not cautious in leading a one-tenth minority into conflict with an overwhelming majority was a fool. You can face a lion one way when you have real artillery, but if you have a powder puff, you have to handle yourself differently—if you want to keep your people alive. For all Stokely's reckless talk of guns and power back then, I still don't think he could tell the difference between a pistol and a powder puff.

Another of the more fashionable arguments advanced at the time was that the misery of Negroes had made them part of the Third World, that their future depended on an alliance between the Third World and Black America. Marcus Garvey, Malcolm X, and Frantz Fanon were to be resurrected. Fanon had carefully said that his views on Africa didn't necessarily apply to the American scene, yet superficial enthusiasts went right ahead and applied them anyway. What we got was an ersatz, dashiki-built instant culture that collapsed when everyone finally got bored with it. The hotheads also seemed to have forgotten that after Malcolm X returned from his pilgrimage to Mecca he was much cooler, that he had been casting about for a way of finding a peaceful coexistence with white people at the time of his assassination.

Malcolm X and his style of black nationalism intrigued me a good deal more than the Hollywood Africans of the black-power school. The more superficial black-power folks did little for Malcolm when he was alive. It was after he was killed that they made a cult of him.

I used to travel 100,000 miles a year in those days, and from time to time I would bump into Malcolm on the road. He was a mesmerizing speaker, the toughest man in debate that I've ever seen. None of us could touch him, not even Dr. King. Whitney Young used to say that the only man who could keep up with Malcolm was George Schuyler, who had a quick wit and a sharp tongue, which by then were in service for the extreme right. I always thought that Malcolm and George made a splendid set of antipodes.

Malcolm used to send me mimeographed invitations to speak or attend his meetings. Everyone else got them as well, but I think I was the only one who answered him. I didn't treat them as throwaways. I had great respect for him as a man. His success at preaching self-denial and accumulating money for farms or small businesses in the cities impressed me enormously.

I didn't agree with his early belief that all white people were devils;

I didn't agree with his anti-Semitism, which became more muted toward the end of his life; and I didn't agree with his sweeping generalization about the church as a devil-in-chief for Negroes. To tell black people that all their troubles came from a single cause—the war of the colors—and that all their troubles would be solved if they could just supplant whites was bad. It created hatred and strife and the false vision that you could solve everything if you just slew the white folks or somehow gained the upper hand without slaying them.

Even so, I had a great regard for him. He was true to his beliefs, a spokesman for Negro rights in places where they needed to be spoken for. It was his background that made him such a forceful speaker: he lived what he was speaking. By cataloguing the wrongs done Negroes in such powerful language, he helped us enormously. Inadvertently, he also helped by creating in white minds the specter of what an aroused, black vengeance squad might do. The white folks began to think that it would be better to deal with me, or Smith or Jones, than to worry about the Muslims. They said to themselves, "We don't want to deal with *those* wild men, so we'll make some concessions." Malcolm didn't intend this particular contribution, but he made it all the same.

What I objected to most in the new thinking was the separatism that was at its heart. Did we destroy *Plessy vs. Ferguson* after so many decades of pain and struggle only to Jim Crow ourselves with superficial ideas of black nationalism? Where had separatism led Marcus Garvey in the twenties? How far had Dr. Du Bois gotten with it in the thirties? I wasn't arguing against separatism in the abstract. I had seen it in action off and on for nearly forty years—and it didn't work.

Black power was only the freshest form of separatism. I watched with increasing dismay as Stokely used the phrase along the path of the Meredith march to Jackson. Stokely yelled it and the crowds roared back, the unreflecting eye of the TV cameras caught it all, and new history was made, even as the old was abused. Those of us who did not endorse or embrace the new concept were rhetorically lynched. I hadn't seen such self-righteous attacks since the Communists discovered their true faith in the thirties and condemned everyone who didn't agree with them to the ash heap of history. But where are those people today?

I was disgusted. Although I had always tried to keep our disagreements within the family, I decided not to stay silent. A few weeks after the Meredith march the N.A.A.C.P. held its annual convention in Los Angeles, a short bus ride from Watts. When my time came to speak, I told the convention that no matter how endlessly everyone tried to explain the term "black power," it meant antiwhite power, going it alone. It had to mean separatism. And separatism, whether on the rarefied, intellectual level of black power or on the wishful level of a secessionist Freedom City in Watts, offered us little except a chance to shrivel up and die. Ideologically it dictated "up with black and down with white" in precisely the same manner that South Africa had reversed that slogan. It was a reverse Mississippi . . . a reverse Hitler . . . a reverse Ku Klux Klan. Some proponents claimed the concept instilled pride of race, but could not the same pride be taught without preaching hatred or supremacy based on race? No matter how often it was clarified and clarified again, "black power" in the quick, uncritical, and highly emotional adoption it received from some segments of a beleaguered people could mean in the end only black death. I meant to have none of it. It was the raging of race against race solely on the basis of color, the fanaticism that had swollen our tears and broken our bodies, squeezed our hearts and taken the blood of our black and white loved ones. What the N.A.A.C.P. wanted, what I wanted, was to include Negro Americans in the nation's life, not to exclude them. America was our land as much as it was any American's—every square inch of every city and town and village. The task of winning our share was not the easy one of disengagement and flight but the hard one of work, of short as well as long jumps, of disappointment—and of sweet success.

I didn't mind getting help or even a little stiff competition from the other wings of the civil rights movement. What angered me was that the people who had been silent—or not even born—when the N.A.A.C.P. was fighting all alone had the nerve to attack us for not doing enough.

C.O.R.E. and S.N.C.C. chose to ignore my warnings and to bet their future on black power. The slogan also swept up a lot of other people, Adam Clayton Powell among them. Before long he was calling Stokely "a new breed of cat," and laughing at me as Roy Week-knees, Whitney Young as Whitey Young, and Dr. King as Martin Loser King. One day I opened my *New York Times* and found that he had accused all of us of being so busy getting white money and the support of white liberals and being led down the primrose path of phony integration that we had lost contact with Negro youth. Adam knew better than to say that the N.A.A.C.P. opposed black power because it was afraid of losing white support. The truth was that 90 percent of our members were Negroes, and that membership dues and contributions supplied the vast bulk of our finances. We did not need white help to survive. C.O.R.E. and S.N.C.C. were both far more vulnerable than we.

When Adam invited me to attend a black power conference on Labor Day, 1966, I turned him down. I did not believe that integration was phony or that white people should be excluded from participating in the civil rights movement. They had created and maintained the problem of white racism; they owed it to themselves and to the nation to help rectify the wrong. Civil rights were not a sham, nor was it true that Negroes couldn't compete successfully with non-Negroes, given equal opportunity. The real challenges that summer were to increase Negro voter registration and put it to use; to open more job opportunities at all levels in private and public employment; to secure adequate housing for slum-shocked ghetto dwellers; to protect poor Negro consumers from unscrupulous merchants, landlords, and credit dealers; to provide high-quality *integrated* education for all American children; to bolster the capital and skills of Negro businesses; to enforce all civil rights, social welfare, and economic legislation; to protect Negroes from police brutality—in short, to make sure that 20 million Negroes had all the rights and privileges and dignity of other citizens. Black was beautiful—I didn't disagree with that. Our African heritage was vital to our culture—I agreed with that point, too. And I believed that we should stand up and demand what we were entitled to as men and women. But I wasn't going to burn down any towns to get it. The N.A.A.C.P. wasn't going to shoot anybody—and it wasn't going to lead anybody to slaughter.

I think that the most concrete legacy of the black power movement was to make the term "Negro" a dirty word. Say it today and you are likely to draw a groan of pain, anger, or disbelief. The rationale for substituting black for Negro was that Negro was a white man's word. That, of course, was true, but I could never see how the word black was much of an improvement. "Black" is in the *Oxford English Dictionary,* just a few volumes ahead of "Negro." There's not a word in the English language that couldn't be considered a white man's word.

Two of the best words are "freedom" and "liberty." If you go back to King John and the Magna Carta, you won't find Negroes or blacks on the fields of Runnymede. What was at stake back then was not an issue of blacks versus whites; it was a matter of liberty for individuals no matter what color they might be. That has been our struggle all along. It made no sense to me to reduce the fight to a clash of colors or to a quarrel over a name.

I think the advice Dr. Du Bois had to offer on this subject long ago is still the soundest. He said, "Suppose we arose tomorrow morning, and Lo! instead of being 'Negroes,' all the world called us 'Cheiropolidi'? Do you really think this would make a vast and momentous difference to you and me? Would you be any less ashamed of being descended from a black man, or would your schoolmates feel any less superior to you? The feeling of inferiority is in you, not in any name. The name merely evokes what is already there. Exorcise the hateful complex and no name can ever make you hang your head."

To the degree that black power helped exorcise the complex, it was useful, but its side effects were extremely destructive. I did not intend to let a slogan sway the N.A.A.C.P. from its fundamental objective: the full participation of Negro Americans in all phases of American life. We realized in that summer of 1966, as we had in the winter of 1909, that racial discrimination corrupts every area of American life. We had tried many techniques to eliminate that social blight, but in everything we had done, we had never sought to isolate the Negro from the mainstream of America. The goal had always been to include the Negro in that mainstream, to create a new sense of dignity and personal worth, to secure equal opportunity. We had plotted the demise of racial discrimination, but at no time had we contemplated ethnicide.

I do not want to attack the motives or sincerity of people like Stokely Carmichael or his successor, H. Rap Brown. They were bold, tough young men who put their bodies on the firing line for S.N.C.C. during its early organizing days in the hostile territory of the Deep South. They were brave, and they were justifiably angry, but during the last years of S.N.C.C., their experiences goaded them to reckless provocations. In the end, they lost their staying power. The N.A.A.C.P. is still with us.

If there is a lesson in this, it is that youth, energy, and passion are not enough to keep the civil rights movement on course. Age, wisdom, and experience are just as vital. One of the saddest things about those years was the way we warred across the generation gap. One of the small examples I recall took place not long after the Meredith march, when S.N.C.C. conceived the idea of organizing a protest during the wedding of Luci Baines Johnson. Dr. King, A. Philip Randolph, Whitney Young, and I sent Stokely a wire asking him to call off the demonstration. We told him we thought it was in extremely poor taste to inject the political and moral judgments of complete strangers into a personal ceremony; that every young woman (including the daughters and sisters of demonstrators) was entitled to private happiness on her wedding day. Luci Baines Johnson was hardly responsible for the race problem or the war in Vietnam. The demonstration was an adolescent and futile attempt to exhibit the egos of the demonstrators. Because S.N.C.C. was part of the civil rights movment, it also stood to implant the wrong ideas in the mind of the country that the movement had wandered from its real purpose and was indulging itself in a malevolent and meaningless shivaree.

I have a copy of the answer we received. It embodied the generation gap at its sharpest:

> Gentlemen,
>   We believe it took some nerve in sending that telegram. You have displayed more backbone in defending Luci than you have shown for the millions of black people being brutalized every day in the United States. You have displayed more backbone in defending Luci than you have shown for the colored people of Vietnam being napalmed by Luci's father. As responsible leaders of so-called civil rights organizations, we suggest that you check your facts as to what SNCC is going to take before you bring the message.
>
>   Yours for black power.

I think that the rhetorical excesses of the black power people and the violence in the cities—understandable as they were—made it easier for lukewarm white folks and our old enemies in Congress to back away from the legislative progress that had been made between 1963 and 1965. The Civil Rights Bill of 1966 was the first victim. Two sections of the bill dealt with the selection of federal and state juries in the South; the third strengthened the power of the Attorney General to intervene in school desegregation cases; the fourth dealt with punishment for those who interfered with the constitutional rights of civil rights people; the most controversial would have made it the national policy of the United States to bar discrimination on the basis of race or religion in the sale or rental of property.

That last provision upset the Republican leadership of Congress. In the House, minority leader Gerald Ford succeeded in watering down the housing section. Then, to my irritation, he tried to eliminate the housing section entirely. In the Senate, Everett Dirksen, full of bullfrog homilies on the sanctity of private property, led the ax men who killed the bill. Dirksen aided and abetted the Southerners, who could not have won on their own, in ducking quorum calls, staging a filibuster, and offering endless opinions on the constitutionality of the proposed bill. With Dirksen's connivance, a cloture vote failed.

It was a serious defeat for us. All we could do was retrench and fight again. I warned the Senate that the Negro was not going away. The government of the United States was going to have to decide either to enact an open housing policy or to endorse by its inaction the unconscionable deprivation and the explosive threat of the ghettos.

As Joe Louis used to say, Senator Dirksen and those Southern Demo-crats could run—but they couldn't hide.

The next two years bore out all my warnings. Nothing could have been more absurd than the shocked surprise with which white America reacted to the terrible riots that were to take place in New-ark, Detroit, then Washington, D.C.—the last reaching to within a few blocks of the White House. The tinder had been smoking for years. All the best efforts of Lyndon Johnson had only nicked segrega-tion in the schools. The unemployment rate of Negroes was two and three times higher than the rate for the rest of the country, and one in every three Negro teenagers was out of work. Of all the new housing built at the time, only 2 percent went to Negroes. The ghettos grew hotter and hotter. The federal, state, and local governments were mincing and maneuvering as the Senate had done over the 1966 Civil Rights Bill, and the separatists and firebrands were practicing the most impassioned kind of racial brinksmanship. The climate was more dangerous than I had ever seen it.

As 1967 opened, we tried on the opening day of the 90th Congress to get the Senate to change Rule 22 so that cloture could be invoked by three-fifths of those present and voting instead of two-thirds. The Senate voted 53–46 to reject the rules change. The vote was a kick in the teeth for civil rights and for other progressive legislation. It aided the extremists, who could cite the vote as one more bit of evidence il-lustrating the futility of working through established channels to gain improvements in civil rights.

At about this same time, the House of Representatives seized on Adam Clayton Powell's legal troubles and denied him his seat. Adam and I had fallen out, but that didn't mean that I was going to walk away from him when he was down. I didn't think that Adam got a fair deal. No one in his right mind could believe that he was the first con-gressman since 1807 whose conduct warranted such punishment. The N.A.A.C.P. insisted that the yardstick applied to him so suddenly be applied to all others in the House whose records deserved it. He was entitled to the same protection that white congressmen had al-ways enjoyed. As things were, it looked like a baseball game in which the umpires had suddenly given one side four outs and the other three.

The action of the House, coming on top of the Senate stonewall on cloture, made it harder than ever for me to argue the merits of keep-ing faith with legislative progress. I had to keep a tight grip on my own feelings in those days; sometimes the arguments of the hotheads seemed very hard to resist.

In February, the atmosphere grew more threatening than ever

after the South delivered up another victim to the hatred. In Natchez, Mississippi, Wharlest Jackson, thirty-six, former local treasurer of the N.A.A.C.P., who had been promoted to the grade of mixer at a plant of the Armstrong Tire and Rubber Company, was murdered by a bomb planted in his pickup truck. I felt that murder more deeply than anything since Medgar Evers's assassination. Wharlest Jackson had a wife, four daughters, and a son. He had fought for the United States during the Korean War; he was a hard worker, a lodge man, an upstanding member of his church. He was killed simply because he had tried to better himself, to get ahead. The funeral was in the Zion A.M.E. Church in Natchez. When I got there, every pew and corner was jammed with mourners. The minister looked us over and pleaded for renewed understanding and faith in the love of God. Most folks stared back at him bitterly. I didn't hear very many amens. I left that day fearing for all of us.

Through the murder, God had offered the United States Senate a second chance to enact a civil rights bill allowing the federal government to punish such assassins. It was hard not to conclude that the killing in Natchez had depended on Congress to act as a roadblock to punishment. Congressmen and everyone else were forever asking Negro Americans to respect and uphold the law. I thought the time had come for Congress to set its own example. At the beginning of 1967, L.B.J. had proposed a new civil rights package. Once again it included measures protecting the right of Negroes to serve on state and federal juries; it gave cease-and-desist powers to the Equal Opportunity Commission; it had open-housing provisions and protection for civil rights activists. In February, President Johnson had called me to the White House to talk over the package; two weeks later Wharlest Jackson was dead, but for the rest of the year, through all the blood and bullets, Congress sat on the President's proposals.

I couldn't believe the delay. A small segment of the Negro community was becoming so disillusioned that it interpreted just about everything that happened as a betrayal. Such people believed that the white world was organized to deprive them of their rights and that every move any white group made was part of a giant conspiracy to hold them down—that the only way to break out was not by the law but with guns.

That summer, I had a run-in with a few of these people. One morning while I was at work, I received a visit from the New York Police Department. The news was unsettling. The police told me that a small band called the Revolutionary Action Movement, whose only other notoriety had come with a plot to blow up the Statue of Liberty, the Washington Monument, and the Liberty Bell, had worked out an elaborate plot to shoot me. The whole notion sounded very farfetched. At first I didn't take it very seriously, but the police department did. They told me that they had been keeping me under surreptitious surveillance for two weeks, and they assigned me an around-the-clock guard.

When I told Minnie what was going on, she was terribly alarmed. The guard went with me everywhere. The protection became a little expensive. I'd invite the guard to eat with me when I went to restaurants. Most of the time they would politely decline; but when they accepted, I had to pick up the tab. "I don't need these cops," I grumped to Minnie one night. But a few mornings later when I woke up and snapped on the radio, I learned that the police had staged a series of wee-hours raids on R.A.M. members in Brooklyn, Queens, Manhattan, and Philadelphia, and arrested sixteen suspected plotters. The dragnet also pulled in thirty weapons, including a machine gun, more than a thousand rounds of ammunition, explosives, a radio receiver and transmitter, and walkie-talkies—a regular little arsenal of terror.

It was reported that R.A.M. had organized a front called the Jamaica Rifle and Pistol Club not far from my home in Queens. The District Attorney said that the suspects had held target practice in National Guard armories in Queens, Brooklyn, and Long Island. And the New York Police Department, which had infiltrated the group, accused two R.A.M. leaders, a school principal and a drifter from Jamaica, of conspiring to kill me. Apparently the idea was to set off ghetto riots across the country by shooting me, Whitney Young, and a number of other civil rights leaders, then making it look as if the blood had been shed by white assassins. At the trial it came out that some of the R.A.M. plotters had worked up a map of my neighborhood—testing the time it would take to flee after a shooting—and locating foliage where gunmen could hide.

I am a harmless fellow. I couldn't see why anyone would want to kill me. Over the years I had received many threats, but they had all come from white racists, not from my own side. Apparently anyone who didn't believe in machine guns was an Uncle Tom. I tried to shrug off the whole business, but Minnie couldn't. She still remembers the trial. One of the police undercover agents testified that while the alleged plot was perking, one R.A.M. member had turned to another and said about me, "What if he's not alone?" The answer was, "We will just have to burn him in her presence." Those are not memories a man's wife forgets easily.

Newark and then Detroit came right after the R.A.M. plot was uncovered. There was no direct connection between the plot and the riots; all were part of the general rage of the times. White America said it just couldn't understand what was going on. More civil rights legislation had been passed during these three years than in the previous hundred. That, of course, was part of the point. You couldn't correct all the damage that had been done since 1864 in three short years; it was unreasonable to expect it. The change of the early sixties had come perilously late. In those months after the Harlem and Watts ghettos went up in flames, the ordinary ghetto dweller elsewhere could see little improvement in his daily life. The new laws passed by Congress applied mostly to the South and meant very little to him. It was easy for him to feel that he had been abandoned by his government and his country, that he was isolated, of no importance in the United States. Nobody could stand those feelings. So he leaned over, picked up a rock, and heaved it at the biggest plate-glass window he could see.

For the next year you could hear the glass shattering and the guns sputtering all across the country. That may have been the worst year in my life. Violence welled up around all of us. Sometimes it was black; sometimes it was white. It was awful that the country could come to such a pass.

One day during the spring of 1968 I flew to Cleveland on a speech and inspection tour. I had my briefcase in hand and my raincoat over my arm and I was walking down one of the long corridors at the airport when I bumped into Dr. King. He, too, was traveling through Cleveland, and he had three very large men at his side.

"Roy," he called out in surprise, "are you traveling all alone?"

"Yes," I answered, not thinking much about it one way or another.

"I don't think you should do that," he said. "It's too dangerous. You should always have someone with you."

We talked for a few minutes, and as he and his men walked off, I watched them make their way through the airport crowds. "Have things really gotten that bad?" I asked myself. Then I shook off the depressing thought, grabbed a cab, and drove into town.

Not long afterward, from across the street of the Lorraine Motel in Memphis, James Earl Ray fixed Dr. King in the crosshairs of his telescopic sight and squeezed a trigger. That rifle shot was my answer.

A FAITH FOR
HARD TIMES

I was working at the office when word of Dr. King's assassination came from Memphis. A rattlesnake had struck the civil rights movement, slipping into its hole before anyone could grab a shovel and crush it. Those bodyguards I had seen with Dr. King on the road several weeks before had not been able to save him. Dr. King, our Great Exhorter, was gone.

That night in Washington, D.C., there were flames and black smudges of smoke only a few blocks away from the White House. The TV news reports the next day caught youngsters hauling their loot to park benches, handling it, picking and choosing whatever caught their eye. There was almost a carnival mood. All that was missing was the calliope. The rioters were not up in arms at the death of Dr. King; his murder had only provided the spark for the riot. It was impossible that his belief in brotherhood and human dignity could lead to such mayhem. The rioters were dragging his dream through the mud.

Even as the carnage was going on, the ABC television station in Manhattan invited me to its studio to talk things over. When I arrived I found Sammy Davis, Jr., on the set. He looked anguished. "I don't see sad faces, people in mourning," he said. "I see laughing and giggling . . . less than forty-eight hours after our leader died: those are not really brothers."

Dr. King's murder and the riots that followed it came only one month after Lyndon Johnson's Commission on Civil Disorders presented its final report on the riots of the previous summer. I served on the commission. One of the last messages I received from Dr. King was a telegram on the commission's work. Thirteen years later his words still burn prophetically:

> The Commission's findings that white racism is the root cause of today's urban disorders is an important confession of a harsh truth. My

only hope is that white America and our national government will heed your warnings and implement your recommendations. By ignoring them we will sink inevitably into a nightmarish racial doomsday. God grant that your excellent report will educate the nation and lead to action before it is too late.

One sentence in that report sounded the warning so clearly that no one could miss it. "White racism is essentially responsible for the explosive mixture which has been accumulating in our cities since the end of World War II." The language was too hard for L.B.J. He could not bring himself to believe it. The churches didn't like the conclusion, either; nor did the clubwomen, the fraternal organizations, and the politicians. They all told us we had done plenty to improve conditions. Millions of whites felt the same way. They couldn't accept the report; they thought things were just fine with the colored: there we were over in our end of town, with our churches, and wasn't a colored boy captain of the basketball team? What were we yelling about?

Millions of more honest white Americans knew that what we reported was true, and I think just about every black American had no doubt about it. During the investigation our commission reporters went to a town in New Jersey that had had a riot: an ordinary American town, not a big city like Detroit or Newark. They were told that before the riot the black community leaders had drawn up a list of sixteen demands and tacked them to the council door because the councilmen refused to allow them into the council chamber for a simple hearing. If even half those demands had been attended to, there would have been no riot in that town, but political flexibility and wisdom seemed to be missing everywhere until the conflagrations began—when, of course, second thoughts came too late.

President Johnson didn't thank us for our conclusions, and I was disappointed in him. The report was the most important government gesture since Harry Truman's Civil Rights Commission committed the government to ending segregation in American life. The conclusions of that commission had also been controversial; President Truman stood by them all the same, but when we reported that America had become two societies, black and white, separate and unequal, L.B.J. seemed to take the conclusion as a personal rebuke and affront. He did not accept and act on it. As a matter of fact, he refused to receive us when the work was done.

We knew very well that our words were powerful. We had discussed them carefully during the closing weeks of our deliberations. I can still see John Lindsay, mayor of New York, yellow legal pad in hand, going over them with us. Without him, the commission would have been seriously reduced in its bite and effectiveness. The bad news had to be delivered. You had to be honest. When you looked at the fact, at the terrible conditions in employment, housing, education, and relations with the police that led to Watts, Newark, Detroit, and all the others, what else could you conclude? Some of the commissioners felt uncomfortable with the white racism formulation, but all 670 pages of that report proved that no matter what you wanted to call it, the attitude of white Americans toward black Americans was the root of the problem.

What President Johnson lost by rejecting his own commission he partly made up for after King's assassination. The murder came as Congress was stalling over the 1968 Civil Rights Bill, the most controversial section of which was its provisions governing fair housing. Senator Edward Brooke of Massachusetts and Senator Walter Mondale of Minnesota had done much to keep the measure alive, and Clarence Mitchell was lobbying with all his skill to get it passed. After Dr. King's assassination, Congress could not resist L.B.J., who pressed harder than ever for passage. The bill went through. I found it impossible to feel much cheer about it. The progress was satisfying, but one more civil rights act was stained with blood.

By the summer of 1968, many of our major objectives had been turned into legislation: we had the 1964 Civil Rights Act and the 1965 Voting Rights Act; there were the School Bill and the Education Bill, the Model Cities Bill and the Rent Supplement Bill; the Teachers Corps; and now the 1968 Act with its housing provisions. The larger problem was one of enforcement, and at just the time when we should have been solving it, the climate couldn't have been worse. Too many whites let the riots and the threats of a few militants turn the cities into battlefields. Law and order were becoming code words for cracking down on Negroes. We were not at war in our cities, and weapons had no place there—but they were in place nonetheless.

The summer of 1968 was a season in the bunker. Militants were after me all the time for one imagined crime after another. There was nothing to do but wait them out. The board of the N.A.A.C.P. was behind me, and I got a good deal of moral support from old friends. One time President Johnson asked me to the White House, and when we had finished the main business at hand, he gave me an earnest look and said, "Roy, now I'm gonna give you some advice. I want you to call me a sonofabitch."

I looked back in surprise. "Now, I know what you're thinking," he went on. "You'd never do it, but you just call me a sonofabitch and it will help you. I won't mind at all."

I laughed. I had come up so high in the world that the President of the United States was inviting me to give him a barnyard dressing down. It was the friendliest offer L.B.J. ever made me, but getting out of the woods with the people who were calling me the country's number-one Uncle Tom wasn't worth the subterfuge. As far as I was concerned, they could go right on howling.

I had some trouble at our convention in Atlantic City that summer. A small group of delegates walked out, saying the usual things—that I might have been good back yonder but that it was time to put me out to pasture. About the same time, a similar insurrection struck C.O.R.E. Blacker-than-thou posing obviously didn't get anyone anywhere: leaders were a target for their followers no matter how militant they tried to sound. That summer C.O.R.E. invited me out to Columbus, Ohio, to make a speech as a gesture of unity. It was a rather tense get-together: there were several dozen security men to guard me when I was supposed to speak. I told the delegates that I was all for racial pride, but that to ask the N.A.A.C.P. to endorse separatism was like asking a sprinkling Methodist to submit to a total immersion. There was no way that such a transformation could come about. I didn't get much applause, but I felt better after the speech. At least we were talking to one another instead of at one another.

The political campaign made the summer one long torment. When Sirhan Sirhan shot Bobby Kennedy in Los Angeles, I came as close as I have ever come to losing faith in the workings of democracy. I had always felt a degree of distance from Bobby Kennedy, partly because of the civil rights foot dragging of J.F.K.'s Administration, partly because he had become senator in New York by defeating Kenneth Keating, a Republican who had always been a very good friend of the N.A.A.C.P. But the older Bobby grew, the more clear matters of race became to him. By 1968 he obviously felt the problem deeply, and he was poised to offer considerable help. With Dr. King scarcely buried and Bobby Kennedy done to death as well, I had to ask myself who was next? Were the rattlesnakes in control of the country?

I was for Hubert Humphrey that summer. He was as good on human rights then as he had been as mayor of Minneapolis long before. I respected Eugene McCarthy and his courage in bucking L.B.J. on the Vietnam War; he had been with us on many civil rights fights, and I liked him personally, but he was no Humphrey. We had a little run-in during the N.A.A.C.P. convention. He invited himself down to Atlantic City and stayed at a Howard Johnson Motor Lodge about

seven blocks from our convention hall. At the time, a group of
N.A.A.C.P. dissidents calling themselves the "Young Turks" was
putting me through the wringer on the N.A.A.C.P.'s program, and
the last thing I needed was for the presidential campaign to spill over
into the convention. The Young Turks were a lot older than their
name suggested, and in the end I had little trouble dealing with them.
When McCarthy sent in his operatives, I had to sit on them, too. It
made for some hard feelings.

I still don't understand why so many people were so hard on Hubert Humphrey that year. Obviously people were angered by the difficulty he had in weaning himself away from Lyndon Johnson and the
Vietnam War; I didn't hold that against him. My concern was that two
separate issues would be linked. Negroes had served loyally and
bravely in all of America's early wars, and at first I thought it was dangerous folly when Stokely Carmichael started yelling, "Hell, no, we
won't go."

So we kept the N.A.A.C.P. from losing itself in the peace movement. The people who had joined the N.A.A.C.P., who had paid their
dues, had signed on for the civil rights fight. They could join the
peace movement on their own if they chose—they were welcome to
do so—but I believed that if we mingled the civil rights and peace
movements we would only weaken our own cause. Later, feelings
against the war ran powerfully and the N.A.A.C.P. came out against
it, but the politics of the issue were exceedingly complex. I felt considerable sympathy for Humphrey as he tried to work his way free.

Toward October Minnie and I thought we might escape the season's political heat by going to Europe; the vacation was wonderful,
but the relief didn't last long. The morning we were due to dock in
New York, I got up early and went out on deck. I confess that I suffer
from a mild case of Norman Rockwell Americanism. I always got out
on deck early whenever we sailed into New York harbor. I liked to
watch the ship steam through the Narrows and see the Statue of Liberty appear before us. No matter how many years passed, the sight
always moved me. That fall of 1968, when the country was in the
middle of an unpopular war and political rhetoric seemed to be tearing it at the seams, it was very reassuring to see that torch aloft over
the harbor.

No sooner did we dock than I found myself in the middle of a terrible mess at the office. While I was away, a young member of the legal
staff named Lewis Steel had published an article in the Sunday *New
York Times Magazine* attacking the Supreme Court for doing far too
little for civil rights. The piece was called "Nine Men in Black Who

Think White." The day after it came out, the N.A.A.C.P. board of directors met and fired Steel. The reverberations were terrible. The American Civil Liberties Union said we were squashing dissent, and there was criticism everywhere. Steel was a sincere young man. He was white, thirty-one years old, and had been working for the N.A.A.C.P. since 1964. He was passionate, but his judgment had not been what it should have. The board called his article "an indefensible rejection of much of the association's major efforts over the last sixty years and of the commitment and sacrifice of countless individuals to that effort." The piece did rather callowly dismiss the role of the Court and of our legal strategy in fighting Jim Crow. My own view was that anyone who believed in Steel's thesis could not honorably choose to remain on the staff. I stood with the board. When Steel left, the entire legal staff resigned. Later I managed to recruit Nathaniel Jones, a brilliant young lawyer who had served on the Verner Commission, to become our new general counsel. He quickly took hold, but it was a long time before the toxins in the air cleared.

The results of the election that November provided evidence of what our long struggle through the courts had attained. We got Mr. Nixon, which was bad luck, but there were other, more positive results. Millions more Negroes were voting in the South, and about 370 Negro candidates won election to local office. This was real progress; no sniping at the Court or at the slow pace of the legal campaigns we had waged for so many years could alter this reality. Beyond the South, Cleveland elected Carl B. Stokes mayor, while Gary, Indiana, elected Richard Hatcher. Both needed votes to win; both had gotten them. In Boston, Louise Day Hicks and the white backlash lost. When I turned off the television set that night, I didn't feel that the election had been a total wash at all.

The change of administration and the departure of L.B.J., however, did throw us right back to the atmosphere of the late Eisenhower years. Richard Nixon invited me to his inauguration, but I stayed home and watched it on television. I was ready to give the new President time to prove himself, but I felt very pessimistic as I watched him take the oath. Among Negroes, I think the shared feeling about President Nixon could be summed up in a very old saw: "He say so good—but he *do* so po'."

At the N.A.A.C.P., our distrust of Nixon dated back to his days as Vice President. On one occasion when he came to address the annual convention, the delegates laid plans to picket him. Thurgood Marshall got wind of the plot, found Minnie, and told her, "They're going to picket Nixon. Where's Roy?" Minnie finally tracked me down at a meeting with the Texas delegation. I had left word that I was not to be interrupted, and when Minnie asked for me, a secretary said, "I can't get him, Mrs. Wilkins. He told me he wasn't to be disturbed."

"Well, *I* can disturb him," Minnie said, and barged right on in and grabbed me. I got the delegates together and told them, "You cannot picket your own guest." They reluctantly agreed and called off the picketing, but when Nixon arrived, they all gave him the coldest shoulder I had ever seen. The delegates just sat there like stone men and women as he talked—looking at him hard.

Not long after the inauguration, President Nixon invited Minnie and me to dinner at the White House. Minnie said she wouldn't go, and I told her she had to. Minnie gave me a look that would have dropped a mule, but finally she agreed to go with me to the party.

We flew to Washington a few days later. You could sense the change in mood as soon as you walked through the door at the White House. Everything was stiff, formal, artificial. After dinner Minnie and I were standing on one side of the dining room having coffee. As we talked, a Secret Service agent came over to us. He said, "The President would like you to join him on the other side of the room, Mr. Wilkins."

We walked over, and as we drew near, President Nixon looked up and smiled. He was very gracious. After a few minutes of small talk, he said to me, "If I do anything wrong, I want you to tell me." I spent the next five years doing so.

The Nixon Administration did all it could to turn back the clock on the progress we had made under Presidents Kennedy and Johnson. Nixon was no George Wallace, of course. He did not try to scuttle the great Civil Rights Acts of 1964, 1965, and 1968, but he was eager to experiment with ideas like bloc grants to federal education—turning money in lump sums over to the states, and letting them dispose of it. This, of course, turned power and money over to the very states that had been resisting the Supreme Court for so long.

On taking office, President Nixon said he wanted to follow "a middle course on integration." He told us his goal was to walk between those who sought "instant integration" and those after "segregation forever." It was beyond me how he could talk about "instant integration" when we were fifteen years beyond the *Brown* decision and the South was still holding out whenever it could. From this aimless fiddling around with desegregation, Nixon went on to undo the Philadelphia Plan, lifting pressure from government to improve minority hiring in the construction trade. Before long Clifford Alexander, the Chairman of the Equal Opportunity Commission, resigned. Senator Dirksen had been after him for "harassing" corporate America into complying with the 1964 Civil Rights Act; Alexander got little support and less action out of the President and had no choice but to leave. After that, it was one hostile act after another. The President said he was going to allow Southern schools more time to comply with September deadlines for school desegregation; the diehards in the Senate began to nibble around the edges of the Voting Rights Act; Daniel Patrick Moynihan called for "benign neglect."

I thought that little phrase was a disaster. In one 1,600-word memo Moynihan provided President Nixon with an outwardly respectable rationale and justification for what the Nixon Administration meant to do all along: let civil rights slide. Moynihan didn't mean for his advice to have this effect, but his eagerness overpowered what should have been better political common sense. In the following years, instead of benign neglect, we got a period of malignant indifference on issues of civil rights and race.

I considered the nominations of G. Harrold Carswell and Clement Haynsworth to the Supreme Court grotesque in their affront to the legal profession and to black Americans. Lewis Powell didn't frighten me as much as William Rehnquist, even though Powell came from the South and Rehnquist from Phoenix. Negroes weren't going to get out in the streets and cheer for Powell, but they could live with him. Warren Burger, I hardly need add, was no substitute for Earl Warren.

The fight against Carswell offered a wonderful display of Clarence Mitchell's lobbying skill. After President Nixon put forth Carswell's name, there was a meeting at the Statler Hilton on Friday the thirteenth. Clarence stood up and said, "Carswell can be beaten." At first no one believed him. Then Senator Roman Hruska said that while Carswell might be mediocre, even mediocrity deserved its representation on the Supreme Court—a blunder that helped us a good deal. Clarence also enlisted Senators Birch Bayh of Indiana and Edward Brooke of Massachusetts, who were lions in that fight. In the end, the outcome turned largely on Senator Margaret Chase Smith of Maine. Senator Bayh knew better than to ask her how she planned to vote on the nomination; she was famous for keeping her counsel and flexibility right up to voting time. What Senator Bayh did was tell her that the White House was putting out word that she would see things its way on Carswell. That did the trick. When the roll call came, she offered a very testy no to the nomination. There was a burst of applause in the gallery. Senator Richard Russell was so mad he demanded the gallery be cleared. The sergeants-at-arms did the job, but they left Clarence sitting there. I always thought the work he did was one of the finest lobbying jobs since Walter White took on Judge Parker.

While the Nixon Administration was preparing its wrecking operations, I had one last battle of my own with a new form of black power.
This time the issue was separate dormitories, dining halls, and black-
studies programs for Negro college students. The issue presented a
terrible problem. I had been against black apartheid all my life, and I
welcomed activism on campus. I was completely in favor of the study
of black history and culture, for racial pride, for reconstructing a history that had been left to die from ignorance or outright hostility. But
I also thought the call for separateness, for isolation, for retreating
from the rest of the campus was a sign of weakness, not strength. Just
when white America thought it must at last give in and open the
doors of opportunity and equality in education wider and wider, a
small group of vociferous young Negroes—including, of all people,
some Negro college students—began chanting, "Ve vant to be
alone."

I saw the whole business as a shameful, self-inflicted form of reverse Jim Crow, and I fought it. Common sense dictated that if black
college kids were going to have to go out and make it in white
America, they had better learn what the white kids learned. The pre-
tentiousness of some of those early black-studies programs was ridiculous. I'm no stuffed shirt, but I do believe that all Americans should
be able to speak English properly. One day I was standing in a line
and a young professor walked up and shook my hand. He said he was
head of the black-studies department of a university not far away.
"Mr. Wilkins," he said, "I want to ax you a question."

I couldn't believe my ears. I stopped him right there. "You're
teaching our children black history and you don't even know how to
pronounce a simple three-letter word?" I asked.

"That's just the way I talk," he told me, an edge coming into his
voice.

"Well, you talk *wrong*," I snapped.

I still feel that way. It is not "axing" anyone too much to know how
to pronounce "ask." What I said about reverse Jim Crow in those
days probably cost me more than anything else I had said since my
black-power–black-death speech in Los Angeles in 1966, but it had to
be done. By all means let us have black studies, but as a strengthen-
ing supplement, as a means toward, not as a substitute for, understanding the world around us. I didn't want black children to become
mesmerized by dashikis while the white kids were thinking about
space suits.

I have a reputation for being a quiet, rather boring fellow, but I felt
those issues passionately, and was quite vociferous about them. One

of the reasons I protested so loudly was that for a time I didn't know how long I would have to get my case across.

During the fall of 1969, while Minnie and I were on vacation, I began to notice a sore spot in my abdomen. I paid little attention to it at first, but in December, the soreness began to nag at me constantly. I called Dr. Farrow Allen, my old friend and personal physician, and made an appointment for a checkup.

Dr. Allen looked me over, then insisted that I get a set of X-rays right away. The X-rays showed that I had two intestinal lesions. Alarmed, Dr. Allen referred me to Dr. S. Arthur Localio, a top surgeon at New York University Hospital. Not long after New Year's in 1970, I checked into the hospital as Dr. Localio's patient.

The surgery went smoothly, but three days later, while Minnie was visiting me, Dr. Localio walked into my room. There was a look of great sadness on his face. Speaking almost in a whisper, he told me that the lesions had been malignancies.

"How long has it been since you had your last operation?" he asked.

"Almost twenty-five years," I said.

"I hope you will be able to go another twenty-five years without any trouble," he told me.

The diagnosis was frightening, but the prognosis turned out just as we had hoped. It has been eleven years now since the operation, and there has been no sign of a recurrence. Dr. Localio's skill was matched only by his compassion, and I have always felt grateful to him.

After this brush with cancer, I thought of retiring, but as my body began to mend I rejected the idea. As the months passed and I began to feel better, it seemed more and more that to retire would be to default just when real fighting was needed. To step down at a time like that seemed like plain cowardice. I stayed.

Those years weren't all tight spots and hard places. I remember one night when Minnie told me to get dressed—because she was taking me out to dinner. We went to the Carlyle Hotel, and when I walked in there were 150 people waiting for me. It was my seventieth birthday—and William Hastie, William Trent, John Morsell, and Mildred Roxborough had arranged a surprise party. Mayor John Lindsay was there, Leontyne Price was there, and so were dozens of personal friends from around the country. I can still see Thurgood Marshall raising his glass. He said, "I've never seen a turtle move ahead without sticking his neck out, and Roy has done that and more." Everyone had a good laugh. I had reached the Biblical age of threescore and ten and I felt no pain. It was one of the easiest mile-stones I ever passed.

Minnie retired from her social-work job in 1971, and was free to travel with me. Having spent so many years on the road alone, I was delighted to have her with me. Our first trip was to Israel, where Hebrew University in Jerusalem gave me an honorary fellowship. The beauty carved out of the desert, the wonderful spirit of the people, the welcome we received from Golda Meir, the grand lady who governed, fascinated us. The following Easter we went to South Africa, where things were a good deal more complicated. I spoke at a convention of one of the few black organizations the government had not yet raided or put out of business. Seeing firsthand what we had read about and condemned for so many years was deeply troubling for both of us. An ugly moment of controversy also swirled up around the visit. After a speech before a group of mixed "coloreds" and whites, I told reporters that many black South Africans had told me that American companies operating in their country should not be pressured to leave, that pressure should be brought to bear on them to create equal opportunities in their plants. What I had been told was that these companies could do much to help black South Africans if only they would do so. I suppose it was a little naïve of me; back home Congressman Charles Diggs pounced on the story and me, as did some other black publications. After the stop in South Africa, it was a breath of fresh and free air to reach Kenya.

At the invitation of the Pentagon, Minnie and I made another trip that year to Italy and Germany to see how equal opportunity was working in the army. For years the N.A.A.C.P. had been monitoring the progress—or lack of it—of minorities in the military. The contrast between the integrated army of the 1970s and the Jim Crow service of World Wars I and II impressed me, but racial strains continued to exist. We will have to be vigilant for a long time to come.

After Minnie retired, she used all her powers to make the idea of retiring attractive to me. I thought about her arguments for quite a while, and then I received a job offer of a visiting professorship from a well-known university "upon my retirement." The offer seemed quite attractive. One of the members of the university's board of trustees followed up on it in a letter urging me to accept. I talked things over with Minnie, and we decided that I would retire on December 31, 1972.

I discussed my plans with three people at the N.A.A.C.P.: Bishop Stephen Gill Spottswood, the chairman of our board; John Morsell, our assistant director; and Mildred Roxborough, a talented administrator and wonderful woman who was our executive assistant. When Bishop Spottswood asked me to postpone retiring for a while, I accepted his advice. I suppose he and I both knew that I did not really want to leave the N.A.A.C.P., but the delay was to be only temporary. I felt that at the age of seventy-two I had to leave the organization to younger heads and hands.

My hope was to announce my retirement at the N.A.A.C.P.'s annual convention that year in New Orleans, but before the convention came, a series of deaths and illnesses struck down our staff. First Warren Howard, our assistant for programs, suffered a cerebral hemorrhage in the office and died the next day. Then Leonard Carter, director of our West Coast region, died. Shortly after that, John Morsell developed cancer.

John's illness hit me very hard. He was one of the finest men I have ever known. He had a brilliant mind, a delightful sense of humor, and a calmness that had helped us through many a crisis. He was a sincere and thoughtful friend with the kind of integrity and dedication to the cause that was very rare. I had counted on him to carry on, and when he died in 1974, I once again postponed my retirement. I didn't feel I could leave the N.A.A.C.P. in the lurch.

John had handled all the administrative work of the N.A.A.C.P. for twenty-one years. As I looked for a replacement for him, I had to assume responsibility for the work he had done, in addition to keeping up my own schedule. Instead of retiring at the comfortable age of seventy-three, I found myself working harder than ever. I suppose my standards for an assistant were too high, for my search tended to drag on. I should have liked to have had Clarence Mitchell take the job more than anyone; but I never discussed it with him, because I believed that his service in the Washington office was too valuable for us to lose. Perhaps I made a mistake in looking for a person with all the qualities that John had. The people outside the organization whom I wanted to hire were not willing to accept the low salaries that the N.A.A.C.P. paid.

While these matters were still in the air, Bishop Spottswood died, and Kivie Kaplan, who had become our president, soon after. The deaths left a terrible hole in our leadership, and I decided that I had no choice but to stay on.

In the fall of 1975, a symposium on civil rights was held at the L.B.J. Library in Austin. I was invited to speak, and Mrs. Johnson invited Minnie and me to be guests at the LBJ Ranch. Justice Earl Warren and Mrs. Warren were the other guests. Johnson looked a bit tired, but he was as full of life as ever. Feeling worn out after a day at the meeting, I announced early that I was going to bed. L.B.J. looked at me a minute and said in polite surprise, "Nobody goes to bed until after the ten o'clock news." He still had three television sets arranged so he could watch the evening news on all three networks at the same time. Johnson laughed his hearty Texas laugh, but I went off to bed. That was the last time I was with him. During that visit, he told Minnie, "Roy never gave me any bad advice when I was President. And he never compromised his position." We heard from him again shortly after Christmas. A few days later he was dead.

The contrast between L.B.J. and Richard Nixon, who was falling into the toils of Watergate, couldn't have been greater. I thought Mr. Nixon would try to be President of all the people; instead, he allied himself with the worst enemies of black children. After stalling on integration, he came out against busing in a way that beclouded the whole issue, splitting the country just when the civil rights laws needed full backing from the White House.

My own views on busing were simple. Anyone who said he was against busing but for equal education for black children was either fibbing or a fool. At the time there were only two alternatives: you could instantly provide equal schools in all neighborhoods—a patent impossibility—or you could use busing, a technique that would work. The emotional outcry that grew up around busing was heavily tinged with racism. For years white folks had not complained when busing was used to maintain segregated schools; they cried out only when we proposed to use it to put an end to *de facto* segregation in the North and to the last Jim Crow enclaves down South.

The busing issue didn't improve when Watergate brought down President Nixon. Gerald Ford wanted Congress to put a five-year limit on busing orders, and in his 1976 State of the Union message he didn't even mention civil rights—not one word for 22 million of his constituents. I thought he had jumped to the forefront of the mob, that he was leading the way against the courts and the Fourteenth Amendment, the *Brown* decision and black children. The way he undermined us was a craven retreat and a capitulation to the lawlessness and ignorance of the people who were fanning the race issue.

In early 1976, before the political primaries began, I said a few nice things about Jimmy Carter at a N.A.A.C.P. meeting. A few days later I received a handwritten note in the mail. It read: "To Roy Wilkins, As a longtime admirer of yours, I was very pleased and honored to hear of the kind words you had to say about me at an N.A.A.C.P. leadership conference. I would always welcome your personal advice or criticism. Your friend, Jimmy Carter."

I looked at that neat, earnest handwriting and shook my head. There was always something of the prize schoolboy about Jimmy

Carter, but it was hard not to like him. History will probably record that he was a good enough President, indicted by the press for making more promises than he kept; but that kind of indictment doesn't really bother me as much as it used to. I've had problems enough of my own along those lines. After I confessed to a weakness or two in an interview, a reporter from *Ebony* magazine said to me, "It takes a pretty strong man to admit he's made mistakes." I thought about that a minute, and told him if I ever met a man over seventy who claimed to have made no mistakes in his life, I'd say to him, "Brother—where are your wings?"

As things turned out, my return to private life became quite a rugged passage. After Bishop Spottswood died, Margaret Bush Wilson, a fifty-six-year-old lawyer from St. Louis, became chairman of the board. Mrs. Wilson's concept of the board's role and function was quite at variance with my own. All through the middle and late 1960s, when the rhetoric of militancy was hottest, the N.A.A.C.P.'s board of directors had stayed right behind me, and their support helped enormously in enduring those terrible years. But suddenly, in the middle 1970s, I found that some board members were quite eager to see me step down. I thought we had worked out an agreement for my retirement in 1977 at our sixty-eighth convention in St. Louis, just a few months before my seventy-sixth birthday, but as time passed, pressure grew for me to retire sooner from a group within the board. All the while N.A.A.C.P. branches were urging that I remain until after the St. Louis convention. I received word of a petition signed by thousands of members urging me to delay retirement until the St. Louis convention. The drift of events led to an unpleasant showdown at the 1976 convention in Memphis. Once I was there, a delegation of branch presidents came to my room at the hotel to urge me to remain.

After that I felt I should share what was going on with the delegates. I walked into the hall, took the podium, and told the convention that for eighteen months I had had to put up with a depressing campaign of pressure. I said to the delegates, "If God is willing, I shall be at the St. Louis convention as an active, directing member of the N.A.A.C.P. family. If the board elects to fire me, I shall have to call on you to let me represent your interests individually."

I didn't have to say anything more. The board of directors decided to postpone the issue of my resignation for several months, and in the end, we agreed to keep to the original plan of setting 1977 for my swan song.

In the winter of 1976 and the spring of 1977, Minnie and I were kept busy traveling to cities where N.A.A.C.P. branches were staging their own testimonial dinners for me. The most thrilling testimonial, though, came from the Association of Local Black Elected Officials, of which Maynard Jackson, the mayor of Atlanta, was president. I appreciated the silver bowl and gift they gave me, but just seeing them—over a thousand strong—gave wings to my heels.

In July 1977, the time came for me to say goodbye. It had been well over fifty years since I had been secretary in the St. Paul branch, and nearly fifty years since the night Walter White first welcomed me to New York City. During the convention there was a great flood of nostalgia and affection from old friends from many national organizations—a balm that did much to heal the pain of the fight in Memphis. It would embarrass me to recall all the things that were said, but in particular I remember when C. Dolores Tucker, a member of the board of directors and secretary of state for Pennsylvania, rose and said, "Roy Wilkins, you have been our Rock of Ages—our Rock of Roy."

No one has ever said anything nicer to me. I told the delegates that while I was retiring from active leadership in the N.A.A.C.P. I would not retire from active participation in the struggle for racial justice. As long as there was breath in my body, I intended to be with them in their fight.

People have been very kind to me these last years. Not long after the convention, Jimmy Carter invited Minnie and me to the White House for a talk. It was a short, pleasant visit, a relief to feel that the Nixon miasma had lifted from the President's quarters. President Carter said he wanted to thank me in person and for the American people for what I had done over the years. As he talked, a feeling of great weariness came over me, and I said, "Mr. President, I know you're very busy," and got up to leave. He seemed a bit surprised, but I couldn't help feeling that the civil rights fight was in the hands of others and that I shouldn't hog the limelight.

In earlier days, I used to travel 100,000 miles and more each year on N.A.A.C.P. rounds. Now I mostly stay home, still within earshot of La Guardia Airport. When I hear the planes taking off for far-off cities and places of trouble, my heart goes with them, but retirement offers a man time for reflection where all before had been a great blur of action.

The events of today bring memories of the past. As I read of the plight of the American hostages in Iran, I thought back to the time I went to Iran as chairman of the American delegation to the International Conference on Human Rights. At that time the Shah was hailed as a great benefactor who had improved the lives of his subjects. Likewise, the news of widespread anti-American feelings in Germany takes my mind back to the enthusiastic response to a message from President Johnson that I was privileged to read on his behalf in Berlin in the spring of 1965.

There have been many nice moments during the years I have been away from the N.A.A.C.P. I continued to write a column for the Register and Tribune Syndicate for years. Enough papers bought it to keep me in touch with people all over the country, and the letters I received were always rewarding. People still call to ask me to give speeches, and colleges have given me honorary degrees—my house is full of photographs and plaques. Not long ago, the Library of Congress asked for my papers and the Smithsonian asked for my mementoes. Minnie packed them up and sent them off; as they disappeared out the door, I couldn't help wondering why anyone would want such a dusty pile.

One September evening in 1979, Minnie and I took off for the Algonquin Hotel. When I first arrived in New York in the 1930s, the Algonquin was one of the few midtown hotels willing to serve Negroes or put them up, and I have been going there ever since. When we arrived on the evening of September 15, we were greeted by a roomful of old friends on hand to celebrate our golden wedding anniversary. Leontyne Price, our dear friend, sang "I Love You Truly," and her beautiful voice fairly rocked the whole hotel. As I thought back on the day when I finally talked Minnie into marrying me—and couldn't find the license—tears came to my eyes. It has been a very long journey from Kansas City to the Algonquin. I wish that every man could be blessed with the love I have known.

Other moments have been disturbing. At a press conference several years ago a young reporter stood up and asked, "Mr. Wilkins, is the civil rights movement dead?" At the time, I told him the question had no value and sat down, but over these past few years, as Jimmy Carter's promises have given way to Ronald Reagan's, and as senators like Strom Thurmond and Jesse Helms have come into such great power, the question troubles me more and more. The answer of course is plainly no, but that does not lay the issue to rest. That it comes up at all is evidence of how much remains to be done.

We do not yet have a society open to the free and full advancement of every citizen, whether or not his ancestors were slaves. Unemployment, faulty education, poor housing—the stewing of the ghettos still mocks our claim to equality for all. An enormous discrepancy exists between the way we talk about equality in the abstract and the value as translated into law and practice. History offers us a peculiar irony: the idea, the value of equality is probably nurtured most by the protests of the very people who do not have it. Without us, without our struggle, the country would have foundered in moral emptiness long ago. We must never lose faith in the justness of our cause and the certainty of our success. We have tried to create a nation where all men would be equal in the eyes of the law, where all citizens would be judged on their own abilities, not their race. We have sought justice, only to be thwarted by old hatreds, obstacles that white people have not had to overcome. But we have never given up—never quit. We have believed in our country. We have believed in our Constitution. We have believed that the Declaration of Independence meant what it said. All my life I have believed these things, and I will die believing them. I share this faith with others—and I know that it will last and guide us long after I am gone.

AFTERWORD

Roy Wilkins died on September 8, 1981, shortly after the manuscript for this book was finished. In assembling his story, he benefited often from the support and shared reminiscences of many old friends. In particular he wanted to thank Arnold Aronson, Herman Anderson, M. C. Bowen, Helen Clayton, Adina Gibbs, Missouri Jeffries, Lewis Martin, E. D. Nixon, Muriel Outlaw, and Joseph Rauh. And to give special thanks to the historical associations of Holly Springs, Mississippi, and the states of Minnesota and Missouri; the Library of Congress; and the libraries of Duluth, Kansas City, the University of Mississippi, and *Newsweek* magazine. Many others helped. He was grateful to all of them.

INDEX